D0207626

FREDERICK DOUGLASS AND IRELAND

FREDERICK DOUGLASS AND IRELAND

In His Own Words

Edited by
Christine Kinealy

VOLUME I

Routledge
Taylor & Francis Group

LONDON AND NEW YORK

First published 2018
by Routledge
2 Park Square, Milton Park, Abingdon, Oxon OX14 4RN

and by Routledge
711 Third Avenue, New York, NY 10017

Routledge is an imprint of the Taylor & Francis Group, an informa business

British Library Cataloguing-in-Publication Data
A catalogue record for this book is available from the British Library

Library of Congress Cataloging-in-Publication Data
Names: Douglass, Frederick, 1818–1895 author. | Kinealy, Christine editor.
Title: Frederick Douglass and Ireland: in his own words/edited by
    Christine Kinealy.
Description: London : Routledge, 2018. | Includes bibliographical
    references and index.
Identifiers: LCCN 2018002282 (print) | LCCN 2018003746 (ebook) |
    ISBN 9781351211109 (set) | ISBN 9780429505058 (1) |
    ISBN 9780429492426 (2) | ISBN 9780815380634 (set) |
    ISBN 9781138495487 (1) | ISBN 9781138495494 (2)
Subjects: LCSH: Douglass, Frederick, 1818–1895—Travel—Ireland. |
    Douglass, Frederick, 1818–1895—Relations with Irish. | Douglass,
    Frederick, 1818–1895—Political and social views. | Slavery—United
    States—History—19th century. | Freedmen—United States—History—
    19th century. | African American abolitionists—Biography. | Ireland—
    Race relations—History—19th century.
Classification: LCC E449.D75 (ebook) | LCC E449.D75 A25 2018 (print) |
    DDC 973.8092—dc23
LC record available at https://lccn.loc.gov/2018002282

ISBN: 978-0-8153-8063-4 (set)
ISBN: 978-1-138-49548-7 (volume I)
eISBN: 978-0-429-50505-8

Typeset in Times New Roman
by Apex CoVantage, LLC

For Michael Kinealy (1955–2017)

Do Mhicheál, mo dheartháir dil,

ach i bhfad nios mó ná sin amháin.

CONTENTS

4 Dublin cont.   158

5 The South – Wexford and Waterford   162

6 Cork   173

CONTENTS

CONTENTS

CONTENTS

CONTENTS

CONTENTS

TIMELINE

1818	Frederick Bailey was born into slavery in Maryland
1827	taught the alphabet – which was illegal
1829	began work in a shipyard
1836	first attempt to escape to the North
3 September 1838	escaped to the North
15 September 1838	Sunday, married Anna Murray in New York
28 May 1845	*Narrative* published
16 August 1845	Saturday, left Boston on board the *Cambria*, bound for Liverpool
27 August 1845	Wednesday, attempted to lecture on board the *Cambria*
28 August 1845	Thursday, arrived in Liverpool
31 August 1845	Sunday, arrived in Dublin that morning
31 August 1845	spoke at Temperance meeting in Celbridge
3 September 1845	Wednesday, first lecture in Ireland – Royal Exchange, Dublin
9 September 1845	Tuesday, lecture in Friends' Meeting House, Eustace Street, Dublin
10 September 1845	Wednesday, lecture in Royal Exchange, Dublin
12 September 1845	Friday, lecture in Friends' Meeting House, Dublin
16 September 1845	Tuesday, spoke on temperance in Richmond Gaol, Dublin
17 September 1845	Wednesday, lecture in Music Hall, Dublin
21 September 1845	Sunday, spoke at temperance meeting near Dublin
23 September 1845	Tuesday, lecture in Music Hall, Dublin
29 September 1845	Monday, spoke at meeting of the Loyal Repeal Association, Dublin
Late September 1845	first Irish edition of *Narrative* was published
1 October 1845	Wednesday, lecture in Music Hall, Dublin
7 October 1845	Tuesday, left Dublin, lectured in Wexford
8 October 1845	Wednesday, lecture in Wexford
9 October 1845	Thursday, lecture in Waterford

11 October 1845	Saturday, arrived in Cork
12 October 1845	Sunday, attended Temperance Festival, Cork
13 October 1845	Monday, spoke in temperance meeting, Cork
14 October 1845	Tuesday breakfast, lecture at Lloyds's Hotel, Cork
14 October 1845	Tuesday afternoon, lecture at City Court-house, Cork
17 October 1845	Friday, lecture in Wesleyan Chapel, Cork
20 October 1845	Monday, spoke at Temperance Institute, Cork
21 October 1845	Tuesday, attended Festival at Temperance Institute, Cork
23 October 1845	Thursday, lectured in Imperial Hotel
25 October 1845	Saturday, in his absence Thomas Auld 'sold' Douglass to his brother, Hugh, for $100
27 October 1845	Monday, lectured in Independent Chapel, Cork
28 October 1845	Tuesday, spoke at Anti-Slavery Soirée, Cork
3 November 1845	Monday, spoke in Independent Chapel, Cork
10 November 1845	Monday, lectured in Independent Chapel, Limerick
12 November 1845	Wednesday, lectured in Independent Chapel, Limerick
21 November 1845	Friday, lectured in Philosophical Rooms, Limerick
5 December 1845	Friday, lectured in Independent Meeting House, Donegall Street, Belfast
9 December 1845	Tuesday, lectured in Wesleyan Methodist Church, Donegall Square, Belfast
11 December 1845	Thursday, lectured in Presbyterian Meeting House, Donegall Street, Belfast
12 December 1845	Friday, lectured in Rosemary Street Presbyterian Church, Belfast
14 December 1845	Sunday, in Liverpool
15 December 1845	Monday, arrived in Birmingham, England
16 December 1845	Tuesday, Birmingham Temperance meeting
19 December 1845	Friday, return to Belfast
23 December 1845	Tuesday, lectured in Independent Meeting House, Donegall Street, Belfast
26 December 1845	Friday, lectured in Presbyterian Meeting House, Donegall Street, Belfast
29 December 1845	Monday, Lisburn Presbyterian Church, Lisburn
31 December 1845	Wednesday, Total Abstinence Meeting, Holywood
1 January 1846	Thursday, lectured in Primitive Wesleyan Church, Donegall Place, Belfast
2 January 1846	Friday, lectured in Methodist Meeting House, Donegall Place, Belfast
6 January 1846	Tuesday, lectured in Commercial Rooms, Belfast Anti-slavery Society (Breakfast)
6 January 1846	Evening lecture on temperance – Lancasterian Schools Rooms, Belfast

7 January 1846	Wednesday, temperance meeting in Presbyterian Meeting House, Donegall Street, Belfast
10 January 1846	Saturday, leaves Belfast
February 1846	variant Dublin edition of *Narrative* is published
18 May 1846	Monday, arrived in London
16 June 1846	Tuesday, Presbyterian Church, Donegall Street, with James Buffum
29 June 1846	Monday, left Dublin following a visit with Buffum and Webb
4 July 1846	Saturday, Buffum and the Hutchinson family returned to the U.S.
8 July 1846	Wednesday, lectured in Primitive Wesleyan Chapel, Donegall Place, Belfast
10 July 1846	Friday, lectured in Methodist Chapel, Donegall Place
13 July 1846	Monday, lectured in First Presbyterian Church, Bangor
16 July 1846	Thursday, Garrison sailed for England on board the *Hibernia*
21 July 1846	Tuesday, attended meeting of Olive Branch, Belfast
22 July 1846	Wednesday, temperance meeting, Independent Chapel, Donegall Street
25 July 1846	Saturday, left Belfast
4–8 August 1846	Tuesday to Saturday, World Temperance Convention, London
24 August 1846	Monday, Meeting of Anti-Slavery League, London
26 September 1846	death of Thomas Clarkson
3 October 1846	Saturday, lectured with Garrison and Henry C. Wright, Belfast Music Hall, Belfast
3 October 1846	Evening – farewell soirée to Garrison in Royal Hotel
6 October 1846	Tuesday, lectured on anti-slavery in Independent Meeting House, Belfast
7 October 1846	Wednesday, Garrison lectured in the Music Hall, Dublin
2 November 1846	Monday, Garrison spoke in the Music Hall, Dublin
4 November 1846	Wednesday, Garrison departed from Liverpool
12 December 1846	Thursday, women abolitionists in England purchased Frederick's freedom from slavery for £150 ($711)
4 April 1846	letter to the *Times*. Departed from Liverpool on board the *Cambria*
15 May 1847	Saturday, death of Daniel O'Connell
Autumn 1847	Frederick and his family move to Rochester
3 December 1847	Friday, launches the *North Star*
1848	signed the Declaration of Sentiments in favour of Women's Rights

10 April 1863	Friday, invited to the White House to meet President Lincoln
1865	Mrs. Lincoln gave Frederick her assassinated husband's favourite walking cane
1867	published appeal for 'impartial suffrage' for the black man
4 August 1882	Friday, death of Anna Douglass
1884	marriage to Helen Pitts
Summer 1887	returned to Dublin
December 1887	spoke in Washington in favour of Irish Home Rule
20 February 1895	Wednesday, died at his home near Washington. Earlier, he had attended a meeting of Women's National Council
1 December 1903	Tuesday, death of Helen Pitts Douglass. She was buried alongside Frederick and Anna in Mount Hope Cemetery in Rochester

ACKNOWLEDGEMENTS

As the book was in its final stages, a debate about Confederacy statues erupted in the U.S. During these, at times, ahistorical discussions, it seemed to me that Frederick Douglass was needed more than ever. While it is heartening to see how Frederick's sentiments and values retain their power through time, it is disheartening to observe that such a divisive atmosphere persists.

Many people have assisted or inspired me during the writing of this book. In particular, I would like to thank the staff of the Royal Irish Academy in Dublin, the Boston Public Library and the Burns Library in Boston. A number of individual librarians and archivists have assisted me. Two in particular stand out – Robert Young of Quinnipiac University and Alan Delozier of Seton Hall University. I acknowledge their help with much gratitude.

Over the years, this project has been assisted and inspired by many people. A special thanks is due to my colleagues on the 'Frederick Douglass Ireland' Committee. They are Nettie Washington Douglass, Kenneth B. Morris Jr, Kristin Leary and Don Mullan. Individually and collectively they do wonderful work to promote the cause of human rights internationally. Nettie and Ken are descended from Frederick – and their illustrious ancestor would be proud of all that they have achieved and how much time they devote to keeping his memory alive. The creation of this committee was the idea of Don Mullan, also a selfless human rights activist, whom I am delighted to call my dear friend. A few years ago, I had the pleasure of traveling to Ireland with Congressman John Lewis, and, while there, I was privileged to hear him deliver the inaugural Frederick Douglass lecture in the Department of Foreign Affairs in Dublin. A few days later, in the company of John Lewis and John Hume I walked across the Peace Bridge in Derry. The spirit of Frederick Douglass (and Daniel O'Connell) lives on in these two great civil rights leaders.

There are many people who are engaged in telling Frederick's story, in different ways, and I have benefited from my interactions with them. Dr. Catherine Shannon and John Walsh in Boston; James Russell in New Bedford and Nantucket; Dr. Tim Madigan in Rochester; Dr. Maureen Murphy in New York; Todd Alllen in New Jersey; Máirtín Ó Muilleoir MLA and Rev. Bill Shaw in Belfast; Gerry Adams TD and Ardmhéara Mícheál Mac Donncha in Dublin; Patrick O'Shea, formerly of the University of Maryland and now President of University College, Cork – they have each helped to promote Frederick's remarkable life story. Andrew Edwards, a brilliant sculptor from Stoke in the north of England, has created two magnificent statues of Frederick, based around the time he was in Ireland, when aged only 27 years old. They are not only visually beautiful, but Andrew has captured the energy and vibrancy of the young Frederick Douglass. Frederick's message of universal compassion is being carried on by Dr. William Smith of Wheelock College. His leadership at the National Centre for Race Amity is an important reminder that we need to remember and learn from moments that have united us as a people, not simply those that have divided us.

My colleagues at Quinnipiac University have embraced my passion for Frederick and have worked with me to create an exhibition and documentary to commemorate Frederick's time in Ireland. Our aim is to make him accessible to students through a variety of different projects and by viewing him through a variety of prisms. I would like to thank, in particular, Rebecca Abbott, Lynn Bushnell, Kevin Convey, Kevin Daly, Paula Fowler, Ann Marie Godbout, Robert Joven, Karla Natale, Sandy O'Hare, Robert Young and President John Lahey.

Many historians are involved in doing wonderful work on Frederick. There are two that I would like to mention. Tom Chaffin has done much to highlight the 'Irish' Frederick, and I have enjoyed my exchanges with him. I am also extremely grateful to David Blight of Yale University for his encouragement for this project.

My friends put up with me and understand that when I am writing, my communications with the outside world are rare. They include Bernadette Barrington, Angela Farrell, Honora Ormesher, Susan Bailey, Gerard Moran, Caroilin Callery, Jason King, Peter Murphy and Ruth Jacob. Special thanks belong to Francine Sagar – who is one of the best proofreaders that I know. Of course, any remaining mistakes are my own.

Finally, my deepest gratitude is for my children, Siobhán and Ciarán, who continue to keep me grounded, and I am grateful for their love, their support and their deeply held humanitarian principles. I recently acquired another son (in law), Dave Marchese. He, and his large Italian family, are a wonderful addition to the Kinealy clan. An essential part of the Kinealy household is a dog. My own dog, Cú, forced me to stop writing at regular intervals so that he could have food or a walk. He was a necessary reminder that there was a world outside of Frederick and beyond this book.

Of course, at the top of this list of people to thank is Frederick himself. Reading his public lectures and his private correspondence made me feel very near to him, which was a great honour. Transcribing the speeches not only brought me closer to the man himself, but during times of pain and sadness, it brought an inner peace and tranquility. I thank him for that.

Although he is now over 200 years old, Frederick's words and vision resonate today.

INTRODUCTION

The year 1845 proved to be a pivotal one both in the history of Ireland and in the personal life of Frederick Douglass. In May of that year, Douglass's autobiography, *Narrative of the Life of Frederick Douglass, an American Slave. Written by Himself*, had been published in the United States to equal degrees of praise and opprobrium;[1] in September, a destructive blight appeared on the potato crop in Ireland, marking the onset of a prolonged and deadly famine. By travelling to the United Kingdom to avoid being captured and returned into slavery, unwittingly Douglass became a witness to this unfolding tragedy, which was to develop into one of the most devastating social disasters in modern European history. Concurrently with the commencement of a famine in Ireland, the 'fugitive' slave, for the first time in his life, felt like a free man, and rejoiced in this transformation as he found his own voice and matured from being an American abolitionist to an international human rights' champion.[2] Neither Douglass nor Ireland would ever be the same afterwards.

Arrivals

Frederick Douglass was born a slave on a plantation in Maryland, with the given name of Frederick Augustus Washington Bailey. Little else about his early life is clear. He never knew who his father was, although he suspected it was the 'owner' of his mother, Harriet. He did not know his precise age, calculating that he had been born in 1817 or 1818. He was mostly raised by his grandmother and only saw his mother occasionally, she dying in 1825 or 1826. In 1827, he became the property of Thomas Auld and, around this time, was taught the rudiments of reading by Sophia Auld, whom Frederick described as 'a woman of the kindest heart and finest feelings'.[3] Teaching slaves to read was illegal, and so she stopped at her husband's insistence, he explaining that if a slave could read and write:

> there would be no keeping him. It would forever unfit him to be a slave. He would at once become unmanageable, and of no value to his master. As to himself, it could do him no good, but a great deal of harm. It would make him discontented and unhappy.[4]

1

Frederick, however, understood that reading and writing would provide him with a pathway to intellectual freedom, and so he persisted in learning in secret. His path to personal freedom was to take some time longer to achieve. He, with five other slaves, plotted to escape to the north in 1836, but the plan was uncovered and they were jailed briefly. A second attempt in 1838 was successful. Frederick subsequently claimed that his determination to escape had been inspired by a number of Irishmen: he had read the speeches of the Irish politician Richard Brinsley Sheridan, and Irish workers on a wharf in Baltimore had encouraged him to run away to the north.[5]

Shortly after arriving in New York, a free state, Frederick was joined by Anna Murray, a free black housekeeper whom he had met in Baltimore the previous year. They were married in September 1838 by James Pennington, also an escaped slave from Maryland, who had pursued a religious vocation. Pennington did not charge the penniless couple a fee.[6] A few days later, the newlyweds moved to New Bedford, a seaport town associated with whaling and regarded as a relatively safe location for runaway slaves. There, partly to protect his 'fugitive' slave status, he changed his surname to Douglass. Under the Fugitive Slave Act of 1793, all citizens, even in the states where there was no slavery, were by law required to assist in returning runaway slaves to their owners.[7] In New Bedford, Douglass was employed on the docks, but mostly as an unskilled labourer because the white skilled labourers refused to work alongside skilled black workers.[8] Regardless of this and other examples of prejudice and segregation, he rejoiced in his new status:

> I found employment, the third day after my arrival, in stowing a sloop with a load of oil. It was new, dirty, and hard work for me; but I went at it with a glad heart and a willing hand. I was now my own master. It was a happy moment, the rapture of which can be understood only by those who have been slaves. It was the first work, the reward of which was to be entirely my own. There was no Master Hugh standing ready, the moment I earned the money, to rob me of it. I worked that day with a pleasure I had never before experienced. I was at work for myself and newly-married wife. It was to me the starting-point of a new existence.[9]

Douglass embraced his freedom in other ways – obtaining a license to preach in the African Methodist Episcopal Zion Church (the only Methodist church in the U.S. that did not practice segregation); subscribing to the *Liberator*, the newspaper of William Lloyd Garrison's American Anti-Slavery Society; and speaking at several abolition meetings. American abolition had split in 1840 into two distinct groups, one led by Garrison and the other by Lewis Tappan in New York.[10] The latter, the American and Foreign Anti-Slavery Society, tended to be more moderate and rejected causes such as non-resistance and women's rights. Tappan also disliked Garrison's heterodox views on the Sabbath. Douglass gravitated towards the more radical society. Following Douglass's contributions at an American Anti-Slavery Society meeting in Nantucket in August 1841, he received an invitation to lecture with the American Anti-Slavery Society for a trial period of a few months. Some months afterwards, he, Anna and their three children, Rosetta, Lewis and Frederick Jr., moved to Lynn in Massachusetts, a centre of abolitionism.[11] Douglass's rise on the anti-slavery circuit was rapid, fueled by his compelling life story, his physical attractiveness and his speaking abilities. The experienced abolitionist Nathaniel Peabody Rogers, who heard Douglass speak in Rhode Island towards the end of 1841, was moved to write:

> This is an extraordinary man. He was cut out for a hero. In a rising for Liberty he would have been a Toussaint or a Hamilton . . . A commanding person – over six feet, we should say, in height, and of most manly proportions. His head would strike a phrenologist amid a sea of them at Exeter Hall, and his voice would ring like a trumpet in the field. Let the South congratulate herself that he is a *fugitive*. It would not have been safe for her if he had hung around the plantations a year or two longer . . . As a speaker he has few equals. It is not declamation – but oratory, power of debate . . . He has wit, argument, sarcasm, pathos – all that first-rate men show in their master efforts. His voice is highly melodious and rich, and his enunciation quite elegant, and yet he has been but two or three years out of the house of bondage.[12]

Interestingly, Rogers also noted that Douglass's speaking style had 'strikingly improved' since he had heard him speak three months earlier. Douglass's oratorical skills led to him being given a position as a permanent lecturer for the Massachusetts Anti-Slavery Society at the beginning of 1842. During the next few years he lectured with other leading abolitionists, including Charles Remond Lenox, the only other black lecturer employed by the Anti-Slavery Society. Less well known is that Douglass lectured alongside Abby Kelley, a passionate abolitionist, feminist and reformer.[13] Kelley was the daughter of Irish Quaker immigrants.[14] During this time, Douglass also developed a close relationship with Garrison, his unofficial mentor.

Doubts, however, were being thrown on the authenticity of Douglass's life story, especially as he had avoided providing precise names or places. To counter such accusations, Douglass decided to write his own autobiography, replete with names. The writing of slave narratives, by both men and women, had become a powerful tool in the armoury of the abolition movement. They simultaneously provided evidence of the brutality of slavery and of the nobility and intelligence of slaves. They were also popular with the public, being more widely read than novels in the Victorian era, some selling in the tens of thousands.[15] The publication of Douglass's *Narrative* marked a milestone in his journey to freedom, but it also put him in danger of being found by his former master and returned to slavery.

While publication of the *Narrative* fuelled the debate about abolition, and consolidated Douglass's position as its leading authority, the excitement and publicity that it attracted put Douglass in serious jeopardy of recapture. According to the *New York Tribune*:

> In the book before us he has put into the story of his life the thoughts, the feelings and the adventures that have been so affecting through the living voice; nor are they less so from the printed page. He has had the courage to name the persons, times and places, thus exposing himself to obvious danger, and setting the seal on his deep convictions as to the religious need of speaking the whole truth.[16]

Douglass's initial motivation for travelling to the United Kingdom had been to seek sanctuary following the publication of his *Narrative*.[17] From Garrison's perspective, the presence of his star performer would also energize his allies across the Atlantic. Douglass spent the first four months of what was to become a twenty-month stay overseas, in Ireland. His initial reason for travelling there was that a Dublin printer, Richard Davis Webb, had agreed to publish an Irish version of the *Narrative* as a way of providing Douglass with funds during his stay.[18] But what had started as a pragmatic reason for visiting Ireland quickly became a personal one when Douglass encountered the ardency of Irish abolitionism and thus, unexpectedly, as part of his own private journey, 'the chattel became a man'.[19]

Douglass's journey across the Atlantic proved to be eventful. He left Boston on 16 August 1845 bound for Liverpool. He did not travel to Europe alone but was accompanied by James Buffum, an abolitionist from Massachusetts.[20] Buffum, a friend of Garrison since 1831, had physically defended Douglass when he had been grabbed off a railway carriage and attacked by a mob in 1841.[21] It was Buffum who had raised most of the money that paid for Douglass's fare, the remainder coming from sales of the *Narrative*.[22] The two men were accompanied by a talented singing family, the Hutchinsons, performers from New Hampshire. The Hutchinson quintet comprised of four brothers, John, Asa, Jesse and Judson, and their sister, Abby.[23] While their close-harmonies and performances were popular with American audiences, their public support for such controversial issues as abolition and women's rights, had proved less so. At a performance in Manhattan in March 1845, for example, they had been warned by local newspapers that demonstrators would attend with 'brickbats and other missiles'[24] to protest against the abolitionist anthem 'Get off the Track'.[25] The group performed it regardless of the threat. Amongst other songs, the Hutchinsons had penned 'THE FUGITIVE'S SONG, *I'll be Free! I'll be Free!*', dedicated to Frederick Douglass and other slaves.[26] Fifty years later, Jesse's brother, John, would sing this melody at Douglass's funeral.[27]

The abolitionist group sailed on board the *Cambria*, a steamship built in 1844. It had the capacity to carry 120 passengers, although only ninety-four undertook this particular journey.[28] The departure of Douglass, Buffum, and the Hutchinson family was noted in Garrison's newspaper, the *Liberator*, which predicted that, 'Their reception, we do not doubt, will be kind, cordial, enthusiastic. In every respect, they are deserving of the confidence, esteem and hospitality of our British friends'.[29] Before they boarded the steamer, Jesse Hutchinson led everybody assembled in singing, 'Home Sweet Home', with its famous chorus:

> There's no place like Home!
> There's no place like Home.[30]

As the ship sailed away, Garrison reported, 'The last thing we saw of Douglass was his waving his hat to us in the distance'.[31] The journey took less than twelve days but it proved to be eventful, reinforcing Douglass's precarious status as being simultaneously a champion of abolition and a runaway slave. In their journal, the Hutchinson family recorded that they were 'accompanied by Frederic Douglas [sic]'.[32] The entry for Monday, 25 August noted:

> Frederic Douglas [sic] had quite an exciting conversation with some of the passengers yesterday evening which caused some excitement. Today the captain invited him to speak but as the sea was rather rough he felt it best to defer it until we reached the Irish channel.[33]

Two days later, as the ship approached Liverpool, the journal entry read, 'At half past six Frederick Douglass attempted to speak on the quarter deck but was gagged down by a few slave holders and their employees'.[34] This incident, described in one sentence by the Hutchinson family, was to attract the attention of the trans-Atlantic press, occupying hundreds of lines of column space. The *Cambria* controversy ran for months, polarizing opinion along the traditional lines of the abolitionist debate. During Douglass's tour of the United Kingdom, he was to recount the incident on the *Cambria* to many audiences.[35] The drawn-out debates demonstrated how controversial Frederick's tour was and how unpalatable his actions were to the pro-slavery body.

The *Cambria* arrived in the bustling port city of Liverpool in the north of England on Thursday, 28 August. There, Douglass and Buffum stayed in the Union Hotel in Clayton Square for two nights. The two men continued on to Ireland, arriving on Sunday morning, having travelled on the overnight steam ship.[36] The Hutchinson family did not accompany them but remained in England where they were contracted to give a number of concerts. Initially, Douglass and Buffum had intended to stay in Ireland only for a few days, but this was extended as Douglass became involved with the Irish publication of his *Narrative*. Undoubtedly also, the American men were encouraged by the warmth of the reception they received and the widespread support for abolition in Ireland.

Douglass and Buffum's hosts in Dublin were Richard Davis Webb and his wife, Hannah Waring Webb.[37] The former, according to Douglass, was, 'the very impersonation of old-fashioned, thorough-going anti-slavery'.[38] Webb's two brothers,

Thomas and James, also businessmen, were both involved in the abolition and temperance movements. It was Richard Webb, a printer and admirer of Garrison, who had promised to publish the Irish version of Douglass's *Narrative*.[39] The Webbs were members of the Society of Friends, or Quakers. Quakers in Ireland formed a close network, which was part of a larger, world-wide, community. Within Ireland, they numbered in the region of 4,500, with approximately 650 residing in Dublin.[40] Many leading Quaker abolitionists were connected through marriage or through attendance at Ballitore, a renowned school in the village of the same name in County Kildare, where there had been a Quaker community since the late seventeenth century.[41] Although Christian, Quakers were religious Nonconformists and thus not part of the dominant Protestant 'Ascendancy' nor of the oppressed Catholic majority. Their distinctive, plain style of dress and of speech, notably the use of 'thee' and 'thou', also marked them out as being different. The Quakers were noted for their commitment to reform and philanthropy, and they were often at the forefront of international progressive causes. The Dublin abolitionists were at the radical end of various reform movements and, amongst other issues, they were supporters of temperance, ending slavery in British India, women's rights and animals' rights. They were opponents of all wars, but especially the recent Opium War in China.[42] Their overt commitment to international social justice must have provided Douglass with a sense of comfort as he settled into his life as an exile.

In Ireland, Douglass and Buffum also had extensive contact with James Haughton, a successful businessman, who was a nationalist and supporter of Daniel O'Connell.[43] Of him, Douglass said, 'there is not to be found a truer, or more devoted, vigilant, working, persevering abolitionist on this side the Atlantic'.[44] Haughton was president of the Hibernian Anti-Slavery Society (HASS), which had been founded by Haughton, Webb and Richard Allen in 1837.[45] Allen was its secretary.[46] Allen's involvement in many humanitarian causes had won him praise from American abolitionists who in an article published in 1842 averred, 'Though his heart is Irish, it beats for the world'.[47] In supporting total and immediate abolition, the Irish society was closer to the approach of Garrison rather than that of the moderate British and Foreign Anti-Slavery Society, which favoured a more gradual approach.[48] Outside of Dublin, Garrison's main support was based in Scotland and Bristol.[49]

The day after he arrived in Dublin, Douglass wrote to Garrison and announced that he was now 'safe in old Ireland'.[50] Douglass's reaction was not unique amongst American abolitionists. For abolitionists in general, and for Douglass in particular, Ireland held a special place in the anti-slavery struggle. A number of prominent abolitionists had visited the country in the previous decades, including Olaudah Equiano, who had toured the country in 1791 for eight months and sold almost 2,000 copies of his autobiography, *The Interesting Narrative of the Life of Olaudah Equiano or Gustavus Vassa, the African*.[51] Like Douglass's over half a century later, Equiano's writings and lectures were important in presenting slavery from the perspective of a former slave.

Another significant visitor was Charles Lenox Remond, a free man, who had been the first black lecturer on behalf of the anti-slavery societies in America, until Douglass.[52] Remond had travelled to England in 1840 to attend, amongst other things, the first World Anti-Slavery Convention. While in London, he had attended an abolition meeting at which O'Connell spoke. Remond was moved to write:

> for thirteen years I have thought myself an abolitionist, but I had been in a measure mistaken, until I listened to the scorching rebukes of the fearless O'Connell in Exeter Hall on 24 June, when before that vast assemblage, he quoted from American publications and alluded to the American Declaration, and contrasted the theory with the practice; then was I moved to think, and feel, and speak; and from his soul stirring eloquence and burning sarcasm would every fibre of my heart contract in abominating the worse than Spanish Inquisition system in my own, I almost fear, devoted country.[53]

Remond visited Ireland in 1841. Webb and his network of Quakers organized a lecture tour for him. His route was very similar to that undertaken by Douglass five years later, with visits to Dublin, Waterford, Cork, Limerick and Belfast. Remond also holidayed with the Webb family in County Clare – an experience that was shared with American abolitionists as Webb wrote a detailed account for publication in the *Liberator*.[54] Remond was universally admired in Ireland and when he left the country, he returned to America with an anti-slavery petition signed by over 60,000 Irish men and women,[55] the first names being those of O'Connell and Father Mathew.[56]

Nathaniel Rogers, a white abolitionist from New Hampshire, also visited Ireland briefly in the wake of the World Anti-Slavery Convention, in the company of Garrison.[57] His admiration was palpable:

> as we stepped ashore from the Glasgow Steamer, [Webb] took us, poste haste, through the crowded streets of the Irish capital, to 160 Great Brunswick Street, his own more than welcome home. There we had a great-souled time with the Webbs, the Allens, and the Haughtons, the Cochrans, the Downeses and the Drummonds. But only for three days . . . We ought to have staid three months. I never saw such a circle as the Dublin one, and never expect to again. It takes Old Ireland to top out *darling* human character. Genius, refinement, heart (a bosom-full of it), simplicity, hospitality warmer than brotherly love, high-souled philanthropy – reform of the most daring cast – I have never felt so much at home anywhere before.[58]

Other guests at the Webb household included Lucretia and James Mott, who also attended the Convention,[59] and Henry Wright, who had first visited Dublin in 1842

7

and stayed on a number of occasions thereafter.[60] In 1849, William Wells Brown, also a runaway slave, visited the Webbs. Richard arranged to print a Dublin edition of his narrative, although under the imprint of Charles Gilpin, a London-based Quaker publisher.[61]

In addition to the hospitality offered to American abolitionists, several Irish people had acquired international reputations as abolitionists. The latter included Richard Madden, a Catholic doctor and nationalist who, following the ending of slavery in the British Empire in 1833, had served in Jamaica and Cuba on behalf of the British government to ensure the fair treatment of former slaves.[62] Madden was also a sympathetic witness during the *Amistad* trial in 1841.[63] The Marquess of Sligo, who owned an estate in Westport, County Mayo, and property in Jamaica, had served as Governor and Vice-Admiral of Jamaica in 1834 and 1835, in order to oversee the transition from slavery to apprenticeship.[64] His outspoken criticism of the cruelty of apprenticeship, and his decision to liberate the slaves (now re-designated 'apprentices') on his own property, had made him a contentious figure in the colony but won him the praise of the Hibernian Anti-Slavery Society.[65] Even more prominent, but also more divisive, was the towering figure of Daniel O'Connell, a Catholic and the founder and leader of the Repeal Association.[66] The Repeal movement sought, through peaceful means, to restore an Irish parliament in Dublin, which had been dissolved as a consequence of the 1800 Act of Union.[67] O'Connell's other interests spread across a broad spectrum of humanitarian issues, ranging from support for the rights of Maoris and Aborigines to campaigning for 'Jewish Emancipation' in the United Kingdom. Moreover, since 1824, O'Connell had been a vociferous supporter of abolition, favouring an immediate and total ending to slavery throughout the world.[68]

Following his election to the British Parliament in 1829, O'Connell had become one of the most powerful advocates of a complete abolition of slavery. In 1832, when asked by a pro-slavery group of merchants and politicians to remain silent on this issue in return for their support on Irish issues, he had responded:

> Gentlemen, God knows that I speak for the saddest people the sun sees, but may my right hand forget its cunning and may my tongue cleave to the roof of my mouth before, to help Ireland, I keep silent on the negro question.
>
> I am for speedy, immediate abolition. I care not what caste, creed, or colour, slavery may assume. I am for its total, its instant abolition. Whether it be personal or political, mental or corporal, intellectual or spiritual, I am for its immediate abolition. I enter into no compromise with slavery; I am for justice in the name of humanity and according to this law of the living God.[69]

In contrast, the London-based Anti-Slavery Society, which had been founded in 1823 by William Wilberforce and Thomas Clarkson, was calling for measures to be adopted to improve slave conditions in the 'British Dominions' and for gradual emancipation that would lead ultimately to complete freedom.[70] O'Connell's unequivocal approach had won the admiration of Garrison, although on a personal level the two men did not get on. Garrison, however, realized the power and influence of the Irish man, whose words featured regularly in the columns of the *Liberator*. In March 1842, when he published a ten-year retrospective of O'Connell's speeches, Garrison predicted, 'They will scathe like lightening and smite like thunderbolts. No man in the wide world has spoken so strongly against the soul-drivers of this land as O'Connell'.[71] Similar to his mentor, Douglass too admired O'Connell, claiming that he had first become aware of him as early as 1838 when the Irish man had refused to shake the hand of the American Ambassador to Britain on the grounds that he was a slave 'breeder'.[72] Significantly, regardless of any differences, in the Preface to the first edition of Douglass's *Narrative*, Garrison referred to the Irish man as 'DANIEL O'CONNELL, the distinguished advocate of universal emancipation, and the mightiest champion of prostrate, but not conquered Ireland'.[73]

Ironically, O'Connell, the most famous Irish abolitionist, was not a member of the Hibernian Society but was more closely aligned with the British and Foreign Anti-Slavery Society, despite its gradualist stance. However, he lectured to and assisted both groups while maintaining his autonomy. Nonetheless, the relationship between O'Connell and the leaders of the Hibernian Society was at times fraught. O'Connell took a different stand on issues close to the heart of the Dublin abolitionists, namely temperance and pacifism. Although O'Connell ostensibly supported temperance, believing that it would increase discipline amongst his followers, he personally did not observe the pledge. And while he disapproved of the use of violence for political ends in Ireland, he viewed pacifism in a qualified sense, two facts not lost on Webb.[74] Even more seriously, following the formation of the Repeal Association in 1840, it had initially accepted funds from slave states in America.[75] The strengthening of the slave states, culminating in the annexation of Texas in 1845,[76] had alarmed O'Connell, and so, after 1843, he had stopped accepting Repeal funds from them, averring:

> I want no American aid if it comes across the Atlantic stained with negro blood; and from my soul I despise any government which, while it boasts of liberty is guilty of slavery, the greatest crime that can be committed by humanity against humanity.[77]

This action led to a number of Repeal associations in America condemning O'Connell, with a number choosing to dissolve, including those located in New Orleans and Baltimore.[78] Furthermore, his lacerating attacks on American slavery proved divisive with the Repeal movement in Ireland. Opposition to his interventions included that of the increasingly influential Young Ireland group who felt the two issues should be kept separate. An editorial in the *Nation* bluntly stated:

Repeal must not be put in conflict with *any* party in the States. The men of the Southern States must not have their institutions interfered with, whether right or wrong . . . We might as well refuse English money because of mill slavery . . . as well as quarrel with Americans because of their domestic institutions.[79]

Following the split in the Repeal movement in 1846, the Young Ireland group were more vociferous in distancing themselves from abolition and showed willingness to accept 'blood-stained' funds from America. Father Kenyon, a Catholic priest and close friend of John Mitchel, even announced, 'If slavery be an evil, then God mend it', which caused a rift with James Haughton.[80] In the same edition, the paper announced it did not want to publish further on the topic on the grounds that 'Irish slavery is an abundantly large branch of the subject for our time and space'.[81] Significantly, the *Nation* was one of the few Dublin newspapers that did not report on Douglass's lectures.

Regardless of O'Connell's separate stand on many issues, the Dublin abolitionists recognized that, when promoting abolition, O'Connell was their 'secret weapon', and so they were willing to overlook his shortcomings and utilize this valuable resource.[82] For example, at the beginning of 1845, O'Connell responded to a request by Haughton, who was a member of the Repeal Association and a personal friend:

With respect to the principles of President Tyler on the subject of negro slavery, I am as abhorrent of them as ever I was; indeed, if it was possible to increase my contempt of slave-owners and the advocates of slavery, my sentiments are more intense now than ever they were, and I will avail myself of the first practical opportunity of giving utterance to them, especially in connection with the horrible project of annexing Texas to the United States. But at the present moment the public mind is so engrossed by other topics of local interest, that an Anti-slavery speech would excite no such attention as it ought. I will, however, avail myself of the first favourable opportunity to express my indignation on the subject, so as to give my sentiments circulation in America.[83]

Overall, the tensions within the Irish and British abolitionist movements showed that, on both sides of the Atlantic, alignments and alliances were complex. Douglass, relatively young and inexperienced, was landed into the centre of this fractious, if passionate, group of Irish abolitionists, not aware of the sensitive fault lines.

As he had promised, Douglass kept in contact with Garrison with a series of letters, which were clearly intended for wider publication in the *Liberator*. When compared with other sources, it is evident that the contents of the letters were not always totally accurate. Understandably, both Douglass and Garrison were keen to show readers in America – from both sides of the slavery divide – the most positive aspect of his reception by Irish audiences.[84] The first letter, dated 1 September and written in Dublin, while expressing delight at being in Ireland, explained that the final stage of the voyage to Liverpool had been marred by an attempt to prevent him from giving a public lecture on board the *Cambria*.[85] Douglass's second letter, again written from Dublin and dated 16 September, concluded with a reflection on how he was being treated in Ireland, which led him to conclude, 'I find myself not treated as a *color*, but as a *man* – not as a thing, but as a child of the common Father of us all'.[86] At the time of writing, Douglass had been in Ireland for two weeks, but his words suggested that a subtle, yet significant, transformation had taken place. Frederick Douglass the free man had replaced Frederick Douglass the fugitive slave.

The early letters and public appearances of Douglass gave little indication of the mounting tensions that were emerging between him and Webb, and between him and Buffum. Even before Douglass had arrived in Europe, his former colleagues from across the Atlantic were casting doubts on his integrity. Maria Weston Chapman, a Boston abolitionist and ardent supporter of Garrison,[87] had asked Buffum to keep an eye on him and report back on his actions. In addition, she had warned Webb to ensure that Douglass would not be tempted to support any rival anti-slavery societies.[88] This was a reference to the British and Foreign Anti-Slavery Society, which was regarded as a rival to Garrison's more radical society. In a follow-up letter, when it became clear that Douglass's tour was a major success, Chapman expressed concern that his new-found celebrity status would go to his head and that he would become 'drunk with vanity'. She also implied that Douglass was motivated by money rather than principles.[89] When Webb, ill-advisedly as it turned out, showed these letters to Douglass, the latter was understandably furious. Chapman, however, defended her actions, saying it was 'in my heart at the time' and suggesting that she had not done 'Friend Douglass any harm'.[90] Douglass waited until the end of March 1846, when he was ensconced in Scotland, to reply directly to Chapman. Informing her that he felt 'disappointed', he added:

> I can assure you Dear Madam that you have mistaken me altogether if you suppose that ethr [sic] the love of money – or the hate of poverty will drive me from the ranks of the old organized antislavery society . . . And although not sustained as I supposed myself to be, I can thus far challenge the strictest scrutiny into all my movements [.] I have neither compromised my self nor the character of my friends. But enough.[91]

Privately, Webb was having issues with his guest. In a letter to Chapman, he lambasted Douglass, describing him as, 'absurdly haughty, self-possessed and prone to take offence'. He added:

> He is in my opinion by much the least likeable and the least easy of all of the abolitionists with whom I have come into intimate association. I think his selfishness intense, his affections weak, and his unreasonableness

11

quite extravagant when he is in the slightest degree hurt or when he thinks himself hurt.[92]

Webb was also annoyed by Douglass's treatment of Buffum, describing his behavior as 'absolutely insolent'.[93] Douglass's interactions, however, probably resulted from having discovered that he was, effectively, being spied on. Moreover, these tensions were a microcosm of wider anxieties and undercurrents within the trans-Atlantic anti-slavery movement. Historian Benjamin Soskis suggests, 'There was a curious ambivalence among American abolitionists towards Douglass's British celebrity, one that reflected their attitudes towards the role of blacks in the anti-slavery movement as a whole'.[94]

If the private Frederick Douglass was proving to be a disappointment to some, the public Frederick Douglass was exceeding all expectations. A month after his arrival in Dublin, Webb informed Garrison, 'The general impression F.D. has made has been highly favourable, both to himself and to his race, by the mother's side'.[95] Douglass's physical appearance was frequently commented on, particularly in the press, and overwhelmingly positively. However, despite flattering reporting on Douglass's appearance, he was clearly viewed through a racial prism. One press report, commenting on his lecture, stated, 'Here the speaker imitated the nasal twang of the old man, in a style curiously characteristic of the negro passion for mimicry'.[96] On a rare occasion, during a lecture in Cork, Douglass expressed annoyance with a local newspaper, the *Cork Constitution*, that had referred to him as 'an excellent specimen of the Negro'. He informed the meeting that he was 'familiar with such epithets in America, and cared little for what their public journals said; but in Cork, in a place of enlightenment, he was not prepared for such language from a public journal', concluding that, 'it looked like a good advertisement from a slave trader'.[97] Privately, his own view of himself was expressed in a frank letter to his friend Francis Jackson, dated 29 January 1846. In it he explained, 'It is quite an advantage to be a nigger here. I find I am hardly black enough for British taste, but by keeping my hair as woolly as possible I make out to pass for at least for half a Negro at any rate'.[98] Douglass, an early fan of photographs, was aware of the importance of creating a positive visual impact. He regarded photography as a democratic art, which was an important tool in counteracting racial stereotypes. His personal interest and his lifelong mission collided, and thus Douglass became the most photographed man in nineteenth-century America.[99]

Although public lecturing had not been Douglass's purpose when he travelled to Ireland, his successful reception encouraged him to give more lectures and both to extend his stay in Dublin and to travel beyond it. In addition to speaking on abolition, Douglass also gave a number of impromptu lectures on his other passion, temperance. In Ireland, Britain and America, there was a strong confluence between the temperance and abolition movements. The three founders of the Hibernian Anti-Slavery Society were also very active in the Irish Temperance Union, with Richard Allen being its secretary.[100] These men were all

Nonconformists, but within Ireland the success of the movement was largely attributed to the activities of a Catholic priest, Father Theobald Mathew. On the afternoon of the day that Douglass arrived in Ireland, following an overnight sea journey from Liverpool, he travelled to Celbridge in County Kildare to attend a temperance meeting. There, he was asked to address the large meeting, thus making it his first public lecture in the country.[101] Following this, Douglass attended a number of other temperance meetings, including one held at Booterstown on Sunday, 14 September, at which Father Mathew – the 'apostle of temperance' – administered 'the pledge', that is, a promise not to drink alcohol.[102] Douglass, already a teetotaller, re-took the pledge from the Irish priest. In return, he was given a silver temperance medallion. Two days later, Douglass spoke on this topic in Richmond Gaol – intemperance being regarded as the source of both crime and poverty. It was the prison in which O'Connell had been incarcerated in 1844.[103]

Douglass's first lecture on slavery took place on Wednesday, 3 September 1845, when he spoke at the monthly meeting of the Hibernian Anti-Slavery Society in the prestigious Royal Exchange in the centre of Dublin.[104] The Hibernian Anti-Slavery Society frequently met at this venue, suggesting the social standing and influence of its members.[105] Douglass's first lecture was well attended, with local newspapers reporting that the venue was 'crowded to excess', with many people being turned away.[106] He spoke to a full audience for about forty-five minutes, and was judged to be overwhelmingly successful. During the course of his first lecture, Douglass praised Daniel O'Connell's role in the abolition movement, which clearly pleased the audience. The local newspapers provided detailed physical descriptions of the 27-year-old visitor, his demeanour and his oratory powers.[107] Two days later, Douglass spoke at a smaller venue in Dublin, the Mechanics Institute. The meeting was again crowded. Douglass told the audience that the day marked the seventh anniversary of his escape from slavery. His oratorical skills were lauded widely in the press. An exception, however, was made in a report in the *Waterford Chronicle*. While averring that 'He spoke with feeling and energy', it further added, 'though a little incoherently'.[108] It was a rare criticism of the increasingly confident young lecturer.

On 9 September, Douglass spoke at the Friends' Meeting House, where the room was described as being 'tolerably well filled'.[109] He returned to this venue on 12 September.[110] When writing to Garrison on 16 September, Douglass was jubilant about the success of his four 'glorious' anti-slavery lectures, describing them as all being 'crowded to over flowing'.[111] In particular, he was delighted at being allowed to speak in a Friends' Meeting House, pointing out, 'When at home, they would almost bolt us out of their yards'.[112] However, his elation was short-lived. Douglass's criticism of some of the churches in America – in particular, the Methodist Church – for refusing to speak out against slavery, was regarded as being inappropriate in a place of worship, and so he was not allowed to use this venue again, much to the annoyance of the Webb brothers.[113]

Douglass's lecture on 17 September was held in a new location, the Music Hall in Abbey Street, which could accommodate up to 3,000 people. To defray the expenses, there was an admission fee: 4*d*. for the body of the house and 2*d*. for the gallery. A second lecture was held in the Music Hall on 23 September, with the same entrance fees being applied. Publicity for the first lecture stated that this venue had been chosen in consequence of the 'inconveniently' crowded state of the lecture room on the previous Wednesday evening.[114] Douglass, however, was more forthright in describing what had happened: 'The Methodists in America supported slavery, and when he exposed their conduct the other night to their friends in Dublin, he had the door of the meeting house closed against him, and he was denied any further sanction from their body'.[115] Fittingly perhaps, the Music Hall was located only doors away from the most prestigious Methodist church in Ireland, situated on Lower Abbey Street.[116] In the course of his second lecture, Douglass had praised both O'Connell and the Roman Catholic Church. In regard to the latter he had stated that the Catholic Church had 'opened to them [slaves] their churches without any distinction'.[117] His comments were not totally accurate. At this stage, the attitude of the Catholic Church in America to abolition was ambivalent. Bishop John Hughes of New York, for example, an influential figure amongst Irish Americans and himself an immigrant, had urged Catholics not to take a stance against an institution that was approved of by the Constitution. Hughes had also led protests against the 1841 anti-slavery petition, at one point claiming that it was a hoax. He also disliked the extremism of abolition and the fact that its leadership was Protestant.[118] Douglass's comments, however, were well received in the largely Catholic city of Dublin.

Douglass's outspokenness regarding Protestant churches was supported by Richard Webb and his brother, Thomas, who challenged the Friends' decision in a letter that was published in both Ireland and in the United States. In it, they vigorously defended Douglass:

> Some Friends fear that Frederick Douglass does not express himself in a sufficiently gentle spirit. Only think of those who have been nurtured in the lap of ease, who have never experienced cruelty, hunger, or the midnight of the mind which is the fate of the bondsman, asking a slave to speak in silken terms of Slavery. Frederick Douglass has drunk the bitter cup to the dregs. His back is even now furrowed with the cow skin, his soul burns with the wrongs he has endured; the slaveholders have done their utmost to make a brute of him.[119]

Following Douglass's final lecture in Dublin, Webb again publicly referred to this incident and 'the sensitiveness of some religious bodies in our city', much to the amusement of the audience.[120] Shortly afterwards, James Webb left the Quakers, followed by Richard in 1851, Douglass's treatment being a catalyst for this action.[121] For Douglass, however, the incident was a warning of the fragility that surrounded the slavery debate, and the sensitivity of the churches when discussing this topic. It also demonstrated that, even in Ireland, there were limits to how he could frame the argument when it came to criticizing organized religion. The issue dragged on on both sides of the Atlantic long after Douglass had left the city.[122] But if religious sensitivities were emerging, they were balanced by increasing public recognition. At Douglass's second lecture in the Music Hall, the Lord Mayor of Dublin, John Arabin, was the Chairperson.[123] Both Douglass and Buffum were subsequently invited to dine with Arabin at his official residence, the Mansion House.

While Douglass was staying in Dublin, Daniel O'Connell – the Liberator – returned from his family home in County Kerry. For many American abolitionists, O'Connell was a source of inspiration. Although he had never visited the country (and refused to do so while slavery continued), engravings of him were frequently sold at the fundraising bazaars held by women's anti-slavery societies in America, and his speeches were reprinted in American newspapers on each side of the slavery divide.[124] O'Connell was also unusual in that he was a Catholic in a movement that, for the most part, had been led traditionally by middle-class Protestants. Douglass was a great admirer of the older man, claiming to have become aware of O'Connell while a slave. He also admitted that he had stayed in Dublin for so long in the hope of seeing the Irish Liberator.[125]

When Douglass encountered O'Connell, the Irish man was in his political twilight. Aged 70, his health was deteriorating, and his ambitions had suffered a major blow when Peel's government had put him in prison in 1844 in retaliation for the holding of a 'monster meeting' in Clontarf, near Dublin, which had been intended to provide a climax to the 'Repeal Year'. In the face of government opposition, O'Connell had, in fact, canceled the meeting. Although O'Connell's imprisonment aroused sympathy, it also demonstrated that Peel was a steely adversary who was willing to risk a civil war rather than grant Repeal. Following the stand down in Clontarf, and his brief incarceration and release, O'Connell did not revive the monster meetings, but focused on regional visits and Repeal dinners. His travels received extensive coverage in the Irish press and showed that, despite his recent setbacks, he was still 'the Liberator', the man who had won Catholic Emancipation for his people in 1829.[126] But age, deteriorating health and the failure of the 'Repeal Year' had all taken their toll. Moreover, the debate over the colleges bill, which paved the way for four new 'Queen's Colleges', or universities, in Ireland, which were to be non-denominational, opened the way for sectarian division and accusations of overt Catholicism. Even more significantly, the Young Ireland faction within the Repeal movement was gaining support. One of the issues on which they disagreed with O'Connell was the question of slavery, many of them deploring his fiery interventions and the impact they had on supporters of Repeal in America.[127] The division came to a head in the summer of 1846 when the leaders of Young Ireland were maneuvered by O'Connell's son, John, to declare publicly their allegiance to moral force tactics. They refused to do so. In the wake of this debate, there were now two Repeal parties in Ireland – at the same time that the British Conservative Party was splitting into two groups, the Peelites and the Protectionists. Thus, politics throughout the United Kingdom were divided and in disarray, and Douglass was a witness to these events.

In Douglass's third letter to Garrison, dated 29 September, he reported on his encounter with O'Connell earlier that evening. It had come about when Douglass attended a Repeal meeting at Conciliation Hall.[128] Although Repeal meetings were held weekly in this venue, it was the ones that O'Connell attended that made them so popular. O'Connell's attendance at the Repeal meeting at the end of September meant that not only was attendance high but 'his presence imparted a life, interest and energy to the proceedings which was in striking contrasted with meetings in his absence'.[129] Because the hall was so full, Douglass could only observe the proceedings from the back. Nonetheless, he was mesmerized and full of praise for the older man's oratorical skills:

> It seems to me that the voice of O'Connell is enough to calm the most violent passion, even though it were already manifesting itself in a mob. There is a sweet persuasiveness in it, beyond any voice I ever heard. His power over an audience is perfect.[130]

During the course of O'Connell's long speech, he referred to the dispute between England and America over the Oregon territory. He opined that:

> While the canker of negro slavery eats the heart's core of America, she can never be strong; while that remains a plague spot on her institutions, Heaven forbids that any country should prosper which was tainted with that infernal system.[131]

O'Connell also spoke at length separately on the topic of American slavery. A number of newspapers, however, omitted this part of his lecture, one simply noting that the Irish Liberator had delivered, 'a long flourish on slavery'.[132]

Following O'Connell's speech, the hall had emptied, enabling Douglass to move to the front, where he was introduced to John O'Connell. John, in turn, introduced him to his father, who invited Douglass on stage to say a few words. Multiple newspaper reports provided additional information, although they varied in detail regarding the length and the contents of Douglass's speech. It was during this speech, that Douglass made the famous 'Black O'Connell' comment – a phrase that was subsequently inaccurately but frequently attributed to O'Connell.[133] The confusion was partly caused by Douglass, who later claimed that the Liberator had introduced him in this way.[134] However, as the contemporary press reports all show, it was Douglass himself who coined this phrase.[135] O'Connell appeared not to comment on Douglass's speech but, when it was over, immediately called the meeting to an end. The meeting was widely reported, including by the Irish provincial press and in English newspapers.[136] Inevitably, there was some variation in detail and in the extent of the coverage. However, none of the press reports suggest that O'Connell made any comment on the speech or on the man who delivered it. O'Connell's speech, with his comments on slavery, was reprinted in the *Liberator* on 24 October, interspersed with comments by Garrison, who was critical of some of the remarks made by the Irishman. Interestingly, Garrison's report did not mention the speech made by Douglass at the end of this meeting.

The varying accounts of this meeting, on both sides of the Atlantic, show the divergences within newspaper reportage but also within memory. Despite subsequent suggestions to the contrary, this was probably the only time the two men, 27-year-old Douglass and 70-year-old O'Connell, met. At this stage, O'Connell was in the latter days of his career, with the Repeal movement about to splinter into two opposing factions, Young Ireland and Old Ireland. Nevertheless, as his speech in Conciliation Hall proved, his passion and eloquence on the issue of anti-slavery remained absolute.

At the weekly meeting of the Repeal Association the following week, O'Connell was not present, but his son, John, spoke at length about the annexation of Texas, and he denounced any Irish American who did not condemn slavery. He was challenged by a member of the audience who argued that 'the slave-holding states showed more liberality towards the Irish emigrants and extended to them with much more readiness the hand of friendship and good fellowship than the cold northern states which pretended to hate slavery with a most cordial detestation and at the same time hated in their heart's core the name of an Irish man (hear hear)'.[137] His comments demonstrated that even before the mass exodus of the Irish to America resulting from the Great Famine, they were experiencing prejudice, and furthermore that the support of Irish Americans for abolition should not be taken for granted. The approval that greeted his comments suggested that support for abolition was complex and conditional and did not easily transfer to the American context. However, during the long debate, there was no mention of the visiting abolitionist from North America who had stood on that stage only one week earlier.

The Hutchinson siblings had not accompanied Douglass and Buffum to Ireland but had remained in Liverpool for three weeks. They first performed in that city on 10 September – in a singing style largely unknown to English audiences. Despite this, they were well received.[138] From Liverpool, they travelled to Ireland, arriving on 21 September. In Dublin, they reunited with Douglass and Buffum and also met James Haughton and the Webbs.[139] Subsequently, they met O'Connell and Father Mathew.[140] Their first concert in Dublin, on 22 September, was poorly attended, which was in strong contrast to their sell-out performances in America.[141] They also performed at a lecture given by Douglass in the Music Hall on 23 September.[142] According to Webb, their singing was the first time there had been music at an anti-slavery meeting in Ireland. He informed Garrison:

> The Hutchinsons are here. They are a delightful troop. They have sung the first songs ever sung at an anti-slavery meeting in Dublin. They have a glorious gift, and nobly they employ it for the good of humanity. Their style of singing is so different from the scientific and artificial style so much in vogue here, that I cannot give an opinion as to their probable success.[143]

Shortly afterwards, the musical siblings travelled back to Britain. They returned to Ireland to perform in a benefit concert in the Music Hall on 13 October, their repertoire including 'The slave's appeal'.[144] When they finally departed, Webb penned 'Farewell to the Hutchinson Family Singers, Ireland, 1845', to mark their departure:

> When you came among us strangers
> Having braved the ocean dangers
> Cold perhaps, at first we met
> Now we part you with regret.
>
> You have sung in accents clear,
> Strains our souls delight to hear –
> Songs of Freedom, pure and holy
> Pleading for the poor and lowly.
>
> Jesse, Judson, John and Asa,
> Gentle Abby we address you;
> Not as strangers now we meet you,
> But in Friendship true, we greet you.[145]

In England, the Hutchinsons gave further performances. In Preston, a town associated with temperance, the concert was billed as 'intended to elevate the tastes and improve the moral and intellectual character of the working classes'.[146] Despite having a style and approach not familiar to those who attend their concerts, they won much praise and a considerable following. One notice of a concert in Manchester, which noted their 'simple harmony and ballad singing in a style which catches hold of the popular feeling to a high degree', added:

> I have seen a whole Athenaeum and Mechanic's Institute, consisting of clerks and working men, with tears coursing down their noses most piteously. They are encored in almost everything they sing, and have considerable comic humour, which, though upon local subjects principally, has caught hold of our Lancashire people most thoroughly.[147]

The Hutchinsons' final concert was performed in Liverpool on 3 July 1846. Douglass, Buffum and Elihu Burritt – an abolitionist from Connecticut – were all in the audience.[148] When the singers sailed out of the city to return home, on the same vessel as Buffum, Douglass was present to bid them farewell.[149]

Douglass, accompanied by Buffum, left Dublin on 7 October 1845. Although over the succeeding twelve months they returned to Dublin on at least two occasions, they never again gave public lectures in the city. Assisted by introductions from the Webb family, the two men had been invited to lecture in a number of other Irish towns and cities. They were initially heading to the city of Cork. As they travelled south, they were accompanied by Richard Webb and Maria Waring, sister of Hannah Waring Webb and sister-in-law of Webb.[150] They stopped in Wexford and Waterford to give some impromptu lectures. Each location had an established Quaker community, and the Waring sisters had family connections in both places, thus facilitating the Americans' visit.[151] Douglass's lectures in the smaller towns of Wexford, Waterford and, later, Youghal achieved less press coverage than those in the larger towns and cities of Cork, Limerick and Belfast. In Waterford, for example, the attendance was euphemistically described as being 'by no means large'.[152] It appears though, that the lectures had been hastily arranged with no notice given to the local press.

Shortly after the American abolitionists left the town, the *Waterford Chronicle* became enmeshed in a public dispute with the *Boston Pilot*. The American paper had written a long column criticizing the Waterford publication for its attack on the 'peculiar American institution' and all Irish Americans who did not support abolition. In turn, the *Waterford Chronicle* wrote a long defence of its position and rebuttal of the *Boston Pilot's* stance. The Irish paper was praised by the *Kilkenny Journal*, which requested that:

> We beg of the *Boston Pilot* when he writes again, to honour the *Kilkenny Journal* also with his disapprobation, for, as polluted as his columns are with the defence of that plague spot, 'his praise is censure, and his censure praise.'[153]

The dispute between the *Boston Pilot* and *Waterford Chronicle* continued into 1846, occupying much column space.[154] It highlighted the difficulties for Irish immigrants in supporting abolition in America. This sensitive topic was one that Douglass did not address in his lectures, but about which he wrote and spoke extensively upon his return to America.

The ultimate destination of Douglass and Buffum was Cork, a city on the south coast, noted for its shipbuilding, brewing, distilling, tanning and butter industries. The nearby city of Queenstown (Cobh), situated on Cork Harbour, was a major port for trans-Atlantic migration – a role that was to increase after 1846. Like other major cities and towns in Ireland, Cork had been a beneficiary of slavery, largely due to the export of beef and butter to plantations in the Caribbean. Other products included salmon, herring and candles, all of which were exported to those islands.[155] In return, Cork and the nearby ports of Youghal and Kinsale received sugar, rum and tobacco produced by slave labour. At the same time, from the late eighteenth century, anti-slavery was gaining traction. In 1792, Anthony Edwards, a local bookseller, produced a sixty-page tract condemning the trade and urging the discontinuation of using produce created from slave labour.[156]

In Cork, Frederick stayed with Thomas and Ann Jennings and their eight children for five weeks at their fashionable home and business premises on Brown Street, close to the River Lee.[157] Thomas, an Anglican, was the manufacturer of 'non-intoxicating' soda water and vinegar.[158] Douglass became a close friend of one of the daughters, Isabel Jennings, and corresponded with her for many years. Isabel's abolitionist credentials were impeccable, she being one of the secretaries of the Cork Ladies' Anti-Slavery Society.[159] Douglass spent almost four weeks in in the city. As he had done in Dublin, he made a number of speeches on temperance, although they were less well publicized than those concerned with abolition. Douglass was a great admirer of Father Mathew, 'the apostle of temperance', who lived in the city, and they were to become friends during this visit, with Father Mathew inviting both Douglass and Buffum to his home for breakfast. Douglass admitted to being surprised by how simply the priest lived, observing privately he believed it was, 'rather too plain, I thought, for so great a man'.[160] Sadly, the men's friendship proved to be short-lived. In 1849, Douglass attacked Father Mathew for not speaking out against slavery during the priest's visit to America.[161] American abolitionists made a similar attack on the Hungarian nationalist Louis Kossuth in the same year for his comparable silence on the issue.[162]

While staying in Cork, Douglass visited Youghal in the company of William Martin. The town was approximately twenty-six miles away. There was a Quaker community, which included Dr. Joshua Harvey.[163] In a letter to Garrison, Ralph Varian, a Cork abolitionist and follower of O'Connell, described Douglass's lecture as being 'crowded', but no newspaper account appears to have survived.[164] According to Varian:

In company with Mr. William Martin, of this city, Frederick Douglass visited Youghall [sic]. They had an overflowing meeting. When Frederick Douglass had concluded his address, a vote of thanks was proposed to him, and carried by acclamation.[165]

In Cork, Douglass gave at least thirteen lectures on abolition and on temperance, which were delivered in a mixture of secular and religious venues. His time in Cork was not without controversy. As in Dublin, Douglass had criticized some of the Protestant churches in America for their stance on slavery and their failure to condemn slave-holders. Again, his views proved to be divisive, especially his criticisms of the Methodist Church in America. In contrast, Douglass praised both O'Connell and the Roman Catholic Church. In regard to the latter he stated that the Catholic Church had 'opened to them [slaves] their churches without any distinction'.[166] His comments were not totally truthful, as the response of Bishop John Hughes of New York demonstrated.[167] As with Dublin, however, Cork was a predominantly Catholic city.

During the course of his lecture in the Court House in Cork on 14 October, and again in the Wesleyan Chapel on 17 October 1845, Douglass criticized a number of Protestant churches in America for enabling and supporting 'the corrupting influences of slavery'.[168] In turn, several ministers who had been present attacked Douglass for pandering to a largely Roman Catholic audience. The Rev. Mackay said that he 'felt offended at the language used by Mr. Douglass'.[169] Newspaper reports of this event offer different emphases in their accounts of the incident, depending on their own political sympathies. Clearly though, while Douglass was welcomed and honoured in Cork, his Irish honeymoon was over. But if Douglass's message was unpalatable to some Irish ears, he was helping to reinvigorate abolition in America. Garrison, in particular, was aware of the propaganda value of Douglass's speeches and the fact that they were garnering the support of so many influential people. The reprinting of one of Douglass's Cork speeches in the *Liberator*, for example, was preceded by the warning, 'Southern Slaveholders read the following proceedings if you wish to know what are the feelings of the People of Ireland, in reference to your nefarious slave system'.[170] In October 1845, while he was in Cork, Douglass learned that he had been 'sold' by his former master, Thomas Auld, to his brother, Hugh Auld, perhaps in response to his new-found notoriety and popularity. The sale price was $100.[171] It was a grim reminder that, regardless of his success in Ireland and his new sense of freedom, 3,000 miles away there was a price on his head and that, under American law, he remained the property of another man.

In spite of the tensions and divisions, Douglass's visit to Cork was a great success. His lectures were also receiving some attention in the British provincial press. For example, the *Leeds Times*, when reprinting one of Douglass's speeches in Cork, preceded it thus:

> Fugitive Slave in Ireland – A week or two ago, a fugitive slave, from the United States, addressed a large public meeting in Cork. His name Frederick Douglas [sic]; he is a negro; and judging from his reputed speech, he seems to be a person of considerable powers of speech. In the course of his address, which was highly applauded, he said, 'I was sold as a slave at a very early age. . . . On 3 September 1838, I made my escape into Massachusetts, a free State, and it is a pleasing coincidence that just seven years after I stood up in the Royal Exchange in Dublin, to unfold to the people of that good city the wrongs and sufferings to which my race in America were exposed' (applause).[172]

Before Douglass left the city, his supporters held a soirée in his honour, and a song was composed for the occasion, 'Cead mille failte to the stranger.'[173] It was written by local poet Daniel Casey,[174] and its chorus was:

> Cead Mille Failthe [sic][175] to the Stranger.
> Free from bondage, chains and danger.

It was sung to the air of 'Old Dan Tucker'. Douglass, who was musically gifted and loved to sing, was so moved by the performance that he 'sang unsolicited with great effect, and power, a noble Abolition song'.[176] A number of placards decorated the room, including one that also said 'Cead mille failte'. These placards were later sent to Anna, Douglass's wife, as a gift from the women of Cork.[177] Douglass was to receive other permanent reminders of his time in Cork. When he left the city, the Mayor, Richard Dowden, sent him a ring – the first ring that Douglass ever owned. In a letter written from Limerick thanking Dowden, Douglass described the gift as 'representative of the holy feelings with which you espoused and advocated my humble cause'. He took to wearing the ring on the little finger of his right hand.[178] The poem sung at the soirée was later reprinted in a collection of Casey's poems, published in 1857, with the explanation, 'The following song, which the celebrated Frederick Douglas [sic] stated was sufficient to compensate for years of slavery may be deemed appropriate, as the recent struggles for Negro Emancipation have attracted such deep attention'.[179] Douglass kept a handwritten copy of the poem, and it was in his personal papers when he died.[180]

From Cork, Douglass travelled to Limerick, on the west coast. Limerick was an overwhelmingly Catholic city, with a population in the region of 50,000. During his stays in Dublin and Cork, Douglass had been accompanied by Buffum.[181] Despite the older man being the more experienced lecturer, the newspapers accounts made it clear that the former slave overshadowed the white abolitionist in terms of popular appeal. Douglass too was aware of this fact. In a private letter to a friend in America he admitted, 'My old friend Buffam finds the tables turned on him completely – the people lavish nearly all of their attention on the negro'.[182] In Cork, Buffum left Douglass to travel to Manchester in the north of England in order to attend a large Anti-Corn Law meeting.[183] Privately, however, the relationship between the two men had become strained. John Hutchinson recorded in his journal that Buffum had confided in him that he had 'had a falling out with Douglass and could not stay with him any longer'.[184] Consequently, Douglass travelled the sixty-five miles to Limerick alone. He remained there for over three weeks, staying with the Fisher family in Lifford House. The Fishers, who were Quakers, were related to Richard Webb. Benjamin Clark Fisher was a successful linen draper and a founding member of the Limerick Anti-Slavery Society. Benjamin had eleven daughters and one son. Douglass struck up a lifelong friendship with Rebecca and Susanna Fisher, who were also fervent abolitionists.[185]

Although Douglass stayed in the city for almost a month, he only gave three public lectures. In addition to talking about his own story, Douglass spoke about the current political situation, especially in regard to the annexation of Texas and the Oregon Question. Douglass's first two lectures in Limerick were in an Independent Chapel, a fact lamented by a local newspaper which believed that it gave a sectarian tinge to his appearances.[186] His final lecture took place in a secular venue, the Philosophic Rooms, and it was chaired by the Mayor. A number of Catholic priests were present. The lecture was part of a farewell soirée, replete with a temperance band and music before and after Douglass's speech. The evening had opened with the singing of the British national anthem, 'God Save the Queen', and towards the end of the evening, Douglass 'sang a beautiful sentimental air'.[187]

In Limerick, Douglass unwittingly courted controversy, this time for criticizing a theatre act that had recently been staged in the city – a 'blackface' minstrel act performed by a Mr. Bateman.[188] Bateman's origins are uncertain, with

one Irish newspaper referring to him as an American comedian who was touring Ireland, although elsewhere he was referred to as Irish.[189] In another review,
he was described as being 'the celebrated imitator of American character'.[190]
Another, however, referred to him as the '*nigger* Comedian'.[191] Douglass had
taken offence at the minstrel part of his programme. In turn, an editorial in the
Limerick Reporter criticized Douglass for attacking Bateman 'so bitterly'.[192]
Douglass, however, remained unconvinced, believing that Bateman and other
minstrel performers were presenting an inauthentic view of slavery, in contrast
to his attempts to present the authentic version.[193] To emphasize his point, Douglass showed his audience in Limerick a number of instruments that were used to
torture slaves.[194] This difference of opinion is perhaps not surprising. According
to the historian Douglas Riach, minstrel shows were popular in Ireland between
1830 and 1860, ironically, at the same time that the Irish abolitionist movement
was most active. He points out that, 'The shows occasioned considerable comment in the press, but surprisingly little, or none, among abolitionists'.[195] Riach
concluded that:

> It is probably that the cause of the Negro in America suffered from the
> failure of the abolitionists in Ireland to condemn as wholly inaccurate the
> image of the Negro most often presented on the Irish stage, and carried to
> America in the minds of countless Irish immigrants.[196]

While in Cork, Douglass had briefly alluded to the issue of whether or not the
Irish were slaves, describing himself as, 'A slave not in the ordinary sense of the
term, not in a political sense, but in its real and intrinsic meaning . . . By the laws
of the country whence I came, I was deprived of myself – of my own body, soul,
and spirit'.[197] Richard Dowden, the Mayor of Cork, had expanded on the difference between the Irish in Ireland and slaves in America, stating, 'They had many
things to do to elevate their own country, but they had not to get rid of the lash, and
the privilege they enjoyed of personal freedom they should strive to extend to all
mankind'.[198] In his first lecture in Limerick, on 10 November, Douglass returned
to the question of Irish 'slavery', tackling the issue head on, challenging the fact
that some Irish people referred to themselves as slaves. He informed his audience:

> He had been met with the objection that slavery existed in Ireland, and
> that therefore there was no necessity for describing its character as found
> in another country (hear, hear). His answer was, that if slavery existed
> here, it ought to be put down, and the generous in the land ought to rise
> and scatter its fragments to the winds (loud cheers). – But there was
> nothing like American slavery on the soil on which he now stood. Negro-
> slavery consisted not in taking away a man's property, but in making
> property of him, and in destroying his identity – in treating him as the
> beasts and creeping things.[199]

Douglass came back to this theme on a number of occasions. In Belfast, for example, he chastised people who did not sufficiently distinguish between 'oppression and slavery'. He explained, 'Slavery was not what took away any one right or property in man; it took man himself'.[200]

Douglass should have returned to Dublin for an event on 20 November but cancelled it, informing Webb, 'a number of young gentlemen here who have become entrusted in me and my mission and are very anxious and have really prepared to give me a soiree on Friday evening next. It seems a pity to disappoint them'.[201] In his final lecture in Limerick, Douglass told his audience that 'Whether home or abroad he would never forget the very kind manner he was received in Limerick'. At this stage, Boston and Maryland must have been distant memories as Douglass was welcomed into Irish homes and listened to with respect. However, Boston and Garrison were brought to mind through the medium of Richard Webb. Both Garrison and Webb desired that Douglass should join forces with Henry Clarke Wright. The peripatetic Wright had been travelling in Europe on behalf of the New England Non-Resistance Society. World peace was an issue close to Webb's heart, and so when Wright had first arrived in Dublin in November 1842, he had found a warm welcome and a willing ally in his schemes.[202] For some months in 1845, Wright had been in Scotland spear-heading a campaign against the Free Church to force them to send back the money that they had accepted from slave-holding states. The Free Church had been founded in 1843 by the Rev. Thomas Chalmers, as he was dissatisfied with the governance of the Presbyterian Church in Scotland.[203] Chalmers had been supported by the Rev. William Cunningham and Rev. Robert Candlish in this decision. Following the schism, or 'Disruption', new churches, schools etc. needed to be built and ministers paid. To finance this new venture, a deputation (which included Cunningham) travelled to America to appeal to churches there for support. Although their appeal was to all Presbyterian churches, the great bulk of their money was contributed by pro-slavery churches in the South.

The actions of the Free Church were opposed by both the British and Foreign Anti-Slavery Society and by Garrisonians, but it was the latter who kept the issue at the forefront of abolitionist debate. Wright, supported by English abolitionist George Thompson, commenced a campaign in Scotland that publicly demanded that the Free Church should return the 'blood-stained' money.[204] Wright's fiery attacks on the Free Church, given under the guise of lectures on slavery, were causing controversy in Scotland and dividing abolitionist opinion.[205] To Douglass, finally independent of being controlled and observed, the suggestion that he join Wright was unattractive for a number of reasons. In a carefully worded letter, he informed Webb:

> Friend Wright has created against himself prejudices which I as an abolitionist do not feel myself called upon to withstand. My mission to this land is purely an Anti slavery one, and although there are other good causes which need to be advocated, I think that my Duty calls me strictly

to the question of slavery. I am qualified for this, if I am for anything, and it would be idle for me to attempt becoming anything else at least under the present circumstances. Friend Wright is identified with doctrines for which I do not wish to seem responsible. He is truly a reformer in general. I only claim to be a man of one idea.[206]

Douglass also added that when he returned to Dublin they could talk further on the matter. At this stage, however, it seemed clear that Douglass did not want to share the stage or to deviate from his anti-slavery message.

From Limerick, Douglass returned to Dublin, again to the Webbs. After a brief stay in the capital city, where he made no public appearances, he travelled to Belfast, in the north of the country. Belfast had a long tradition of involvement with anti-slavery. In 1791, the republican group the United Irishmen[207] had welcomed Olaudah Equiano (also known as Gustavus Vassa) there.[208] Like Douglass fifty years later, Equiano had initially travelled to Dublin to oversee the publication of the fourth edition of his autobiography.[209] Vassa's personal testimony, *The Interesting Life of Olaudah Equiano*, had proved to be a bestseller in both Ireland and Britain.[210] As had been the case elsewhere, the abolition movement in Belfast had faded in the wake of the 1807 legislation outlawing the slave trade throughout the British Empire and making it illegal for British ships to be involved in the trade. It had revived in the 1830s, and until the founding of the Hibernian Anti-Slavery Society in Dublin, Belfast had been the most active part of Ireland in terms of agitating for abolition.[211] In September 1830, a large meeting had taken place in the town to call for the 'complete abolition' of slavery.[212] In 1832, the committee of the Belfast Anti-Slavery Society passed a resolution that:

> The real friends of freedom and humanity ought to be satisfied with nothing less than the immediate abolition of slavery throughout the British dominions; and that the electors of Belfast be earnestly recommended to withhold their support from every candidate not known as the decided advocate of this principle.[213]

Following the replacement of slavery with the apprenticeship system, the Belfast committee continued to agitate against that.[214] The committee's Protestant origins and leanings, however, were evident, with one of its founding members, the Rev. Dr. Edgar, saying that they 'represented the feelings of the great capital of Protestant Ulster'.[215] The Belfast group was later absorbed into the British and Foreign Anti-Slavery Society. In October 1841, Remond had visited Belfast. In the same year, the local Anti-Slavery Society issued a twelve-page appeal to the Christian churches in America whom they believed 'have cast the shield of their protection over the unrighteous dealers in slaves', asking them to refuse to have any dealings with slave-holders.[216] The appeal was signed by James Morgan, James Standfield and Francis Calder – the men who would host Douglass a few years later. Following Remond's visit, there was little abolitionist activity until the visit of Henry

Wright in December 1844. Wright's focus was on the 'Send Back the Money' campaign – an issue that was already polarizing opinion.[217]

In 1845, the town of Belfast was rapidly industrializing, becoming a centre of linen production and shipbuilding. In contrast to other parts of Ireland that Douglass had visited, which were predominantly Catholic, Belfast was predominantly Protestant, with Presbyterians in the majority.[218] A further difference was the fact that while anti-slavery societies in the south largely allied with Garrison and the American Anti-Slavery Society, the majority of abolitionists in Belfast were supporters of the British and Foreign Anti-Slavery Society, which was aligned with the American and Foreign Anti-Slavery Society. Douglass skillfully negotiated this divide – perhaps too skillfully for those watching his progress from Boston. However, as Douglass's visit showed (and Remond's and Wright's before him), the Belfast abolitionists were willing to work with Garrisonians.

Douglass left Dublin on 4 December, travelling the whole route to Belfast by horse and carriage, as bad weather meant that he missed his train connection. Even before he arrived, notices had been placed around the town and in the local papers announcing his lectures, one advertisement stating that he had already lectured in other parts of Ireland 'to large assemblies, who were delighted at the powerful eloquence displayed by the talented Lecturer'.[219] Douglass's hosts were the Belfast Anti-Slavery Society, which was an auxiliary of the British and Foreign Anti-Slavery Society. Two leading members of the Society, James Standfield and Francis Calder, accompanied the visitor around the town.[220] Of Standfield, Douglass wrote, 'I was much pleased with his face and more so with his conversation. I observed a heartiness about him, a little uncommon to those of his age', which he tempered with the comment, 'He was somewhat fearful I might disappoint them'.[221] The Society had arranged for Douglass to stay at the Victoria Hotel, at their expense. Staying in a public venue as opposed to a private home was not as pleasant as Douglass might have anticipated. He confided in Webb his new lodgings were 'Comparable comfortable', but that:

> The friends have placed me here they say to make me accessible to everyone that wishes to see me. They have gained their purpose thus far "still they come". I can thus far truly say that everyone that hears me seems to think that he has a special claim on my time to listen to his opinion of me, to tell me just how much he condemned and how much he approved – very well, let them come. I am ready for them although it is not the most agreeable.[222]

Upon arrival in Belfast, Douglass had privately confided to Webb that:

> here as elsewhere the enemies of anti-slavery have been busy in creating prejudice against me on the grounds of my heterodoxy. From what I can learn, the Methodist minister in Cork as well as Dublin have written here against me. Do you see mine will be no bed of roses.[223]

Fearing that religious venues might be closed against him as they had been in Dublin, he was particularly pleased to find that he was allowed to lecture in a number of Protestant churches: on the first night, he spoke in an Independent Church; the second lecture took place in the Wesleyan Methodist Chapel, Donegall Square; the third, in the Presbyterian Meeting House, Donegall Street; and the fourth in the Presbyterian Church on Rosemary Street. By occupying these spaces, Douglass believed that he was striking a direct blow at American Protestant churches who supported slavery.[224]

Douglass's first lecture in Belfast took place on 5 December. He started off with his hallmark humility, saying 'He felt considerable embarrassment in thus standing before intelligent people, for the purpose of instructing them'.[225] He then explained to his audience why their involvement was so important:

It will pain the conscience and anguish the heart of the slaveholder, to hear that, in the sacred soil of the Emerald Isle, the inhabitants of the Irish Athens, the emporium of commerce and seat of enterprise, interested themselves on behalf of the poor persecuted negro.[226]

He finished with a blistering attack on the country of his birth, perhaps the most damning that he had so far made:

Let the Americans, when they come here, feel that they are not looked upon as Christians, while they continue to trade so largely in the bodies of their fellow-men. He wanted the people here, and everywhere, to rise up, in indignant remonstrance, to tell the Americans to tear down their star-spangled banner, and, with its folds, bind up the bleeding wounds of the lacerated slaves. (Great cheering).[227]

In his fourth lecture, before he travelled to Birmingham in England for a temperance meeting, Douglass alluded to the Free Church and its taking of money from slave-holders. He informed the meeting of his intention to go to Scotland after Belfast in order to take the fight directly to those who had accepted the money. During the course of this address, he juxtaposed the actions of men of the church with those of Daniel O'Connell, 'the mere secular politician', who had 'disdained to take money from slave-holders.[228] Although this comment was greeted with 'cheers', being compared unfavourably to a Catholic nationalist must have galled a number of listeners. Subsequent favourable references to O'Connell were omitted by the Protestant press.[229]

As had been the case elsewhere, the Mayor of the town – in this case, Andrew Mulholland – chaired a number of the lectures. Douglass's success in Belfast also extended to book sales, he informing Webb, 'Well all my books went last night at one blow. I want more. I want more'.[230] Writing the next day, Douglass predicted that he could sell over 100 books in one evening.[231] As an indication of his newfound wealth and responsibilities, Douglass bought himself a watch on

6 December that cost £7-10*s* and which he described as 'a mighty good one'.[232] As he was reminiscing about this purchase five decades later, it was clear that the watch represented so much more than simply an instrument for keeping time, because, as a slave:

> I could hardly indulge in the hope of some day owning a watch, yet in those hope-killing days of my slave life I did think I might some-where in the then dim and shadowy future, find myself the happy owner of a watch, a real English 'bull's eye', such as a sailor, a regular sea-captain 65 years ago, might sport, with heavy chain and seal, from the watch fob of his pants. If a man in those days had a watch, it was not allowed to remain a secret to the outside world. It was a sign of wealth and respectability.[233]

Webb had organized for Douglass to travel to Birmingham in mid-December to meet people involved in abolition and to speak at a temperance meeting. Birming-ham was a centre of abolitionism, having welcomed Equiano there in 1790.[234] Douglass urged that Webb break this engagement on his behalf, believing his time would be better spent in Belfast and Scotland. Douglass also alluded to the coldness of one of the organizers when writing to him.[235] Regardless of his res-ervations, a week following his arrival in Belfast, Douglass travelled to England, where he spent over a week in Birmingham, partly as the guest of Joseph Sturge, one of the founders of the British and Foreign Anti-Slavery Society and, like Douglass, a committed advocate of temperance.[236] Douglass's misgivings initially appeared to be accurate. One of the first people he met was the Congregationalist minister John Angell James who, in 1840, had suggested that the churches should turn their backs on slave-holders. Douglass, describing their brief encounter, said, 'I found him not only cold towards me, but absolutely suspicious of me'. James also questioned Douglass as to his religion, an issue which Douglass refused to be drawn on. Nonetheless, at the end of their meeting, James purchased a copy of the *Narrative*.[237] In contrast, the veteran abolitionists Joseph Sturge and William Boultbee both welcomed him into their homes.[238] John Cadbury, who had initially invited Douglass:

> received me kindly – was rather afraid I would not come – acting on his fears he had left my name off the bill announcing the evening meeting. On talking with him, I found he felt the meeting to be a very important one – and himself measurably responsible for its success or failure. We soon parted. I left with the impression he doubted my ability to interest the audience.[239]

Douglass returned to Ireland on 19 December. He immediately wrote to Webb to let him know that he was 'again safe in old Ireland'. He also gave a lengthy account of the people he had met and how they had treated him. Regarding the actual temperance meeting, he reported:

> The meeting went on swimmingly. It was very edifying. I thought I perceived strong evidence that the committee did not intend to let me speak – they acted for a long time [as] though I were not there and as though they had not invited me. Six or seven speeches had been made. The interest of the meeting was on the decline – we had been together nearly three hours – a strong current set toward the door – at this moment the committee – as if waked by a clap from the sky – turned to me and asked me to second a resolution. I rose, was recognized by the President – proceeded – a few minutes and the current turned toward the door was turning towards the platform. I spoke 25 minutes amid cheers and sat down amid loud cries of good.[240]

Newspaper reports of the meeting corroborate Douglass's account. He had not been named as one of the invited speakers, and he only received a brief mention in the press when it was noted, 'several other able speeches were delivered'.[241] But if the professional reception afforded to Douglass was disappointing, personal relations proved to be more satisfying, with Douglass admitting, 'I fell in love with Mr Sturge, and had a good time . . . Father Boultbee is a fine old man, he cried like a child when I left – God bless him in his decline'.[242]

While Douglass was happy to be back in Belfast, the lectures given following his trip to Birmingham received a mixed reception when it came to the issue of the Free Church. He was also disappointed to find that his reception in the town was not as unreservedly open as it had been elsewhere in Ireland. Douglass made a public allusion to this treatment in the course of his lecture on 23 December, when he claimed that for the first time he had been asked to provide credentials. He also stated that there were rumours circulating that he was an imposter.[243] This skepticism was in strong contrast to the warm welcomes that he had received in other parts of the country and must have been a reminder of his initial reason for writing his *Narrative*.

In Belfast, Douglass became caught up in the controversy regarding the Free Church of Scotland's acceptance of money from American slave-holders. The 'Send Back the Money' campaign was to become a major part of Douglass's mission over the next year and was to polarize the British and Irish abolition movements. The reasons why he changed his mind about this issue, having unequivocally rejected any involvement only a few weeks earlier, are not clear but appear to be rooted in the town's strong Presbyterian links. Immediately on arrival in Belfast, Calder had given Douglass leaflets about the Free Church, leading Douglass to the realization, 'It will be necessary to say much about them here'.[244] Two days after arriving, he wrote to Webb that Belfast 'is the very hot bed of Presbyterianism and free churchism, [and] a blow can be struck here, more effectively than in any other part of Ireland. One nail drove in a sure place is better than a dozen driven at random'. On these grounds, he explained 'I think it will be of the utmost importance that I remain here a much longer time than that allotted in the first instance'.[245]

Douglass's increasingly unequivocal stand on the 'Send Back the Money' issue, which came to dominate his public appearances, proved to be divisive, and it weakened support for him, especially amongst Presbyterians in Belfast. While the local press continued to give extensive coverage to his lectures, the *Banner of Ulster* and the *News-Letter* made clear their disapproval of Douglass's criticisms of the Free Church, believing that it was damaging the cause of abolition.[246] Douglass responded to the criticism that he was being too harsh on the Free Church by saying: 'It was for her salvation he did it – it was for her purification he did it – it was for the redemption and disenthralment of his race from the chains of slavery he did it'. He also refuted claims that he was opposed to religion, a charge often leveled at followers of Garrison.[247] Privately, however, Douglass did attend church while in Belfast, a fact which he shared with Webb, although adding, 'tis not a sin in itself'.[248] The growing storm did not remain confined to the lecture venues, but was spilling into the letter pages of the local newspapers. The *Banner of Ulster* published a number of letters written by 'Civis' attacking Douglass and his supporters for their condemnation of American churches.[249] The fact that the proprietor of the *Banner*, George Troup, was himself Scottish and a founding member of the Free Church, although also an opponent of slavery, helps to explain the paper's stance.[250] Members of the Anti-Slavery Society wrote a response to Civis, which the Rev. Nelson hand-delivered to the *Banner* – but the letter mysteriously disappeared and was not published.[251] The dispute between the Anti-Slavery Society and Civis, and between the Anti-Slavery Society and the *Banner*, dragged on, overshadowing the true purpose of Douglass's mission to Ireland.[252] The dispute divided abolitionist opinion and even the press, with the *Northern Whig* opining that Nelson had been 'treated unfairly by the *Banner*', accusing the paper of being 'in this instance, the tool of the reverend slavery gentlemen'.[253] Battle lines were being drawn which would thicken over the coming months.

Although controversy was raging around him, Douglass refused to be swayed from a conviction that had now become central to his whole mission. Some years later, he explained that being in Belfast, a Protestant town, helped him to realize that the actions of the Free Church opened up the debate about the role of Protestant churches in America in regard to slavery, an issue he had repeatedly talked about in his lectures. Moreover:

> That church, with its leaders, put it out of the power of the Scotch people to ask the old question, which we in the north have often most wickedly asked – 'What have we to do with slavery?' That church had taken the price of blood into its treasury, with which to build free churches, and to pay free church ministers for preaching the gospel . . . this church, through its leading divines, instead of repenting and seeking to mend the

mistake into which it had fallen, made it a flagrant sin, by undertaking to defend, in the name of God and the bible, the principle not only of taking the money of slave-dealers to build churches, but of holding fellowship with the holders and traffickers in human flesh. This, the reader will see, brought up the whole question of slavery, and opened the way to its full discussion, without any agency of mine.[254]

Douglass gave three further lectures on abolition in early January. On the first night, 1 January, he was joined by Buffum, who shocked the audience with a display of the instruments of torture used on slaves. Douglass's final anti-slavery public event in Belfast took place on 6 January, when he was honoured with a breakfast. William Sharman Crawford, a progressive member of the British parliament and Irish landowner, attended.[255] A number of female abolitionists were also present who, inspired by Douglass, formally incorporated themselves into the Belfast Auxiliary Female Anti-Slavery Society. During the event, Douglass was presented with a pocket Bible, bound with gold, 'Presented by the Belfast Auxiliary to the British and Foreign Anti-Slavery Society'. Douglass, despite the controversy that he had courted in the town, responded by saying 'Wherever else I feel myself a stranger, I will remember I have a home in Belfast'.[256] It was a poignant reminder that the young man, who was a fugitive in his country of birth, indeed had no home and was 3,000 miles apart from his family.

As Douglass prepared to depart from Belfast to Scotland, he gave two final lectures on the other topic close to his heart – temperance. He delivered the first one on the evening of the farewell breakfast, and his second lecture on the following day. Buffum was again present and spoke, suggesting that publicly at least the two men had reconciled. A religious note was inserted into the lecture by Buffum, who chastised the audience by saying:

> He had been in the South as well as the North of Ireland, and was struck with the contrast. In the former, temperance and sobriety; in the latter, much intemperance yet prevailed. Was not this not a shame on Protestants, who in many things thought themselves superior to Roman Catholics? He and his friend, Douglass, had been most kindly, and hospitably entertained by Father Matthew [sic], who, under God, had been rendered the blessed instrument of carrying forward a great reformation.[257]

Douglass departed from Belfast on 10 January. He left with a number of gifts and goods: from Dublin, a blanket given to him by James Webb; from Cork, a ring given by Richard Dowden and a silver temperance medal from Father Mathew, while the placards from the soirée in his honour had been posted to his wife; in Belfast, he had received a pocket Bible from local abolitionists and a history book from the supporters of temperance. To this, he had added a watch that he purchased for himself. But more than the presents that he valued so much, during his time in Ireland, Douglass had received respect and admiration wherever he went.[258] Regardless of any disagreements that had arisen, the telling of his life story and his message about abolition had been overwhelmingly well received. As a writer and a lecturer, he had been praised. Just as importantly, in each part of Ireland he visited, he had walked the streets in the company of white men and white women without ever being accosted or insulted. Before departing Ireland, Douglass wrote his fifth letter to Garrison in which he reflected on his time in the 'Emerald Isle'. Despite any slights or setbacks, his sense of liberation was palpable, summed up in his phrase, 'I breathe and lo! The chattel becomes a man'.[259] For Douglass, acquiring a sense of identity and of self worth must have been particularly satisfying because, in so many ways, he defied easy definition: he was no longer a slave, but was not free; he was neither fully black nor fully white; he was a husband and a father, but living a solitary existence; he was a public celebrity, but his finances were precarious. Regardless of all of these contradictions, in Ireland, Douglass for the first time felt like a man – and that appeared to make all other ambiguities bearable.

From Belfast, Douglass travelled to Scotland, from whence he planned to go to England in March. His visit to Britain had again been facilitated by letters of introduction provided by Webb and other Irish Quakers.[260] In Scotland, which was the home of the Free Presbyterian Church, Douglass continued with the 'Send back the money' campaign.[261] In a letter dated 29 January 1846, Douglass outlined his commitment to raising the Free Church issue, even though it meant that abolition meetings were now 'of the most soul churning character'.[262] Ultimately, as in Belfast, it was to prove to be divisive to the abolitionist cause and personally damaging to Douglass. Regardless, the crusade that Douglass had commenced in Belfast dominated his actions for the next few months. Writing to Edmund Quincy,[263] the secretary of the Massachusetts Anti-Slavery Society, in late April 1846, he enthused:

> I think next year – you will have to devote a larger space in your report to Scotland. It has been & is to be the battle field of old organized Anti slavery action. It is now all in a blaze of anti-slavery excitement.[264]

In Scotland, Douglass was reunited with Buffum, their differences apparently forgotten. On a number of occasions, they also spoke alongside Wright and Thompson, two key figures in the 'Send Back the Money' campaign. Before leaving Edinburgh, a 'fruit soirée' was held in the city's Music Hall to honour the four abolitionists. The Hall was described as being 'overflowing', with those present as 'respectable', while a large portion of those who attended were 'ladies'.[265]

Although in his public letters Douglass appeared pleased with the progress made in Scotland and the impact of the 'Send Back the Money' campaign, in a private letter to his 'sister', Harriet Bailey,[266] dated May 1846, he admitted that he had been feeling ill and out of sorts:

> My underlip hung like that of a motherless colt[.] I looked so ugly that I hated to see myself in a glass.

There was no living for me. I was snappish. I would have kicked my old grans 'dadda'! I was in a terrible mood – 'dats a fact! old missus – is you got any ting for a poor nigger[267] to eat!!!

Douglass broke his despondent mood by purchasing a second-hand fiddle, and 'I had not played ten minutes before I began to feel better . . . as lively as a crikit [sic] and as loving as a lamb'.[268] Douglass included in his letter to Harriet a letter for his wife, 'Dear Anna'. Because Anna could not read or write, he requested Harriet to read it 'over and over again till she can fully understand its contents'.[269]

When Douglass left Belfast in early January, he had expressed the intent of returning in July.[270] In fact, together with James Buffum, he returned to Belfast to give a lecture in mid-June. While the two men were warmly received by their abolitionist friends, they were not totally welcomed. The *News-Letter* noted their arrival with the brief comment that: 'We perceive by placards posted through the town that Mr. Frederick Douglass has returned to Belfast, after his anti-slavery agitation tour in Scotland, and is about to deliver a public lecture on his favorite theme'.[271] Douglass's only lecture was made at the Church of Rev. Nelson. He preceded his main comments by saying that doubts about him having been a slave had been quelled and 'Thus the question is settled that I am what I represent myself to be'.[272] He then returned to the theme of 'Send Back the Money'. Douglass informed the audience that initially in Scotland he and Buffum had been 'coldly received', but that now the 'greatest anxiety and excitement were felt on the subject, by people from all classes of society'.[273] These neutral comments disguised how polarizing the topic was proving to be. During his lecture, Douglass also suggested – erroneously – that O'Connell had never accepted money from slave-holders.[274] In fact, O'Connell's position on this question had been far more ambiguous.[275] However, comparing a section of the Presbyterian Church unfavourably with a Catholic nationalist was a pointed dig by Douglass.

From Belfast, the two men visited Dublin, as Buffum, who was planning to return home, wanted to say goodbye to his Irish friends. They gave no public lectures in Ireland's capital city, Richard Webb explaining that 'their object being to rest a while after their stormy campaign in Scotland'.[276] From Dublin, Douglass returned to Britain. In England, Douglass spoke at a number of anti-slavery meetings, now mostly travelling alone. There, the focus of his lectures was more general than when speaking in Presbyterian strongholds, he describing his experiences as a slave and talking about the recent death of Rev. Torrey in prison[277] and the Mexican War, with fewer references to the actions of the Free Church.[278] In Birmingham, he once more lectured alongside Sturge, Cadbury and Boultbee, veterans of the abolitionist movement, whom he had met a few months earlier at a temperance meeting. Again, his focus reflected that of English anti-slavery societies, he talked about the duties on slave-grown sugars and using the produce of free labour.[279]

In mid-May, Douglass attended the annual general meeting of the British and Foreign Anti-Slavery Society in London. One of the speakers was the MP,

William Sharman Crawford, who referred to Douglass's visits to Belfast in warm terms. Following a brief discussion about the Free Church, Douglass was asked to address the meeting:

> In lengthy speech of considerable fluency, he denounced the conduct of the Free Church, and joined in the recommendation that the money which had been accepted should be returned. Mr. Douglas [sic] was proceeding to detail the state and condition of the coloured and slave population of the southern states, when Gentleman in the body of the meeting suggested that as the day was far advanced a separate meeting should be held for the purpose of hearing Mr. Douglas's statement.

The chairperson, Joseph Sturge, agreed and promised that, during the week, notice of the meeting would be provided by public placards.[280] It was quite a victory for supporters of Garrison. However, Douglass's willingness to speak at this meeting seemed to surprise Garrison and may have re-awakened fears that Douglass was becoming a little too independent.[281] If Garrison had seen the contents of a letter written by Douglass to veteran English abolitionist Elizabeth Pease, his fears would have been confirmed.[282] In response to a question about non-resistance, he declared, 'I think there is a *slight* difference between us. I am against taking life . . . and yet I can conceive of circumstances when it would not only be right – but our bounden duty to use physical force'.[283] Douglass's response was a clear rejection of Garrison's embrace of non-resistance. Instead, it was more in keeping with O'Connell's pragmatic views on pacifism.

Douglass's new-found independence was perhaps most evident in his handling of the re-publication of the *Narrative*. Douglass's initial purpose in travelling to Ireland had been that Richard Webb, a printer by trade, had promised to publish it, thus creating the first non-American version of the memoir. Writing to Garrison from Dublin on 16 September, Douglass explained that, 'our stay is protracted in consequence of publication here of my narrative'.[284] The Irish edition of the *Narrative* appeared within weeks of Douglass being in the country.[285] It cost 'half a crown',[286] which Douglass used as living expenses 'without seeking pecuniary aid from any assemblage'.[287] Early sales were buoyant. Webb informed Garrison, 'I have printed an edition of 2,000 copies of his Narrative, and 100 are already sold in a few days in Dublin alone.'[288] At the end of November, he reported:

> Upwards of 600 copies of his book have been already disposed of, and this is a very large sale when it is considered that the book is little more than two months published, and that the whole of this sale has been private, and with hardly any assistance from the booksellers. A large portion of this sale has been owing to the zealous and energetic co-operation of the Jennings family, of Cork, who are among the warmest and most efficient of your coadjutors on this side of the Atlantic.[289]

The rapid sales of the *Narrative*, and Douglass's need for income, led to a second Dublin version being published in early 1846, which included some changes suggested by Douglass.[290] An even more extended third Irish edition of the *Narrative* appeared in May 1846.[291] The second copy printed appears to have acted as a stop-gap, as Douglass was running out of copies to sell. This version appeared with the publication date of 1845, thus leading to confusion with the first Irish edition. Furthermore, the version that appeared in May 1846 was officially designated the second edition. To avoid confusion between the two *Narratives* published in 1846, the earlier one has been referred to as the 'variant' edition.[292]

The changes that were incorporated into the three Dublin printings, mostly at Douglass's insistence, provide an insight into the transformation that had taken place in the fugitive slave during the short space of time that he had been outside America. While the first Irish edition of the *Narrative* had essentially been a replica of the Boston publication, with some minor style changes to make it more suited to Irish and British readers, Douglass intervened to ensure that the two subsequent printings reflected his own interests. The flyleaf of the later editions included a resolution of the Hibernian Anti-Slavery Society welcoming Douglass to Ireland. Its inclusion could be considered a tribute to the Irish abolitionists who, within the space of only a few weeks, had made such an impression on Douglass, and vice versa. The resolution was followed by a new image of Douglass and a poem by John Greenleaf Whittier, which appeared on the title page.

Webb had a hand in some of the changes. It was his suggestion that an appendix be included, entitled 'An Address to the Friends of the Slave', which was an appeal on behalf of the annual Anti-Slavery Bazaar in Boston. When writing to Maria Weston Chapman, Douglass explained he had been happy to comply with this request:

> from no sordid motive, but because I believe it to be a powerful instrument in affording means to carry on our important anti-slavery Machinery . . . though I consider myself as forming a humble part of that machinery I have never received any pecuniary aid directly from it.[293]

It was clear that even though at the time of writing he was in Scotland and some months had passed since Webb had shared the contents of Chapman's letter with Douglass, her claim that the runaway slave was motivated by money and vanity still rankled.

Webb had also suggested that the second Irish edition be made 'shorter and thicker', a change approved by Douglass who, with an eye to aesthetics, had told Webb to, 'Get as good, and if you can get better paper than that used in the first edition'.[294] However, his other interventions were to go far beyond simply ornamental changes, with Douglass effectively taking editorial control of the contents. These more substantive changes signified a new-found sense of independence by Douglass. Both the Boston and first Irish editions commenced with a preface written by Garrison and a letter of endorsement written by Wendall Philips – two white abolitionists. This was not unusual because, 'Even though it was desirable for ex-slaves to write their stories, dominant racist doctrine still mandated that relationship be established whereby whites functioned as those who sanctioned black voices'.[295] Garrison and Philips remained in the Irish editions but their position was usurped when a preface written by Douglass himself was inserted in front of the original preface in the two subsequent printings. At the end of the preface, Douglass proclaimed, 'I am an American slave, who has given my tyrant the slip. I am in a land of liberty, with no man to make me afraid'.[296] An extended version of the preface was reprinted in the second Irish edition (although the third to be printed) which appeared only two months later in 1846.[297]

In the new preface, Douglass explained that his reasons for leaving the United States had been 'Threefold' and that they had, to a large extent, been achieved:

> I wished to be out of the way during the excitement consequent on the publication of my book; lest the information I had there given as to my identity and place of abode, should induce my owner to take measures for my restoration to his 'patriarchal care.' For it may not be generally known in Europe, that a slave who escapes from his master is liable, by the Constitution of the United States, to be dragged back into bondage, no matter in what part of the vast extent of the States and their territories he may have taken refuge.
>
> My next inducement was a desire to increase my stock of information, and my opportunities of self-improvement, by a visit to the land of my paternal ancestors.
>
> My third and chief object was, by the public exposition of the contaminating and degrading influences of Slavery upon the slaveholder and his abettors, as well as the slave, to excite such an intelligent interest on the subject of American Slavery, as may react upon my own country, and may tend to shame her out of her adhesion to a system so abhorrent to Christianity and to her republican institutions.
>
> My last object is, I am happy to say, in a fair way of being accomplished. I have held public meetings in Dublin, Wexford, Waterford, Cork, Youghal, Limerick, Belfast, Glasgow, Aberdeen, Perth, and Dundee, within the five months which have elapsed since I landed in England. An edition of 2,000 copies of my Narrative has been exhausted, and I am in great hopes that before my visit to Great Britain shall be completed, thousands and tens of thousands of the intelligent and philanthropic will be induced to co-operate with the noble band of American abolitionists, for the overthrow of the meanest, hugest, and most dastardly system of iniquity that ever disgraced any country laying claim to the benefits of religion and civilization.[298]

Overall, the inclusion of a preface written by Douglass meant that the *Narrative* could no longer be viewed as 'a key text of Garrisonian abolitionism, anchored firmly in the moral territory of the United States', but its inclusion placed both the *Narrative* and its author in the forefront of the trans-Atlantic abolition movement.[299]

Additionally, Douglass included a response to A. C. C. Thompson, who had publicly accused him of writing a 'lying narrative'.[300] Extracts of Thompson's accusations had first appeared in the *Delaware Republican* and had been reproduced in the *Liberator* of 12 December 1845. In a letter to Garrison dated 27 January 1846, Douglass outlined his own refutation of Thompson, the same one that would appear in the new edition of the *Narrative*. For Douglass, the exchange with Thompson served an important purpose. Although Thompson had sought to discredit Douglass's story, he had, inadvertently, corroborated it, albeit from a pro-slavery perspective. Ironically, therefore, Thompson's writings had validated Douglass's story in a way that the publication of the Boston edition of the *Narrative* alone had not been able to do, leading Douglass to thank Thompson 'for the testimony he bears to the substantial truth of my story'.[301] The inclusion of the arguments of a white apologist for slavery, arguments that Douglass was able to mock and use to his own advantage, challenged and inverted the accepted conventions and practices regarding white authority. In keeping with his statement made in his own preface, Douglass truly was 'in a land of liberty, with no man to make me afraid'.[302]

A number of Douglass's demands caused tension with Webb. This included numerous discussions over the inclusion of an image. Douglass realized the importance of positive representations of black people as a way of refuting racist caricatures. He had not liked the image that had been used in the Boston and first Dublin editions, and so he suggested that no picture be included in subsequent editions. As a compromise, he agreed to allow a new image of himself to be included.[303] However, sales of the *Narrative* in Belfast proved to be so buoyant that on 22 December he wrote to Webb, 'Please send me fifty books so that I may have them by Tuesday night, with or without the portrait'.[304] The second publication was not ready, however, until February/March 1846, by which time Douglass was in Scotland. Douglass was unhappy with Webb's choice of image in the variant Irish edition, and so he obtained a new image for the third Irish printing. But he remained dissatisfied with this one also, believing that the engraving that he had commissioned in Scotland did not do justice to the original portrait.[305] Subsequent versions of the *Narrative* published in Britain reverted to using the original, unattributed image that had appeared in the original Boston version.[306]

More controversially, Douglass wanted to include in the appendix to the second Dublin edition endorsements by two Protestant ministers, Dr Nelson and Dr Drew, whom he had met while lecturing in Belfast. The passion of many Protestant ministers on the slave question was twofold, combining a humanitarian abhorrence of the cruelty of the system with, just as importantly, a horror that slaves were 'deprived of access to the scriptures'.[307] The desire to proselytize would have been anathema to Webb and his fellow Quakers who viewed the slave question through a prism of humanitarianism and social justice, not the need to convert. Webb was also aware of the religious sensitivities that were embedded in Irish society. However, when Webb objected on the grounds that it might introduce a sectarian dimension, Douglass stuck to his ground, arguing the opposite to be the case, curtly informing him, 'I have no time to discuss the question, nor is it necessary'.[308] His answer was not only an act of defiance against Webb, but perhaps even more so against the anti-clerical Garrison. Douglass's vision prevailed, and so the third Dublin printing included endorsements by the two ministers, in addition to favourable newspapers reviews.

According to a recent biographer, Douglass 'revered' the final Dublin edition of the *Narrative*.[309] Both the preface and the refutation of Thompson had helped the cause of abolition and authenticated his story, while the tributes by the two Protestant ministers had struck a blow at American churches who were complicit with slavery. The endorsements provided by the ministers must also have been personally gratifying; Dr Drew's endorsement in the *Narrative* described Douglass as 'a metaphysical illustration of a mind bursting all bonds, and winning light and liberty for his own good, and for the good of millions!'[310] Just as importantly from Douglass's perspective, the commercial success of the Irish *Narratives* meant that he gained financial independence, the income from the sales paying for his living expenses. His precarious financial situation may have accounted for his numerous and, at times, brusque letters to Webb throughout the spring regarding sales and income from the *Narrative*. Webb, in turn, revealed his own frustrations with the process in a number of letters to his Boston friend, Maria Weston Chapman. In one, written in late February 1846, he revealed an acerbic side to his nature when he repeated a comment that he had heard about Douglass, that he was 'a sort of reclaimed wild beast & that it don't do to gauge him by our civilized rules'.[311] Regardless of this mean-spirited private comment, and the public disagreements between the two men, Webb continued to assist and support Douglass long after the latter had left Dublin. Moreover, Douglass, aware that he had treated Webb badly, apologized to him in late April 1846, explaining his pugnacious attitude was a form of self-defence, and 'I have had this armor on ever since I came into Scotland'.[312] Overall, the Irish editions that appeared in 1846, which included Douglass's own preface and appendices, suggest that within only months of arriving in Europe, the author of the *Narrative* had found a new confidence and his own voice. Less than a year after the first publication of the Boston *Narrative*, Douglass had asserted his determination to own his life story, to control his image and to manage his message. Douglass, the fugitive slave, had been replaced by Douglass, the confident black voice of trans-Atlantic abolition.

Regardless of Douglass's private squabbles and considerable public triumphs, there is no doubt that his personal loneliness continued. Writing to Garrison in mid-April, in a letter not meant for publication, he admitted 'I long to be at home . . . Be it ever so humble, there is no place like home'.[313] This feeling was probably exacerbated by the fact that both Buffum and the Hutchinsons would be returning to America in July 1846. When Douglass had first reached London a number of sympathetic abolitionists, understanding that he was missing his family, offered to raise money so that they could join him in England. The gesture horrified Garrison who wrote, 'While we greatly admire this spirit of sympathy and generosity, we must express our conviction that the cause here cannot spare him so long as he will probably remain abroad, should his family be removed'.[314] Just as alarming for Garrison was the fact that Douglass was consorting with his rival abolitionists, leading him to comment in the columns of the *Liberator*, 'Considering the hostile position of the London Committee to the American A.S. Society, we are not a little surprised that Douglass should have complied with their invitation to make a speech at the meeting of the British and Foreign Anti-Slavery Society'.[315] Shortly afterwards, Garrison announced that he would be joining Douglass in Britain – ostensibly accepting an invitation by the Glasgow Anti-Slavery Society. Garrison left Boston on 16 July 1846.[316]

It was not only his former colleagues in Boston who were watching Douglass's activities. Despite being 3,000 miles distant and there being a delay in communication of about four weeks, it was inevitable given Douglass's high profile that his movements would be followed by those opposed to abolition. The incident on the *Cambria* provided an early insight into how polarizing and observed Douglass's actions would prove to be. His personal popularity and professional successes (despite the 'Send Back the Money campaign') must have been anathema to slave-holders and their supporters. One pro-slavery newspaper, while referring to the 'slanderous speeches of Frederick Douglass in Ireland, Scotland etc.', claimed that he had been 'pampered up and sent over to England to slander southern slave-holders'. The article concluded by asking, 'Is there not a law for punishing such persons?'[317] These responses were inevitable in the light of Douglass's many successes and constant media attention. Moreover, the extensive newspaper coverage of Douglass's speeches meant that the churches in America were in the spotlight in a way that would not have been welcomed by them.

In early July, Douglass attended a large Anti-Corn Law meeting in Manchester in the company of Elihu Burritt, from Connecticut.[318] His praise for 'the learned blacksmith' was fulsome:

> I have seldom met with an American in whose presence I have felt more at home. They are all more or less tainted with prejudice against color so that I generally feel like keeping my distance from them – for fear of being repulsed. People who seemed in America – pretty free from those taints – when compared with people here – disclose the taints.[319]

A few days later, Douglass returned to Belfast, his visit being timed to coincide with the annual meeting of the General Assembly of the Presbyterian Church in Ireland.[320] Only days prior to this, 'after a warm discussion', the General Assembly of the Free Church of Scotland had decided *not* to send back the money.[321] A large part of the Assembly's discussion in Ireland was concerned with slavery, with a committee being appointed to examine it in more depth. A local newspaper observed Douglass unobtrusively attending the meetings of the General Assembly, sitting in the public gallery.[322] During his visit, Douglass gave a series of lectures in the town and its vicinity.[323] On 13 July, when lecturing in Bangor, Sharman Crawford was present, demonstrating that Douglass still had the support of powerful people within Ireland. Moreover, during his introductions, Crawford referred to Douglass as his 'friend'.[324] As usual, Douglass balanced his support for abolition with his devotion to temperance. His penultimate public event in Belfast took place on 21 July when he was an invited guest at the inaugural meeting of the Olive Branch, a temperance organization.[325] His final lecture was also on temperance and took place in the Independent Chapel on Donegall Street. At the end of the meeting, a number of people took the pledge. A few days later, the Belfast Total Abstinence Association presented Douglass with an inscribed book on ancient and modern history. It was dated 25 July 1846.[326] At this point it appeared that this was to be Douglass's final appearance in Belfast, as he had no plans to return to Ireland.[327] The arrival of Garrison, however, was to force Douglass to change his plans.

Douglass's time in Belfast coincided with a visit by Belfast-born Rev. Thomas Smyth, a Presbyterian minister from Charleston in South Carolina. Smyth supported slavery, but with reservations, believing, amongst other things, that slaves should be educated. When the Free Church deputation had visited America, they had sought him out and he had given them financial assistance. Smyth's visit to Belfast was intended to coincide with the annual meeting of the General Assembly of the Presbyterian Church. Douglass took the opportunity of Smyth's visit to lambast him and his support for the Free Church, pointing out, 'In America, he dared not challenge Dr Smyth, he would soon be put down; but here, on the Belfast soil, under the protection of British law, the truth was not in danger'.[328] The fact that Smyth was not invited to attend the Assembly was a telling victory for Douglass and for trans-Atlantic abolition. When sharing a platform with Douglass a few days later, Rev. Nelson thanked the General Assembly for their action, adding:

> The American Churches would see by the letter sent out in reply to theirs, that we are neither to be enjoyed nor deceived by their labored and studied, but flimsy apologies for slavery. But especially would they hear, by the exclusion of Dr. Smith [sic], that even when a native of our own town of Belfast becomes untrue to the great cause of freedom, we, as Churches, are determined, by refusing him admission to our Assembly, to settle practically and forever, our fixed resolve to have no fellowship with slaveholders.[329]

Despite repeated requests, Smyth had refused to join Douglass in a public debate. An encounter came about, however, following some public comments made by Smyth impugning Douglass's character, including accusing him of visiting a brothel in Manchester. Douglass's staunch allies in Belfast, Standfield and Nelson, intervened on his behalf and requested that Smyth recant. Douglass also demanded a retraction, but when it failed to materialize, the former slave employed solicitors to act on his behalf. Following this, Smyth did issue a public apology, admitting that the comments 'I incautiously made, on the report of third parties, were unfounded'.[330] The apology appeared in the Belfast newspapers, a demand that had been insisted on by Douglass, but it only appeared after Douglass had left the town and returned to England.[331] It was a complete back-down by a prominent white minister of the Presbyterian Church who was known on both sides of the Atlantic. For Douglass, it was both a personal and a moral victory, but not one without some anguish. At the height of the dispute between the two men, placards appeared throughout Belfast carrying the distasteful slogan, 'Send Back the Nigger'.[332] It was a rare, but offensive, reminder to Douglass that racism existed on both sides of the Atlantic.

Concurrently with Douglass's return to Ireland in July 1846, his American mentor, William Lloyd Garrison, was making arrangements to join him. He left Boston in mid-July on board the *Hibernia*. It was his third trip to Britain. The origins of his visit ostensibly lay in a meeting organized by the Glasgow Anti-Slavery Society on 21 April 1846, at which Douglass, George Thompson and Henry Wright had spoken on the topic of 'Send Back the Money'. During the course of his speech, Thompson had publicly extended an invitation to Garrison to visit Britain and support them.[333] Garrison had agreed on the grounds that his visit would strengthen links between abolitionists on both sides of the Atlantic and that he could add his voice to the 'Send back the money' campaign. The *Liberator* newspaper further explained, 'From every side, the cry is ever coming up to him, to "come over and help us," with the native logic, the keen sagacity, and the earnest eloquence which mark his public speeches'.[334] However, an additional, if unspoken, motive might have been to keep an eye on his protégé, who had been so warmly welcomed by English abolitionists, particularly the British and Foreign Anti-Slavery Association, traditional foes of Garrison's American Anti-Slavery Society. The *Liberator* also announced that after Garrison had attended to business in London, he would tour with Douglass.[335]

Garrison's return to British shores pleased his supporters in Dublin. Richard Webb travelled to Liverpool to be part of the group who welcomed him at the beginning of August.[336] Following his arrival, Garrison went straight to London, where he stayed with the veteran abolitionist, George Thompson, the president of the British Anti-Slavery League. There, Garrison announced that a further purpose of his visit was to found a new anti-slavery league, which would be trans-Atlantic.[337] Like so many abolitionists, Garrison was an advocate of temperance, and he and Douglass attended the first World Temperance Convention, which was held in London from 4 to 8 August in the Literary Institute on Aldergate Street. The Convention had evolved out of a discussion at the second World Slavery Convention, which had been held in London in 1843.[338] The thirty-one American delegates to the Temperance Convention included the Rev. Dr. Beecher (Ohio), Rev. Samuel Cox[339] and Rev. A. Wheelock (both New York), Henry Clapp, Henry C. Wright and Elihu Burritt (all from Massachusetts).[340] Burritt, however, left early due to illness. Although Garrison attended, he did not do so as a delegate, while Douglass was listed as the delegate representing Newcastle upon Tyne.[341] A number of friends from Ireland were present, including James Haughton and Richard Allen. Despite his non-delegate status, Garrison attempted to introduce a discussion about slave-owners and temperance, but the topic had been banned on the grounds that it would excite 'strong feeling' and 'destroy the harmony of the meeting'.[342] From the official Proceedings of the Convention it appears that Douglass remained unusually quiet throughout the debates, but on day three, he seconded a motion concerned with limiting the sale of alcohol in the state of New York.[343] Cox and Beecher proposed that it be modified, but the motion carried. What the official proceedings do not record is that during the Convention, Cox made a 'bitter remark' concerning Douglass.[344] Cox, a Presbyterian minister in Manhattan, was an adversary of Garrison. By a twist of fate, he had been responsible for bringing another runaway American slave, James Pennington, into the ministry.[345] And it was Pennington who had married Douglass and Anna in Manhattan in 1838.

On day four of the Convention, at Clapp's suggestion, the meeting was turned over to Irish delegates to talk about the progress of temperance there, it being regarded as a model for other places. During the discussion, Haughton read an address from the Irish Temperance Union.[346] While Douglass may not have spoken much during the Convention, he spoke extensively on both temperance and slavery at an auxiliary event in the Covent Garden Theatre on Friday, 7 August. In fact, his speech was so long that the chairman intervened to remind him about the time, much to the dismay of the audience, who had cheered him loudly.[347] Cox, who was also present, was outraged by Douglass's interventions. He followed up with 'a long denunciatory letter published in the *New York Evangelist* and other American papers'.[348] Cox's letter and Douglass's long and impassioned response were both re-published by the American Anti-Slavery Society.[349] On day five, smaller numbers attended, but Allen spoke about the success of the temperance movement in Ireland, where there was an estimated four million teetotallers. He lamented, however, that they were overwhelmingly from the poorer classes in the country. During the day, there was a brief discussion about Douglass's comments made in Covent Garden on the previous evening, but the contents of the discussion were not recorded in the Proceedings.[350] Although Douglass may not have featured largely in the record of the Convention, his presence was captured in pictorial form by one of the London newspapers.[351] Out of a group of approximately forty men and one woman, Douglass was the only black person present at the Convention. When viewed in this context, his presence and impact were remarkable.

On 17 August 1846, leading British, Irish and American abolitionists met at the 'Crown and Anchor Tavern' in London. Garrison, Douglass, Webb and Haughton were present.[352] The main purpose of the gathering was to create a new transAtlantic organization that would be an auxiliary to the American Anti-Slavery Society. Throughout the meeting, Garrison held centre stage, speaking a number of times. In contrast, Douglass was relegated to being a subsidiary speaker. This discrepancy was evident from a leading American abolitionist newspaper which gave extensive coverage to Garrison, followed only with the brief observation that 'Mr. Douglass succeeded him'.[353] To an observer or reader of the newspaper accounts, there could be no doubt that a pecking order had been re-established and that Douglass had been returned to his traditional, subservient position – namely, that of being in Garrison's shadow.

After London, Garrison planned to travel to Glasgow, lecturing en route. Following Glasgow, he intended to visit Belfast, Dublin and Cork and then loop back to Liverpool for his return to America.[354] He anticipated leaving Liverpool on 20 October.[355] Garrison did not expect to lecture in Dublin or Cork, but only to see friends in these cities. At some stage, he changed his mind, however, and delayed his return until 4 November.[356] During his extended stay, Garrison lectured with Douglass at a number of venues in Britain. Their initial focus was a criticism of the Free Church of Scotland, but this was replaced by attacks on the new Evangelical Alliance for equivocating on the issue of slave-holders being admitted into Christian churches. By doing so, in the uncompromising tones that were a trademark of Garrison when speaking on religious matters, both men clearly offended some members of the Presbyterian Church. In Scotland, the heart of Presbyterianism, such criticisms were particularly sensitive. A newspaper report of a meeting held on 21 October opened by stating:

> When we entered, Douglass, the runaway slave, was haranguing his audience from the pulpit – for Brighton Street chapel was the place of meeting. This 'fugitive,' by the bye, is a singularly-gifted individual, of whose speeches one may with all safety pronounce this opinion, that what of them is 'true is not new, and what is new is not true.' Aware of this, his coadjutors have him, generally speaking, first disposed of, in the shape of what we may venture to call tentaculum or feeler, wherewith he sounds the moral depths of his audience, so that those who are to come after him may know what hidden shoals to steer clear of.

The article also pointed out that while the gathering was 'technically called' an anti-slavery meeting, 'the slavery question, of course, was never mooted'.[357]

It was not just in Scotland where Douglass and his mentor were disappointing and alienating audiences by their almost exclusive focus on the failings of the Protestant churches. Garrison's brief visit to Belfast, accompanied by Douglass, proved to be one of the most controversial aspects of his whole visit, with even Douglass's loyal allies, Standfield and Nelson, wanting to create distance between themselves and Garrison. Douglass and Garrison reached Belfast at the beginning of October 1846. Even before the two men arrived in the town, several local newspapers expressed reservations about the purpose of the visit. They were mostly concerned about Garrison's sustained and embittered attacks on many Protestant churches. The *Belfast News-Letter* was in the vanguard of criticizing Garrison and his uncompromising stand on religion, condemning him for his 'ceaseless enmity' to the Protestant evangelical churches.[358] Tellingly, Garrison's first talk in Ireland took place not in a religious building, but in the Belfast Music Hall.

On 3 October, Garrison, with Douglass at his side, gave a lunch-time lecture in the Music Hall. Attendance was reported as being relatively low, with only an estimated 220 people attending, many of whom were female. Just as telling, only one minister was present on the platform party. Even before the lecture took place, Garrison had been taunted by the editor of the *News-Letter* for his 'infidel' sympathies and the fact that no church had offered him space to speak.[359] Again, throughout the meeting, Garrison took the lead, with Douglass simply introducing the older man. Following Douglass's opening speech (which was an extended panegyric to Garrison), a number of ministers were invited to join them on the platform. This clumsy gesture was an indication that the ministers were not comfortable giving their endorsement to the American visitors. Overwhelmingly, the tone of the meeting was fractious. During the course of Garrison's long speeches (he spoke twice), he attacked the editor of the *News-Letter*, who was sitting with other journalists. It provided another awkward moment for those who had come to hear a speech on abolition, and it added to the general bad feeling of the meeting. Garrison's pointed attacks on the Free Church led to audible hisses from the audience. Garrison, however, claimed that he welcomed the hisses as sounding like 'American music to his ears'.[360] Undaunted, he continued his attack on various American churches and the newly created Evangelical Alliance, which had convened in London in the summer of 1846.[361] Garrison also made a number of *ad hominem* attacks on two leading members of the Alliance, the Rev. Samuel Cox and Rev. Clarke.[362] Such attacks must have made uncomfortable listening for Douglass who, in the course of a lecture in Belfast in June, had praised the Alliance for refusing to have a union with slave-holders.[363]

Garrison's comments were challenged by a minister in the audience and by a supporter of the Free Church, who had travelled from Scotland to hear the lecture. Overall, Garrison's unequivocal criticisms proved divisive and unpopular, they being received with as many hisses as cheers.[364] The meeting came to a premature conclusion when the chairman, James Tennant, felt that he could no longer control it.[365] Newspaper accounts of the meeting differed slightly in terms of the information they provided.[366] The report in the *Belfast Commercial Chronicle*, while less antagonistic to Garrison than the *News-Letter*, confirmed that the meeting was deeply contentious.[367] The *Chronicle* also reported that Garrison had ended his speech by condemning the Irish in America and their apathy on the abolition question – a topic that had been avoided by Douglass during the previous twelve months.[368] In every way, this bad tempered affray was a far cry from the warm welcome that had been accorded to Douglass only a few months earlier.

Although Garrison left Belfast the following day, the controversy continued. His uncompromising comments resulted in copious correspondence to the local newspapers, much of it negative. One letter pointed out that, though advertised as an anti-slavery meeting, its focus had been to denounce religious ministers.[369] Another letter to the *News-Letter*, from 'Sara', who claimed to have been present at the meeting in the Music Hall in Belfast, was critical of Garrison and Douglass. The author pointed out that the meeting had been poorly attended, suggesting their unpopularity.[370] Garrison had spent only two days in Belfast, and while there he had lectured for approximately two hours, but the American had left behind him an abolition movement that was more divided than ever before.

From Belfast, Garrison travelled to Dublin without Douglass. When Garrison had visited Ireland in 1840, he had established friendships with many people who later hosted Douglass, including the Webbs, the Allans and the Haughtons. Like Douglass five years later, he had stayed with the Webbs, and while there, O'Connell had called on him.[371] By 1843, however, O'Connell had distanced himself from the American abolitionist leader, referring to him as 'a maniac in religion'.[372] On the coach journey to Dublin, Garrison admitted that he cried when he witnessed the poverty of the people; like Douglass, he was unaware that he was witnessing the onset of the Great Famine. In Dublin, Garrison stayed with the Webbs, and, during his stay, he had his photograph taken.[373] Regardless of his stated intentions, he did lecture in Dublin, in the Music Hall on Abbey Street on the evening of 7 October.[374] It attracted little press attention.

Following his lecture, Garrison travelled on to England. He did not make it to Cork as he had hoped, it being too far to reach in his limited time frame.[375] He briefly returned to Dublin, where he gave a final lecture, again in the Music Hall, on 2 November 1846. He spoke alongside Henry Wright and George Thompson, but without Douglass.[376] Like the first lecture, this one received little press attention, although a report in the *Freeman's Journal* described the attendance as 'thin but respectable'.[377] Ironically, the next act to appear at this venue was a group of 'Ethiopian performers' who were famous for their 'Nigger melodies'. Their highly successful repertoire included songs such as, 'Come Darkies Sing'.[378] It was the first time they had appeared in Ireland.[379] They were described as attracting 'fashionable and numerous crowds'.[380]

At the meeting in the Belfast Music Hall on 3 October, it had been announced that although Garrison was leaving Belfast, Douglass would be staying in the town and would lecture there on Tuesday evening, 6 October. His audience for what was to be his final appearance in Belfast (and, indeed, in Ireland) was described as 'respectable'. According to the *News-Letter*, it was 'composed principally of ladies and little boys', and when Douglass came forward to speak he was 'received without any demonstration of applause'.[381] The lecture itself lacked the humour and self-deprecation that had been a hallmark of Douglass's early lectures. In what was predominantly a negative tirade, Douglass expressed a number of frustrations with the abolition movement in the United Kingdom. He commenced by saying that:

> on coming to this country, he expected to find but one opinion as to the conduct of the American slave-holders, that whatever feeling existed with reference to slaveholding in the United States, but one opinion was entertained of the [same] in this Christian land; but in that idea he had

45

been sadly disappointed, for recent events had disclosed for what he could not have supposed existed in the minds of any Christians, in this country.[382]

Echoing themes from Garrison's lecture, a large part of Douglass's speech was devoted to attacking the Evangelical Alliance. Slavery itself was no longer being attacked, but the churches who worked with slave-holders were now the main enemy. The two lectures drew angry responses, which also appeared in the press. They were led by a Methodist minister, the Rev. Daniel M'Afee, who had challenged Garrison during his lecture and been cheered for doing so.[383] In the twelve months that he had spent in Ireland, Douglass had honed his skills as a lecturer, but the 'Send Back the Money' campaign, which had come to dominate Douglass's speeches in the previous ten months, had lost him the support of those who had welcomed him to Ireland less than a year earlier. Furthermore, his uncompromising attacks appeared to be having little impact on the actions of the Free Church. According to the historian Ian Whyte, Douglass's exclusive focus on the 'Send Back the Money' campaign was part of a series of 'misjudgments' made by him at this time.[384] Douglass's final lecture in Ireland was, nonetheless, an inglorious way to end a tour that had achieved so much in the cause of abolition.

While the 'Send Back the Money' crusade had dispirited abolitionists, Douglass's time in Ireland had galvanized women within the movement. The impact of this revival was felt by women's societies on both sides of the Atlantic. Women had formed a considerable part of Douglass's audiences in all parts of Ireland. Their presence reflected the nature of anti-slavery in general, it being one of the few social movements where it was generally acceptable for women to operate in the public sphere. Although women rarely spoke, they were active in raising donations, collecting signatures for and signing petitions, and providing goods for sale at bazaars and other fundraisers. Within Ireland, the involvement of women in anti-slavery had a long pedigree that paralleled the contribution of Irish men. In 1792, for example, Dublin Quaker Mary Birkett had written 'A Poem on the African Slave Trade', which was sub-titled 'Addressed to her own sex'.[385] The poem was noteworthy for encouraging women not to be passive but to boycott slave-produced goods. In 1829, when a Negro's Friends' Society was formed in Ireland, women created their own counterpart organizations throughout the country.[386] In 1838, 75,000 Irish women had signed a petition which they sent to Queen Victoria asking her to intervene to end the apprenticeship system.[387] Apprenticeship was outlawed shortly afterwards. Similarly to the men's associations, the women's societies faded following its ending.

Douglass's visit to Cork had given a boost to the local women abolitionists, who increased their efforts in sending items to the annual Anti-Slavery Bazaar in Boston.[388] The bazaar, which was organized by the Boston Female Anti-Slavery Society, was an important source of fundraising for the movement. That year, the bazaar ran from December 1845 to January 1846 and was held in Faneuil Hall. Although Douglass was 3,000 miles away, his influence was evident. The items for sale included memorabilia relating to Douglass, notably, 'An excellent Daguerreotype of Frederick Douglass' and 'a kit-kat portrait of Frederick Douglass, by W.P. Brennan',[389] a young artist from Lynn. Moreover, the Boston hall was ornamented with the same placards, saying, '*cead mille failte*', with which the Cork abolitionists had decorated their room for the reception held to honour Douglass. Afterwards, the Boston Society recorded that 'We had the pleasure of giving them to Mrs. Douglass, agreeably to his request'.[390] The Boston bazaar also included many items that had been donated by abolitionists in Ireland.[391] These included:

> the elegant selection of writing materials . . . from R. D. Webb, and Anne Allen, of Dublin, [which] attracted continual admiration, and contributed greatly, especially the latter, to the pecuniary success of the occasion. An oil-picture of Derrynane Abbey, the seat of O'Connell, was presented by James Haughton, with the autograph and seal of the Liberator. A water-color sketch of Lough Attry [sic] and the Twelve Pins of Benahola, surrounded by the Highlands of Connemara, of County Galway, was presented by R. D. Webb, and looked at with great interest, as from the pencil of the well-known Irish novelist, Samuel Lover, known here not as an artist, but as the author of 'Roy O'Moore', 'Handy Andy', and other works of much celebrity as delineations of Irish character. The paper folder from Cork, made of the Mossgiel Thorn which shaded the dwelling of Burns,[392] the Bogoak ornaments from Dublin.[393]

Douglass's visit had a similar impact in the north of Ireland. While his lectures in Belfast proved increasingly controversial, an unexpected outcome was the creation of the Belfast Female Anti-Slavery Society in January 1846.[394] They, in turn, appealed to women throughout Ulster to organize. Their source of inspiration was evident in a message from the Belfast Society to the Boston Ladies' Anti-Slavery Society:

> The information communicated during the late visit of Frederick Douglass to Belfast, has aroused many ladies within our precincts to deep feeling on behalf of the suffering victims of Slavery in the United States; – and this feeling has brought with it a sense of responsibility as to the use of all available influence towards putting down that flagrant sin against God and against man. Those sentiments and considerations have led to the formation of the Belfast Ladies' Anti-Slavery Association; on behalf of which I now address thee. As we are personally far removed from the scene of action, our first step is to open a correspondence with our American sisters, in the hope that the expression of cordial sympathy with those who have to bear "the burden and heat of day," may tend still further to stimulate and to cheer them in their arduous conflict with public sentiment and public iniquity.[395]

In late 1846 and 1847, as food shortages took their toll on Ireland, the women abolitionists apologized that the distress in the country meant that they were unable to donate a larger number of goods. This was true in Belfast where many of the women abolitionists became involved in the Ladies' Relief Committee, which had been formed at the beginning of 1847. A member of both groups was redoubtable octogenarian Mary Ann McCracken, sister of a hero of the 1798 rebellion.[396] Clearly, the Famine diverted these women in terms of their activism, as throughout Ireland many of them worked to alleviate the suffering in Ireland. In 1849, as the Famine continued to devastate the country, Webb bewailed the fact that 'All that goes in the Dublin box is contributed by very few persons and the number of our helpers is not increased but diminished from year to year'.[397] Two years later, the Cork Ladies' Association reported to the women in Boston that 'the famine years have exercised a very depressing influence, and tho' the country is now as well off as before 1846, still that amount of prosperity is not enough to allow us to send money to America'.[398]

Douglass's arrival in Ireland had coincided with the arrival of a less welcome newcomer – *phytophthora infestans* – a topic on which he had little to say.[399] As early as October 1845, however, reports of Douglass's lectures were vying with news of the spread of this previously unknown potato disease. At this stage, nobody, including the American visitor, understood that they were witnessing the onset of the greatest human subsistence crisis to occur in the nineteenth century – Ireland's Great Famine. Moreover, at this stage, nobody was aware that what initially seemed to be a one-year failure would, in fact, due to the repeated reappearance of the potato disease, transform from a temporary subsistence crisis into a deadly famine. Increasingly, reports of the failure were appearing extensively in the newspapers, and at times, they were situated next to reports about Douglass, which he read avidly.[400]

While Douglass did not comment on the tragedy that was unfolding before his eyes as a result of the potato failure, he did remark on the abject poverty that he witnessed. He addressed the issue most frankly after he left the country in January 1846, in letters sent from Scotland to Garrison. In them, Douglass expressed sympathy with the poor of Ireland: 'I had heard much of the misery and wretchedness of the Irish people, previous to leaving the United States, and was prepared to witness much on my arrival in Ireland. But I must confess, my experience has convinced me that the half has not been told'. He described, in detail, the poverty he had witnessed in Dublin and its vicinity, saying of the living circumstances, 'I see much here to remind me of my former condition', likening the situation of the Irish poor to 'the same degradation as the American slave'. Despite this comparison, Douglass attributed the poverty not to political reasons but to personal failings – alcohol and intemperance. He explained, 'The immediate, and it may be the main cause of the extreme poverty and beggary in Ireland, is intemperance'.[401] By stating this, Douglass demonstrated insensitivity to Irish social conditions and history. Such an interpretation, however, was common amongst proponents of temperance – the desire for moral reform that underpinned the temperance movement viewed alcohol, poverty and crime as being intricately linked.[402] It was also in keeping with Douglass's strong views on drinking, he seeing alcohol as the root of many evils amongst his fellow slaves. He told one audience in Belfast that 'Even when a slave, he had not degraded himself by this vice, and inwardly felt his superiority over his drunken white master, who in this respect was the greater slave of the two'.[403] Yet, by making such a judgment on the Irish poor, Douglass was displaying a rare lack of compassion for his fellow oppressed people.[404]

What is, perhaps, more surprising is that when Douglass returned to Ireland in the autumn of 1846, it was evident that the country was undergoing a famine, with newspapers reporting deaths from disease and starvation daily. The suffering of the Irish poor did not seem to register with Douglass, although, again, it is apparent that he did read the Irish newspapers to find out how his lectures were being reported.[405] Nonetheless, while Douglass may have said little in regard to the humanitarian crisis while he was in Ireland, it is clear that he was aware of it while travelling in Britain. In March 1847, he is recorded as having sent a sum of two pounds and ten shillings to the Belfast Ladies' Society, which was assisting with Famine relief.[406] It was a generous contribution and donated without any press attention.[407]

When Douglass left Ireland in October 1846, he returned to what had become his 'lonely Pilgrimage' lecturing in Britain, often together with Wright and Robert Smith of the Anti-Slavery League, in an attempt to promote the new trans-Atlantic league. He was missing his family and anxious to return to his anti-slavery activities in America. On 12 December 1846, Douglass officially became a free man, a legal process that women abolitionists in England had commenced in the summer. His 'purchase of freedom' was instigated by Anna Richardson of Newcastle in the north-east of England. Anna was related to Ann Jennings, who had hosted Douglass in Cork.[408] As with so much in his life, the purchase of his freedom was bittersweet. The idea of 'purchasing' freedom proved unpalatable to a number of abolitionists, including Wright, who begged him not to touch the 'Certificate of Freedom', warning that if he did so:

> You will lose the advantages of this truly manly, and to my view, sublime position; you will be shorn of your strength – you will sink in your own estimation, if you accept that detestable certificate of your freedom, that blasphemous forgery, that accursed bill of sale of your body and soul; or even, by your silence, acknowledge its validity.[409]

Douglass politely, but firmly, disagreed. As he succinctly explained, it was a means of 'restoring myself to myself'.[410] In less than thirty years of life, Douglass had been categorized as a slave, a fugitive, an exile, and now, a free man. Although he could return home without fear of capture, he had promised Garrison that he would stay in Britain until the following summer.[411] In the event, Douglass only remained until April 1847, at which point he had been away from home for twenty months.

Douglass returned to America in 1847 on the same ship as he had arrived in, the *Cambria*, but now he travelled as a free man. Before leaving London, he gave a powerful farewell address in which he quoted O'Connell:

> America presents to the world an anomaly, such as no other nation ever did or can present before mankind. The people of the United States are the boldest in their pretensions to freedom, and the loudest in their profession of love of liberty; yet no nation upon the face of the globe can exhibit a statute-book so full of all that is cruel, malicious, and infernal, as the American code of laws. Every page is red with the blood of the American slave. O'Connell once said, speaking of Ireland—no matter for my illustration, how truly or falsely—that "her history may be traced, like the track of a wounded man through a crowd." If this description can be given of Ireland, how much more true is it when applied to the sons and daughters of Africa, in the United States? Their history is nothing but blood! blood! – blood in the morning, blood at noon, blood at night! They have had blood to drink; they have had their own blood shed.[412]

Douglass was to use a variation of this quote from O'Connell on a number of other occasions during his career, significantly without the same qualification as to its veracity that he had used before a British audience.

Douglass's changed status on his return journey to Boston did not protect him from discrimination. Just as he had experienced prejudice on his crossing to Liverpool, he experienced it on the return leg of his journey, when again he was not allowed to travel as a first-class passenger. But the intervening twenty months had wrought many changes in Douglass's confidence and outlook. His response to this treatment was to write from his Liverpool hotel, prior to the voyage, to the London *Times* – at that time probably the most influential and prestigious newspaper in the world.[413] His letter was reprinted in many Irish and British newspapers, causing universal outrage. The owner of the shipping company, Samuel Cunard, even became personally involved, writing to the *Times:*

> No one can regret more than I do the unpleasant circumstances respecting Mr. Douglass's passage; but I can assure you that nothing of the kind will again take place in the steam-ships with which I am connected.[414]

It was a brilliant propaganda coup and a testament to the impact that Douglass had had during his stay in the United Kingdom.

In September 1846, as Garrison had been preparing for his controversial visit to Ireland, Thomas Clarkson, the veteran of British abolition, died.[415] In May 1847, as Douglass was reengaging with his life and family in America, Daniel O'Connell passed away, in Genoa, on his way to see the Pope. The death of these two gigantic figures in the anti-slavery movement marked the end of an era in that struggle. Both men had witnessed the ending of the slave trade and the abolition of slavery in most British possessions. And both had fought in their final years to end slavery in America and elsewhere. They left behind a movement that was divided on both sides of the Atlantic. When Douglass had first appeared in Ireland, it seemed that he could be a unifying figure with abolition. Unfortunately, his early successes were skewed by his preoccupation with the 'Send Back the Money' campaign and his public devotion to his mentor, Garrison. His return to America as a free man marked a new beginning, however, as he was not just liberated from slavery, but also from living in the shadow of Garrison. More tellingly, his time overseas had given him a renewed sense of social justice. The young man who had arrived in Ireland in August 1845 concerned with the single issue of slavery had transformed into a champion of the oppressed wherever they existed. This was evident in a letter written to Garrison in February 1846:

> though I am more closely connected and identified with one class of outraged, oppressed and enslaved people, I cannot allow myself to be insensible to the wrongs and sufferings of any part of the great family of man. I am not only an American slave, but a man, and as such, am bound to use my powers for the welfare of the whole human brotherhood. I am not going through this land with my eyes shut, ears stopped, or heart steeled. I am seeking to see, hear and feel all that may be seen, heard and felt; and neither the attentions I am receiving here, nor the connexion I hold to my brethren in bonds, shall prevent my disclosing the results of my observations. I believe that the sooner the wrongs of the whole human family are made known, the sooner those wrongs will be reached.[416]

Many receptions were held in honour of Douglass's return.[417] In New York, one function was hosted by 'coloured people' to pay tribute, and Garrison appeared during the event.[418] Unfortunately, the sense of freedom and equality that Douglass had experienced while travelling in the United Kingdom must have quickly dissipated when back in America. An early incident on board a riverboat on the Hudson, when a female abolitionist had tried to secure for Douglass a cabin place, the preserve of whites only, resulted in inches of column space and frenzied opprobrium being heaped on him. Even the *Liberator* was critical of Douglass and his champion for trying to subvert the rules 'by stealth', averring, 'they must be conquered openly, and through much suffering'.[419] Moreover, Douglass's new sense of confidence and purpose were not appreciated by all who opposed slavery. An article in the *Northern Christian Advocate*, which opposed both slavery and Garrison, reported on a lecture by Douglass and Remond in the autumn of 1847. Of Douglass they said:

> He is the same whose recent visit to England has made so much noise. He is an intelligent looking, youngerly mulatto. A fellow of strong native sense, quick wit, considerable theatrical address, more assurance, and unbounded powers of sarcastic mimicry . . . In other respects . . .

Douglass lacks the modesty which is becoming in all public speakers, and especially one in his circumstance . . . He strengthens the prejudice of those who say, 'Allow the coloured class to arise at all in society and they will tread you underfoot'.[420]

Clearly, regardless of his notoriety, Douglass was not immune to insults, which continued throughout his life, one historian characterizing them as the 'racist circumstances that were a consequence of accepted ways of life, modes of behaviour, and manners of speech in the everyday American world: the enforcement of Jim Crow practices on boats and trains and in churches from New York to New Hampshire, as well as racist jokes, cold handshakes, slips of the tongue, and the spurious side-comments that accompanied Douglass as he traversed the country to speak of his experiences as a slave'.[421]

Back in America, Douglass returned to the anti-slavery circuit, sometimes accompanied by his friend, Remond. He proved indefatigable in spreading his message, writing in October 1847:

I am at home again. Since I left home, less than three months ago, I have travelled more than 8,000 miles – spoken to more than 60,000 persons – held 100 conventions, and delivered not fewer than 150 lectures – written numerous letters for the press – had a number of private interviews with friends – many stern debates with enemies – been mobbed once – experienced some rebuffs and many hardships; yet here I am, in the bosom of my dear family, the embodiment of health, and in the best of spirits, for all of which I desire to feel sincerely grateful to God, whose servant I trust I am.[422]

During his lectures, Douglass spoke about his recent experiences in Ireland and Britain. When exhorting his audiences to overthrow slavery, 'he pointed to the triumphs of the efforts of O'Connell and others which had brought emancipation to the Catholics of Ireland'.[423]

Significantly, following his return home, Douglass made a number of changes in his life that indicated his new felt independence. At the end of 1847, he moved his family to Rochester in New York. While doing this, Douglass was also preparing to start his own newspaper, the *North Star*, together with Martin Delany.[424] It commenced publication on 3 December 1847, and in the first edition, he explained his motives, which included his desire for universal social justice:

We are now about to assume the management of the editorial department of a newspaper, devoted to the cause of Liberty, Humanity and Progress. The position is one which, with the purest motives, we have long desired to occupy. It has long been our anxious wish to see, in this slave-holding, slave-trading, and Negro-hating land, a printing-press and paper, permanently established, under the complete control and direction of the immediate victims of slavery and oppression.

At the same time, Douglass's newly found agency, confidence and determination to champion the cause of black people were evident:

> It is scarcely necessary for us to say that our desire to occupy our present position at the head of an Antislavery Journal, has resulted from no unworthy distrust or ungrateful want of appreciation of the zeal, integrity, or ability of the noble band of white laborers, in this department of our cause; but, from a sincere and settled conviction that such a Journal, if conducted with only moderate skill and ability, would do a most important and indispensable work, which it would be wholly impossible for our white friends to do for us.[425]

Douglass was productive in other ways: in response to a request from the Rochester Ladies' Anti-Slavery Society, he wrote *The Heroic Slave, a heartwarming Narrative of the Adventures of Madison Washington, in Pursuit of Liberty*, his only work of fiction, which was first published in 1852.[426] *The Heroic Slave* was sold in Britain, where the distributor described it as a 'thrilling narrative'.[427]

Increasingly, Douglass was distancing himself from Garrison both ideologically and spatially. An early indication of Douglass's new-found sense of autonomy came in May 1847 during a lecture when Garrison suggested his return had been motivated by a love of his country. Douglass rejected this by saying, 'I cannot agree with my friend Mr. Garrison in relation to my love and attachment to this land. I have no love for America, as such; I have no patriotism. I have no country'.[428] Their differences came to a head over the issue of whether the American Constitution was pro-slavery or not. Garrison believed that it was. Douglass publicly announced his change of heart on this matter in an editorial in the *North Star* in early 1849.[429] In 1851, more public differences emerged between the two men over what actions should be taken to end slavery. At this stage, the former colleagues became implacable enemies, still fighting for abolition, but no longer from one platform. Douglass's disagreements with Garrison also damaged his relationship with Remond and with George Thompson, the latter remarking that Douglass's new ventures were making 'herculean attempts to wash the Ethiop white'.[430] Douglass fell out with other people with whom he had previously been close. In March 1848, he criticized the Hutchinson family for performing in New York in front of the leader of the Whig Party, Henry Clay.[431] In the following year, he ended his relations with Father Mathew over the latter's refusal to speak out against slavery during a tour of America. In a long statement, Douglass referred to his own time in Ireland, when 'we were received by no one in a manner more gratifying to our feelings or who manifested a deeper interest in the anti-slavery cause, than he'.[432] Douglass's actions showed the complexity of the anti-slavery issue and how contingent his relationships were with his fellow abolitionists.

They can also be seen as part of the process of Douglass finding his own voice as he emerged from Garrison's shadows.

Following his return, women continued to play a pivotal role in Douglass's life. In 1848, Douglass attended the Seneca Valley Convention. He was the only black man present and was one of the small number of men to sign the Declaration of Sentiments in favour of women's suffrage. He explained his position:

> In this denial of the right to participate in government, not merely the degradation of woman and the perpetuation of a great injustice happens, but the maiming and repudiation of one-half of the moral and intellectual power of the government of the world . . . I would give woman a vote, give her a motive to qualify herself to vote, precisely as I insisted upon giving the colored man the right to vote; in order that she shall have the same motives for making herself a useful citizen as those in force in the case of other citizens. In a word, I have never yet been able to find one consideration, one argument, or suggestion in favor of man's right to participate in civil government which did not equally apply to the rights of woman.[433]

Douglass's outspoken support for women's rights, which was evident throughout his life, was an important part of his humanitarian crusade that was no longer limited to the single issue of slavery.

Back in America, Douglass continued to show an interest in Ireland. Her relationship with the British political system – of which he was an admirer – continued to perplex him. In 1848, he wrote in the *North Star* unsympathetically about 'The Wrongs of Ireland':

> The wrongs of Ireland. – The most determined enemy to 'Saxon rule' will find it difficult to make out a case of very peculiar hardship for Ireland – that is, heavier taxation or a more rigorous Government than falls to the lot of the other portions of Great Britain. The miseries of Ireland – those of them that can be effected by legislation, are more the effect of past than of present misgovernment. The Protestant establishment, to which all are forced to contribute, either in the form of tithes or church rates, a monstrous iniquity, which is felt not less severely a majority of the people of England and Scotland, than it is by the Roman Catholics and other dissenters of Ireland.[434]

Given that Ireland was then undergoing a third year of devastating famine, such comments seemed particularly insensitive.

When speaking in Rochester in 1850, building on the theme of a number of speeches that he had given in Ireland, Douglass challenged the idea that Irish people were slaves:

It is often said, by the opponents of the anti-slavery cause, that the condition of the people of Ireland is more deplorable than that of the American slaves . . . Yet I must say that there is no analogy between the two cases. The Irishman is poor, but he is not a slave. He may be in rags, but he is not a slave. He is still the master of his own body, and can say with the poet, 'The hand of Douglass is his own.' 'The world is all before him, where he to choose;' and poor as may be my opinion of the British parliament, I cannot believe that it will ever sink to such a depth of infamy as to pass a law for the recapture of fugitive Irishmen! The shame and scandal of kidnapping will long remain wholly monopolized by the American congress. The Irishman has not only the liberty to emigrate from his country, but he has liberty at home. He can write, and speak, and co-operate for the attainment of his rights and the redress of his wrongs.

In the same speech, he added:

Far be it from me to underrate the sufferings of the Irish people. They have been long oppressed; and the same heart that prompts me to plead the cause of the American bondman, makes it impossible for me not to sympathize with the oppressed of all lands.[435]

The comparisons between the Irish poor and black people continued to fascinate Douglass and show how his analysis and understanding was evolving. In 1854, in an address entitled 'The claims of the Negro, ethnologically considered', he claimed, 'an educated man in Ireland ceases to be an Irishman; and an intelligent black man is always supposed to have derived his intelligence from his connection with the white race. To be intelligent is to have one's negro blood ignored'.[436] He went on to say, in a section entitled 'The Effect of Circumstances upon the Physical Man', that:

The day I landed in Ireland, nine years ago, I addressed . . . a large meeting of the common people of Ireland, on temperance. Never did human faces tell a sadder tale. More than five thousand were assembled; and I say, with no wish to wound the feelings of any Irishman, that these people lacked only a black skin and wooly hair, to complete their likeness to the plantation negro. The open, uneducated mouth – the long, gaunt arm, the badly formed foot and ankle – the shuffling gait – the retreating forehead and vacant expression – and their petty quarrels and fights – all reminded me of the plantation, and my own cruelly abused people.

He qualified his comments by adding:

Yet *that* is the land of Grattan, of Curran, of O'Connell, and of Sheridan. Now what I have said is true of the common people, the fact is, there are no more really handsome people in the world, than the educated Irish people. The Irish man educated, is a model gentleman; the Irishman ignorant and degraded, compares in form and feature with the negro![437]

Similarly, Douglass's views of Irish Americans continued to develop. Shortly after returning home he wrote of the Irish in America that 'In every position, they are the most valuable, and, when properly guided, advised, and temperate, the most useful of any class of people in the country. We could not get on without them'.[438] At times, however, their inertia on the slavery issue, and their open support for the pro-slavery Democratic Party, frustrated him. In a speech delivered before the American Anti-Slavery Society in New York in 1853 he explained:

Let me now call attention to the social influences which are operating and cooperating with the slavery party of the country, designed to contribute to one or all of the grand objects aimed at by that party. We see here the black man attacked in his vital interests; prejudice and hate are excited against him; enmity is stirred up between him and other laborers. The Irish people, warm-hearted, generous, and sympathizing with the oppressed everywhere, when they stand upon their own green island, are instantly taught, on arriving in this Christian country, to hate and despise the colored people. They are taught to believe that we eat the bread which of right belongs to them. The cruel lie is told the Irish, that our adversity is essential to their prosperity. Sir, the Irish-American will find out his mistake one day. He will find that in assuming our avocation he also has assumed our degradation. But for the present we are sufferers. The old employments by which we have heretofore gained our livelihood, are gradually, and it may be inevitably, passing into other hands. Every hour sees us elbowed out of some employment to make room perhaps for some newly-arrived emigrants, whose hunger and color are thought to give them a title to especial favor. White men are becoming house-servants, cooks, and stewards, common laborers, and flunkeys to our gentry, and, for aught I see, they adjust themselves to their stations with all becoming obsequiousness. This fact proves that if we cannot rise to the whites, the whites can fall to us.[439]

The Civil War and the ending of slavery did not end Douglass's intermittent feuds with Irish Americans. In 1883, the Supreme Court's overturning of a civil rights act introduced by Congress in 1875 for the purpose of guaranteeing more equal treatment for African Americans, angered Douglass. He singled out Irish Americans for their role in perpetuating segregation. In a powerful speech delivered in Lincoln Hall he claimed:

Perhaps no class of our fellow citizens has carried this prejudice against color to a point more extreme and dangerous than have our Catholic

Irish fellow-citizens, and yet no people on the face of the earth have been more relentlessly persecuted and oppressed on account of race and religion than have the same Irish people . . . Fellow citizens! We want no Black Ireland in America.[440]

If Douglass was frustrated by Irish Americans, his admiration for the now-dead O'Connell continued. Even before arriving in Dublin, Douglass had been aware of the towering figure of O'Connell as a voice in the international abolition movement, and, as a number of Douglass's speeches demonstrated, he was aware of the Repeal movement's desire to restore a parliament in Ireland. But while praising O'Connell on a number of occasions, he avoided overtly political comments relating to the 'Irish question', as his speech in Conciliation Hall showed. When on that occasion Douglass witnessed O'Connell address his followers, he was mesmerized by his oratory eloquence and the 'calming sweetness' of his voice – both attributes that Douglass himself possessed as a speaker. Moreover, Douglass had unobtrusively observed O'Connell, the man not the politician, earlier that day and noted his playful interaction with a group of children on the streets of Dublin. In 1862, he again described his first sighting of O'Connell on the streets of Dublin seventeen years earlier:

> I once saw a swarm of little boys following the great O'Connell from square to square in the city of Dublin, all forgetful of their poverty and wretchedness, despising wind and rain and mud and cold, treading with bare feet upon the melting snow,[441] swept up by a joyous enthusiasm, which drew me along with them. They made the Welkin ring with ecstatic praises of the great Irish Liberator.
> Why did they thus follow and shout? . . . There walked before them the manhood of all their dreams, and every Irishman of them felt larger and stronger for walking in the shadow of this one great Irishman.[442]

In recalling his first view of O'Connell, Douglass conjured up an irresistible combination of the public and the private man – and brief though their encounter had been, O'Connell's words and humanity would remain with Douglass for the rest of his life.

On numerous occasions, Douglass mentioned O'Connell in his speeches. On 1 August 1848, the anniversary of total emancipation in the West Indies, Douglass addressed an audience of black and white people in Rochester at an annual commemoration organized by black activists.[443] The main topic of his speech was the revolutions in Europe, a number of which were still unfolding. He averred that the events in France in February had unleashed a 'general insecurity . . . over the crowned heads of Europe'. In his speech, his admiration for England was obvious, he praising 'brave and strong old England . . . England the heart of the civilized world' – a devotion that was subsequently criticized.[444] Douglass added:

Ireland, too, the land of O'Connell, among the most powerful that ever advocated the cause of human freedom – Ireland, ever chafing under oppressive rule, famine-stricken, ragged and wretched, but warm-hearted, generous and unconquerable Ireland, caught up the inspiring peal as it swept across the bosom of St. George's Channel, and again renewed her oath, to be free or die. Her cause is already sanctified by the martyrdom of [John] Mitchell [sic], and millions stand ready to be sacrificed in the same manner.[445]

In 1851, Douglass's own newspaper, now named the *Frederick Douglass Paper*, included a long retrospective on O'Connell to mark the fourth anniversary of his death. It praised the Irish man, asserting that:

No Patriot, we believe, ever encountered more opposition in his struggles, or encountered more obloquy and contempt from his fellows; nor is there an instance when reproach and insult have been more solidly changed to respect and praise.[446]

In a speech given in Canandaigua in 1857, on the theme of West Indian emancipation, Douglass told his largely black audience: 'Who would be free, themselves must strike the blow'. It was a phrase frequently used by O'Connell and, in turn, was taken from a poem written by Lord Byron: 'Hereditary Bondsmen, know ye not Who would be free themselves must strike the blow'.[447] Douglass went on to say:

When O'Connell, with all Ireland at his back, was supposed to be contending for the just rights and liberties of Ireland, the sympathies of mankind were with him, and even his enemies were compelled to respect his patriotism.[448]

While his admiration for O'Connell remained constant, Douglass came to criticize O'Connell's successors, 'the Duffys, Mitchell's [sic], Meaghers, and others, men who loved liberty for themselves and their country, but were utterly destitute of sympathy with the cause of liberty in countries other than their own'. Furthermore, like many abolitionists, he came to detest John Mitchel for his subsequent open support of slavery following his arrival in America in 1853.[449] At the end of 1854, Douglass issued public appeal to the Irish man in the columns of his newspaper entitled 'Going, going, not gone', asking Mitchel to desist from interfering in the slavery debate.[450] His suggestion fell on deaf ears.

Surprisingly, in his 1855 autobiography, Douglass says little about his time in Ireland. He did reminisce, however, that Irish songs reminded him of those that he had heard on plantations, as they contained 'a tinge of melancholy' and 'the same wailing notes'.[451] While there is no mention of Daniel O'Connell in the 1855 autobiography, in Douglass's 1882 biography, he paid fulsome tribute to the Irish man. He talked about O'Connell 'welcoming' him to Ireland 36 years earlier and implied a closer relationship than had, in fact, existed. He wrote:

> In introducing me to an immense audience in Conciliation Hall, he playfully called me 'the Black O'Connell of the United States'; nor did he let the occasion pass without his usual denunciation of our slave system.[452]

There is no contemporary evidence that this introduction took place. Nonetheless, Douglass was full of admiration for the older man's oratory:

> His eloquence came down upon the vast assembly like a summer thunder shower upon a dusty road. He could stir the multitude at will, to a tempest of wrath, or reduce it to the silence with which the mother leaves the cradle side of her sleeping babe. Such tenderness – such pathos – such world-embracing love! And, on the other hand, such indignation – such fiery and thunderous denunciation, and such wit and humour I never heard surpassed, if equaled, at home or abroad.[453]

In Douglass's opinion, 'No trans-Atlantic statesman bore a testimony more marked and telling against the crime and curse of slavery, than did Daniel O'Connell'.[454]

In one of Douglass's final public speeches made in defence of the black republic of Haiti, only two years before his death, he again paid tribute to the Irishman, with a reference that he had used on many prior occasions:

> It was once said by the great Daniel O'Connell, that the history of Ireland might be traced, like a wounded man through a crowd, by the blood. The same can be said of the history of Haiti as a free state.[455]

Forty-six years after meeting O'Connell, the Irishman that Douglass had first admired as a young slave continued to inspire him.

Returns

Douglass returned to Britain in 1859 – again to escape from a tricky situation – in this case, possible arrest in the wake of the controversial and unsuccessful slave uprising at Harper's Ferry. Douglass had not been directly involved, but there was a fear that he would be targeted anyway.[456] As in 1845 and 1846, therefore, he came seeking sanctuary, again 'to protect himself from the violence of the Southern slaveholders'.[457] He stayed for a few months, lecturing in England and in Scotland, where over a decade earlier he had proved to be an uncompromising critic of the Free Church.[458] During his public lectures, Douglass was frequently called on to explain the split with Garrison. During one lecture, he explained:

The Garrisonians say – Yes. They hold the Constitution as a slaveholding instrument, and will not cast, or vote, or hold office, and denounce
all who vote or hold office, no matter how faithfully such persons labor
to promote the abolition of slavery. I, on the other hand, I deny that the
Constitution guarantees the right to hold property in man, and believe
that the way to abolish slavery in America is to vote such men into power
as will use their powers for the abolition of slavery.[459]

Overall, Douglass was warmly received, and none of the rancor of fifteen years
earlier was evident but, while lecturing in Scotland, he received news that his
10-year-old daughter had died, which caused him considerable sadness.[460] The situation led to Douglass curtailing his tour and returning to America unannounced.[461]

The years following Douglass's second return to America were years of
increasing hostility between the Southern states and the Northern states as the
former moved towards secession. The armed hostilities which broke out in 1861
represented decades of growing divisions, with the issue of slavery playing a central role. From the outset, Douglass hoped that the war would mean an ending to
slavery and, eventually, to granting citizenship to all black people. To this end,
he began to campaign for black soldiers to be allowed in the Union army, a plea
that was too radical for many. The way in which the Civil War was perceived in
Ireland, particularly by his Quaker friends, was of interest to Douglass.[462] The
outbreak of a war in America had dismayed the pacifist Quakers in Dublin. They
hoped that its outcome would be beneficial to slaves, but they viewed the conflict
as arising from 'the ambition and imperialism of the Northern states'.[463] In the
early phase of the war, Douglass himself was suspicious of Lincoln's stance on
slavery and, fearing the worst, even contemplated emigration to Haiti.[464]

It was not until 1 January 1863, in fact, that President Lincoln introduced
the Emancipation Proclamation, which freed more than three million slaves. At
this stage, the war was not going well for the Union and there was a shortage of
recruits. Douglass welcomed the Proclamation but took a pragmatic view of the
reasons it had been passed at this time. At a meeting at Cooper Union in New
York City he announced the Proclamation to be 'the great event of the century –
of our whole history'. He likened its impact to that of Catholic Emancipation in
Ireland, adding 'Though wrung out by the stern dictates of military necessity, it
was in reality a moral necessity'.[465] Following this, Douglass travelled thousands
of miles, calling on black people to enlist. He also published a number of long
and considered rationales of his position, which included 'Men of Color to Arms',
which was published in March.[466] In April, he published one of his most powerful writings, entitled 'WHY SHOULD A COLORED MAN ENLIST?' In it, he
argued:

You are a member of a long enslaved and despised race. Men have set
down your submission to Slavery and insult, to a lack of manly courage. They point to this fact as demonstrating your fitness only to be a

servile class. You should enlist and disprove the slander, and wipe out the reproach.

He also cautioned, 'The War for the Union, whether men so call it or not, is a war for Emancipation'.[467]

The Proclamation had not been welcomed by all in the North, who regarded its impact as having been to turn the Civil War into an Abolition War. In an attempt to win more recruits, President Lincoln introduced a form of conscription, or draft, commencing in New York. The so-called Draft Riots, which took place in July 1863, were ostensibly in opposition to a newly introduced draft. However, they turned into an attack on black people in the city, with Irish Americans being in the forefront of the violence. Douglass said of this incident:

> Though this mob was nominally against the draft which had been ordered, it poured out its fiercest wrath upon the colored people and their friends. It spared neither age nor sex; it hanged negroes simply because they were negroes, it murdered women in their homes, and burned their homes over their heads, it dashed out the brains of young children against the lamp posts, it burned the colored orphan asylum, a noble charity on the corner of 5th ave., and scarce allowing time for the helpless two hundred children to make good their escape, plundering the building of every valuable piece of furniture; and colored men, women, and children were forced to seek concealment in cellars or garrets or wheresoever else it could be found until this high carnival of crime and reign of terror should pass away.[468]

The progress of the riots was followed in Ireland, with some of the press supporting the idea that the draft was probably unconstitutional. The *Irish Times*, without mentioning the involvement of any Irish people, took the message of the violence to be, 'If the South cannot be conquered by volunteers, it should be conquered'.[469] Another Irish newspaper, again ignoring the role played by Irish Americans in perpetuating the violence, included an article praising the 'courageous, self-sacrificing spirit' of many Catholic priests in the city during the rioting.[470]

Douglass's impact and importance during the War can be judged by the fact that, on 10 August 1863, he was invited to the White House to meet President Lincoln. Douglass later admitted to feeling nervous, 'as I had never been in the White House before, and had never spoke to a President of the United States before'.[471] The two men met again a year later, this time at Lincoln's behest. At this stage, people were war-weary, with some describing it disparagingly as simply an 'abolition war'. Douglass was summoned to the White House for a third meeting in March 1865, but he was prevented from entering by two officious policemen. Unruffled, Douglass asked an officer to 'Just say to Mr. Lincoln that Fred. Douglass is at the door'.[472] It was a moment of levity in a moment that revealed the depth of prejudice. The following month, President Lincoln was assassinated.

A tribute to the impact that Douglass had made on Lincoln was revealed when Mrs Lincoln gave the president's favourite walking cane to Douglass.[473] Despite the loss of a President that he had come to admire, the passage of the Thirteenth Amendment in January 1865, outlawing slavery throughout the country, and the symbolic surrender by Robert E. Lee in April, effectively marking an end to the War, gave Douglass great hope that out of four years of bloodshed, a new, more egalitarian, nation would emerge.[474] He was to be disappointed.

The years following the Civil War were tumultuous on both sides of the Atlantic. In Ireland, a new wave of physical force republicanism had attempted another uprising in 1867. It had been unsuccessful. In America, emancipation and living in a country torn apart by a domestic war presented a number of new challenges for Douglass. In January 1867, he made an appeal for 'impartial suffrage' for the black man. During the course of his speech, he made a reference to Ireland and O'Connell that he had used on many previous occasions: 'What O'Connell said of the history of Ireland may with greater truth be said of the negro's. It may be "traced like a wounded man through a crowd, by the blood"'. More positively, this was followed with: 'Yet the negroes have marvelously survived all the exterminating forces of slavery, and have emerged at the end of two hundred and fifty years of bondage, not morose, misanthropic, and revengeful, but cheerful, hopeful, and forgiving.'[475] Later in the speech, he again referred to Ireland, saying:

> Look across the sea. Is Ireland, in her present condition, fretful, discontented, compelled to support an establishment in which she does not believe, and which the vast majority of her people abhor, a source of power or of weakness to Great Britain?[476]

It was a trope Douglass used frequently, even though it was now over twenty years since he had been in Ireland. The lasting impression made by Ireland was also apparent in his 1882 biography in which he paid fulsome tribute both to his time in the country and to O'Connell. In turn, one Irish newspaper paid tribute to 'the great coloured orator' for his praise of the Irishman.[477]

In the post-war years, Douglass's status as the most famous black American, while giving him stature and celebrity, inevitably also brought controversy and contempt. In 1883, for example, the first day of the meeting of the National Convention of Colored Men held in Louisville, was spent wrangling about the fitness of having Douglass as the chairman. The obstruction was led by 'A small but pugnacious minority'. According to one of the opposition, Douglass was 'a man who had never done anything for his race, but all for himself'.[478] An even larger storm was to break the following year. In 1884, Douglass married Helen Pitts, his wife Anna having suffered a fatal stroke in 1882. He had met Pitts when Douglass was working as the recorder of deeds in Washington and she was employed in his office. Even before they met, Pitts was involved in a number of reform issues, including temperance, she being a delegate at the national meeting of the Temperance Union in 1876.[479] Her family were also abolitionists. The marriage was controversial for a number of reasons: Pitts was a social activist and outspoken feminist; she was twenty years Douglass's junior; and she was white. Family members on both sides disapproved. Newspapers on each side of the Atlantic reported on the marriage, mostly unfavorably. The *New York Times*, showing no regard for accuracy, reported:

> Frederick Douglass, the colored leader was married in this city [Washington] this evening to Miss Helen M. Pitts, a white woman formerly of Avon, N.Y. . . . The first wife of Mr. Douglass, who was a colored woman, died about a year ago. The woman he married today is about 35 years of age, and was employed as a copyist in his office. Mr. Douglass himself is about 73 years of age and has daughters as old as his present wife.[480]

One Scottish newspaper informed its readers, 'An American paper has the following dubious announcement: – Fred Douglass's second marriage has made him a still stronger supporter of women's suffrage than he was before.'[481] In September 1886, he having resigned his position as recorder, Douglass and Helen sailed for Britain, where they expected to spend a year travelling in Europe, the now 69-year-old Douglass viewing this as his final visit.[482] This time, however, Douglass did not cross the Atlantic, fleeing from the threat of capture and lecturing for an income, but he travelled as a free man and an affluent tourist. Moreover, he and his wife travelled as first-class passengers. As Douglass explained on arrival in Liverpool:

> Then I came as a slave, now I come as a freeman; then as an alien; now as a citizen; then I was young, now I am comparatively old; then to plead the cause of my brethren in bonds, now to tell of their freedom and progress.[483]

The visitor who had travelled to Liverpool four decades earlier had changed in other ways. Shortly before departing, Douglass was a guest of the Wendell Phillips Club in Boston. His former travel companion, James Buffum, was present. In his speech, Douglass paid a generous tribute to his one-time mentor and one-time foe, Garrison: 'I have often been asked where I got my education. I have answered, from the Massachusetts Abolition University, Mr. Garrison, president'.[484] It was a more mature and mellowed man who was making the journey across the Atlantic. Douglass's presence did not capture the attention of the British media as it had done previously, but his celebrity status was confirmed by the appearance of a number of newspaper articles and images about his visit.[485]

On the voyage to Liverpool, the vessel stopped briefly at the port of Queenstown (now Cobh), near the city of Cork. Douglass and Helen were on deck to see the first sight of land, observing 'numerous little huts clinging for dear life apparently, while the barren mountain side itself was seared with dark lines which marked the stone walls by which it was divided'. It prompted Douglass, who was 'gazing sadly on those shores he first saw forty-one years ago', to remark, 'Poor barefooted Ireland'.[486] Regardless of Douglass's sympathy for Ireland and her struggle for independence, he had always been a great admirer of the British political system. He claimed that a highlight of his stay in Britain was a visit to the Colonial Exhibition, which Douglass thought 'epitomises the glory and the power and genius of the British Empire'.[487] Another highlight, in contrast to the former, was, while in London, Douglass heard William Gladstone, the leader of the Liberal Party and Home Rule advocate, speak in the House of Commons. He was full of praise for the elderly statesman, describing his argument in support of Home Rule as 'masterly and convincing'.[488] Douglass and his wife also wanted to combine their visit to the United Kingdom with a tour of the Continent, he being unable to do that forty years earlier because he had no rights of citizenship and so was unable to obtain a passport. While in Europe they also visited Egypt to explore a culture that had long fascinated Douglass. In addition to travelling there as a tourist, he admitted to:

> an ethnological purpose in the pursuit of which I hoped to turn my visit to some account in combating American prejudice against the darker colored races of mankind, and at the same time to raise colored people somewhat in their own estimation and thus stimulate them to higher endeavors. I had a theory for which I wanted the support of facts in the range of my own knowledge.[489]

In July 1887, Douglass completed his European tour with a final, brief visit to Ireland. He did so because he desired 'to once more look into the faces and hear the voices of the few remaining friends who gave him sympathy and support during his visit 41 years ago'.[490] Within Dublin, news of his impeding visit caused excitement, albeit amongst a new generation of activists. Writing to him in London at the beginning of June, Wilhelmina Webb, a relative of the now-dead Richard and Hannah, encouraged him to visit sooner rather than later,[491] explaining that people would scatter for their holidays in a month's time.[492] In a subsequent letter she warned him, 'I hardly know whether there are any outside our immediate circle, except James Haughton's family, left of your old friends in Dublin'.[493] Richard Allen had also passed away a few months earlier,[494] but his son wrote to Douglass, asking:

> if you and Mrs Douglass can come and see me here in Old Ireland – there are still hearts which beat true to you and your people, and I should be glad to unite a few of your old Friends, or the descendants of them, to meet you.[495]

It was not until the end of July 1887 that Douglass travelled to Ireland. He was alone, as Helen had returned to the United States, her mother having become ill during her absence.[496] Although Douglass had kept a detailed diary of his tour of Europe and North Africa, it did not extend to Ireland, the final entry being made on 5 June 1887, when he 'dined with Mrs Lucas and Charlotte' in Bedford Square in London.[497] The diary did, however, include the names and addresses of his Irish friends.[498] Largely for reasons of time, Douglass only stopped in Dublin, where he again visited the Webb family on Great Brunswick Street, but this time with Alfred, eldest son of Richard, who had died in 1872. According to Alfred, Douglass came 'to renew old memories of the 40s'.[499] Douglass reminisced on his earlier journey to Ireland, under very different circumstances:

> In Dublin, the first city I then visited, I was kindly received by Mr. Richard Webb, Richard Allen, James Haughton, and others. They were now all gone, and except some of their children, I was among strangers. These received me in the same cordial spirit that distinguished their fathers and mothers. I did not visit dear old Cork, where in 1845 I was made welcome by the Jennings, the Warings, the Wrights, and their circle of friends, most of whom I learned had passed away. The same was true of the Neals, the Workmans, the McIntyres, and the Nelsons at Belfast. I had friends in Limerick, in Waterford, in Eniscorthy [sic], and other towns of Ireland, but I saw none of them during this visit. What was true of the mortality of my friends in Ireland, was equally true of those in England. Few who first received me in that country are now among the living. . . I missed the presence of George Thompson, one of the most eloquent men who ever advocated the cause of the colored man, either in England or America. Joseph Sturge and most of his family had also passed away. But I will pursue this melancholy enumeration no further, except to say that, in meeting with the descendants of anti-slavery friends in England, Ireland and Scotland, it was good to have confirmed the scriptural saying, "Train up a child in the way he should go and when he is old he will not depart from it."[500]

While many of those who had welcomed Douglass to the capital city during his first visit had since passed away, other things had not changed, notably, the poverty and intermittent famines that still stalked the mass of the population. Again, much as he had done on his earlier visit, Douglass tried to understand the causes of such distress. Interestingly, he did not view alcohol as a factor in creating the poverty, which was in marked contrast to his explanation forty years earlier when he had combined his passion for abolition with his zealousness for the cause of temperance. Clearly, the statesman who returned to Ireland was very different from the 27-year-old 'fugitive' slave who had visited the country in 1845.

On the eve of his return visit to Ireland, Douglass published a reflection on the condition of the country. In it, he demonstrated a more nuanced and politicized understanding of Ireland than he had forty years earlier. He was particularly concerned with the on-going poverty of the Irish people and their long struggle for freedom. This time, he placed the suffering within the context of their being a colonized people who had endured 'centuries of oppression and sorrow'.[501] Douglass also reflected on the religious and other differences between the north and the south of the country – differences that had intensified in the decades following the Great Famine. Again, he explained the contrast through a colonial prism, in this case, the denial of many civil rights to Catholics, thus making them second-class citizens. Douglass's overall conclusion was that Irish poverty, suffering and religious divisions resulted from their colonial status. For him, the solution lay in Ireland becoming independent.

Douglass's visit coincided with another struggle for independence taking place in Ireland, the constitutional Repeal movement of the 1840s being replaced by another peaceful political movement known as Home Rule. His Dublin host, Alfred Webb, had, since the late 1860s, been involved in nationalist causes, he being appointed treasurer of the Home Rule League in 1873 and, in 1890, being elected a Home Rule member of the British Parliament.[502] Just as abolition had divided Irish American opinion in the 1840s, the Irish demand for independence, Home Rule, divided African American opinion in the 1880s. This was largely due to the feeling that Irish Americans had been weak on, or opposed to, abolition. Douglass, however, made a distinction between the Irish in Ireland and the Irish in America.[503] In August 1886, he wrote a letter to the *Boston Pilot* stating that he had 'never allowed the unfriendly attitude of Irish men in this country toward colored people to dim my vision as to the just rights of Irishmen at home'.[504] However, despite his sympathy for Home Rule, Douglass also wanted to understand the alternative perspective. To this end, he read a publication written by a leading Ulster Unionist and Wesleyan Minister, William Arthur, whose pamphlet *Shall the Loyal be deserted and the Disloyal Placed over them?* had sold over 50,000 copies.[505] In it, Arthur had predicted that Home Rule would result in civil war.[506]

In 1886, before traveling to Europe, Douglass had showed sympathy with the Home Rule agitation in Ireland and with William Gladstone, the English politician who was trying to resolve it. At an abolitionist dinner in Boston, he told his audience:

> I shall remember your injunction to extend your sympathy to all men oppressed; and I shall not hesitate to declare my own entire sympathy with that grand old man, Mr. Gladstone, in his endeavors to remove the reproach of oppression from England and to extend the desired liberty to Ireland.[507]

Around the same time, he published an eighteen-page article entitled 'Thoughts and Recollections'. In it, he unequivocally supported Home Rule, explaining that he had two reasons for so doing: 'First, because Ireland wants "Home Rule", and Secondly, because it will free England from the charge of continued oppression of Ireland'. He closed the article with a statement redolent of the words of O'Connell: 'I am for fair play for the Irishman, the negro, the Chinaman, and for all men of whatever country or clime, and for allowing them to work out their own destiny without outside interference'.[508] In 1887, when he heard that a number of women in England had signed a petition of sympathy in relation to the ongoing poverty and evictions in the country, he wrote to one of the organizers:

> I have just read your message of sympathy to Ireland, and am deeply moved by it. It carries me back to those dark days in my history when every honest word of sympathy with me and my oppressed brethren was worth more than silver and gold. Such words saved me from despair, were a consolation in sorrow, and a harbinger of hope for the future. Your words will be a balm to every bruised Irish heart.[509]

In December 1887, only months after his return from Ireland, Douglass attended a meeting in Washington in support of Home Rule. Sir Thomas Grattan Esmonde and the Hon. Arthur O'Connor, two Home Rule MPs, attended, as did eight senators and fifty-two members of Congress. Senator John J. Ingalls presided.[510] Twenty thousand people had accompanied the speakers to the hall. Douglass, who was part of the platform party, was the final speaker, doing so, 'after great applause'. He commenced with typical self-deprecation, saying, 'This is not my hour. England does not want to know what Frederick Douglass has to say on the subject of Home Rule for Ireland', but he was encouraged to continue. He made fun of the fact that he was the only black speaker by saying he had attended 'to give color' to the proceedings. During his well-received speech, he alluded to his meeting with O'Connell in a way that suggested that the two men were allies in their struggle for social justice.[511] The meeting passed a resolution thanking Gladstone for his 'manly efforts on behalf of the Irish'.[512] The assembly, and Douglass's presence at it, were reported in the British press.[513] Douglass, who had avoided talking about Irish politics in the 1840s, had now become an outspoken champion of Home Rule. He had become a black O'Connell, although perhaps not in the way he had intended when he first coined the phrase.

Regardless of his advancing years, a further sign of Douglass's international view of social justice came in June 1889, when he accepted the position as Consul General of Haiti. When announcing the appointment, the *New York Times* referred to him as 'the best-known negro in the United States'.[514] As with so much in his life, the appointment was controversial, in no small part because Haiti – the first black republic in the world – had been boycotted and not officially recognized by America from 1806 to 1862. During this time, Garrison's Anti-Slavery Society had repeatedly agitated for their recognition.[515] Moreover, for largely strategic reasons, in the 1880s, America was considering making itself a protectorate over the island – a move Douglass regarded as unnecessary and hostile.[516] In July 1891, Douglass and Helen returned to Washington, where Douglass resigned his post. A few months later, the Haitian government paid tribute to Douglass by naming him their commissioner in the World's Fair that was to be held in Chicago in 1893. Ironically, its focus was to celebrate the 400th anniversary of Christopher

Columbus's arrival in the New World in 1492. On 2 January 1893, Douglass delivered a lecture on Haiti in the Haitian Pavilion at the Fair. It was one of the finest speeches of his life, in which he denounced America's imperial ambitions towards Haiti and explained her deep-rooted dislike of the black republic. During the course of his oration, he likened the history of Haiti to the history of Ireland, employing his favourite quote from O'Connell. It was now almost fifty years since his meeting with the Irishman, but Ireland and O'Connell continued to influence Douglass's political thought. Douglass's experiences in Haiti also led him to update his 1882 autobiography.[517] He was now 75 years old and showed no signs of slowing down.

Irish newspapers ran occasional articles on Douglass, although his time spent in Ireland appeared to have been forgotten. In September 1892, a Dublin newspaper featured Douglass in a series entitled 'Prominent People'. Setting the tone for a saccharine piece of writing, they described him as 'a man whose history has been one long romance'.[518] No mention was made of his visit to the country in 1845. In the same year, Douglass was involved in another campaign that must have caused him considerable anguish. In 1892, when lynching – an unpalatable aspect of life in post–Civil War America – was at its peak, Douglass wrote an article for the *North American Review* speaking out against this activity. He attributed the increase in lynchings to 'the material rise of the negro', which had provoked acts of race hatred.[519] His article, in turn, was discussed by newspapers in Britain and Ireland.[520] One commentary that appeared in the *Glasgow Evening Post* rejected the interpretation by the 'honourable gentleman', positing that, 'nothing is more patent than that those miscreants had outraged white women'.[521] One English newspaper, in response to news of another lynching, alluded to Douglass's visit in 1859:

> When Frederick Douglass, the negro orator, and the friend of John Brown, came to England before the outbreak of the great civil war to plead the cause of the slaves he expressed himself as astonished and delighted to find himself treated with much greater courtesy and respect in an old Monarchical country than he had ever raised in Republican America.

It added, 'We have, however, always to remember that we have no such temptations to treat negroes as an inferior race as are daily and hourly presented to our trans-Atlantic kinsmen' and posed the question that if there was an influx of negroes into the country 'how long would it be before a social prejudice sprang up similar to in America?' The article concluded with a statement that negated all that Douglass had spent his life fighting against: 'The average Englishman is incontestably higher than the average negro, and knows himself to be so; and no good can accrue from pretending out of politeness that things are otherwise'.[522] To counter such prejudice and propaganda, a young black activist, Ida Wells, decided to travel to England. She had first risen to prominence when, aged only 22, she had refused to give up her first-class seat in a railcar when asked to do so by a conductor.[523] Before taking the anti-lynching campaign to England she asked Douglass for letters of support. Despite her being over forty years younger than Douglass, he admired Wells's work and agreed to help.[524] Her mission may even have reminded him of his own journey in 1845, when he had tried to win over British public opinion. Douglass's support was clearly valued because, in British press reports, Wells was described as being 'accredited' by Douglass.[525] In gratitude for his assistance, Wells celebrated 'Douglass Day' each year following her mentor's death.[526]

Douglass died on the evening of 20 February 1895. Earlier that day, he had attended the Women's National Council, the convention of the National Women's Suffrage Association, of which he was a member. During the conference, he had been escorted to the platform by his lifelong friend, Susan B. Anthony.[527] He died in his home near Washington while telling Helen about his day's activities. To the end, he was campaigning for a worthy cause. Douglass's remains were taken to Rochester, where he was buried alongside his first wife, Anna, in Mount Hope Cemetery.[528]

Douglass's death meant that his life story could be retold to a new generation. One newspaper account of his life referred to him as 'one of the foremost figures in the gallery of American's distinguished citizens'.[529] It was a subtle, but important, acknowledgement that he was not simply a champion of black people, but a champion of all Americans. News of Douglass's passing was reported throughout the world, although it attracted surprisingly little attention in Ireland. The *Belfast News-Letter* of 26 February 1895 included a paragraph about his funeral referring to him as 'the departed champion of freedom'. Their bitter differences with him in 1846 appeared to have been forgotten. The *Northern Whig* also noted his passing and referred briefly to his time in England.[530] At the far end of the country, while noting his death, the *Cork Constitution* stated that he had been Minister to Haiti.[531] No reference was made to his successful visit to the city fifty years earlier. The *Belfast News-Letter* which, at the time of Douglass's departure from the country in October 1846, had become his implacable enemy, reported on the funeral in Rochester, noting that during his lying-in state in the City Hall, 'all classes of the community reverently passed round the bier of a man who had done so much for the emancipation of his fellow-man from that serfdom of which he had been a victim'.[532] In contrast, British newspapers made reference to his visit there in the 1840s and the lasting impression he had made.[533] One Scottish newspaper asserted, 'He frequently visited Britain and created a deep impression by his oratory'.[534] Other papers, by referring to him as 'the famous American orator', recognized his international stature as a citizen and representative of America – a status he had been denied for the first twenty-eight years of his life.[535]

While most obituaries and eulogies were overwhelmingly positive, a number were more measured, one English provincial newspaper opining, 'Though not the greatest man of his race, Frederick Douglass was undoubtedly its most successful orator'.[536] A less palatable article appeared in a provincial newspaper, entitled, 'A Remarkable Mulatto', and stated:

> He was a mulatto, not a negro; and the people who cherish the idea that the negro will ultimately be placed on a level with the white man in the scale of civilisation cannot point to Douglass as example of this process. We are afraid there is nothing in the history of the Southern negroes since the emancipation to encourage the belief in their potential capacity.[537]

In death, as in life, Douglass divided people. Within the House of Representatives, a proposal that the House should adjourn to honour the passing of Douglass was opposed by the Democrats, with many southern members speaking vehemently against it. It was finally carried by thirty-two against twenty-five.[538]

Conclusion

Frederick Douglass was not the only black abolitionist to visit Ireland and Britain, but he was the most famous at the time and the most acclaimed and commemorated since then.[539] He was no stranger to such notoriety. During his lifetime, he had become a celebrity, as requests for his autograph testified,[540] as did the fact that two biographies had been published before Douglass's death.[541] During his stay in Ireland and Britain, Douglass was a favourite on the lecture circuit. This was not simply because of his compelling life story or his oratorical skills. Douglass was charismatic. His time in the United Kingdom coincided with that of another escaped slave, Moses Roper. Roper's early life story was similar to Douglass's, and he had also published his own narrative in 1837, which had been republished by the English Quaker printer, Charles Gilpin, in 1843.[542] He too was lecturing in Britain in 1846. Although Roper's audiences in 1846 were said to be large, he did not attract the same public attention or newspaper column space as Douglass.[543] Moreover, today Roper is largely forgotten.

Douglass's twenty-month exile spent in the United Kingdom has generally been judged by historians to have been successful, one even claiming that while he was there, his time was spent 'lecturing to wildly enthusiastic audiences'.[544] To some extent, this statement is true, but it ignores the complexity of Douglass's interaction with those whom he met and how his message increasingly became less about his own story and more about creating an alliance to expose those who sustained slavery, most notably the churches. A close reading of the newspapers reveals that Douglass's dogged adherence to the 'Send Back the Money' campaign proved divisive and ultimately damaging to his reputation, at least in the short term. This was clear from his reception in Belfast in October 1846, which was markedly different from how he had been received in December 1845. Moreover, his support for Garrison's uncompromising and, at times, bombastic, attacks on the Evangelical Alliance alienated some who had previously admired him in Ireland and in Scotland. The two men did not lecture as equals. In Garrison's presence, Douglass was reduced to a mere auxiliary, a warm up for the older man. And the warmth, self-deprecation and humour that had so charmed his Irish audiences over the preceding year disappeared. One of the things that this episode demonstrated was that Douglass had outgrown Garrison. Upon his return to America a few months later – as a free man – Douglass sought to distance himself from Garrison, initially geographically, but increasingly ideologically. And the independent Douglass thrived.

Historian David Blight has argued that it was in the years after Douglass returned to America, and notably during the Civil War, that his political and personal growth matured and reached new levels of sophistication.[545] His time in Ireland provided the foundation for this further growth. There, he realized many first and landmark moments. Furthermore, his personal and intellectual liberation was unleashed in Ireland in a way that it had not been in America, where he had been relegated to standing in the shadow of Garrison.

Without his experiences in Ireland, it is unlikely that Douglass would have had the confidence or the skills that he required to strike out on his own, especially in the precarious world of newspaper ownership. Just as importantly, his experiences in Ireland proved to be a political awakening. In Ireland, Douglass witnessed poverty such as he had never seen before, except in the slave plantations.[546] During his visit in 1846, the tragedy of the Famine was starting to inflict its deadly blow, although, at this stage, nobody was aware of its longevity or the enormity of the destruction it would cause. How could over one million *white* people starve to death at the heart of the richest empire in the world? When Douglass first arrived in Ireland, he had been in the early stages of his political and intellectual development, yet, as Don Mullan has written:

> One senses from his letters that while he was not yet equipped with the tools to incisively analyze the political and economic causes of hunger and deprivation endured by a colonized people . . . his politicization was, nonetheless, underway.[547]

Staying with the Webbs and meeting other Irish Quakers gave Douglass an insight into how even middle-class professionals could still be second-class citizens. At this stage, Quakers (like Jews) could not be members of the British parliament.[548] Like free black people in America, they were denied the right to attain the highest levels of public office. Tellingly, the three founders of the Hibernian Anti-Slavery Society were Nonconformists, and so they were personally familiar with social exclusion. For their part, Catholics had only been granted the right to be members of the British parliament in 1829. Even though they were the majority in Ireland, they too knew what it was like to be discriminated against and to be denied civil liberties. Within Ireland, simplistic ideas of freedom and liberty, and of white privilege, were challenged, a fact that was not lost on Douglass.

Many of the people whom Douglass encountered in the south were Repealers, even if not followers of O'Connell. Here, he was in a country that disavowed slavery but in which the majority of the people believed that they were not free. Irish nationalists frequently described themselves as being 'slaves' – an idea that was rejected by Douglass, perhaps most forcibly in a speech made in Limerick where he drew a distinction between being a slave and being oppressed, arguing that, 'Negro-slavery consisted not in taking away a man's property, but in making property of him, and in destroying his identity'.[549] In his view, Irish people were not slaves: they were free to move around, to emigrate, to protest against their treatment and to effect change. To invert Douglass's own words – Irish men and women *owned* themselves. No, they were not slaves . . . but he also understood that they were not free. Clearly, Ireland's colonial status helped Douglass to marshal his arguments against slavery, even, at times, borrowing the language of the Repeal movement and frequently quoting its illustrious leader.

Douglass had to further negotiate how to balance his respect for colonized Ireland with his admiration of Britain. The British government had liberated its slaves in 1833, yet it kept the Irish people in a subjugated state. This process may have been further complicated by his own admission that Britain was 'the land of my *paternal* ancestors'.[550] By such a statement, Douglass inserted himself personally into the trans-Atlantic discourse concerned with slavery, colonization and oppression. Regardless of any deficiencies, Douglass found much to admire in the British system of government and liked to point to the fact that there was more freedom under the British *monarchy* than in the American *republic*.[551] So why were Irish people oppressed and impoverished? In the 1840s, Douglass was a zealous advocate of temperance, and he regarded alcohol as the root of much poverty. Many years later, when Douglass spoke in favour of Home Rule, he referred to the centuries-old oppression of Ireland as the cause of its suffering and lack of economic progress. He regarded it as 'a land which has been for ages the scene of misrule and social misery' yet which was, paradoxically, 'the land of Burke and Sheridan, of Grattan and Curran, of O'Connell and Father Matthew [sic]; a land renowned in song and story for its statesmen, orators, patriots, and heroes'.[552] The men that Douglass so fondly spoke of were Irish patriots, yet they combined their love of their country with an international love of liberty that transcended nationality. All of these experiences and ideas enabled Douglass to recalibrate his approach to subjugation and persecution, as well as to liberty and freedom. When Douglass arrived in Ireland he admitted that he was concerned with one issue only – slavery – but when he left, he had come to believe that his cause was part of a universal struggle for justice. The same day that he heard O'Connell speak in Conciliation Hall, he wrote to Garrison, quoting part of the Irish man's speech: 'I am the friend of liberty in every clime, class and colour. My sympathy with distress is not confined within the narrow bounds of my own green island. No – it extends itself to every corner of the earth'.[553] Only a few weeks later, Douglass echoed these words, writing:

> I confess I should be ashamed to lift up my voice against American slavery, but that I know the cause of humanity is one the world over. He who

really and only feels for the American slave, cannot steel his heart of the woes of others; and he who thinks himself an abolitionist, yet cannot enter into the wrongs of others, has yet to find a true foundation for his anti-slavery faith.[554]

Even after 1846, memories of Ireland continued to influence Douglass's actions. At key junctures in Douglass's life – from reading speeches of Irish patriots when still a slave, to being encouraged to escape to the North, to applying the words of O'Connell to an understanding of other colonized peoples – Douglass was influenced by Irish people and by Ireland's history. Douglass's admiration for the Irish, however, was tempered by his observation of the Irish in America and their avoidance of siding with abolition. This matter had also concerned O'Connell, who, in his magnificent 'Cincinnati Letter' of 1843, lambasted his fellow Irishmen across the Atlantic:

How can the generous, the charitable, the humane, the noble emotions of the Irish heart, have become extinct among you? How can your nature be so totally changed as that you should become the apologists and advocates of that execrable system which makes man the property of his fellow man – destroying the foundation of all moral and social virtues – condemns to ignorance, immorality, and irreligion, millions of our fellow-creatures – renders the slave hopeless of relief, and perpetuates oppression by law; and, in the name of what you call a Constitution!

It was not in Ireland you learned this cruelty. Your mothers were gentle, kind, and humane. Their bosoms overflowed with the honey of human charity. Your sisters are, probably, many of them still among us, and participate in all that is good and benevolent in sentiment and action. How, then, can you be so depraved? How can your souls have become stained with a darkness blacker than the negro's skin?[555]

Why were the Irish ardent abolitionists at home, but not when in America?[556] There is no single explanation for this change: fear of competition for the lowest jobs; allegiance to the Democratic Party, who were pro-slavery but immigrant-friendly; unwillingness to criticize an institution that was legal in a country that had given them shelter; the Protestantism and anti-religion stance of leading abolitionists; and reluctance to draw attention to themselves in the face of American nativism as embodied in the Know Nothing Party. All of these factors probably played a part. Angela Murphy has further suggested that it is necessary to 'look at how irreconcilable calls for action from their ancestral and their adopted countries shaped their negotiation of identity as a distinct group within a slave-holding republic'.[557]

If the impact of Ireland on Douglass was considerable, what was the impact of Douglass on Ireland?

Despite some dismay with his attacks on American Protestant churches, Douglass's words and presence reenergized the anti-slavery movement within the country. Shortly following his arrival, Webb informed Garrison that he had 'occasioned deep interest in the anti-slavery cause, and many who never thought on the subject at all, are now convinced that it is a sin to neglect'.[558] Some of the legacies of Douglass's visit were tangible. His influence on women abolitionists was particularly powerful. Like Garrison, Douglass was a supporter of women's rights, a stance that was considered too radical by many Irish and British abolitionists. In reality, it even proved too radical for many American male abolitionists, with few of them signing the Declaration of Sentiments in 1848. Douglass was an honorable exception. When in Ireland, he forged many deep, and even lifelong, friendships with a number of strong women.[559] A number of female abolitionist groups were revitalized or initiated due to his visit. They, in turn, strengthened their trans-Atlantic links, with the Ladies' Anti-Slavery Bazaar in Boston being an immediate beneficiary. In 1855, English-born Julia Griffiths, friend of Douglass and one-time tutor and assistant editor, visited Ireland. In Dublin, she spent time with the female abolitionists who now sent goods to the Rochester Bazaar rather than to the Boston one. In Belfast, she met with the Ladies' Anti-Slavery Society. Griffiths reported that wherever she travelled, people remembered Douglass and still wanted to help him.[560] The role of women in the movement remained close to his heart. In his third autobiography, Douglass wrote:

> When the true history of the anti-slavery cause shall be written, women will occupy a large space in its pages; for the cause of the slave has been peculiarly a woman's cause. Her heart and her conscience have supplied in large degree its motive and mainspring. Her skill, industry, patience, and perseverance have been wonderfully manifest in every trial hour.[561]

For the men abolitionists of Belfast, Douglass's legacy was more ambiguous. In the town which was the heartland of Presbyterianism in Ireland, the once-strong abolition movement never recovered from the polarizing impact of both the 'Send Back the Money' campaign and the attacks on the Evangelical Alliance. The Belfast Anti-Slavery Society disbanded in 1852, Calder remaining convinced that these two crusades had caused irreparable damage.[562] Douglass's victories have to be set against this shortcoming; they include his obtaining sterling testimonials from the Rev. Drew and the Rev. Nelson and his personal and professional triumph over the Rev. Smyth. These actions alone constituted a significant blow to the American churches who upheld slavery. Moreover, Douglass proved himself able to transcend the age-old divisions in Ireland between Catholics and Protestants, and between nationalists and supporters of the Union, not to mention the more recent divisions between the two branches of the abolition movement.

Regardless of controversies and conflicts, in the post-Famine decades, anti-slavery continued in Ireland, as evidenced by the warm welcomes given to intermittent visitors. But it never achieved the dazzling heights of the 1840s, when both Remond and Douglass were welcomed, and Garrison visited twice. During this time also, abolition had the support of Irish political leaders from across the political and religious spectrum, including O'Connell, Father Mathew, Richard Madden, Sharman Crawford and the Marquess of Sligo. In Britain, the veteran Thomas Clarkson inspired universal respect, while many politicians supported abolition, albeit for various motives, and Prince Albert would attend meetings, thus giving the movement royal approval. Overwhelmingly, abolition in Ireland and Britain was a cause that all classes in society could support and endorse. Black abolitionist Samuel Ward, visiting in 1854 and again in 1855, opined: 'It was with the greatest delight that I found, in every part of England, Ireland, Scotland, and Wales, that abolitionism is not a mere abstract idea, but a practical question of grave importance'.[563]

One aspect of Douglass's visit that has been largely overlooked is the time that he devoted to his other passion, temperance. It is no coincidence that his first and final lectures in Ireland during his four-month visit were on this topic. In fact, within a few hours of arriving in Ireland, Douglass spoke at a temperance meeting. A personal highlight was meeting Father Mathew on a number of occasions and being invited to breakfast at the priest's home. Although already a teetotaller, Douglass retook his vow:

> So entirely charmed by the goodness of this truly good man was I, that I besought him to administer the pledge to me. He complied with promptness, and gave me a beautiful silver pledge. I now reckon myself with delight the fifth of the last five of Father Mathew's 5,487,495 temperance children.[564]

Before Douglass left the country, following his stay, his final public appearances were at two temperance meetings. This tells us about the personality of the young Douglass. For him, part of owning himself was tied in with the need for sobriety and control over his own person. Moreover, any deviation would mean not only letting himself down, but his people. And, as a representative of his people, that is slaves, his public actions and manners, like his clothes, were always immaculate. Creating the right impression fitted in with Douglass's perpetual concern with the image that he presented to the outside world. Throughout the rest of his life he remained committed to temperance, but he never seemed as fervent about it as he had been during his time in Ireland and Britain.

Writing in 1999, Alan Rice contended that Douglass 'arrived in Britain as the raw material of a great black figure; [but left] . . . in April 1847 the finished independent man, cut from a whole cloth and able to make his own decisions about the strategies and ideologies of the abolitionist movement'.[565] Over the last few years, there has been increasing attention paid to Douglass's time in Ireland at the outset of his tour and the impact that Ireland had on his subsequent development. This reevaluation has led one historian to state, 'Although from a young age he possessed the inclination to be a leader, Ireland was the site where this trait blossomed, free of the concern of retribution'.[566] As the documents in this volume attest, the impact of Ireland on Douglass was immense. His escape from slavery in 1838 had physically freed him; the 'purchase' of his freedom by women abolitionists in England had legally freed him; but it was in Ireland that he found intellectual and emotional freedom. Evidence of this new-found liberation was provided by Douglass in the second Dublin edition of the *Narrative*, when he responded to a pro-slavery critic in America:

> If anyone had told me seven years ago that I should ever be able to *dictate* such a Narrative, to say nothing of *writing* it, I should have disbelieved the prophecy. I was then a mere wreck; Covey had beaten and bruised me so much that my spirit was crushed and broken. Frederick the Freeman is very different from Frederick the Slave. To judge me now by what I was then, is to do me great injustice. I feel myself a new man. Freedom has given me new life. The change wrought in me is truly amazing.[567]

As the Irish editions of the *Narrative* confirm, it was during this part of his sojourn that Douglass discovered both his personal and political agency. During his time in Britain he honed these skills, and, following his return home, he consolidated the lessons learned while outside the country. His experiences both nationally and internationally fused, enabling Douglass to become one of the most prolific and respected Americans of the nineteenth century and beyond, one who devoted his life to 'the cause of humanity'.[568] It was in Ireland that the 27-year-old runaway slave both found himself and freed himself. In Douglass's words, the chattel had become a man, and in the process, the American abolitionist had blossomed into a champion of human rights.

A note on the documents

In light of the hundreds of thousands of words written by Douglass himself and even more words written about him, is there anything new to say?[569] As the documents that follow testify, Douglass, over 200 years after being born into slavery, still has fresh things to say to us. And, just as importantly, his message remains relevant.

The documents that follow tell the remarkable story of Frederick Douglass in Ireland from a range of contemporary sources, but primarily newspapers, which allow the voice of the young Douglass to emerge. In the mid-nineteenth century, Ireland had a lively national and regional press. It was part of a long tradition of reading news, going back to the establishment of the *Belfast News-Letter and General Advertiser* in 1737. The *News-Letter* was Presbyterian, reflecting the religion of the majority of people in Belfast. The majority of the newspapers subsequently published out of Belfast had a Protestant focus and, in the 1840s, were opposed to the nationalist movement. The *Banner of Ulster*, for example, had been founded in 1842 to uphold orthodox Presbyterian principles. A more moderate voice was provided by the *Northern Whig*, which first appeared in 1832 and had a liberal unionist focus. By the 1840s, together with the *News-Letter*, it was one of the leading papers in the town. At the time of Douglass's visit, the only local Catholic newspaper in Belfast was the *Vindicator*, which had been founded in 1839 and was a supporter of O'Connell. In Dublin, the nationalist press was particularly vibrant. The *Freeman's Journal* had been founded in Dublin in 1763 and was Ireland's first nationalist newspaper. It was followed in 1828 by the *Pilot*, largely at the initiative of O'Connell, who realized the value of the press in the propaganda war for winning hearts and minds. The *Nation*, which had been founded in 1842 by the group of Repealers known as Young Ireland, added a new dimension to the medium due to their focus on both politics and culture as a way of creating an Irish national identity.[570] The *Nation* was also longer than other papers, with much space devoted to history, literature and poetry.[571] By the time of Douglass's arrival, Young Ireland were questioning O'Connell's leadership, slavery being one area of division. They believed the Liberator devoted too much time to this issue, and they had no qualms about accepting money from slave-holders. In Cork, the *Cork Examiner* was one of the leading provincial newspapers with a reach beyond the county. It had been founded in 1841 and was a supporter of O'Connell. Irish newspapers had a reach beyond the literate and those who could afford to purchase them. There was an established tradition of local priests or schoolmasters reading the news aloud. After 1840, the Repeal Association established reading rooms throughout the country to help disseminate information and improve literacy in the country.

During his four visits to Ireland in 1845 and 1846, Douglass received extensive newspaper coverage, most of which was overwhelmingly positive. At end of 1845, however, he was competing for newspaper space with the appearance of a new form of potato disease, railway speculation, the launch of O'Connell's new Repeal campaign and, from America, the annexation of Texas – a topic which Douglass addressed in a number of lectures. By the time of his final visit in October 1846, the potato blight and food shortages of the previous year had now developed into a national famine and were taking up much column space. Surprisingly, it is something on which Douglass said little.

Douglass's early lectures in Ireland provide many insights into his life as a slave that, in later periods, he avoided. As he explained in his 1855 autobiography:

> I have often refused to narrate my personal experiences in public anti-slavery meetings . . . I have never based my opposition to slavery on a basis so narrow as my own slavery, but rather on the indestructible and unchangeable laws of human nature, every one of which is perpetually and flagrantly violated by the slave system.[572]

In addition to telling his own story (which also served as a way of encouraging purchase of the *Narrative*), Douglass was anxious to expose the complicity of some of the American churches in not turning their back on slave-holders, an issue that proved to be controversial. When he reached Belfast in December 1845, his main concern changed to the 'Send Back the Money' campaign. By the time Garrison joined him in Belfast in October 1846, this issue, together with an uncompromising condemnation of the Evangelical Alliance, was their main focus. The newspapers chart this change and the negative impact it had on his interactions with his audiences and, in fact, with a number of newspapers themselves.

Reports of Douglass's lectures that appeared in the Irish press were occasionally reprinted in newspapers in Britain and, more frequently, America. In this way, newspapers played a crucial role in facilitating the international flow of ideas. This process had been expedited by the development of steam shipping, railways and telegraphs, all of which had brought about a communications revolution. As a result, news from Ireland could reach Boston in as quickly as three weeks. For Douglass, it was particularly important that his words should be read by as wide an audience as possible. Douglass regarded newspaper coverage of his words as an important part of swaying public opinion and winning the propaganda war against slavery. For these reasons, he believed that sympathetic press coverage was of enormous benefit to the slave.[573] Douglass himself read the accounts of his lectures and would report to Webb and Garrison and his other correspondents about their reception. After giving his first lecture in Belfast, he wrote to Webb that 'The papers of this morning took a favourable notice of my meeting last night and a deep interest appears to be excited'.[574] Three months later, he informed an audience in Lisburn:

> Several of the lectures which he had delivered since he came to Ireland, had been published in the newspapers and had found their way against the western breeze, and been copied into American papers which were sent to him by friends. This showed the advantage of which the press could be to the slave.[575]

The fact that Douglass's lectures were very well attended, even when an entrance fee was charged, would also have been heartening to abolitionists observing from America. Ten years following his time in the United Kingdom, Douglass reflected more fully on the role of the press in promoting his mission:

> It has happened to me – as it has happened to most other men engaged in a good cause – often to be more indebted to my enemies than to my own skill or to the assistance of my friends, for whatever success has attended my labors. Great surprise was expressed by American newspapers, north and south, during my stay in Great Britain, that a person so illiterate and insignificant as myself could awaken an interest so marked in England. These papers were not the only parties surprised. I was myself not far behind them in surprise. But the very contempt and scorn, the systematic and extravagant disparagement of which I was the object, served, perhaps, to magnify, and to render me of some account, whether deserving

or not. A man is sometimes made great, by the greatness of the abuse a portion of mankind may think proper to heap upon him. Whether I was of as much consequence as the English papers made me out to be, or not, it was easily seen, in England, that I could not be the ignorant and worthless creature, some of the American papers would have them believe I was.[576]

On his return to America, the fact that Douglass devoted himself to founding and editing a newspaper, the *North Star*, reinforced the importance of this medium of communication in Douglass's crusade.

Newspaper reports provide a level of detail that is not usually available elsewhere. By providing the names of the platform party and the other speakers present, they allow a more complete picture of the Irish anti-slavery movement in the 1840s to be glimpsed. It is clear that Anglicans, Catholics, Presbyterians and Quakers all hosted and listened to Douglass, demonstrating that Irish anti-slavery cut across religious boundaries. Additionally, the newspapers give tantalizing insights about those who came to hear Douglass. The most common word used when describing the audience was 'respectable', or it was filled with 'men of influence' or graced with the presence of 'ladies', including, on occasion, the 'daughters of Tradesmen' – and even children were mentioned as spectators. Inevitably, given the location, the audience was white – making Douglass's plea for a 'Black O'Connell' more poignant and pertinent. Newspaper reportage uniquely makes it possible to gauge the reaction of the audience through the comments provided in parentheses, ranging from 'Cheers', to 'Hear, hear', to 'Loud cheering', to 'Sensation', to 'Laughter', or, far less usually, 'Hisses' or even 'Silence'. Tellingly, the warm cheers and enthusiasm that had attended much of Douglass's initial lectures dissipated during his brief return accompanied by Garrison. While we know that Douglass's lectures were well attended, and that at some of the early ones people had to be turned away, we do not know the motivation of those who attended. Was it through curiosity or conviction? Or, later, was it to observe the conflict that accompanied the 'Send Back the Money' campaign? The imposition of a charge at many of the secular lectures, sometimes of as much as six pence, reveals something about the social composition of the audiences.

How was Douglass perceived? In addition to content, the newspapers convey a sense of the deportment and delivery style of the young speaker and his engagement with his audience. His voice was frequently commented on, it being described as 'well toned and musical' and his 'selection of language most happy'.[577] Another newspaper reported, 'He was much admired as a speaker, possessing as he does, a fine soft, mellow, and sonorous voice'.[578] Douglass was praised for his 'his manly and eloquent address',[579] and his 'manly dignity of manner, which must win him the attention of any audience before whom he may appear'.[580] On both sides of the Atlantic, the Victorian use of the term 'manly' was considered the highest praise that could be bestowed.[581] At his initial lectures, Douglass spoke for approximately forty-five minutes, but as he grew in confidence, he lectured for longer periods. In his later lectures, he spoke for up to two hours, usually having been preceded by speeches by local abolitionists and by his travelling companion, Buffum. Nonetheless, we are told he held the 'breathless attention' of his audiences.[582] Reporting on his very first lecture in Dublin, the *Pilot* opined, 'we have never seen a more enthusiastic meeting of our fellow citizens'.[583] A report from Cork averred that Douglass gave 'one of the most eloquent and impressive discourses ever heard'.[584] From the reports of his lectures, it is possible to gain a sense of how he kept the audiences engaged with a delivery that included theatricality, humour, mimicry and pathos. He often commenced with a self-deprecating statement about his own inadequacy as a public speaker – and then went on to prove the opposite to be the case. As with everything he did, his public actions were underpinned by a desire to challenge racial stereotypes. And, as the newspapers demonstrate, he excelled as a lecturer, sharing many of the attributes that he so admired in O'Connell. Moreover, his lectures in Ireland were delivered extemporaneously, making their range and fluency, and cogent lines of reasoning, even more impressive.

Douglass's handsome physical appearance was frequently commented on. Images from this period show that he dressed fashionably and impeccably. Yet, in describing Douglass's physical appearance to their readers, even when doing so favourably, the newspapers occasionally revealed their own deep-rooted prejudices and reversion to stereotypes. This was evident in the following reports. When he lectured in Waterford, the journalist wrote 'Mr. Douglas [sic] speaks the English language fluently, and has rather a good delivery'.[585] A report from Cork stated:

> Mr. Douglas [sic] rose in compliance with the wishes of the company, and proceeded to address them with the ease and grace of a gentleman – a gentleman of nature and society. Evidently, from his colour and conformation, he is descended from parents of different race, his appearance is singularly pleasing and agreeable. The hue of his face and hands rather a yellow brown or bronze, while there is little, if anything, in his features of that peculiar prominence of lower face, thickness of lips, and flatness of nose, which peculiarly characterize the true Negro type.[586]

The process of reporting in the nineteenth century was labour intensive. At public meetings, journalists were usually provided with a table. They each brought a large number of sharpened pencils. While they attempted to record verbatim, inevitably there were discrepancies in the coverage by different papers, and, depending on the paper's politics, in emphasis and interpretation. To allow for these biases, a variety of different newspapers have been included in the documents, from High Church Tory to Catholic nationalist, to Presbyterian unionist, and everything in between. To reflect these differences, in some cases, two or more accounts of the same lecture have been included in the Documents. An example of the subtleties – and politics – of reporting occurred following Douglass's first lecture in Belfast on 5 December 1845. During the course of his speech, Douglass paid fulsome tribute to Daniel O'Connell for his opposition to slavery. The *Northern Whig* covered this mention but omitted to include any record of audience reaction. The *Banner of Ulster*, when it mentioned this part of the lecture, recorded two instances of 'cheers'. The Catholic, and pro-O'Connell, *Vindicator* noted 'applause', 'vehement applause' and more 'applause'. The *News-Letter* omitted any mention of the reference to O'Connell. These differences reflected the divergent opinions of newspapers in Belfast in the 1840s. In the case of the '*Cambria* incident', a number of accounts have been provided which demonstrate interesting variations in opinion on both sides of the Atlantic. A small selection of letters from those who hosted Douglass and interacted with him first-hand have also been provided, as have Douglass's letters to Garrison about his Irish experiences. These letters were intended for publication and can therefore be regarded as part of the crusade. Douglass's letters confirm the early triumph and sense of freedom which he experienced at being in Ireland.

Newspapers formed a vital part of the propaganda war in the crusade against slavery. While the majority of Irish and British newspapers agreed that slavery was a bad thing and ought to be ended (although they differed as to when and how), American newspapers were polarized on the issue. As the extracts from *Boston Pilot* and its dispute with the *Waterford Chronicle* show, being liberal on Irish issues did not mean support for abolition. This dispute, as with the *Cambria* incident, additionally reveals how closely each side was watching the other, regardless of the distance. Furthermore, the impact of such reporting seems to have been considerable. Moses Roper, another runaway slave writing in his own *Narrative*, explained the value of British and Irish support: 'We look very much to Great Britain and Ireland for help. Whenever we hear of English or Irish doing good to black men, we are delighted and run and tell each other the news'.[587] His comment implies that the spread of news was not confined only to the literate but was passed by word of mouth, thus reaching those who were the object of such sympathy.

The passage of time has not diminished the vibrancy and potency of Douglass's lectures. They speak not merely to those who were fortunate enough to hear him lecture in Ireland in 1845 and 1846, or to those who read his speeches in the newspapers, or to those groups, poor and illiterate, who were told of his message through word of mouth. Douglass's reach was far greater than this. He possessed a rare ability to speak to later generations, especially to those who struggled for social justice. In this sense, Douglass's words have proved to be timeless and universal.

Notes

1 The first edition of the *Narrative* was published in Boston by the Anti-Slavery Office, at No. 25 Cornhill. It included a ten-page preface written by Garrison.
2 Douglass himself used the word 'transformation' in his letter to Garrison dated 1 January 1846.

3 Frederick Douglass, *Narrative of the Life of Frederick Douglass, an American Slave, Written by Himself* (Boston, MA: Anti-Slavery Office, 1845), p. 32.

4 Ibid., p. 33.

5 Douglass made these claims in his *Narrative* and again during his speech in Conciliation Hall on 29 September. See, 'Repeal Association', *Dublin Evening Mail*, 1 October 1845. Douglass may have confused Sheridan with another Irish politician, Arthur O' Connor, a United Irishman.

6 Christopher L. Webber, *American to the Backbone: The Life of James W. C. Pennington, the Fugitive* (New York: Pegasus Books, 2011).

7 The full title was 'An Act respecting fugitives from justice, and persons escaping from the service of their masters'. It had been passed by George Washington in February 1793. In 1850, a more draconian Fugitive Slave Act was passed.

8 Douglass had learned the skilled trade of calking when working on the wharves of Baltimore.

9 Douglass, *Narrative*, pp. 116, 117.

10 Lewis Tappan (1788–1873) was born in Massachusetts. He and his brother Arthur owned a successful silk company. In 1830, the Tappans met Garrison and gave him financial support, although their business suffered as a consequence. In 1833, he helped found the American Anti-Slavery Society (AASS). Tappan was a strict Calvinist and evangelical, and he was disturbed by Garrison's attacks on Protestant churches. He left the AASS in 1840, disapproving of the election of a woman to a committee.

11 At this stage, the Douglass children were Rosetta (1839–1906), Lewis (1840–1908) and Frederick Jr. (1842–1892). There would be two more children, Charles Remond (1844–1920) and Annie (1849–1860).

12 Nathaniel Rogers, *Miscellaneous Writings of Nathaniel Rogers* (New Hampshire: W. H. Fisk, 1849), pp. 203–204.

13 Leigh Fought, *Women in the World of Frederick Douglass* (Oxford: Oxford University Press, 2017), pp. 76–77.

14 Dorothy Sterling, *She Didn't Know Her Place. Abby Kelley and the Politics of Antislavery* (New York: W.W. Norton and Co., 1992); Abby Kelley Foster in: www.encyclopedia.com/people/social-sciences-and-law/social-reformers/abigail-kelley-foster, accessed 5 July 2017.

15 Julia Sun-Joo Lee, *The American Slave Narrative and the Victorian Novel* (Oxford: Oxford University Press, 2010).

16 'Narrative of the Life of Frederick Douglass. . . ', *New York Tribune*, 10 June 1845.

17 A number of escaped slaves produced narrative accounts of their experiences. For example, Charles Ball, also from Maryland, published *Slavery in the United States: A Narrative of the Life and Adventures of Charles Ball, a Black Man* (John Thompson, *The Life of John Thompson, a Fugitive Slave: Containing His History of 25 Years in Bondage, and His Providential Escape, Written by Himself* (Worcester: John Thompson, 1856). His origins also were in Maryland. In 1831, the British Anti-Slavery Society had published the first account of slavery by a black woman, Mary Prince, *The History of Mary Prince: A West Indian Slave* (London: F. Westley and A. H. Davis; Edinburgh: Waugh and Innes, 1831).

18 Richard Davis Webb (1805–1872) was an Irish Quaker publisher. He had been one of the three founders of the Hibernian Anti-Slavery Association in 1837, which initially was focused on ending the system of apprenticeship that had accompanied the 1833 legislation outlawing slavery in parts of the British Empire. His brothers, James Henry and Thomas, were also abolitionists, as was his wife, Hannah Waring, a member of the Waterford Quakers. All four attended the Anti-Slavery Convention in London in 1840. Richard Webb eventually resigned from the Society of Friends, his individual approach to radical issues being increasingly at odds with the Friends' desire for public consensus.

19 'Breakfast to Mr Frederick Douglass', *Belfast Commercial Chronicle*, 6 January 1846. In his speech, the actual phrase used by Douglass was 'the chattel becomes a man'.

20 James Needham Buffum (1807–1887) had been born in Maine. Originally a Quaker, he abandoned his religion when he became a devoted supporter of the radical abolitionist, William Lloyd Garrison. In later life, he entered politics, serving as mayor of Lynn from 1869 to 1875 and as a Massachusetts legislator in 1873.

21 See Buffum's Obituary, *New York Times*, 13 June 1887.

22 Douglass to Maria Weston Chapman, marked private, 29 March 1846, Kilmarnock, Scotland, in John R. McKivigan (ed.), *The Frederick Douglass Papers: 1842–1852*. Series 3, Correspondence, vol. 1 (New Haven, CT: Yale University Press, 2009), p. 99.

23 More often, the Hutchinsons performed as a quartet, without Jesse.

24 Tom Maxwell, 'A History of American Protest Movement: How the Hutchinson Family Singers achieved Pop Stardom with an Anti-Slavery Anthem', https://longreads.com/2017/03/07/a-history-of-american-protest-music-how-the-hutchinson-family-singers-achieved-pop-stardom-with-an-anti-slavery-anthem/, accessed 14 May 2017.

25 'Get off the track' was written by N.P. Rogers. It was also referred to as 'The Emancipation Song'.

26 *Liberator*, 4 July 1845.

27 *New York Times*, 21 September 1897.

28 Dale Cockrell, *Excelsior: Journals of the Hutchinson Family Singers, 1842–1846* (Stuyvesant, NY: Pendragon Press, c. 1989), p. 315.

29 *Liberator*, 22 August 1845.

30 'Home Sweet Home' was written by the American lyricist John Howard Payne (1791–1852) and English composer Sir Henry Bishop (1786–1855) for an opera that was first produced in London in 1823, called *Clari: or the Maid of Milan*. The song became enormously popular, especially during the American Civil War, when it was sung by soldiers on both sides of the conflict.

31 *Liberator*, 22 August 1845.

32 *Journals of the Hutchinson Family Singers*, p. 316. Within the Journals, Frederick Douglass is spelled in a variety of ways.

33 Ibid., p. 320.

34 Ibid., p. 321.

35 For example, *Glasgow Argus*, 22 January 1846.

36 Steam ships sailed every evening from George's Pierhead in Liverpool to Kingstown Harbour near Dublin, with departures at either 8.00 pm or 10.00 pm. See, 'For Dublin . . .', *Liverpool Mail*, 16 August 1845.

37 Hannah Waring Webb (1809–1862) was married to Richard Davis Webb. Hannah welcomed many abolitionists into her Dublin home. Together, they had four children, Alfred John Webb (1834–1908), Richard Webb (1835–1882), Deborah Webb (1838–1921) and Anne Webb (1839–1868). Alfred later became a nationalist Member of the British Parliament.

38 *Liberator*, 10 October 1845.

39 Shortly following his marriage to Hannah in 1833, Richard formed a partnership with fellow printer, Robert Chapman, also a Quaker, but stricter in his observances than Richard. His wife was a cousin of Hannah.

40 Richard S. Harrison, *Richard Davis Webb: Dublin Quaker Printer* (Skibbereen: Red Barn Publishing, 1993), p. 2.

41 The Ballitore school was established in 1726 and was open to non-Quaker children, one of its most famous pupils being Edmund Burke. It was known for its enlightened and modern approach to education, its subjects including history and science.

42 The Opium War (1839–1842) was a conflict between Britain and China over the latter's sovereignty regarding the import of the drug opium. Britain wanted this trade to continue, as it created a favourable trade surplus for them. The Treaty of Nanking in

1842 concluded the war, by which, among other impositions, China was forced to cede Hong Kong to Britain. A second Opium War took place from 1856 to 1860.

43 Christine Kinealy, *Daniel O'Connell and the Anti-Slavery Movement: 'The Saddest People the Sun Sees'* (London: Pickering and Chatto, 2011).

44 *Liberator*, 10 October 1845.

45 One of their first actions was to arrange for English abolitionist George Thompson (1804–1878) to speak in Dublin on 11 August 1837. Thompson was a friend of Garrison.

46 Richard Allen (1803–1886), a successful Dublin draper, was active in the abolition, temperance, peace and other radical movements. He was ably supported by his wife, Anne Webb, whom he had married in 1828. In 1830, he opened his own successful business at 52 High Street, where the family also lived. He was a supporter of Garrison and known on both sides of the Atlantic for his devotion to anti-slavery and other reform issues.

47 Anon, 'Sketch of a Foreign Incendiary', *The Liberty Bell* (Boston, MA: Anti-Slavery Fair, 1842), pp. 67–70, p. 70.

48 Following the ending of the apprenticeship system in 1838, the Anti-Slavery Society disbanded. In 1839, the British and Foreign Anti-Slavery Society was founded, which was dedicated to ending slavery internationally rather than just in British possessions.

49 Harrison, *Quaker Printer*, p. 33.

50 Douglass to Garrison, 1 September 1845. For full text see Documents.

51 Olaudah Equiano (c. 1745–1797) was born in Africa but given the name Gustavus Vassa by one of his owners. A successful seafarer, he eventually bought his own freedom. His narrative became a bestseller in Britain and Ireland.

52 Charles Lenox Remond (1810–1873) was born in Massachusetts. His father was a former slave. In 1838, he commenced lecturing for the American Anti-Slavery Society. After 1842, he and Douglass lectured together, and Douglass named his third son after him in 1844. Following Douglass's return to the U.S., the men subsequently disagreed as Douglass moved further away from Garrison's position.

53 Letter from Charles Lenox Remond, London, 30 June 1840, to Charles B. Ray, *Colored American*, reprinted in the *Liberator*, 16 October 1840. Interestingly, Lenox had sent the letter for publication in a newspaper with a black readership.

54 Harrison, *Quaker Printer*, p. 26; the *Liberator*, 24 September 1841.

55 'The Anti Slavery Cause', *Nenagh Guardian*, 10 November 1841.

56 The first signatures on the petition were those of Daniel O'Connell and Father Mathew. The petition proved to be controversial amongst Irish Americans, with some declaring it to be a hoax and urging Irish immigrants not to support abolition. The petition inflamed existing tensions on the slavery question.

57 'The Anti Slavery Cause', *Nenagh Guardian*, 10 November 1841.

58 Rogers, *Miscellaneous*, p. 253.

59 See Harrison, *Quaker Printer*, p. 25.

60 Henry Clarke Wright (1797–1870) was born in Connecticut. In 1823, he married wealthy widow Elizabeth Stickney, who encouraged his interest in reform issues, which included pacifism, abolition and feminism. Irish abolitionists first became acquainted with him through his articles in the *Liberator*. Handsome, charming and passionate, the Webb family, including the children and Hannah's sister, Maria, were enamoured by Wright, although Joseph Poole came to regard him as a 'humbug'. See Harrison, *Quaker Printer*, p. 46.

61 Harrison, *Quaker Printer*, p. 68. William Wells Brown (c. 1814–1884) was born into slavery in Kentucky. He escaped to Ohio in 1834. In 1847, he published the *Narrative of William W. Brown, a Fugitive Slave, Written by Himself* (Boston, MA: The Anti-Slavery office, 1847), which became a bestseller in the U.S. Although he spent three

years lecturing in Europe, including the United Kingdom, he never aroused the same public interest as Douglass. His freedom was 'purchased' in 1854.

62 Madden wrote about his experiences in *A Twelvemonth's Residence in the West Indies, During the Transition from Slavery to Apprenticeship; with Incidental Notice of the State of Society, Prospects, and Natural Resources of Jamaica and Other Islands* (Philadelphia: Carey, Lea and Blanchard, 1835. 2 vols).

63 Richard Madden (1798–1886) was born in Dublin. In 1833, he was appointed a special magistrate in Jamaica, where he was in charge of carrying out the abolition of slavery. He subsequently moved to Havana to look after freed slaves.

64 Howe Peter Browne, 2nd Marquess of Sligo (1788–1845), travelled to Jamaica with his wife and children. As thanks for liberating people on his own estate, he was given silver candlesticks (which the family still possess), and the town of Sligoville was named in his honour.

65 Address of the Hibernian Anti-Slavery Society to the People of Ireland, 18 September 1837.

66 Richard Madden, the Marquess of Sligo and Daniel O' Connell were all praised by black abolitionist Samuel Ringgold Ward, who visited the UK in 1853:

> I do hope that Irish abolitionists will be true to emigrants, exhorting them to save themselves from the abominations of pro-slaveryism, and rebuking those who ruthlessly trample upon the Negro – who found friends in O'Connell and Madden, and who now, for the best of reasons, blesses the names of Richard Webb, Mr. Jennings, the Marquis of Sligo, and the Right Honourable John Wynne.
>
> Ward, *Autobiography of a Fugitive Negro: His Anti-Slavery Labours in the United States, Canada and England* (London: John Snow, 1855), p. 384.

67 The Loyal National Repeal Association was launched in July 1840 with the aim of winning self-government for Ireland (although within the British Empire). Like the Catholic Association, it was dedicated to only using legal and constitutional means. The way in which it raised funds, employed a permanent staff, used publicity and mobilized its supporters made it far more sophisticated than other contemporary political movements.

68 Kinealy, *Saddest People*, pp. 21–22. O'Connell was persuaded to support anti-slavery by Liverpool abolitionist James Cropper.

69 This story was retold by Wendell Phillips and others, Wendell Phillips, *A Lecture Delivered at the Academy of Music*, New York, 12 May 1868, in Wendell Phillips, *Lectures and Speeches* (New York and London: Street and Smith, 1902), pp. 188–89. A different version to the one above appeared in Wendall Philips, Daniel O'Connell, *The Irish Patriot* (Boston, MA: Lee and Sheppard, 1884), p. 24.

70 Its full title was The Society for the Mitigation and Gradual Abolition of Slavery Throughout the British Dominions. It disbanded when the apprenticeship system was abolished in 1838. One of its main tactics had been mass petitioning. Two of its founders, William Wilberforce (1759–1833) and Thomas Clarkson (1760–1846), were veterans of early English anti-slavery and part of the original so-called 'Apostles'.

71 Garrison to George W. Benson, Boston, 22 March 1842, in William Lloyd Garrison, *The Letters of William Lloyd Garrison: No Union with the Slaveholders, 1841–1849* (Cambridge, MA: Harvard University Press, 1973), p. 63.

72 Kinealy, *Saddest People*, pp. 64–71. The ambassador was Andrew Stevenson, and the issue was widely reported in newspapers on both sides of the Atlantic and even discussed in the Congress.

73 Douglass, *Narrative*, Preface to Boston edition.

74 Richard Webb to Maria Weston Chapman, 2 February 1843, Anti-Slavery Collection, Boston Public Library (BPL), MS 1.2, vol. 13, p. 7.

75 'The O'Connellites and the Hibernian Anti-Slavery Society', *Freeman's Journal*, 2 May 1843.

76 In 1846, the slave states were Alabama, Arkansas, Delaware, Florida, Georgia, Kentucky, Louisiana, Maryland, Mississippi, Missouri, North Carolina, South Carolina, Tennessee, Texas and Virginia.

77 Quoted in the *Liberator*, 2 May 1845.

78 See Kinealy, *Saddest People*, pp. 120–123.

79 *Nation*, 13 January 1844. The paper did not provide coverage to Douglass's lectures, but during his time in Dublin printed an article saying they had received a letter from the U.S. defending slavery – they commenting, 'we rejoice to hear', Ibid., 1 November 1845.

80 The dispute between Haughton and Fr Kenyon, and between Haughton and the *Nation*, was carried out in the columns of the paper 'Negro Slavery – Mr Haughton', *Nation*, 20 February 1847.

81 Ibid., 'Answers to Correspondents'.

82 Harrison, *Quaker Printer*, pp. 8–19, 30–31; quoted in McKivigan, *The Frederick Douglass Papers*, pp. 79–80.

83 Letter from Daniel O'Connell, Merrion Square, Dublin, to James Haughton, dated 4 February 1845, in W. J. Fitzpatrick, ed., *Correspondence of Daniel O'Connell* (London: John Murray, 1888).

84 For example, Douglass told Garrison in his letter of 16 September 1845 that all of his lectures were 'crowded to over-flowing'. The *Freeman's Journal* (FJ) reported that the lecture on 9 September was only 'tolerably well filled' (*FJ*, 10 September 1845). In the same letter, Douglass talks of four lectures; in fact, he gave five in the first two weeks. Historians generally have taken his accounts of his travels on face value, for example, John F. Quinn, '"Safe in Old Ireland": Frederick Douglass's Tour, 1845–1846', *The Historian*, vol. 64, no. 3–4 (2002), 535–550, pp. 537–538.

85 *Liberator*, 26 September 1845.

86 Ibid., 10 October 1845.

87 Maria Weston Chapman (1806–1885) of Boston was an ardent abolitionist and devoted follower of Garrison. She was suspicious of Douglass, as her letters to Webb testify.

88 Maria Chapman, Boston, to Richard Webb, Dublin, 26 June 1845, BPL, Anti-Slavery Collection Online, https://archive.org/details/extractsofthree100chap, accessed 9 May 2017.

89 Ibid., 23 January 1846.

90 Ibid., 24 February 1846.

91 Douglass to Maria Weston Chapman, marked private, 29 March 1846, Kilmarnock, Scotland, in McKivigan, *Frederick Douglass Papers*, p. 99.

92 Richard Webb to Maria Chapman, Boston, 16 May 1846, quoted in Tom Chaffin, *Giant's Causeway: Frederick Douglass's Irish Odyssey and the Making of an American Visionary* (Charlottesville: University of Virginia Press, 2014), p. 45.

93 Ibid.

94 Benjamin Soskis, 'Heroic Exile: The Transatlantic Development of Frederick Douglass 1845–1847', www.yale.edu/glc/soskis/fr-3.htm, accessed 10 July 2017.

95 Webb to Garrison, 2 October 1845, reprinted in the *Liberator*, 24 October 1845.

96 *Belfast News-Letter*, 26 December 1845.

97 'Anti-Slavery Meeting', *Cork Examiner*, 20 October 1845.

98 Douglass to Jackson, 29 January 1846, Anti-Slavery Collection (BPL), MS A. 1.2. v.16., p. 13.

99 John Shauffer et al., *Picturing Fredrick Douglass: An Illustrated Biography of the Nineteenth Century's Most Photographed American* (New York: Liveright, 2015), passim.
100 *Freeman's Journal*, 4 November 1846. The Irish Temperance Union had been established in May 1839. R. D. Webb was the treasurer and Richard Allen the secretary. James Henry Webb and Thomas Webb and Haughton were also on the committee. The temperance meetings were held in Hallbride Street on every Thursday evening, and they often talked about slavery. All of these men were also members of the Hibernian Anti-Slavery Society, which held monthly meetings in the Royal Exchange on Dame Street.
101 'To the Editor of the Freeman', *Freeman's Journal*, 3 September 1845.
102 Second letter, Father Mathew had travelled to Booterstown to preach at the opening of a new church, *Cork Examiner*, 12 September 1845.
103 Seán McConville, *Irish Political Prisoners, 1848–1922: Theatres of War* (Hove: Psychology Press, 2003), p. 45.
104 The Royal Exchange – now City Hall – was opened in 1779. An accident in 1815 due to overcrowding, resulting in the death of nine people, led to the introduction of stricter crowd restrictions. Douglass, in a letter to Garrison, claimed that he spoke twice at this venue, but there is no newspaper account of the second meeting.
105 Lewis Perry and Michael Fellman, *Antislavery Reconsidered: New Perspectives on the Abolitionists* (Baton Rouge, LA: Louisiana State University Press, 1979), p. 151.
106 'Slavery', *Freeman's Journal*, 8 September 1845.
107 Ibid.
108 *Waterford Chronicle*, 6 September 1845. The venue was incorrect.
109 *Freeman's Journal*, 10 September 1845.
110 Ibid., 11 September 1845.
111 In the letter, he spoke of two appearances at the Royal Exchange – he did not mention his appearance in the Mechanics Institute, which was referred to in the *Waterford Chronicle*, but the paper was possibly confusing the venue.
112 Douglass to Garrison, 16 September 1845. Letter Two – see Vol. 2.
113 The letter was written on 17 September 1845. It was published by Garrison's *Liberator* on 24 October 1845.
114 *Freeman's Journal*, 16 September 1845.
115 Ibid., 18 September 1845.
116 The chapel opened in 1823, although its origins dated back to 1747. In 1845 and 1846, its minister was the Rev. Adam Clarke, a Primitive Wesleyan. Clarke does not seem to have attended in any prominent role Douglass's meetings. See John Wesley Etheridge, *The Life of the Rev. Adam Clarke* (Dublin: John Mason, 1858).
117 This claim was made at a lecture in the Music Hall in Dublin on 23 September, 'Anti-Slavery Society', *Freeman's Journal*, 24 September 1845.
118 See Kinealy, *Saddest People*, pp. 93–99.
119 The letter was written on 17 September 1845. It was published by Garrison's *Liberator* on 24 October 1845.
120 *Freeman's Journal*, 3 October 1845.
121 Harrison, *Quaker Printer*, pp. 69–70.
122 William Shortt, himself a Wesleyan, wrote a number of letters to the press and to Douglass on this matter, which Douglass joked were anything but short. See 'American Slavery', *Liberator*, 30 January 1846.
123 Following this meeting, Mayor Arabin invited Douglass to dine at his official residence, the Mansion House.
124 *Liberator*, 18 December 1845.

125 'The Repeal Movement', *Dublin Evening Post*, 29 September 1845.

126 The Catholic Emancipation Act of 1829 enabled Catholics throughout the United Kingdom to stand for election in the British Parliament in London.

127 Although the moderate William Smith O'Brien was the nominal leader of the Young Ireland group, it also included the fiery John Mitchel and the young, charismatic, Thomas Francis Meagher. In 1848 and 1849 the three men were sentenced to treason and transported. Eventually, Mitchel and Meagher would support opposite sides in the Civil War. See Kinealy, *Repeal and Revolution, 1848 in Ireland* (Manchester: Manchester University Press, 2009).

128 Conciliation Hall, which was located on Burgh Quay in Dublin, had opened in October 1843 as a meeting place for the Loyal National Repeal Association. As far as possible, it had been built from Irish materials. The weekly Repeal meetings were held on Mondays.

129 'The Repeal Association', *Statesman and Dublin Christian Record*, 30 September 1845.

130 Douglass to Garrison, Letter Three, 29 September 1845. See Vol. 2.

131 'The Repeal Association', *London Standard*, 1 October 1845.

132 Ibid.

133 For example, Quinn, 'Safe in Old Ireland', p. 541.

134 Frederick Douglass, *The Life and Times of Frederick Douglass: From 1817–1882, Written by Himself* (London: Christian Age Office, 1882), pp. 205–206; 'Frederick Douglass', Obituary, *London Daily News*, 22 February 1895.

135 See for example, *Dublin Weekly Register*, 29 September 1845.

136 For example, 'The Repeal Association', *Newry Telegraph*, 2 October 1845; *Kilkenny Journal, and Leinster Commercial and Literary Advertiser*, 4 October 1845; 'Loyal National Repeal Association', *Limerick Reporter*, 3 October 1845.

137 'Conciliation Hall', *Freeman's Journal*, 7 October 1845. Although the *Nation* provided full coverage of the Repeal meeting, no mention was made of Douglass's contribution, *Nation*, 4 October 1845.

138 *Liverpool Mercury*, 12 August 1845. John Wallace Hutchinson, *Story of the Hutchinsons* (tribe of Jesse) (Boston, MA: Lee and Shepard, 1896), p. 156.

139 Ibid.

140 Cockrell, *Journals of the Hutchinson Family*, p. 325.

141 Hutchinson, *Story of the Hutchinsons*, p. 156.

142 'Anti-Slavery Society', *Freeman's Journal*, 24 September 1845.

143 Richard Webb, Dublin, to Garrison, 2 October 1845, *Liberator*, 24 October 1845.

144 'The Inimitable Henry Russell: The Celebrated Hutchinson Family', *Dublin Evening Packet and Correspondent*, 11 October 1845.

145 Quoted in Scott Gac, *Singing for Freedom: The Hutchinson Family Singers and the Nineteenth-Century Culture of Reform* (New Haven, CT: Yale University Press, 2008), p. 208.

146 *Preston Chronicle*, 22 November 1845.

147 'Anti Slavery Minstrels from America', *Anti-Slavery Reporter*, 24 December 1845, p. 236.

148 'Departure of the Hutchinson Family for America', *Manchester Times*, 11 July 1846.

149 Ibid.

150 Maria Waring, sister-in-law to Richard Webb, belonged to a network of Irish women who were both feminists and abolitionists. She escorted Douglass to Wexford and was captivated by him, regarding him as the most impressive abolitionist she had ever met. She and her sister are largely ignored in Fought's book, *Women in the World of Frederick Douglass*.

151 The father of the Waring sisters was a draper, initially in Wexford, but they moved to Waterford when the sisters were young. Richard Webb's mother, Deborah Sparrow, was also from Wexford.

152 *Wexford Independent*, 15 October 1845.

153 'American Slavery', *Kilkenny Journal*, reprinted in *Waterford Chronicle*, 25 October 1845.

154 'Boston Pilot', *Waterford Chronicle*, 4 July 1846.

155 Nini Rodgers, *Ireland, Slavery and Anti-Slavery: 1612-1865* (New York: Palgrave Macmillan, 2007), pp. 127–128.

156 Anthony Edwards, *An Essay on the Slave Trade: Enumerating Its Horrors, and Shewing the Vice of Encouraging It by the Consumption of West-India Productions: And also Shewing the Certainty of Its Abolition by the Disuse of Them* (Cork: Printed by Anthony Edwards, bookseller, Castle-Street, 1792).

157 The Jennings' premises were at 11 and 12 Brown Street. See, *The County and City of Cork Post Office General Directory for 1842–1843* (Cork: Jackson, 1843), p. 45.

158 Jennings also patented an improved stopper for mineral water bottles, see *Reporatory of Patent Inventions, July to December 1854*, vol. xxiv (London: Macintosh, 1855), p. 284.

159 Cork Ladies' Anti-Slavery Society in *The County and City of Cork Almanac, Calculated & Adapted by C. Thompson* (Cork: Jackson, 1843), p. 79.

160 Douglass to Garrison, Letter Four, 28 October 1845. See Vol. 2.

161 'Father Mathew', *North Star*, 17 August 1849.

162 The attack was penned by Gerrit Smith in *Frederick Douglass Paper*, 25 May 1852 and 3 June 1852. In his articles, Smith praised O'Connell's principled stand.

163 Harvey's Dock in Youghal is named after this Quaker family.

164 Varian to Garrison, 2 December 1845, *British and Foreign Anti-Slavery Reporter*, 10 December 1845.

165 Ralph Varian to William Garrison, 10 November 1845, *Liberator*, 12 December 1845.

166 This claim was made at a lecture in the Music Hall in Dublin on 23 September, 'Anti-Slavery Society', *Freeman's Journal*, 24 September 1845.

167 Kinealy, *Saddest People*, pp. 100–101.

168 *Southern Reporter*, 18 October 1845.

169 *Cork Examiner*, 20 October 1845.

170 *Liberator*, 12 December 1845.

171 'The Anti-Slavery Standard', *National Anti-Slavery Standard*, 5 March 1846.

172 'A Fugitive Slave in Ireland', *Leeds Times*, 15 November 1845; see also, *Hampshire Advertiser*, 8 November 1845.

173 *National Anti-Slavery Standard*, 12 February 1846.

174 *The County and City of Cork Almanac for 1843* (Cork: Jackson, 1843) lists a Daniel Casey residing at the academy at 2 Lavitt's Quay in Cork City, p. 11.

175 More usually, *Cead Mille Failte*, meaning 'One hundred thousand welcomes'.

176 'St Patrick's Temperance Hall', *Cork Examiner*, 28 October 1845.

177 *Liberator*, 23 January 1846.

178 Douglass to Dowden, 11 November 1845, reproduced in McKivigan, *The Frederick Douglass Papers*, p. 66. The original is in the Cork City and County Archives (Dowden Papers, Ref: U140/L/029).

179 'To Frederick Douglass, the Fugitive Celebrated Slave', in Daniel Casey (ed.), *Cork Lyrics or Scraps from the Beautiful City* (Cork: Nash's Printing, 1857), p. 76.

180 The original manuscript copy is in the Library of Congress, www.loc.gov/item/mfd.36011/, accessed 4 April 2017.

181 'American Slavery', *Limerick Reporter*, 11 November 1845.

182 Douglass to Francis Jackson, Holist Street, Boston, 29 January 1846, Anti-Slavery Collection, (BPL) MS A. 1.2. v.16., p. 13.

183 The Corn Laws kept the price of corn artificially high. Many abolitionists supported their removal, seeing this as a way to bring cheap food (particularly bread) to the poorer classes.

184 *Hutchinson Story*, p. 164.

185 Liam Hogan, 'Frederick Douglass's Journey from Slavery to Limerick' (1845), www.academia.edu/8116691/Frederick_Douglass_s_Journey_from_Slavery_to_ Limerick_1845_, accessed 3 March 2017.

186 'American Slavery', *Limerick Reporter*, 11 November 1845.

187 Ibid., 25 November 1845.

188 'The "inimitable Bateman" was touring Ireland', *Freeman's Journal*, 12 September 1845.

189 *Clare Journal and Ennis Advertiser*, 30 October 1845.

190 'The Theatre', *Galway Mercury, and Connaught Weekly Advertiser*, 18 October 1845.

191 'Ballinasloe Fair', *Galway Vindicator, and Connaught Advertiser*, 11 October 1845.

192 *Limerick Reporter*, 11 November 1845.

193 This point is made by Kathleen Gough, *Haptic Allegories: Kinship and Performance in the Black and Green Atlantic* (London: Routledge, 2013), p. 166.

194 *Limerick Reporter*, 11 November 1845.

195 Douglas C. Riach, 'Blacks and Blackface on the Irish Stage, 1830–60', *Journal of American Studies*, vol. 7, no. 3 (December 1973), 231–241, p. 231.

196 Ibid., p. 241.

197 Douglass speaking at City Court House, Cork, reported in 'Interesting Narrative of Fugitive Slave', *Southern Reporter and Cork Commercial Courier*, 16 October 1845.

198 Ibid., Speech by the Mayor of Cork.

199 *Limerick Reporter*, 11 November 1845.

200 *Banner of Ulster* (Belfast), 5 December 1845.

201 Douglass to Webb, 16 November 1845, Anti-Slavery Collection (BPL), MS A. 1.2. v.15, p. 2.

202 Harrison, *Quaker Printer*, pp. 32–33.

203 Rev. Thomas Chalmers (1780–1847) was born in Fife in Scotland and ordained into the Presbyterian Church in 1803. In 1832, he was appointed Moderator of the Church of Scotland. He was interested in both Church reform and poor law reform.

204 George Shepperson, 'Thomas Chalmers, The Free Church of Scotland, and the South', *The Journal of Southern History*, vol. 17, no. 4 (November 1951), 517–537, p. 520.

205 'The American Prayer Meeting', *Northern Warder and General Advertiser for the Counties of Fife, Perth and Forfar*, 27 November 1845.

206 Douglass to Webb, 10 November 1845, in McKivigan, *Frederick Douglass Papers*, pp. 63–64.

207 Inspired by the revolutions in America and France, the Society of United Irishmen was formed in late 1791 and appealed to Irish people to put aside their religious differences and work together for an Irish republic. The leader of the movement was a Protestant solicitor, Theobald Wolfe Tone. A rising in 1798 was unsuccessful and resulted in the execution or exile of many of the movement's leaders, including Henry Joy McCracken, whose sister Mary Ann became a prominent abolitionist in Belfast.

208 Olaudah Equiano (c. 1745–1797), known in his lifetime as Gustavus Vassa, was born in Africa (modern-day Nigeria) and captured and sold into slavery when a young boy. He purchased his own freedom with money earned as a skilled sailor and navigator. Also see, Nini Rodgers, 'Equiano in Belfast: A Study of the Anti-Slavery Ethos in a Northern Town', *Slavery & Abolition: A Journal of Slave and Post-Slave Studies*, vol. 18, no. 2 (1997), pp. 73–89.

209 Olaudah Equiano, *The Interesting Narrative of the Life of Olaudah Equiano, or Gustavus Vassa, the African, Written by Himself* (Dublin: 1791, printed for, and sold by, the author. Sold also at the Dublin Chronicle Office, by W. Sleater, No. 28, Dame-Street, and the other booksellers in Dublin).

210 *Belfast News-Letter*, 20 December 1791, contains a detailed advertisement for the publication. It stated that it was available from Samuel Neilson, the editor of the *United Irish Northern Star*, an abolitionist and one of Equiano's hosts during his time in Belfast.

211 'Anti-Slavery Meeting', *Northern Whig*, 10 December 1832.

212 'Belfast Anti-Slavery Meeting', *Belfast News-Letter*, 17 September 1830.

213 William Dool Killen, D.D., *Memoir of J. Edgar, etc.* (Belfast: C. Aitchison, 1867), pp. 17–18.

214 Robert Workman, Chairman and James Carlile, Secretary to Belfast Anti-Slavery Society to Lord Howick, Secretary of War, 23 November 1837, in 'British Colonial Slavery', *Northern Whig*, 2 December 1837.

215 'Abolition of Slavery', *Dublin Morning Register*, 23 June 1838.

216 Belfast Anti-Slavery Society, *To the Christian Churches of the United States: The Address of the Belfast Anti-Slavery Society* (Belfast: H. McKendrick, 1841), pp. 1, 12.

217 Daniel Ritchie, '"The Stone in the Sling": Frederick Douglass and Belfast Abolitionism', *American Nineteenth Century History* (2017), 245–272, p. 3, https://doi.org/10.1080/14664658.2017.1371924, accessed 15 October 2017.

218 In 1810, only around 25,000 people lived in Belfast; by 1841, this number had increased to 70,000.

219 'Mr Frederick Douglass', *Belfast Vindicator*, 29 November 1845.

220 Lieutenant Francis Anderson Calder (1787–1855) had served in the Royal Navy. In addition to abolition, he campaigned on behalf of animal rights, between 1843 and 1855 paying for ten public water-troughs in Belfast for the use of cattle. A memorial fountain was erected to him in Queen's Square in Belfast in 1859.

221 Douglass to Webb, 5 December 1845, Anti-Slavery Collection (BPL), MS A. 1.2. v.15, p. 85.

222 Ibid., Douglass to Webb, Belfast, Victoria Hotel, 6 December 1845, MS A. 1.2. v.15, p. 86.

223 Ibid., Douglass to Webb, Belfast, 5 December 1845, MS A. 1.2. v.15, p. 85.

224 Ibid., Douglass informed Webb about this victory 'in the face of letters prejudicial to me both from Cork and Dublin', Douglass to Webb, 6 December 1845, MS A. 1.2. v.15, p. 86.

225 'Mr Frederick Douglass's Address', *Banner of Ulster*, 9 December 1845.

226 'Belfast Anti-Slavery Meeting', *Vindicator*, 10 December 1845.

227 'Mr Frederick Douglass's Address', *Banner of Ulster*, 9 December 1845.

228 'Douglass's Fourth Address', *Banner of Ulster*, 16 December 1845.

229 For example, a positive reference to O'Connell only appeared in 'Anti-Slavery Meeting', *Vindicator*, 31 December 1845.

230 Frederick Douglass to Richard Davis Webb, December 6, 1845, Anti-Slavery Collection (BPL), MS A. 1.2. v.15, p. 86.

231 Ibid., Douglass to Webb, Belfast, 7 December 1845, MS A. 1.2. v.15, p. 87.

232 Ibid.

233 Frederick Douglass, *The Story of My First Watch* (New York: New York Standard Watch Company, 1893).

234 Birmingham Museums commemorated Equiano's visit in 2007, www.equiano.net/project.html, accessed 4 May 2017.

235 Douglass to Webb, 6 December 1845, American Anti-Slavery Collection (BPL), MS A. 1.2 v.15, p. 86. Douglass only mentions the surname, Cadbury. Richard Tapper

Cadbury (1768–1860) had attended the 1840 World Anti-Slavery Convention. He financed his son's tea, coffee and chocolate business. His son, John Cadbury (1801–1889), also supported temperance and abolition.

236 *Belfast Commercial Chronicle*, 7 January 1846.

237 Douglass to Webb, 20 December 1845, Anti-Slavery Collection (BPL), MS A. 1.2 v.15, p. 89.

238 Boultbee was a veteran of the Anti-Slavery movement. He attended the 1840 World convention in London and was captured in the painting by Benjamin Robert Haydon. During the meeting, he sympathized with the excluded women delegates, www.wwhp.org/Resources/Slavery/mottdiary1840.html, accessed 10 October 2017. Boultbee was involved in other radical movements, including being a member of the Birmingham Political Union, a precursor of Chartism.

239 Douglass to Webb, 20 December 1845, Anti-Slavery Collection (BPL), MS A. 1.2 v.15, p. 89.

240 Ibid.

241 'Birmingham Temperance Society', *Aris's Birmingham Gazette*, 22 December 1845. Interestingly, at the conclusion of the meeting the matter of the potato failure in Ireland was raised, and it was suggested that distillation should be suspended, as had been done in England in 1796 and 1797 and in Ireland in 1809 'with the most complete success'.

242 Douglass to Webb, 20 December 1845, Anti-Slavery Collection (BPL), MS A. 1.2 v.15, p. 89.

243 *Belfast News-Letter*, 26 December 1845.

244 Douglass, Belfast, to Webb, 5 December 1845, Anti-Slavery Collection (BPL), MS A. 1.2. v.15, p. 85.

245 Ibid.; Douglass, Belfast, to Webb, 6 December 1845, MS A. 1.2. v.15, p. 86.

246 *Banner of Ulster*, 2 January 1845; *Belfast News-Letter*, 6 January 1845.

247 'American Slavery', *Belfast Commercial Chronicle*, 27 December 1845.

248 Douglass to Webb, 7 December 1845, Anti-Slavery Collection (BPL), MS A. 1.2. v.15, p. 87.

249 Letter to Editor of the *Banner of Ulster*, 19 December 1845.

250 For more on George Troup (1811–1879), see George Elmslie Troup, *Life of George Troup, Journalist* (Edinburgh: Macniven and Wallace, 1881), pp. 8–12.

251 'American Slavery', *Belfast Commercial Chronicle*, 27 December 1845.

252 'Anti Slavery Meeting – Mr Douglass's Address', *Banner of Ulster*, 30 December 1845.

253 'The Anti Slavery Cause and the General Assembly', *Northern Whig*, 8 January 1846.

254 Frederick Douglass, *My Bondage and My Freedom* (New York: Miller, Orton & Mulligan, 1855), pp. 381–382.

255 'Breakfast to Mr Frederick Douglass', 7 January 1846.

256 *Northern Whig*, 8 January 1846.

257 'Lectures on the Evils of Intemperance and the Benefits of Total Abstinence from All intoxicating drinks, Belfast. Lecture by Frederick Douglass, the Fugitive Slave', *Belfast Commercial Chronicle*, 12 January 1846.

258 During a soirée in his honour in Cork, he admitted, 'He confessed that he had not contemplated such respect at the hands the Irish people as he received since he landed in this country', in 'Entertainment to Frederick Douglass at St. Patrick's Temperance Hall', *Southern Reporter and Cork Commercial Courier*, 30 October 1845.

259 Douglass to Garrison, Letter Five, 1 January 1846. See Vol. 2.

260 Webb to Garrison, 2 October 1845, *Liberator,* 24 October 1845.

261 *Northern Whig*, 18 June 1846.

262 Douglass to Jackson, 29 January 1846, Anti-Slavery Collection (BPL), MS A. 1.2. v.16., p. 13.

263 Edmund Quincy (1808–1877) was son of Josiah Quincy, President of Harvard University. His conversion to abolition came about as a result of the murder of Elijah Parish Lovejoy in 1837. Lovejoy (b. 1802), an American Presbyterian minister and abolitionist, had been murdered by a pro-slavery mob. Quincy was an inventor and an author who contributed to the *Liberty Bell* and the *Liberator* and, after 1844, was editor of the *National Anti-Slavery Standard*.

264 Douglass, Glasgow, to Quincy, 28 April 1846, quoted in McKivigan, *Frederick Douglass Papers*, p. 119.

265 'Anti-Slavery Soiree', *Dundee Courier*, 16 June 1846.

266 Harriet Bailey (1818–1900), whose slave name had been Ruth Cox, had also grown up in Talbot County in Maryland. She escaped in 1842. Douglas mistakenly believed that she was his younger sister. Harriet lived in the Douglass household until her marriage in 1847.

267 In the letter, Douglass uses the *n* – word, which has been reprinted.

268 Douglass to Harriet Bailey, 16 May 1846, FD Collection, Library of Congress, quoted in McKivigan, vol. 1, pp. 124–135.

269 Ibid.

270 *Belfast Commercial Chronicle*, 6 January 1846.

271 'Frederick Douglass', *Belfast News-Letter*, 16 June 1846.

272 'American Slavery', *Belfast News-Letter*, Friday, 19 June 1846.

273 'Return of the Fugitive Slave to Belfast', *Northern Whig*, 18 June 1846.

274 *Northern Whig*, 16 June 1846.

275 Kinealy, *Saddest People*, pp. 92–94.

276 Richard Webb to *National Anti-Slavery Standard*, 30 July 1846.

277 Charles Turner Torrey (1813–1846) was an American Congregationalist minister and outspoken abolitionist. He organized one branch of the Underground Railway and personally freed hundreds of slaves. He used his arrest to challenge the constitutionality of slave-holding but was unsuccessful. He died of tuberculosis while in prison.

278 'Annual Meeting of Birmingham Anti-Slavery Society', *Birmingham Journal*, 4 July 1846.

279 For example, Douglass spoke at the annual Anti-Slavery Society meeting in Birmingham on Monday, 29 June, when he was the star attraction and the focus was on these topics, *London Daily News*, 1 July 1846.

280 Ibid., 'British and Foreign Anti-Slavery Society', 19 May 1846.

281 'Reception of Douglass in London', *Liberator*, 26 June 1846.

282 Elizabeth Pease (1807–1897) was involved in many reform issues, including abolition, women's rights, anti-vivisection, world peace and temperance. She attended the 1840 World Slavery Convention, though she had to sit with the other women in the galleries. She was, however, represented in Haydon's famous portrait.

283 Douglass to Pease, Belfast, 6 July 1846, in McKivigan, *Frederick Douglass Papers*, pp. 141–142.

284 Douglass to Garrison, Letter Two, 16 September 1845. See Vol. 2.

285 Frederick Douglass, *Narrative of the Life of Frederick Douglass, an American Slave, Written by Himself* (Dublin: Webb and Chapman, 1845).

286 In old money, two shillings sixpence.

287 *Cork Examiner*, 17 October 1845. As Douglass's popularity spread, and religious venues were no longer made available, entrance fees were charged at a number of events.

288 Richard Webb, Dublin, to Garrison, 2 October 1845, reprinted in the *Liberator*, 4 October 1845.

289 Richard Webb, Dublin, to Garrison, 30 November 1845, reprinted in the *Liberator*, 26 December 1845.

290 The precise date of publication of the variant edition is unclear, but Douglass had expected the variant edition would be available on 16 February 1846. See, Douglass, Dundee, to Francis Jackson, 29 January 1846, Anti-Slavery Collection (BPL), MS A. 1.2. v.16., p. 13.

291 Fionnghuala Sweeney refers to the extended edition that appeared in March 1846 as the 'variant edition'. She points out that despite the date of its appearance, it gave 1845 as its publication date. See Fionnghuala Sweeney, ' "The Republic of Letters": Frederick Douglass, Ireland, and the Irish *Narratives*', *Éire-Ireland*, vol. 36, no. 1 & 2, *Earrach/Samhradh* (Spring/Summer 2001), pp. 47–65.

292 Ibid. Sweeney located a rare surviving copy of the variant edition in Goldsmith's Special Collection of Economic Literature, Senate House, University of London. See Sweeney, 'Republic of Letters', p. 48.

293 Douglass, Kilmarnock, to Maria Weston Chapman, 29 March 1846, marked 'Private', Massachusetts Collection Online, http://ark.digitalcommonwealth.org/ark:/50959/7s75fx18h, accessed 8 June 2017.

294 Douglass, Scotland, to Webb, undated but probably mid-January.

295 Patricia J. Ferreira, 'Frederick Douglass and the 1846 Dublin Edition of His Narrative', *New Hibernia Review*, Volume 5, Number 1, Earrach/Spring 2001, 53-67, p. 62.

296 Frederick Douglass, *Narrative of the Life of Frederick Douglass, an American Slave, Written by Himself*, Second Dublin edition. [With a portrait.] (Dublin: Webb & Chapman, 1846). p. vi.

297 Douglass, *Narrative*, Second Dublin edition.

298 Ibid., Preface.

299 Fionnghuala Sweeney, *Frederick Douglass and the Atlantic World* (Oxford: Oxford University Press, 2007), p. 16.

300 Absalom Christopher Columbus Americus Vespucious Thompson (1821–1877?) had resided in Talbot County in Maryland, close to where Douglass had lived when a slave. He could, therefore, claim to have known Douglass and the other people mentioned in the *Narrative*. His rejection of Douglass's interpretation of events first appeared in the *Delaware Republican*. Absalom had originally been named Anthony but changed his name in law in 1838 (*Laws of Maryland Passed by the General Assembly*, Annapolis, 1838, ch. 360). His father, also Absalom Thompson, was a famous surgeon.

301 Preface to the second Dublin edition, p. vi, and Appendix, he again thanks Thompson p. cxxvii.

302 Ibid., p. vi.

303 See, John Stauffer, Zoe Trodd, Celeste-Marie Bernier, Henry Louis Gates Jr., Kenneth B. Morris Jr., *Picturing Frederick Douglass: An Illustrated Biography Of The 19th Century's Most Photographed American* (New York: Liveright, 2015).

304 Douglass to R. D. Webb, 22 December 1845, Anti-Slavery Collection (BPL), MS A. 1.2. v.15, p. 90.

305 Ibid., Frederick Douglass, Glasgow, to R. D. Webb, 16 April 1846, MS A. 1.2. v.16, p. 16; Frederick Douglass to R. D. Webb, 10 February 1846, Dundee; MS A. 1.2. v.16, p. 32. (see also Documents).

The engraving that appeared in the third Dublin edition (May 1846) was done by Joseph Swan (1796–1872), a Manchester-born engraver who worked out of Glasgow. At the bottom of the image it says 'Swan. Sc', *sc* (or, sculpsit, sculpebat, sculp) meaning it was engraved. The engraving for the first Dublin edition (according to photo book) was done by Henry Adlard. Adlard (1799–1893) was an English engraver who worked in London.

306 Sun-Joo Lee, *The American Slave Narrative and the Victorian Novel*, pp. 4–7.

307 Speech by Rev Isaac Nelson, Primitive Wesleyan Chapel, Donegall-Place, Belfast, 'Anti-Slavery Meeting', *Northern Whig*, 9 July 1846.

308 MS A. 1.2. v.16, p. 32 Frederick Douglass, Glasgow, to R. D. Webb 16 April 1846 (see Documents).

309 Patricia J. Ferreira, 'Frederick Douglass and the 1846 Dublin Edition of His Narrative', *New Hibernia Review*, Volume 5, Number 1, Earrach/Spring 2001, 53–67, p. 63.
310 Appendix to second Dublin edition of *Narrative* (1846), p. 132.
311 R. D. Webb to Maria Weston Chapman, February 26, 1846 (BPL, Weston Papers, MS A. 9.2. v.22, p. 26).
312 Ibid., Douglass to Webb, 26 April 1846, MS A. 1.2. v.16, p. 38.
313 Douglass, Glasgow, to Garrison, 16 April 1846, reprinted in McKivigan, *Letters*, p. 108.
314 'Reception of Douglass in London', *Liberator*, 26 June 1846.
315 Ibid.
316 'Mr Garrison's Mission to the British Islands', *Liberator*, 24 July 1846.
317 *Wilmington Journal*, 6 February 1846; *The Green-Mountain Freeman*, 9 April 1846, also noted a lecture by the 'Self-Emancipated Slave' in Belfast.
318 'Great Meeting of the Council of the League', *Aberdeen Herald and General*', 11 July 1846.
319 Douglass to Elizabeth Pease, Belfast, 6 July 1846, McKivigan, *Letters*, p. 142.
320 *Belfast Vindicator*, 16 June 1846.
321 *Tyrone Constitution*, 3 July 1846.
322 'FD was spotted sitting in a gallery seat', *Banner of Ulster,* 10 July 1846.
323 *Northern Whig*, 9 July 1846.
324 Ibid., 18 July 1846.
325 'Temperance', *Preston Chronicle*, 25 July 1846.
326 Ibid.
327 'Temperance Meeting', *Belfast Commercial Chronicle*, 22 July 1846.
328 'Anti-Slavery Meeting', *Northern Whig*, 9 July 1846.
329 'Anti-Slavery Meeting in Bangor', *Northern Whig*, 18 July 1846.
330 'The Anti-Slavery Standard', *National Anti-Slavery Standard*, 10 September 1846.
331 'Mr Frederick Douglass and Rev. Dr. Smyth', *Northern Whig*, 8 August 1846.
332 Webb believed that Smyth was behind these placards, Richard Davis Webb to Maria Weston Chapman, 16 July 1846 (BPL), Weston Papers, MS A. 9.2. v.22., p. 75.
333 William Lloyd Garrison, Walter M. Merrill, Louis Ruchames, *The Letters of William Lloyd Garrison: No Union with the Slaveholders, 1841-1849* (Cambridge, Mass.: Harvard University Press, 1973), p. 326.
334 *Liberator*, 24 July 1846.
335 Ibid.
336 *Letters of Garrison*, p. 359.
337 'Mr. Garrison in England', *National Anti-Slavery Standard*, 10 September 1846.
338 Thomas Beggs, 'The Proceedings of World Temperance Convention' (London; C. Gilpin, 1846), p. 281.
339 Samuel Hanson Cox (1793–1880) was an American Presbyterian minister. In the 1820s, he was mobbed for his anti-slavery views. In a speech in London in 1833, he put the blame for the origin of American slavery on the British government, which was much quoted. The Tappan brothers were members of his congregation, although African Americans were not welcome. In summer of 1846, Cox was one of the founders of the Evangelical Alliance, but fell out with the British members over what he regarded as insults to America over the slavery question.
340 *Appendix to Report of Executive Committee of the American Temperance Union* (New York: American Temperance Union, 1846), p. 39.
341 The Appendix lists Frederic [sic] Douglass as delegate from Newcastle Upon Tyne, a city in the north of England, p. 132.
342 Ibid., Proceedings Day One, p. 21.
343 Ibid., Proceedings Day Three, p. 37.

344 Douglass, *My Life and Bondage*, p. 387.
345 Christopher L. Webber, *American to the Backbone: The Life of James W. C. Pennington, the Fugitive Slave Who Became One of the first Black Abolitionists* (New York: Open Road Media, 2011), Epilogue.
346 Temperance Convention, Proceedings Day Four, p. 50.
347 'Temperance Convention: Meeting at Convent Garden Theatre', *Christian Register*, Boston, 12 September 1846.
348 Douglass, *My Life and Bondage*, p. 387.
349 *Correspondence The Rev. Samuel H. Cox, D. D., of Brooklyn, and Frederick Douglass, A Fugitive Slave* (New York: Office of the American Anti-Slavery Society, NASSAU STREET, 1846), p. 142.
350 Temperance Convention, Proceedings Day Five, p. 47.
351 The *Liberator* said that Douglass's image appeared in the *Pictorial*. In fact, it appeared in the *Illustrated London News* of 15 August 1846.
352 Richard Webb sent a full account of the meeting to the National Anti-Slavery Society – the paper describing him as their 'Dublin Correspondent', *National Anti-Slavery Standard*, 10 September 1846.
353 Ibid.
354 Garrison, *Letters*, p. 418.
355 Garrison to Richard D. Webb, Edinburgh, 25 September 1846, Garrison, *Letters*, p. 428.
356 Letter from William Lloyd Garrison, Liverpool, [England], to Elizabeth Pease Nichol, 12 October 1846, www.digitalcommonwealth.org/search/commonwealth:cv43qt23t?view=commonwealth%3Acv43qt25c, accessed 4 July 2016.
357 'American Slavery', *Dumfries and Galloway Standard*, 28 October 1846.
358 'American Anti-Slavery Agitators', *Belfast News-Letter*, 2 October 1846, Tuesday, 20 October 1846.
359 Ibid.
360 'Anti-slavery meeting', *Belfast News-Letter*, 6 October 1846.
361 About 900 Protestant churchmen, mostly from Britain and America, convened on London in the summer of 1846 for the purpose of forming an international Protestant union. In November the British churchmen formed their own alliance and excluded slave-holders from it. See 'The Evangelical Alliance and the Antislavery Crusade J. F. Maclear', *Huntington Library Quarterly*, vol. 42, no. 2 (Spring 1979), pp. 141–164.
362 'Anti-slavery meeting', *Belfast News-Letter*, 6 October 1846.
363 'American Slavery', *Belfast News-Letter*, 19 June 1846. However, in *My Life and Bondage* Douglass recanted and wrote of the American minister, 'some of them went there merely to weave a world-wide garment with which to clothe evangelical slaveholders'.
364 For example, the meeting of 3 October 1846 was hurriedly ended by the chairman, see *Belfast News-Letter*, 6 October 1846.
365 'Anti-Slavery Meeting', *Belfast Commercial Chronicle*, 5 October 1846; 'Anti-Slavery Meeting – William Lloyd Garrison', *Belfast News-Letter*, Tuesday, 6 October 1846.
366 This negative account appeared in the *Belfast News-Letter* of 6 October 1846.
367 *Belfast Commercial Chronicle*, 5 October 1846.
368 Ibid.
369 I. Steen, Belfast, to the editor of the *Belfast News-Letter*, 6 October 1846.
370 Sara to editor of *Belfast News-Letter*, Tuesday, 6 October 1846.
371 Garrison to Daniel O'Connell, 8 December 1843, *Letters of William Lloyd Garrison*, p. 230.

372 Ibid., p. 231.
373 Wendell Phillips Garrison, Francis Jackson Garrison, *William Lloyd Garrison, 1805–1879: The story of his life told by his children* (New-York, The Century Co., 1885-1889), p. 176. In 1846, three photographic studios were listed in Dublin: Topham and Co. Photographic Gallery, 27 Park Row; the Queens Photographic Rooms, 31 Great Brunswick Street; Debrewil Alexander Doussin, 57 Upper Dorset Street. (Slater Directory for 1846).
374 *Freeman's Journal*, 7 October 1846.
375 *Liberator*, 30 October 1846.
376 *Freeman's Journal*, 24 October 1846.
377 'Anti-Slavery Meeting', *Freeman's Journal*, 9 October 1846.
378 *Freeman's Journal*, 4 November 1846; Friday, 6 November 1846.
379 *Freeman's Journal*, 26 October 1846.
380 Ibid., 30 October 1846.
381 *Belfast News-Letter*, 9 October 1846.
382 Independent Meeting House Donegall St; 'Anti-Slavery Meeting', *Belfast Commercial Chronicle*, 10 October 1846.
383 'The Rev. Daniel M'Afee on the Late Anti-Slavery meetings in Belfast', *Belfast Protestant Journal*, 10 October 1846. M'Afee was a Methodist minister.
384 Iain Whyte, *Send Back the Money!: The Free Church of Scotland and American Slavery* (Cambridge: James Clarke & Co., 2012), p. 127.
385 The poem is available at www.brycchancarey.com/slavery/mbc1.htm, accessed 4 May 2016.
386 Kinealy, *Saddest People*, pp. 38–42.
387 Ibid; Fenton, p. 63.
388 'Cork Ladies Anti-Slavery Society', *Southern Reporter and Cork Commercial Courier*, 5 September 1846.
389 A kit-kat portrait is a particular size of portrait, less than half-length, but includes the hands.
390 The *Liberator*, 23 January 1846.
391 'Twelfth National Anti-Slavery Bazaar', *Liberator*, 23 January 1846.
392 The Scottish poet, Robbie Burns (1759–1796).
393 *Liberator*, 23 January 1846.
394 *Belfast News-Letter*, Tuesday, 6 January 1846.
395 This letter is from Maria Webb, Belfast, to the secretary of Boston Ladies Anti-Slavery Society, *National Anti-Slavery Standard*, 16 April 1846.
396 See, Christine Kinealy, 'The Women of Belfast during the Great Famine' in Patrick Fitzgerald and Anthony Russell (eds), *John Mitchel, Ulster and the Great Irish Famine* (Kildare: Irish Academic Press, 2017), chapter one.
397 Webb to Anne Warren Weston, 5 July 1849, in Clare Taylor, *British and American Abolitionists: An Episode in Transatlantic Understanding* (Edinburgh: Edinburgh University Press, 1974), p. 337.
398 Isabel Jennings to Mary Estlin, 24 March 1851, in E. M. Oldham, 'Irish Support for the Abolitionist Movement', *Boston Public Library Quarterly* (October 1958), 175–187, p. 183.
399 An oomycete caused the potato disease known as late blight. This was a new form of disease and, at the time, the antidote to it was unknown. At this stage, approximately 40 per cent of the Irish population depended on potatoes as a subsistence crop.
400 For example, *Northern Whig*, 9 December 1845.
401 Douglass to Garrison, 26 February 1846.
402 This view was clearly stated in the World Temperance Convention in 1846, which Douglass attended. See Proceedings.

403 'Lectures on the Evils of Intemperance and the Benefits Total Abstinence From All Intoxicating Drinks, Belfast. Lecture by Frederick Douglass, the Fugitive Slave', *Belfast Commercial Chronicle*, 12 January 1846.

404 *Boston Pilot*, reprinted in 'Refuge of Oppression', *Liberator*, 24 April 1846. In it, Douglass's descriptions of the Irish poor were, in turn, chastised in the columns of the *Boston Pilot* – a newspaper opposed to the abolitionists – who challenged his words and concluded that he 'would seem to have visited queer places in Dublin', quoted in the *Liberator*, 24 April 1846.

405 Douglass to Webb, 6 December 1845, Anti-Slavery Collection (BPL) MS A. 1.2. v.15, p. 86.

406 'Belfast Ladies Association for the Relief of Irish Destitution', Supplement to *Northern Whig*, 9 March 1847.

407 Multiply by 100.

408 'Beyond the Pale: Frederick Douglass', *Cork - University College Cork Irish Review*, no. 24 (Autumn 1999), 80–95, p. 91.

409 Wright to Douglass, Doncaster, 12 December 1846, in McKivigan, *Letters*, pp. 179–181.

410 'Our London Letter', *Dundee Courier*, 20 October 1886.

411 Douglass to Garrison, Carlisle, 2 January 1847, McKivigan, *Letters*, pp. 190–191.

412 Farewell Speech to the British People, at London Tavern, London, England, 30 March 1847, *Farewell Speech of Mr. Frederick Douglass Upon His Return to America, Delivered at the Valedictory Soiree Given to Him at the London Tavern on March 30, 1847*, London, 1847.

413 Douglass to Editor of (London) *Times*, 6 April 1847.

414 Ibid., S. Cunard to editor of *Times*, 13 April 1847.

415 *Downpatrick Recorder*, 10 October 1846.

416 Letter from Douglass to Garrison, Scotland, 26 February 1846, *Liberator*, 27 March 1846.

417 'Frederick Douglass', *Liberator*, 7 May 1847; Ibid., 'Reception of Frederick Douglass at the Belknap-Street Church, Boston', 21 May 1847.

418 'Reception of Frederick Douglass by the Colored People', *Liberator*, 21 May 1847.

419 'American Colorphobia', *Liberator*, 11 June 1847.

420 Reprinted in the *Liberator*, 22 October 1847.

421 Ferreira, 'Frederick Douglass', p. 61.

422 Letter from F.D, dated Lynn, Mass, 13 October 1847, 'Last Campaign of Frederick Douglass', *Essex Standard*, 28 January 1848.

423 'Anti-Slavery Convention', *Liberator*, 25 June 1847.

424 Martin Delany (1812–1885) was born to a free mother and slave father. Regardless of various obstacles to his studying medicine, he became a physician and during the Civil War served as both a recruiter and a surgeon for 'coloured troops'.

425 Editorial, *North Star*, 3 December 1847.

426 It was first published by John P. Jewett and Company.

427 'New Story by Mrs Beecher Stowe', *Cheltenham Chronicle*, 28 April 1853.

428 'Country, Conscience, and the Anti-Slavery Cause: An Address Delivered in New York, New York, May 11, 1847', *New York Daily Tribune*, 13 May 1847.

429 *North Star*, 9 February 1849.

430 George Thompson to unknown correspondent, 15 August 1851, Taylor, *British and American Abolitionists*, p. 381.

431 *North Star*, 17 March 1848.

432 Paper written by Frederick Douglass, 'Father Mathew', undated [1849], www.loc.gov/resource/mfd.21032/?sp=1, accessed 4 September 2017.

433 Douglass, *Life and Times*, 1882, pp. 424–425.

434 Frederick Douglass (*North Star*), Reprinted in *Leicestershire Mercury*, 11 November 1848.

435 *The Nature of Slavery: Extract from a Lecture on Slavery, at Rochester*, 1 December 1850. *My Life and Bondage*, p. 433.

436 Frederick Douglass, *The Claims of the Negro, Ethnologically Considered: An Address Before the Literary Societies of Western Reserve College at Commencement, 12 July 1854* (Rochester: Lee, Mann and Co., 1854), p. 20.

437 Douglass, *The Claims of the Negro, Ethnologically Considered*, pp. 30–31.

438 *Clare Journal, and Ennis Advertiser*, 1 June 1848.

439 *The Slavery Party: Extract from a Speech Delivered Before the A. A. S. Society, in New York*, May, 1853. Reprinted in *My Life and Bondage*, pp. 451–456.

440 Douglass, *Life and Times*, p. 973.

441 This observation took place on 28 September 1845 in Dublin. It was not snowing.

442 Douglass, 'Age of Pictures' c. 1862, reprinted in John Stauffer et al., *Picturing Frederick Douglass*, pp. 141–142.

443 Jeffrey R. Kerr-Ritchie, *Rites of August First: Emancipation Day in the Black Atlantic World* (Baton Rouge, LA: Louisiana State University Press, 2007), pp. 7–8.

444 For example, Kerr-Ritchie dismisses Douglass's devotion to England on the grounds that 'It smacks of Anglomania, ignores British complicity in colonialism, and is mute on the maltreatment of native minorities . . . The lack of black abolitionists' criticism in their speeches and writings toward Great Britain is noticeable. This was less because they were Anglophiles and more because their primary objective was to end American slavery and that required support from political elites as well as from the general populace', in Jeffrey R. Kerr-Ritchie 'Black abolitionists, Irish supporters, and the brotherhood of man, Slavery & Abolition', *A Journal of Slave and Post-Slave Studies*, vol. 37, no. 3, (2016) 599–621, p. 618.

445 Speech at West India Emancipation celebration, Rochester, New York, 1 August 1848, *The North Star*, 4 August 1848. Douglass subsequently came to condemn Mitchel for his stand on slavery when he made his home in the U.S.

446 'O'Connell', *North Star*, 21 August 1851.

447 These lines appear in the epic poem, 'Childe Harold', Canto ii, stanzas 73–77, which was written by Lord George Byron between 1812 and 1818.

448 'West India Emancipation', speech delivered at Canandaigua, New York, 3 August 1857.

449 Frederick Douglass, *Life and Times of Frederick Douglass* (OP: 1892; New York: Collier, 1962), p. 238. Douglass's third autobiography was first published in 1881, but extended and revised in 1892.

450 'Going, Going, Not Gone', *Frederick Douglass' Paper*, 22 December 1854.

451 Douglass, *My Bondage and My Freedom*, p. 98.

452 Douglass, *Life and Times*, p. 205.

453 Ibid.

454 Ibid., p. 206.

455 Frederick Douglass, 'Speech on Haiti' (Chicago: Violet Agents, 1893).

456 *Belfast News-Letter*, 3 December 1859.

457 'Mr Frederick Douglass on the Harper's Ferry Insurrection', *Leeds Times*, 24 December 1859.

458 'Mr Frederick Douglass' Lecture on the American Constitution', *Glasgow Herald*, 27 March 1860.

459 Ibid., Tuesday, 27 March 1860.

460 'Mr Douglass in Ayr', *Paisley Herald and Renfrewshire Advertiser*, 31 March 1860.

461 'F- D—', *Newcastle Daily Chronicle*, 29 June 1860.

462 In his private collection he had a copy of William L. Barrington, *Reflections on Some of the Results of the Late American War: Being a Lecture Delivered in the Friends' Institute Molesworth St, Dublin on Thursday, March 29 1866* (Dublin: Webb and Sons, 1866).

463 Harrison, *Quaker Printer*, p. 71.
464 David W. Blight, *Frederick Douglass' Civil War: Keeping Faith in Jubilee* (Baton Rouge, LA: Louisiana State University Press, 1991), pp. 122–130.
465 'Frederick Douglass on the Proclamation', *New York Times*, 7 February 1863.
466 'Men of Color to Arms', *Douglass' Monthly*, 21 March 1863.
467 'Why Should a Colored Man Enlist?' *Douglass' Monthly*, April 1863.
468 Douglass, *Life and Times*, p. 361.
469 'American Affairs', *Irish Times*, 31 July 1863.
470 'Honorable Conduct', *The Irishman*, 15 August 1863.
471 Douglass, *Life and Times*, pp. 795–800.
472 'Frederick Douglass' in Allen Thorndike Rice (ed.), *Reminiscences of Abraham Lincoln by Distinguished Men of His Time* (New York: North American Publishing, 1886), 185-193, p. 191.
473 'Through Slavery to Fame . . . The Life and Adventures of Frederick Douglass', *New York Times*, 27 December 1880.
474 This point is argued eloquently by Blight in *Frederick Douglass' Civil War*.
475 Frederick Douglass, 'An Appeal to Congress for Impartial Suffrage', *The Atlantic*, January 1867.
476 Ibid.
477 'O'Connell on Slavery', *Wexford People*, 29 May 1886.
478 'Coloured Men in Council: Disorderly Beginning. Opposition to Fred Douglas as Chairman', *New York Times*, 25 September 1883.
479 Fought, *Frederick Douglass Women*, p. 238.
480 'Marriage of Frederick Douglass Washington', *New York Times*, 25 January 1884.
481 No title, *Dundee Evening Telegraph*, 31 December 1884.
482 'Our London Letter', *Dundee Courier*, 20 October 1886.
483 'Fred Douglass in Europe,' *New York Times*, 17 October 1886.
484 Wendell Phillips Club, who gave him a dinner at the Revere House on Saturday evening, September 11, 1886, http://teachingamericanhistory.org/library/document/the-nations-problem/
485 *The Graphic*, 13 November 1886.
486 Helen Pitts Douglass, 'Diary Entry', 24 June 1886, Library of Congress (LoC) p. 20, www.loc.gov/resource/mfd.01002/?sp=20, accessed 12 October 2017.
487 'Our London Letter', *Dundee Courier*, 20 October 1886.
488 Douglass, *Life and Times*, p. 677.
489 Ibid., p. 702.
490 'Fred Douglass in Europe', *New York Times*, 17 October 1886.
491 Wilhelmina, a relative of Richard's, was involved in the women's suffrage movement. See International Council of Women, *Report of the International Council of Women: Assembled by the National Woman Suffrage Association, Washington, DC, U.S. of America 1888* (Washington: R. H. Darby, printer, 1888), p. 42. Wilhelmina was part of an Irish delegation.
492 Wilhelmina Webb, 'Ardkill', 5 June 1887, Frederick Douglass Papers, LoC, www.loc.gov/resource/mfd.06009/?q=1887&sp=3. She wrote again on 24 June after hearing that Helen was returning to America and expressing hope Frederick would still visit Ireland, www.loc.gov/resource/mfd.06009/?q=1887&sp=35, accessed 5 September 2017.
493 Ibid., Wilhelmina, 10 July 1887, www.loc.gov/resource/mfd.06009/?q=1887&sp=104, accessed 4 September 2017.
494 For Allen's obituary see, *Irish Times*, 20 January 1886, or *The British Friend*, vol. 44 (1886), p. 45.
495 Allen, 9 June 1887, to Douglass, Frederick Douglass papers, LoC, General Correspondence, www.loc.gov/resource/mfd.06009/?q=1887&sp=7

496 Ibid., Douglass to Helen, 28 June 1887, Carlisle. Although he missed Helen and had only five weeks remaining, Douglass was determined to visit Dublin, www.loc.gov/resource/mfd.06009/?q=1887&sp=50

497 Ibid., Frederick Douglass, Diary Entry, 5 June 1887, 'Diary of Tour of Europe and Africa', p. 65. www.loc.gov/resource/mfd.01001/?sp=67, accessed 3 October 2107.

498 Ibid., The Irish names listed in Douglass's diary were:

Mrs Wilhelmenia Webb, Ardkill, Killiney, Co. Dublin
Mrs Susana Webb, 9 Belgrave Road, Rathmines, Dublin
Mr and Mrs Abraham Shackleton, Clondorrach, Foxrock, Co. Dublin
Miss Deborah Webb (daug. R.D.W.) 9 Granville Road, Dublin
~~Mrs Susanah Webb of Rathmines~~
Mrs John Webb, Ardkill, Killiney, Co. Dublin, Ireland
Thomas Henry and Elizabeth Emily Webb, Primrose Hill, Kingstown, Ireland.

499 Alfred Webb, Marie-Louise Kegge (ed.), *The Autobiography of a Quaker Nationalist* (Cork: Cork University Press, 1999), p. 66.

500 Douglass, *Life and Times*, pp. 668–669.

501 Frederick Douglass, *Thoughts and Recollections*, 1887. For full text see Vol. 2.

502 Webb, *Autobiography*.

503 Lauren Onkey, *Blackness and Transatlantic Irish Identity: Celtic Soul Brothers* (London and New York: Routledge, 2010), p. 60.

504 'Frederick Douglass Explains', *Boston Pilot*, 7 August 1886, quoted in *Blackness and Transatlantic Irish Identity*, p. 60.

505 Michael R. Watts, *The Dissenters: The Crisis and Conscience of Nonconformity*, p. 265.

506 William Arthur, *Shall the Loyal Be Deserted and the Disloyal Placed Over Them? An Appeal to Liberals and Nonconformists* (London: Bemrose and Sons, 1886). A copy of this pamphlet was in Douglass's personal collection and now in his papers in the Library of Congress, www.loc.gov/item/mfd.35013/, accessed 19 September 2017.

507 Frederick Douglass, Speech on 11 September 1886, 'The Nation's Problem', http://teachingamericanhistory.org/library/document/the-nations-problem/

508 Thoughts and Reflections, p. 18.

509 Douglass quoted by Mrs John Mills, 'Message of sympathy from women of England' in *Freeman's Journal*, 12 July 1887.

510 'To Help the Irish Cause', *New York Times*, 15 December 1887.

511 Irish American Association, *Grand Reception to Arthur O'Connor Esq., M.P. and Sir Thomas H. Grattan Esmonde, Bart., M.P. at Masonic Temple, Washington, DC* (Washington, DC: William H. Moore, 1887), pp. 21–23.

512 'Great Home Rule Meeting in Washington', *Daily Gazette for Middlesbrough*, 16 December 1887.

513 'Great Home Rule Meeting in Washington', *London Daily News*, 16 December 1887.

514 'Making a Harrison Party', *New York Times*, 29 June 1889.

515 'Haiti', *Liberator*, 19 December 1845.

516 Lecture on Haiti. For extracts of this speech see Vol. 2.

517 'Book Reviews – No Title', *Zion's Herald*, 8 February 1893.

518 'Prominent people,' *Evening Herald*, 26 September, 1892.

519 These acts of violence against black people were most intense between 1890 and 1920, with the peak year in 1892.

520 'A negros view of lynching' appeared in *Glasgow Evening Post*, 13 August 1892, and *Cork Constitution*, 15 August 1892.

521 'Noted and Comments', *Glasgow Evening Post*, 16 July 1892. In the same article they described Douglass as a 'believer in the Immaculate Nigger'.

522 'Coloured Folk in England', *Lichfield Mercury*, 24 August 1894. This article originally appeared in the *Daily Telegraph*.

523 Ida Bell Wells-Barnett (1862–1931) was an African American journalist, editor, suffragist and civil rights leader. See Patricia A. Schechter, *Ida B. Wells-Barnett and American Reform, 1880–1930* (Chapel Hill, NC: University of North Carolina Press, 2003).

524 Fought, in *Frederick Douglass's Women*, argues that despite the difference in age and experience, Douglass respected Wells as an equal, pp. 283–284.

525 *Western Daily Press*, 3 August 1894.

526 For more on 'Douglass Day', see Schechter, *Ida B. Wells-Barnett and American Reform*, pp. 102–103.

527 'Death of Fred Douglass', *The New York Times*, 21 February 1895.

528 When Helen died in 1903, she was buried in an adjoining plot. Susan B. Anthony, who died in 1906, was also buried in the Mount Hope cemetery in Rochester.

529 'Through Slavery to Fame . . . The Life and Adventures of Frederick Douglass', *New York Times*, 27 December 1880.

530 'Death of a Celebrated American', *Northern Whig*, 22 February 1895.

531 'Death of Fred Douglass', *Cork Constitution*, 22 February 1895.

532 'Funeral of Mr Frederick Douglass', *Belfast News-Letter*, 27 February 1895.

533 For example, 'Death of a Famous American Orator', *Daily Gazette for Middlesbrough*, 21 February 1895.

534 *Dundee Evening Telegraph*, 21 February 1895.

535 *St James's Gazette*, 21 February 1895; 'Death of Mr Frederick Douglass', *Leeds Mercury*, 21 February 1895.

536 'Notes on News', *Yorkshire Evening Post*, 22 February 1895.

537 'A Remarkable Mullato', *Banbury Advertiser*, 28 February 1895.

538 'Scene in the US House of Representatives', *Greenock Telegraph and Clyde Shipping Gazette*, 22 February 1895. The division was also reported in the *Dublin Evening Herald*, 'The Late Frederick Douglass', 22 February 1895.

539 There a number of plaques throughout Ireland dedicated to Frederick Douglass. In Belfast, he features in a mural on the 'Solidarity Wall'. There are plaques to him in Cork and Waterford.

540 Gilbert Barnett, Brooklyn to Mister Douglass', 23 July 1887, Frederick Douglass Papers, LoC, General Correspondence, www.loc.gov/resource/mfd.06009/?q=1887&sp=25, accessed 11 September 2017.

541 Frederic May Holland, *Frederick Douglass: The Colored Orator* (New York: Funk & Wagnalls Company, 1891); James M. Gregory, *Frederick Douglass. The Orator* (New York, 1893).

542 Moses Grandy, *Narrative of the Life of Moses Grandy: Late a Slave in the United States of America* (London: C. Gilpin, 1843), p. 71, in Lunsford Lane, Moses Grandy, and Thomas H. Jones, William L. Andrews (eds.), *The Lives of Moses Roper* (Chapel Hill: University of North Carolina Press, 2003), p. 183.

543 No title, *Montrose, Arbroath and Brechin Review; and Forfar and Kincardineshire Advertiser*, 3 July 1846. Roper was usually described as the 'quondam slave'; 'Lecture on American Slavery', *Armagh Guardian*, 18 August 1846.

544 Henry Louis Gates Jr., 'Evelyn Brooks Higginbotham', *African American Lives*, p. 239.

545 Blight, *Civil War*, passim.

546 Douglass was not the only black abolitionist to compare the poverty of the Irish to that of the black population in America. Ward, visiting five years later, was similarly appalled, and, similar to Douglass, he also noted that the sympathy displayed by the Irish in their native country for abolition dissipated when they arrived in the U.S.

547 Don Mullan (ed.) *Narrative of the Life of Frederick Douglass* (Dublin: A Little Book Company, 2011), p. 15. This edition was published to mark the visit of President Barack Obama to Ireland.

548 See, Harrison, *Quaker Printer*.

549 'Frederick Douglass', *Limerick Reporter*, 11 November 1845.

550 Preface, *Narrative* (1846, Irish edition).

551 'Letters from Frederick Douglass', Belfast, 1 January 1846, *Liberator*, 30 January 1846.

552 Douglass, *Thought and Reflections*.

553 Frederick Douglass, *Dublin to Garrison*, Letter Three, 29 September 1845, *Liberator*, 24 October 1845.

554 'Letter from Frederick Douglass, Montrose, Scotland,' 26 February 1846, *Liberator*, 27 March 1846.

555 Daniel O'Connell, *Letter of Daniel O'Connell on American Slavery to the Cincinnati Repeal Association* (Dublin: Cornmarket, 1843).

556 This matter has continued to frustrate and divide scholars. See, for example, Noel Ignatiev, *How the Irish Became White* (London: Routledge, 1996); Kinealy, *Saddest People*, etc.

557 Angela F. Murphy's recent book on American slavery, *Abolition, Immigrant Citizenship, and the Transatlantic Movement for Irish Repeal* (Baton Rouge: Louisiana State University Press, 2010), p. x.

558 R. Webb to Garrison, 2 October 1845, quoted in the *Liberator*, 24 October 1845.

559 Fought, in *Women in the World of Frederick Douglass*, argues that 'His race, his enslaved status, his ability to read, his self-emancipation, his success as a speaker and newspaper editor, the way in which he lived every aspect of his life in opposition to racism, his understanding of equality between the sexes, his intellectual development . . . all emerged from the world of women', p. 1.

560 Griffiths's letters were published in *Frederick Douglass Paper*, 23 November 1855.

561 Douglass, *Life and Times* (1892), p. 570.

562 D. Richie, ' "The stone in the sling": Frederick Douglass and Belfast abolitionism', in *American Nineteenth Century History* (2017), 245–272, p. 19.

563 Samuel Ringgold Ward, *Autobiography of a Fugitive Negro: His Anti Slavery Efforts in the United States, Canada and England* (London: John Snow, 1855), p. 301.

564 Douglass, Cork, to Garrison, Letter Four, 28 October 1845, *Liberator*, 28 November 1845.

565 Alan J. Rice, 'Triumphant Exile: Frederick Douglass in Britain, 1845–47,' in Alan J. Rice and Martin Crawford (eds.), *Liberating Sojourn: Frederick Douglass and Transatlantic Reform* (London and Athens: University of Georgia Press, 1999), p. 3.

566 Patricia J. Ferreira, 'Frederick Douglass in Ireland: The Dublin Edition of His "Narrative"', *New Hibernia Review / Iris Éireannach Nua*, vol. 5, no. 1 (Spring 2001), pp. 53–67.

567 Appendix, Douglass, *Narrative*, second Dublin edition, p. cxxvii.

568 As Fionnghuala Sweeney has observed, 'Douglass's emergence as a major figure in American politics and letters owed as much to his international as his national activities'.

569 The Frederick Douglass Papers project commenced in 1793, initially out of Yale University, but more recently works out of Indiana University-Purdue University, Indianapolis. It has been successful in identifying and documenting part of Douglass's correspondence, etc. The Gilder Lehrman Centre in Yale was opened in 1998 with the generous support of two businessmen. Its mission is to provide a centre for the 'Study of Slavery, Resistance, and Abolition'. St Thomas University in Rochester provides online resources. The Documenting the South project at the University of

North Carolina is 'a digital publishing initiative that provides Internet access to texts, images, and audio files related to southern history, literature, and culture' are amongst those who have helped make sections of Douglass's work available on line. At the time of publication of these two volumes, there had been no attempt to collate Douglass's Irish speeches in one place.

570 Ann Andrews, *Newspapers and Newsmakers: The Dublin Nationalist Press in the Mid-Nineteenth Century* (Liverpool: Liverpool University Press, 2015).

571 In the 1840s, most newspapers were four pages long, the first page devoted to advertisements.

572 Douglass, *My Bondage and My Freedom*, p. vi.

573 'American Slavery: Lecture in Lisburn', *Belfast Commercial Chronicle*, 31 December 1845.

574 Douglass, Belfast, to R. Webb, 6 December 1845, Anti-Slavery Papers (BPL), MS A. 1.2. v.15, p. 86.

575 'American Slavery: Lecture in Lisburn', *Belfast Commercial Chronicle*, 31 December 1845.

576 Douglass, *My Life and Bondage*, 1855, pp. 380–381.

577 'Anti-Slavery Breakfast', *Cork Examiner*, 15 October 1845.

578 'Festival at the Temperance Institute, Cork', *Wexford Independent*, 25 October 1845.

579 'Anti-Slavery Meeting', *Belfast Commercial Chronicle*, 13 September 1845.

580 'Slavery', *Freeman's Journal*, 8 September 1845.

581 For more on the use of the term 'manly', see Elsa Nettels, *Language and Gender in American Fiction: Howells, James, Wharton, and Cather* (Charlottesville: University of Virginia Press, 1997), pp. 5–6. The word was also applied to another runaway slave, William Wells Brown, a contemporary of Douglass. See Paula Garrett and Hollis Robbins (eds.), *The Works of William Wells Brown: Using His 'Strong, Manly Voice'* (Oxford: Oxford University Press, 2006).

582 Speech by Rev. Nelson, Primitive Wesleyan Chapel, Donegall-Place, Belfast; 'Anti-Slavery Meeting', *Northern Whig*, 9 July 1846.

583 'Slavery', *Pilot*, 8 September 1845.

584 'Public Meeting', *Cork Examiner*, 15 October 1845.

585 'American Slavery', *Wexford Independent* from the *Waterford Freeman*, 15 October 1845.

586 'Anti-Slavery Breakfast', *Cork Examiner*, 15 October 1845.

587 Moses Grandy, *Narrative of the Life of Moses Grandy; Late a Slave in the United States of America* (London: C. Gilpin, 1843), p. 71, in William L. Andrews (ed.), *The Lives of Moses Roper, Lunsford Lane, Moses Grandy, & Thomas H. Jones* (Chapel Hill: University of North Carolina Press, 2003), p. 183.

The following texts are transcribed and annotated by Christine Kinealy.

Punctuation, spelling and capitalization, as far as possible, remain faithful to the original text. Dates, addresses and salutations have been aligned to the left.

DOCUMENTS

PRELIMS

Publication: *Liberator* (Boston, Massachusetts)[1]
Date of Publication: Friday, 4 July 1845
Title: 'THE FUGITIVE'S SONG, *I'll be Free! I'll be Free!*'.

DEDICATED to Frederick Douglass and other Fugitives, by Jesse Hutchinson, Jr. Also, 'Get off the Track,' and the various other Songs of the Hutchinsons.[2] For sale by BELA MARSH.[3]

Letter: James Haughton to the *Liberator*
Publication: *Liberator*
Date of Publication: Friday, 25 July 1845
Title: 'LETTER FROM JAMES HAUGHTON[4] – THE LEAGUE AND AMERICAN SLAVERY'.

35 ECCLES-STREET, DUBLIN, 2 July 1845.

DEAR FRIEND:[5] I do not often write to you, but I often think of you, and I occasionally send you a newspaper, to let you know how we are going on here. I read of your doings with much interest, and although you approach slowly towards the accomplishment of your great end, yet it is cheering to believe that your progress is right onward; that every day you are gaining fresh strength, so as to be able to feel a moral certainty that your labours are approaching to a consummation. You have indeed great difficulties to contend against, but they seem to be melting away rapidly, before the attacks of yourself and those valued friends who are laboring with you. In conjunction with a few others here, I endeavor to aid your efforts, as opportunity arises. I send you the enclosed, to let you see a late attempt I made to influence public opinion in England. The League has a great circulation, which made me anxious to have my letter published in it; and, if inserted there, I knew it would be seen by the 'soul-drivers' in America, who have the impudence to profess themselves friendly to freedom of trade, while they deny any rights to their fellow-men, whom they retain in bondage. I was very glad to see the manner in which O'Connell's speech on the Texas question was received in your land.[6] Your pro-slavery folks now *feel* that the much-loved leader of the Irish people is really in earnest in his detestation of their infernal system. Our people feel with him on the subject; but most of our other popular leaders are disposed to pass by the question of slavery altogether, and accept the aid and sympathy of the devil himself, if he offered it, to assist them in carrying out their views. I think their views are legitimate; but I fear their accomplishment will be retarded, if not altogether overthrown, by the willingness that is evinced to avail of unholy influences. You seem disposed to stand firmly on the rock of principle, and therefore man's improvement drags slowly along.

Our temperance movement is the most blessed work we have in hand. It has indeed done wonders for our people. I am often amazed at their firmness, and at the happy change that has taken place in their habits, when I witness the indifference of our wealthy classes to the great reformation which is going on around them. It is still almost entirely confined to the poor, and among these, I expect that education is surely but slowly laying the foundation for greater happiness and higher civilization in this country. R.D. Webb[7] keeps up such a lively correspondence with some of the best spirits on your side the of water, that I am made acquainted with a great deal that passes among you. My heart and feelings are with you and the 'old organization';[8] and I deeply regret that some who laboured with you are not now found in your ranks. What is the meaning of Rogers's strange conduct?[9] I am unable to find any excuse for him. I did think him a noble man, who would have been as true to you and the cause as steel, but he now seems disposed to stab both to the heart. I deeply regret his conduct. I think of him as a great man fallen, and am truly sorry for him. My friend Bradburn too gone off![10] I have little or no faith in the value of political action, and still less faith in the actors, they are so constantly led astray by a false expediency. I had no intention of writing you this morning, and I have penned these few lines in haste for to-morrow's packet.[11] I hope we shall some way or other get a few copies of Frederick Douglass's *Narrative*. Your extracts from it are most interesting.

I remain your affectionate friend, JAMES HAUGHTON.

1

THE JOURNEY TO LIVERPOOL

Editorial
Publication: *Liberator*, reprinted from the *US Gazette*
Date of Publication: Friday, 22 August 1845
Title: 'DEPARTURE OF FREDERICK DOUGLASS, JAMES N. BUF-FUM,[12] **AND THE HUTCHINSON FAMILY'.**

These widely known and widely beloved friends left us on Saturday last, in the steamer *Cambria*, for Liverpool.[13] Heaven give them a speedy and prosperous passage, and grant them a safe return home in the course of the next year! They need no credentials, no letters of introduction, on the other side of the Atlantic. Their names, services and talents are known by all in England, Scotland, and Ireland, who take any interest in the cause of emancipation here, or who are familiar with what is going on in the musical world. Their reception, we do not doubt, will be kind, cordial, and enthusiastic. In every respect, they are deserving of the confidence, esteem and hospitality of our British friends. Sorry are we, with a great multitude also, to part with them, even for a twelvemonth; but, remembering that 'the field is the world,' and that they are not to be idle in it, but, if possible, more active and efficient than ever, we are reconciled to the separation. They will create a sensation, we opine, before their return.

We arrived from our Pennsylvania excursion just in season to bid them farewell. The noble steamer lay off in the stream, ready in a few moments to commence her pathless journey across the mighty deep. At the suggestion of Jesse, a circle was formed by us all, when the gifted 'family' sung 'Home, sweet home,' with deep pathos and thrilling effect; and as the last strain died upon the air, the bell sounded, and, giving a final clasp of the hand, we bade each other adieu. The last thing we saw of Douglass was his waving his hat to us in the distance. Soon may he stand, where he has never yet stood, on a soil which cannot tolerate slavery, and among a people, who neither despise nor persecute a man on account of the complexion which it has pleased the Creator to bestow on him!

On Friday evening, a crowded and most enthusiastic meeting was held in the spacious Lyceum Hall, Lynn,[14] which was addressed by Douglass, Buffum and others, and at which the Hutchinsons sung in their inimitable strains; after which, the following resolutions, offered by Henry Clapp, Jr.,[15] were adopted by acclamation:

Resolved, As the sense of this great gathering of the inhabitants of Lynn and vicinity, that we extend to our esteemed fellow-citizens, *Frederick Douglass* and James N. Buffum – whose proposed departure for England has brought this 'uncounted multitude' together – our heartiest good wishes for a successful issue of their journey.

Resolved, That we are especially desirous that *Frederick Douglass*, who came to this town a fugitive from slavery, should bear with him to the shores of the Old World, our unanimous testimony to the fidelity with which he has sustained the various relations of life, and to the deep respect with which he is now regarded by every friend of liberty throughout our borders.

Resolved, Also, that we rejoice to welcome among us on this occasion our distinguished guests – 'The Hutchinson Family' – from New-Hampshire, feeling it no small honor that their farewell song should have been poured into our hearts; – and we unite with innumerable friends of humanity in every part of our country, in at once regretting that our gifted friends are to leave us, and congratulating Old England that she is about to receive in their presence, so large an accession to their musical and philanthropic ability.

Alluding to the Hutchinson vocalists, the *N. Y. Courier and Enquirer* says, 'They contemplated going across the water last year; but the sudden death of a beloved and favorite brother so weighed down their spirits, that they for some time thought they should sing no more in public, but stay at home the remainder of their days, to comfort their aged and afflicted parents. But our music-loving public would not long do without them, and last spring they were again welcomed by thousands upon thousands of delighted and sympathizing hearers, in this, and other of our large cities. They are now bound for England, and will carry with them the best wishes and affectionate regards of all in this country who have ever heard them or heard of them – and who has not?'

The Hutchinsons, whose delightful and melodious singing, drew thousands to listen to them when in this city, have determined to venture across the Atlantic, and warble a while in England. Their absence will be felt here, but we shall have a pleasure in hearing of their success among the strangers they go to; notwithstanding, we would be more pleased it they remained at home.

Article
Publication: *Liberator*
Date of Publication: Friday, 3 October 1845
Title: 'FREDERICK DOUGLASS'.

A pro-slavery American, in London, writes to the editor of the *Boston Times*, respecting the pro-slavery row on board the steamer *Cambria*, as follows:

The steamer *Cambria*, on her last home ward trip, brought over a large number of passengers, and, as is usual, they represented the four quarters of the globe,

Englishmen and Americans, however, forming the majority – and a very agreeable party they would have been, if a colored person named DOUGLASS, had not interfered to disturb the good feeling which at first prevailed on board the floating palace *Cambria*. I have been informed that this Douglass was a steerage passenger, and yet he was allowed to visit the quarter deck and mingle with first class cabin passengers, to the great annoyance of some of them. He conversed in a very loud tone every day, upon his favorite topic, slavery, and finally he so far prevailed over the good nature of the popular commander, Capt. Judkins,[16] as to obtain his consent to announce that a lecture on slavery would be delivered by Douglass on the quarter-deck. The steward rung the bell, which was the signal for the lecture to commence. Ladies and gentlemen were promenading, as usual, on the quarter deck, when they were much annoyed by the harangue of Douglass. He heaped the most outrageous abuse on the Americans, calling America the home for blackguards, and said that Americans occupied that home. His abuse became so violent, that two or three gentlemen took the subject up – a singular scene ensued – there was sharp shooting on both sides. Some low Scotchmen took the negro's part, and told him to give it to the Yankees; while the ladies and several Englishmen turned their backs upon this ignorant calumniator and left the deck, fearful that hard words would end in hard blows. One Englishman, who had owned two hundred slaves in Jamaica, stood forward and stated that his whole property had been swept away by the laws of his country – that his estates were valueless since his slaves were liberated by the British government; but that he was strongly opposed to slavery and the slave trade; he could not, however, listen to such low abuse as Douglass had been permitted to utter in a mixed company, and he proceeded to talk down the negro. Other gentlemen expressed great disgust at Douglass's conduct, and a row being soon likely to take place, Capt. Judkins was appealed to, and the negro was not permitted to vomit his foul stuff any longer on the quarter-deck. He was very annoying to most of the passengers during the whole voyage, and if there had been a Southerner on board, his carcass would no doubt have been food for sharks. It is certainly to be regretted that such fellows are ever permitted to annoy cabin passengers in this way, merely because two or three of their comrades wish to get up an excitement, and hear their leaders abuse America and Americans. Capt. Judkins should not have permitted this fellow to open his lips on the quarter-deck.

Article
Publication: *Southern Reporter and Cork Commercial Courier*[17]
Date of Publication: Thursday, 23 October 1845
No Title.

The *New York Herald* states that an extraordinary scene took place on board the Columbia [sic] in a recent trip to England. A coloured passenger named Douglass is stated to have addressed an abolition speech to the passengers, from the quarter-deck, and that in consequence, a row ensued. (From *Liverpool Albion*)

Editorial
Publication: *Liberator*
Date of Publication: Friday, 31 October 1845
Title: 'FREE DISCUSSION OF SLAVERY'.

The following dastardly article appears in the *Oneida Whig*, a paper printed in Utica, N.Y. – and one peculiarly venomous toward the anti-slavery movement: Frederick Douglass, the negro orator, who passed through this city some months since, has gone to Europe. Upon his arrival in Dublin he wrote a letter to the *Boston Liberator*, giving the particulars of his voyage. Among other things he mentioned that he made a speech on slavery, by and with the consent of the captain. There were men, according to his own story, of every nation, and creed, and practice, on board the steamship upon which he had embarked, and yet he was allowed to *insult the feelings* of his fellow passengers by the English Lieutenant, who had charge of her Majesty's vessel. We do not know in what terms to characterize such conduct. If Mr. Douglass had not enough of the gentleman about him to appreciate what was due to those in whose company he had fallen, most assuredly a man holding office in the royal navy should have treated with more regard the national and personal feelings of those who had placed themselves under his guidance and protection. Men of every nation, kindred and creed contribute to the support of his English owners, and shall they have their honest opinions, or their bigoted prejudices, if you will, trampled underfoot? Shall their characters be maligned, their actions held up to scorn, by one who has no more rights on board than any one of them all, and shall the man to whose guidance they entrust themselves, and to whom they must necessarily look for protection of person and feeling, sanction and promote the outrage? The slaveholders on board that disgraced steamship were as much entitled as other men to honorable treatment, and yet the John Bull who governed allowed them to be publicly insulted. What would he have done, if some slaveholder had desired to make a speech upon the horrors of English rule in the East Indies, descanted feelingly upon the knavery, bloodshed and famine that have followed with tireless foot upon the track of the English armies? What if some Yankee had shown up in all its horror, the opium war on China? What if some Dutchman, Frenchman, or American, had spoken with the burning indignation which they deserve, of the multiplied enormities and oppressions of the British power, of the ten thousand abuses of British rule? What would he have done? His wrath would have known no bounds. Englishmen were his passengers, under his care, and neither he nor they would submit to such an outrage upon their national sensibilities. His duties as commander, called on him to protect them, and that protection they should have. And yet he allowed a brand of discord to be thrown among his passengers; he allowed the representatives of a class of men, among whom, Lord Morpeth said, in his letter to Mrs. Chapman, he had found as much warm-heartedness, intelligence and piety as he had ever known, to have their characters assailed, their feelings scorned. We trust that all

Americans, from all sections of the country, will avoid that vessel as they would the plague, and then perhaps the insolent captain will learn to act like a gentleman.

Editorial
Publication: *Liberator*
Date of Publication: Friday, 31 October 1845
Title: 'A JUST REBUKE'.

It gives us peculiar pleasure to copy the following indignant animadversions on the atrocious article we have placed in the 'Refuge of Oppression' from the *Oneida Whig*, respecting Frederick Douglass on board the *Cambria*; because it is from another Whig paper – the *Albany Evening Journal*. It required a second look to assure our eyes that this paragraph really appeared in a Utica instead of a South Carolina or Alabama paper. And though actually written and printed in a Free State, it fails to persuade us that it is either wrong or impertinent to discuss the question of Slavery anywhere and everywhere.

FREDERICK DOUGLASS, as it appears, was solicited by a number of the passengers on board the Steamer, to speak of Slavery, the horrors of which he had endured. He declined until the permission of the Captain of the vessel was obtained, and then very properly acquiesced. It was therefore, his right to speak, and their privilege to hear. And it was equally the privilege of those who did not want to hear, to keep away. The passengers who asked had taste, for this stigmatized 'Negro Orator' is a man of high intellectual, moral and social worth. We hazard little in assuming that in all the qualities that become a man, he is the superior of those by whom he was so rudely insulted on board that Steamer. Slavery claims to enjoy the sanction of Divine as well as human laws. With such high pretensions, it may not shrink from discussion. Nor would it do so if it had any confidence in the strength or justice of its cause. PATRICK HENRY, GEORGE WASHINGTON, and THOMAS JEFFERSON freely discussed the evils and publicly deplored the existence of Slavery. May not 'Frederick Douglass,' a gifted and eloquent man, who has escaped from stripes, manacles and dungeons, lift up his voice against Slavery! Yes! He may, and he will, in defiance of all who threaten or rail at the North or the South – *'in spite of lamentations here or elsewhere.'*

Article
Publication: *Liberator*
Date of Publication: Friday, 28 November 1845
Title: 'Incident on the *Cambria*. Meeting of the Committee of the Glasgow Emancipation Society'.

At a meeting of the Committee of the Glasgow Emancipation Society, Oct. 18, 1845, it was unanimously resolved: – 'That the cordial thanks of this Committee be tendered to Captain Judkins, of the steam-packet *Cambria*, for his firm and noble conduct in vindicating the rights of the oppressed Americans, in the person of Frederick Douglass, who, by the Constitution and laws of the American Union, is a slave, when he was insulted, and threatened with violence, by slaveholders and their abettors, on his recent passage from Boston to Liverpool in said steamer *Cambria*.' Voted, – 'That this resolution be signed by the Chairman and Secretaries, and presented by the latter to Captain Judkins.'

GEORGE WATSON, Chairman.

Editorial
Publication: *National Anti-Slavery Standard* (New York City)[18]
Date of Publication: Thursday, 18 December 1845
Title: 'Pro-Slavery. THE ABOLITION RIOT ON THE ATLANTIC'.

My attention has recently been called to an article published in a Massachusetts paper, which contains an extract from a letter written by "one of the Hutchinson family," in relation to the disturbance on board the English steamer *Cambria*, on her return trip to England, in August last. The Hutchinsons were passengers, and any statement published by them must be recognized as correct until contradicted, and then, of course, a difference of opinion must exist in the minds of those who may read the two statements, one of which I propose to give, and which can be substantiated by a reference to the passengers on board at the time.

We left Boston on Saturday, the 16th of August, with 95 cabin passengers, including the "Hutchinson family." In the second cabin, or steerage, were about a dozen passengers, including a fugitive slave, by the name of "Frederick Douglass," and a celebrated Massachusetts Abolitionist, by the name of "Buffum." I shall pass over various incidents which transpired on the voyage, which might, and which ought to, excite the strongest indignation against the Commander, (Judkins,) believing the one will be sufficient to condemn him in the minds of every American. It is a custom (known by all who have ever crossed in these steamers,) for the Captain to give, the day before arrival into port, a champagne dinner; I say it is a custom known to all. I have often crossed, and as it has always been practiced, I conclude it is as much of an established rule, as it is for the Captain to say grace at the table one moment, and curse some poor steward or sailor the next. The day before our arrival in Liverpool, the party was given, as usual. Among the number who enjoyed this party was Capt. Charles H. E. Judkins. When he came on deck, Mr. "Jesse Hutchinson," by the request of this "Mr. Buffum," his three brothers, perhaps a half a dozen Englishmen, and probably the negro himself, asked the Captain if he would allow Mr. Douglass to make some remarks on the subject of Slavery, and occupy the promenade deck for that purpose. He, the Captain, immediately gave his assent, and ordered one of his stewards to ring the hand-bell in different parts of the ship, and request all the passengers to retire to the deck. It was done, and when they had all met, probably not twenty of the hundred passengers knew for what purpose they had been called together. The Captain then came forward and said, "Some of the passengers had expressed a desire to hear Mr. Douglass speak on the subject of Slavery. Mr. Douglass was a fugitive slave, and could speak from experience of this institution. He was a man, who, although black, could put many of us to the blush," &c. &c.; and closed his address by adding, "Those who do not like or wish to hear him can go below." A portion of the American passengers retired to the saloon, myself among the number, to take into consideration the propriety of expressing our feelings in some proper way, that the public might know the respect, or want of respect, paid to Americans on board this steamer. While we were consulting we were disturbed by a noise on deck. We went up and found all in a state of great excitement. It originated, I learned, as follows, and that these are the facts there can be no doubt. Douglass commenced by referring to philanthropic England, and the example she had shown us by freeing her slaves. He then proposed to read some of the slave laws in the different States, and commenced with Georgia. He had proceeded but a few moments when a gentleman, a citizen of Connecticut, interrupted him, and said, "It was enough to be compelled to hear him, as a mouth-piece of the Captain, insult Americans with his remarks; but if he had any State laws to read, to read them, and not attempt to palm off any of his abolition tracts as the laws of Georgia or any other State. He had lived many years in Georgia, and was well acquainted with her laws, and knew he was not reading any of them." The insulting reply was – "He was not aware before that there was any American blackguards on board, but," – He had said enough, and there was not an American on board that ship who would have submitted to a further insult from a negro, captain, or crew. The Captain, who was in the mess-room, came aft and interfered. He said, "he was commander of the *Cambria* – he was an Englishman – he had given Mr. Douglass permission to speak, and if he was disposed, he might go on, and he would protect him; but if he (Douglass) would take his advice, he would leave the deck and his hearers, with contempt." He, of course, went. The Captain then said, and repeated, "that he did not care a damn for his passengers. Gentlemen, you have drank my health, you have drank success to my ship, for which I thanked you; but I wish you to understand I don't care a d – n for you." The Captain is unable to plead the excuse that he did not know there was any objection among the passengers to hear Douglass speak. Before he commenced, I went to him and reminded him of the probability of its ending in a disturbance, telling him the subject of Slavery was one upon which Americans were very sensitive; and without questioning his privileges as commander, he ought to consult the feelings of his passengers, a good portion of whom were Americans. His reply to me was what I did not expect. I will refrain from mentioning it, believing enough has been said to show the feelings entertained by Captain Charles H. E. Judkins towards Americans. Your correspondent returned to America in the same steamer, and under the same person's command. He more than once told some of his passengers "that he did not care a d – n for them. He was independent and above them all – they could be pleased or not; it mattered not a d – n to him." One hint with regard to the mission of Douglass and Buffum to England. A few days before I left Liverpool, I saw in a Dublin paper an advertisement announcing that Mr. Douglass, a fugitive American slave, would lecture on the horrors of American Slavery. Is there to be a movement by the Abolitionists to secure, directly or indirectly, the assistance of Dan. O'Connell and the Irish to further their hypocritical movements? It is too bad that Americans can be found who will attempt to vilify our country as these wandering Abolition lecturers do, both at home and abroad. TRAVELLER.

P. S. – If I recollect, Mr. Hutchinson referred to a gentleman from New Orleans who took an active part in the disturbance. There was no passenger south of Philadelphia, which will account for the quiet manner in which it was passed over. (From the *New-York Herald*)

Editorial
Publication: *Liberator*
Date of Publication: Friday, 2 January 1846
Title: 'THE BOSTON OLIVE BRANCH'.[19]

Friend Garrison:

In the *Boston Olive Branch* of Dec. 13th, 1845, directly under the editorial head, is a most scandalous article, (which shows to the light of day the dark and malignant heart of the writer) headed in capitals as follows:

ABOLITION RIOT ON BOARD THE BRITISH STEAMER *Cambria* IN AUGUST LAST.

There are conflicting stories about this affair. At best, it was a very disgraceful affair, and cannot but hurt, if not ruin the reputation of C. H. E. Judkins, her commander. There can be no doubt Judkins meant to insult his American passengers; indeed, he told several of them that he did not care a d – n for them; he was independent, and above them all; they could be pleased or not, it mattered not a d – n to him. This was said, because some of them objected to his ringing the bell without notice of the cause, to call them on deck to hear a negro, named Douglass, slander and libel his country, by gross misrepresentations about its laws and institutions. No man of common sense, whose intentions were honest, could suffer his passengers thus to be insulted by a miserable negro, whose only consequence is his ability to tell an unsustained tale of horror, which his present position shows, must have been mainly false. But these political insults are not all which are offered to the travelling public on this line of steamers.

The rest of the article is made up of censures on the same line of steamers in permitting the Governor of Canada to have the ladies' cabin in going out in the *Brittania*; and the editor says he 'gathers these facts from New-York papers' – *Bennett's Herald*, perhaps.[20]

Rev. T. F. Norris,[21] a professed minister of the gospel of peace and good will to man, editor of the *Olive Branch*, an emblem of peace, and a *professed* religious paper, calls his fellow-man a '*miserable negro.*' A man created in the image of God, who made of 'one blood all nations to dwell upon the face of the earth', is thus stigmatized as a '*miserable negro,*' although it is evident he has more of the Anglo-Saxon blood in his veins than the African, and a man of noble powers of mind. 'A negro named Douglass, slander and libel his country, by gross misrepresentation about its laws and institutions.' That is, in plain English, he talked about the institution of slavery, and read to his audience the laws of slaveholding States, in regard to slavery. Shocking affair this, on board a British steamer!!

Rev. T. F. Norris, member and advocate of Odd Fellowship, Free Masonry, &c. &c. and reviler of abolitionists, calls the pro-slavery riot on board the *Cambria* an '*abolition riot,*' and says it 'cannot but hurt, if not ruin the reputation of C. H. E. Judkins'. Probably Rev. T. F. Norris would ruin the reputation of C.H. E. Judkins for his independence and manly character in this affair, if he could, to please slaveholders. 'There are conflicting stories about this affair,' says the editor of the *Olive Branch*. Why does not the editor publish the statement of Mr. Douglass, which appeared in the *Liberator* of Sept. 26, dated Dublin, Sept. 1, relating to this affair? He writes like a man, not like a '*miserable negro,*' nor like a '*miserable*' white man, nor like Rev. T. F. Norris.

'A man is known by the company he keeps,' is an old saying. If I see a stranger come into the community to take up his abode, and observe that he behaves well – takes all pains to get the good opinions of the moral, and religious, and most respectable part of the community in which he resides, caring little or nothing about the opinion of the vicious, the drunkard, or the profane – I set him down as a man possessing a virtuous mind and noble soul; but if I see a man coming among us, who despises the good opinion of the virtuous, the religious, the moral, caring nothing what they think of him, and at the same time is very careful to give no offence to, but seek the good opinion of the most wicked, degraded, tyrannical, debauched class of the community, and associates with them, I am not at a loss to determine his character – he belongs to the most depraved class – he is a vicious man. The latter character, in my opinion, represents the editor of the Boston *Olive Branch*. The above quotation from the *Olive Branch* must give pain and grief to every noble soul, who feels for the oppressed everywhere – who would 'undo the heavy burdens, and let the oppressed go free,' – who wishes to extend liberty to every human being, white or black, throughout the world – who hates the finger of scorn pointed at a man, because he was once a slave, and has a skin not coloured like his own. The above article from the *Olive Branch* gives joy to none but tyrants, slaveholders, and their abettors – to the most corrupt and degraded class in the community – to the scorner of God's poor – to the open reviler of the principles of abolition.

Is there any difficulty in determining to what class the editor of the *Olive Branch* belongs? I think not, especially when I consider his paper to be a vehicle for love stories, love tales, novels, &c. to corrupt the minds of youth; when I consider him to be the champion of Odd Fellowship, Freemasonry, &c. and boasting that his paper has the largest circulation of any paper in New-England.

Before reading the preceding article in the *Olive Branch*, I had bought one copy of the 'Narrative of Frederick Douglass, written by himself,' which I lent to my neighbors; but since I read that article, I have purchased *one dozen copies* more, to spread abroad in the community, that they can see how a '*miserable negro*' can write, and for them to see what a noble soul he possesses, notwithstanding slavery laid her iron grasp upon him in his most early life. It is my firm conviction that Frederick Douglass possesses a soul, so noble, pure and heavenly, that it is as much above that of T. F. Norris, as T. F. Norris is above the common monkey, or the ourang utang [sic].

A FRIEND TO LIBERTY. (from the Boston *Olive Branch*, 13 December 1845)

Letter: Frederick Douglass, Dublin to Thurlow Weed [22]
Date of Publication: Monday, 1 December 1845
Publication: *National Anti-Slavery Standard* (from the *Albany Evening Journal*)
Date of Publication: Thursday, 15 January 1846
Title: 'LETTER FROM A FUGITIVE SLAVE'.[23]

Great Brunswick Street,[24]
  Dublin, Dec. 1st, 1845
  DEAR SIR: – Allow me to thank you for your noble and timely defence of my conduct on board the British steamship *Cambria*, during her passage, 27th August, from Boston, United States, to Liverpool, England; and also to thank you for the friendly manner with which you regard and treat every movement tending to improve and elevate my long enslaved and deeply injured race.

In attempting to speak on board the *Cambria*, I acted in accordance with a sense of duty, and with no desire to wound or injure the feelings of any one on board. My object was to enlighten such of our passengers as wished to be enlightened, and to remove the objections to emancipation, and false impressions concerning Slavery, which I had heard urged during our passage.

Nor should I have done this, but that our popular and gentlemanly commander, as well as a most respectable number of our passengers, gave me a pressing invitation to do so. It is clear that Slavery in our country can only be abolished by creating a public opinion favorable to its abolition, and this can only be done by enlightening the public mind – by exposing the character of Slavery, and enforcing the great principles of justice and humanity against it. To do this with what ability I may possess, is plainly my duty. To shrink from doing so on any fitting occasion, from a mere fear of giving offence to those implicated in the wickedness, would be to betray the sacred trust committed to me, and to act the part of a coward.

The question to be answered is: – Had the passengers, through the Captain, a right to ask me to give them my views of Slavery? To ask the question is to answer it. They had as much right to ask me my views on that subject, as those on any other subject. To deny that they had such right, would be to deny that they had the right to exchange views at all. If they had the right to ask, I had a right to answer, and to answer so as to be understood by those who wished to hear. But then, it will be said, the subject of Slavery is not open to discussion. Who say so? The very men who are continually speaking and writing in its favor? But who has a right to say what subject shall or shall not be discussed on board of a British steamer? Certainly not the slaveholders of South Carolina, nor their slaveholding abettors in New-York, or elsewhere. If anyone has such a right, the ship's commander has. Now, all I did on the occasion in question was in perfect agreement with the wishes of the Captain, and a large number of our most respectable passengers.

The English papers have had much to say respecting the affair, and of course, have in all cases taken a view favorable to myself. I say of course, not because I regard English journalists more disposed to pursue an honorable course in general than those of America; but because they are all committed against negro slavery within their own dominions and elsewhere; and in this, whatever may be said of them in other respects, they hold a decided advantage over those of America.

The whole conduct of the Americans who took part in the mob on board the *Cambria*, was in keeping with the base and cowardly spirit that animated the mob in Lexington, Kentucky, which murderously undertook to extinguish the light of Cassius M. Clay's noble paper,[25] because his denunciations of Slavery were offensive to their slaveholding ears. Not being able to defend their "peculiar institution" with words, they meanly – and I may add foolishly – resort to blows, vainly thinking thus to cover up their infamy. When will they learn that all such attempts only defeat the end which they are intended to promote! as it only calls attention to an institution which can pass without condemnation only as it passes without observation. The selfishness of the slaveholder, and the horrible practices of Slavery, must ever excite in the true heart the deepest indignation, and most absolute disgust.

"To be hated, it needs but to be seen."

Again accept my thanks, and believe me to be most gratefully, yours.
FREDERICK DOUGLASS.

2

DUBLIN

Letter: James Haughton describing a Temperance Meeting
Date of Letter: Monday, 1 September 1845
Publication: *Freeman's Journal*
Date of Publication: Wednesday, 3 September 1845
Title: 'TO THE EDITOR OF THE FREEMAN'.

35, Eccles-street, 1st Sept. 1845.

DEAR Sir – Three great meetings have been recently held in our city, which, owing to the press of other matters on the columns of our papers have been but slightly noticed by the editors of the press. They were held at the Grand Canal Harbour, on the City-quay, and in a field near Donnybrook. An account of the latter was given in the *Nation*.[26] To it the editor appended some friendly remarks, which convey the idea, that these open air teetotal meetings are monotonous affairs.[27] This is an erroneous idea. It is true that these vast assemblages of our people are of a similar character; but they do not, on that account, become tiresome; there is a moral beauty about them which prevents this; and there is besides, something very pleasing and very noble in the view of thousands of human beings collected together for the furtherance of a good object. The eye does not soon tire with looking at a beautiful prospect, composed of lofty hills, of cultivated plains, and wooded vallies [sic]; neither does it turn away in disgust at the constantly recurring sight of the rolling ocean; nor is it easily fatigued by the pencilled beauties of a finely executed picture. To my mind these are not more enchanting than a congregation of happy faces collected under the canopy of Heaven, and brightening up under the influence of conscious integrity of purpose. To me, it seems, that a meeting of a large number of men and women assembled, for the promotion of peace and good order, must ever be a sight beautiful to look at; a sight demanding the sympathy of the patriot, the politician, and the press.

The advocates of teetotalism do regret that the astonishing progress of that great movement does not excite deeper feeling of interest in our public writers, so that all our population should be constantly informed of its progress in different localities. It is a movement which has already shed abroad more happiness in Ireland than any other which could be named, and it is calculated beyond any other agency yet known, to elevate and enlighten the moral and intellectual character of our people. It is a movement which should interest all good men in its favour. I trust its advocates are not influenced by the paltry feelings of vanity which seek for personal notoriety, but that the noble feeling of anxiety to carry onward a great principle, conducive to human happiness, actuates them. It is for this purpose that I desire and entreat the more zealous cooperation of the press; I believe it cannot be more worthily or more usefully engaged; and I am sure its talented writers can readily invest our meetings with a constantly renewed and living interest. The advocates of teetotalism are often accused of overheated enthusiasm, but it is by men who do not witness our proceedings; who look coldly on at a distance, and who need to have their icy imaginations a little thawed under the enlivening influences of our open air meetings. They are noble meetings, they are glorious meetings. I hope the people will long appreciate their value, and that they will continue gladly and joyously to assemble at the call of the good men, Father Mathew[28] and Father Spratt.[29]

I have not a very poetic imagination, but I am not so unimpassioned as to feel cold on witnessing such a scene as occurred at Celbridge yesterday. Many of your city readers are acquainted with that locality. They have wandered among the beauties of the Salmon Leap, and sleepiness did not steal over them as they listened to the "monotonous" roll of its boiling waters, and they have enjoyed the many other natural and highly cultivated beautiful scenes in that neighbourhood. Mr. Brennan, who is much devoted to the cause of teetotalism, induced Father Spratt to hold a meeting at Celbridge; notices of his intention to do so were posted up some days beforehand, and the consequence was that the entire population of that district were in motion yesterday, and at three o'clock a great concourse of people assembled in a field a short distance from the village, and which was kindly lent for the occasion, by Mr. Cooney. Some five or six bands, some of whom came a distance of several miles, met us; they collected the multitude as they passed along, and when we all assembled together we were indeed an imposing concourse. Many thousands were there. Among them were a considerable number of elegantly attired ladies, who came on private cars, to witness the joyousness of the scene. I hope they carried away with them some impressions that will make them, if they be not already members of that body, of which Father Mathew is the acknowledged head and leader, think seriously of their duties to society in that respect.

Our meeting at Celbridge was rendered remarkable by the presence of Frederic [sic] Douglass, a coloured man, who was, only a few years ago, a slave in America, but who had the manliness and the courage to assert his right to liberty by running away from bondage. I say manliness and courage; for it needs the exercise of both to risk the perils and dangers which the poor Negro must encounter when he determines to flee away from his enslaver. Mr. Douglass is a fine-looking man, possessed of a full flow of natural eloquence, which must make him a popular orator before any audience. He spoke warmly in favour of teetotalism, and was much applauded. He said, feelingly, he was not accustomed to such kind treatment from white men.

123

A large number of members were added to our society. I expect the railroad contractors will soon discover the value of Father Spratt's labours in that locality. We remained about three hours on the ground, when several of us repaired to the hospitable residence of the Rev. Mr. Woods, in Celbridge, by whom we were courteously and elegantly entertained at dinner; and, after spending a day and an evening which will be long remembered with pleasure by us and by thousands, the friends who accompanied Father Spratt from town returned with him, and repaired to local temperance meetings, to give them an account of our happy day. Father Spratt again delivered the pledge in Bride-street and French-street halls. The latter was greatly crowded by a well-dressed and attentive audience.

I hope, my dear Sir, you will soon give this letter a place in your columns. As the bee goes about from flower to flower gathering sweets, yet stealing no beauties away, so would I recommend all men to renew their store of happiness, by extracting fresh supplies at temperance meetings, at those exhaustless stores whence we may ever draw supplies, and never make ourselves unwelcome visitors.

Faithfully yours, JAMES HAUGHTON.

Anti-Slavery Meeting
Lecturer: Frederick Douglass
Date of Lecture: Wednesday, 3 September 1845
Location: Royal Exchange, Dublin
Publication: *Freeman's Journal*
Date of Publication: Monday, 8 September 1845
Title: 'SLAVERY'.

The Hibernian Anti-Slavery Society held their usual monthly meeting in the Royal Exchange,[30] on Wednesday night.[31] The lecture-room was crowded to excess; very many persons must have gone away for want of accommodation. The great attraction of the evening was Mr. Frederick Douglass, an American of colour, who was but a few years ago a slave. He stated it as a curious circumstance in his life, that on that very day, seven years ago, he ran away, or took away his own body and limbs from his master in Baltimore. Mr. Douglass is a man highly gifted by nature with natural eloquence, and he details the evils of slavery, and its complete violation of all the rights of humanity, with a manly dignity of manner, which must win him the attention of any audience before whom he may appear. He has come to Ireland to plead the cause of the oppressed black man, and we can assure him of a hearty welcome. He is accompanied by Mr. James Buffum. They were both received by the meeting in such a manner as must have satisfied them that they have the sympathy of the Irish people in their worthy labors. The chair was taken by Mr. R. D. Webb, who introduced these strangers to the meeting. Mr. Douglass spoke for about three-quarters of an hour, and was most enthusiastically cheered throughout. When he spoke of O'Connell as the admired of all who loved liberty and hated oppression the world over, the assembly arose and expressed their hearty approval of the noble course pursued by the Liberator in several rounds of applause. We cannot afford space for even an outline of Mr. Douglass's eloquent and feeling address; he defined what slavery was, saying it was a system which made a chattel of a man – which tore the husband and wife asunder, and which deprived men of all of their rights as human beings; and he asked, should not such a system as this be abolished? which appeal was met by a willing response in the affirmative – indeed, we have never seen a more enthusiastic meeting of our fellow-citizens.

Mr. Douglass was followed by Mr. Buffum, who also gave some interesting and some most appalling details of slavery in his country. The Chairman made a solemn and beautiful appeal to his auditors as Irishmen, as patriots, and as true lovers of liberty, to be consistent advocates of freedom, and to spurn with contempt the sympathy of the guilty slave-holder.

Mr. James Haughton read a beautiful poem on slavery from the *Argus*. He urged the people to give some practical proof of their anxiety to procure liberty for the black man, and showed them how they could do so by giving up the use of tobacco, which is slave-grown produce. He described tobacco as a filthy weed, and the use of it as a custom abhorrent to all feelings of delicacy and cleanliness – that it was, moreover, an expensive luxury, which could be readily dispensed with – but, above all, he implored the people to give it up for the sake of the poor, oppressed black men. Mr. Haughton also encouraged the people by *example* and precept to establish linen and woollen articles for cotton in their clothing, for the double purpose of discouraging slave-grown cotton, and encouraging the use of home manufactured and home produced yarn and woollen goods. The meeting separated at ten o'clock.

Anti-Slavery Meeting
Lecturer: Frederick Douglass
Date of Lecture: Wednesday, 3 September 1845
Location: Royal Exchange, Dublin
Publication: *Pilot*
Date of Publication: Monday, 8 September 1845
Title: 'Slavery'.

The Hibernian Anti-Slavery Society held their usual monthly meeting in the Royal Exchange on Wednesday. The lecture room was crowded to excess; very many persons must have gone away for want of accommodation. The great attraction of the evening was Mr. Frederic [sic] Douglass, an American of colour, who was but a few years ago a slave. He stated it as a curious circumstance in his life that on that very day seven years ago he ran away, or took away his own body and limbs, from his master in Baltimore. Mr Douglass is a man highly gifted by nature with natural eloquence, and he details the evils of slavery, and its complete violation of all the rights of humanity, with a manly dignity of manner, which must win him the attention of any audience before whom he may appear. He has come to Ireland to plead the cause of the oppressed black man and we can assure him of a hearty welcome. He is accompanied by Mr. James

Buffon [sic]. They were both received by the meeting on that night in such a manner must have satisfied them that they have the sympathy of the Irish people in their worthy labours. The chair was taken by R. D. Webb, who introduced these strangers to the meeting. Mr. Douglass spoke for about three quarters of an hour, and he was most enthusiastically cheered throughout. When he spoke of O'Connell as the admired of all who loved liberty and hated oppression the world over the assembly rose and expressed their hearty approval of the noble course pursued by the Liberator in several rounds of applause. We cannot afford space for even an outline of Mr. Douglass's eloquent and feeling address – he defined what slavery was, saying it was a system that made a chattel of a man, which tore the husband and wife asunder, and which deprived men of all their rights as human beings; and he asked, should not a system as this be abolished? which appeal was met with a willing response in the affirmative. Indeed we have never seen a more enthusiastic meeting of our fellow citizens. Mr Douglas [sic] was followed by Mr. Buffon [sic] who also gave some very interesting, and some most appalling, details of slavery in his country. The Chairman made a solemn and beautiful appeal to his auditors, as Irishmen, as patriots, and as true lovers of liberty, to be the consistent advocates of freedom, and to spurn, with contempt, the sympathy of the guilty slave-holder.

Mr James Haughton read a beautiful and interesting poem on slavery from the *Argus*.[32] He strongly urged the people to give some real practical proof of their anxiety to procure liberty for the black man, and shewed them how they could by giving up the use of tobacco which is slave grown produce. He described it as a filthy weed, and the use of it a custom abhorrent to all feelings of delicacy and cleanliness; that it was moreover an expensive luxury which could be readily disposed with, above all, he implored the people to give it up for the sake of the poor oppressed black man. Mr. Haughton also encouraged the people by *example* and precept to substitute linen and woollen articles for cotton in their clothing, for the double purpose of discouraging slave grown cotton and encouraging the use of home manufactured and home produced yarn and woolen goods.

The meeting separated at 10 o'clock. The room was overcrowded throughout the evening, and notice was given that Mr. Douglass would speak there again on that day week.

Anti-Slavery Meeting
Lecturer: Frederick Douglass
Date of Lecture: Wednesday, 3 September 1845
Location: Royal Exchange, Dublin
Publication: *Drogheda Argus and Leinster Journal*
Date of Publication: Saturday, 13 September 1845
No Title.

The Hibernian Anti-Slavery Society held their usual monthly meeting in the Royal Exchange, on Wednesday night. The lecture-room was crowded to excess;

very many persons must have gone away for want of accommodation. The great attraction of the evening was Mr. Frederick Douglass, an American of colour, who was but a few years ago a slave. He stated it as a curious circumstance in his life, that on that very day seven years ago he ran away, or took away his own body and limbs from his master in Baltimore. Mr. Douglas [sic] is a man highly gifted by nature with natural eloquence, and he details the evils of slavery, and its complete violation of all the rights of humanity, with manly dignity of manner, which must win him the attention of any audience before whom he may appear. He has come to Ireland to plead the cause of the oppressed black man, and we can assure him of a hearty welcome. He is accompanied by Mr. James Buffum. They were both received by the meeting in such a manner as must have satisfied them that they have the sympathy of the Irish people in their worthy labours. – from *Freeman*.

Anti-Slavery Meeting
Lecturer: Frederick Douglass
Date of Lecture: Friday, 5 September 1845
Location: Mechanics' Institute, Dublin [33]
Date: Friday, 5 September 1845
Publication: *Waterford Chronicle* [34]
Date of Publication: Saturday, 6 September 1845
No Title.

There was a meeting of the Antislavery society held in the lecture room of the Mechanics Institute last evening.[35] The room (a pretty large one) was crowded. Among the speakers was a coloured man named Frederick Douglas [sic] who had escaped from slavery, as he told the meeting, that day seven years ago. He had been a slave in the state of Maryland and he ran away from that into the state of Massachusetts, as the northern states are bound by federal agreement to deliver up runaway slaves, if reclaimed, he had continued his flight to Ireland where at last he thought himself safe. He spoke with feeling and energy, though a little incoherently, of the condition of the negro, whether free or in bonds, in the boasted land of liberty, saying that there was no place of sanctuary for them, neither the altar of God, or the battlefield of liberty.

Advertisement
Publication: *Freeman's Journal*
Date of Publication: Monday, 8 September 1845
Title: 'American Slavery'.

American Slavery. Frederick Douglass, recently a Slave in the United States, intends to deliver a Lecture on American Slavery in FRIENDS' MEETING HOUSE, EUSTACE STREET TOMORROW (Tuesday) EVENING, the 9th instant at Eight o'clock.

Doors to be open at half past Seven o'clock. Free Admission. No Collection.

Anti-Slavery Meeting
Lecturer: Frederick Douglass
Date of Lecture: Tuesday, 9 September 1845
Location: Friends' Meeting House, Dublin
Publication: *Freeman's Journal*
Date of Publication: Wednesday, 10 September 1845
Title: 'AMERICAN SLAVERY'.

Yesterday evening, Mr Frederick Douglas [sic], a young man of colour, who described himself as being formerly a slave in America, delivered a lecture in the Friends' Meeting House, Eustace Street, on the subject of slavery in the United States. The house was tolerably well filled, and a considerable portion of the audience were respectably dressed females. The speaker entered on the subject at some length, and depicted in very fervent terms, the horrors of slavery drawing his illustrations from his own experience, while labouring under the 'lash' of the 'driver'! His narrative, which almost entirely consisted of personal adventures, interspersed with some general observations on the abominable system, was listened to with great attention, and drew forth repeated intimations of applause from his sober auditors.

Mr. Douglass, by the natural intelligence which he possesses, and the manner in which he communicated his views, never permitted the interests of his hearers to flag, while he denounced with vigour and energy, the hideous system of slavery as inconsistent with religion, morality, and social order, and proved that man – no matter what colour the sun may have burned upon his brow, or in what clime his breath may have been first drawn, was a free agent, entitled to the free exercise of his own energy for the advancement of his own happiness and advantage, as he is capable of exhibiting the highest mental and moral qualifications.

Anti-Slavery Meeting
Lecturer: Frederick Douglass
Date of Lecture: Tuesday, 9 September 1845
Location: Friends' Meeting House, Dublin
Publication: *Dublin Evening Packet and Correspondent*
Date: Thursday, 11 September 1845
Title: 'ANTI-SLAVERY MEETING'.[36]

A great anti-slavery meeting was held on Tuesday evening, under the auspices of the Hibernian Anti-Slavery Society, in the Friends' Meeting-house, Eustace-street,[37] it being lent most kindly by that benevolent Society for the truly Christian purpose of assisting to free the oppressed – of shaking off the chains from the limbs of the black man wherever he is held in cruel bondage. This Meeting-house is very neat and commodious. It was crowded in every part by a most respectable audience who manifested the interest they felt on the subject before them, and their respect for the feelings of the Society of Friends, by a quiet and silent attention to the speakers.

The proceedings were opened by Mr. R. D. Webb, who, in a short introductory address, introduced to the meeting two American gentlemen, (Mr. Frederick Douglass and Mr. James Buffum.) The meeting was called for the purpose of hearing these gentlemen give some details relative to slavery in their country, they having visited Ireland for that purpose. Mr. Douglass is a colored man, who only a few years ago was a slave. His frame is robust, he is above the middle size, and has a very pleasing expression of countenance.

We can only give a mere outline of his manly and eloquent address, which occupied an hour and twenty-five minutes, during which time he deeply interested his audience. He is possessed of great natural eloquence, and his language and style bespeak a cultivated mind. Yet he apologized to his hearers by telling them that he had never received a single day's school education. He is now about twenty-seven years of age, and it is now just seven years since he ran away from a master who denied him all the rights of a human being – who had scarred his back with stripes, the marks of which would remain with him through life. Mr. Douglass combated the argument which said that Irishmen have no right to meddle with slavery in America, and said the same reasoning would confine action on the subject to the States in which it existed, which would be tantamount to its eternal perpetuation. He spoke of Irish sympathy and Irish agitation on the subject with warm and grateful feelings; and said they were of incalculable value to the cause of freedom in his country, if he had a country, for he was, even now, liable in all the States of the Union to be seized and carried away into interminable bondage. He declared that the principles of abolition Societies in America were peace principles, that they only sought to obtain their ends by moral and Christian means, by bringing the public opinion of the world to bear upon the iniquitous system of slavery in America. That these means were, under the blessing of Almighty God, producing the desired results: and as a proof of this, he stated that the prejudice against colour in the free States engendered by slavery in the south, was greatly mitigated. Only two years ago, a coloured man, and a white man too, if he kept company with a black brother, was liable to be insulted wherever he went, to be dragged out of railroad cars, and other public conveyances, to be kicked and abused and spit upon. The wrist of his own right arm was broken by a brutal outrage of the kind on his person. But now matters are happily changed; the coloured man can now travel without insult in most of the free States. This happy change has been caused by improved public opinion – by glorious efforts and agitation in Ireland and in England, and in Scotland, on the question, as well as in America. Americans are very sensitive to the opinion of the world. He implored his audience to keep up this opinion, by making every American slaveholder, every American apologist of slavery who sets his feet upon our soil, feel that he was in a land of freedom, among a people who hated oppression, and who loved liberty; liberty for all, for the black man as well as the white man – to make them feel that they breathed a pure anti-slavery atmosphere.

Here Mr. Douglass alluded to some proofs of Irish honest feeling on this subject, which elicited some expressions of applause, but these were promptly suppressed because of the place in which the meeting was held. Mr. Douglass related a circumstance which occurred on board the *Cambria*, on which vessel he and his friend had taken passage from America. Some slave-owners and a few advocates of their vile system were on board, but a greater number of the passengers were friends of liberty, and his presence among them excited a great interest; they were anxious, on hearing a history of his life, to hear him deliver a lecture on slavery. This, after a request from the captain, he consented to; but such is the impudent and overbearing nature of slaveholders, that these men actually threatened to throw him overboard for daring to speak in their presence. This desperate resolve was quietly met by a noble-hearted Irishman, a Mr. Gough, who told the reckless trafficker in human flesh and bones, that two could play at that work. So great was the violence exhibited by these bad men, that the captain had to call on his boatswain to bring up the shackles to put them in irons, to prevent a fatal exhibition of their wicked feelings. Here was a striking illustration of slaveholding sentiment. When men could act thus on the deck of a British ship, and within sight of the green hills of Ireland, we may imagine what must be their brutality in Cuba and New Orleans.

Mr. Douglass was followed by Mr. Buffum, who exhibited a collar of iron, with three long prongs, which was taken from off the neck of a young female slave who ran away and escaped out of the house of bondage. Some manacles, and a whip – whose lashes were twisted thongs of leather – almost as hard as iron; he held these up and rattled them before the audience, and said – Abolitionists in America are charged with infidelity; but they repudiated the slander, they loved Christianity, the Christianity of the blessed Savior, but they disowned the Christianity which used such irons as these to manacle their brethren, and such whips as that to tear the flesh of their fellow-men. Mr. Buffum spoke at some length in an interesting strain. He and his friend intend to remain some time in Ireland to enlist our feelings in their Godlike mission, and as they come under the introduction of the Hibernian Anti-Slavery Society, and have been lent the Meeting-house of the benevolent Society of Friends, the public may rest satisfied that they are mere matters of truth, whose statements may be relied on.

The proceedings of the evening were terminated about 10 o'clock by an appeal by Mr. James Haughton, to the ladies who favored the meeting with their presence, to send in articles for the Boston Anti-Slavery Bazaar, before the 13th of November, to Mrs. Allen, High-street; Mrs. Webb, Great Brunswick-street; or to the Messrs. Haughton, Eccles-street, who would take charge of them, and forward them to America. He doubted not their judgment as well their feelings was warmed on the present occasion, and he entreated them not allow their sympathies for the oppressed to be a mere matter of feeling, but to exhibit it in a tangible manner. We are glad that our countrymen evince, on all suitable occasions, a just abhorrence of slavery, and we trust the wants of those at home, who are in need of help, will not be forgotten.

Anti-Slavery Meeting
Lecturer: Frederick Douglass
Date of Lecture: Tuesday, 9 September 1845
Location: Friends' Meeting House
Publication: *Limerick Chronicle*
Date of Publication: Saturday, 13 September 1845
No Title.

An anti-slavery meeting was held on Tuesday evening, under the auspices of the Hibernian Anti-Slavery society, in the Friends Meeting-house, Eustace street, when Mr. R. D. Webb introduced to the meeting two American gentlemen, Mr. Frederick Douglass and Mr. James Buffum. Mr. Douglas [sic] is a coloured man, who a few years ago was a slave. Both denounced the slave system, and exhibited a collar of iron with three prongs, which was taken from off the neck of a young female slave, who ran away and escaped out of the house of bondage.

Anti-Slavery Meeting
Lecturer: Frederick Douglass
Date of Lecture: Tuesday, 9 September 1845
Location: Friends' Meeting House, Dublin
Publication: *Nenagh Guardian*
Date of Publication: Wednesday, 17 September 1845
No Title.

An anti-slavery meeting was held on Tuesday evening under the auspices of the Hibernian Anti-Slavery Society, in the Friends' Meeting House, Eustace-street, when Mr. R. D. Webb introduced to the meeting two American gentlemen, Mr. Frederick Douglas [sic] and Mr. James Buffum. Mr. Douglas is a coloured man who, a few years ago, was a slave. Both denounced the slave system, and exhibited a collar of iron with three prongs, which was taken off the neck of a young female slave, who ran away and escaped from a house of bondage.

Advertisement
Publication: *Freeman's Journal*
Date of Publication: Friday, 12 September 1845
Title: 'American Slavery'.

AMERICAN SLAVERY FREDERICK DOUGLASS, recently a Slave in the United States, intends to deliver a Second Lecture on American Slavery, in the Friends' Meeting House, EUSTACE-STREET, on THIS EVENING (Friday), the

12th instant, at Eight o'clock. Doors to be open at half-past Seven o'clock. Admission Free. No collection.

Anti-Slavery Meeting
Lecturer: Frederick Douglass
Date of Lecture: Friday, 12 September 1845
Location: Friends' Meeting House
Publication: *Dublin Evening Post*
Date of Publication: Saturday, 13 September 1845
Title: 'Anti-Slavery Meeting'.

ANTI-SLAVERY MEETING. Another very numerously attended Anti-Slavery meeting was held yesterday evening in the Friends' Meeting House, to hear a lecture on the horrors of slavery by Mr. Frederick Douglass, a man of colour, who was formerly a slave himself.

In his lecture of last night, Mr. Douglass alluded in forcible language to the Anti-Christian nature of slavery, and he denied the Christian name to slaveholders. He described the nature of the system, and put his audience in full possession of it, by illustrations, taken from his own personal experience while in bondage, and reading some extracts from papers published in the slave-holding states of his country – which proved in a clear and convincing manner, the horrible nature of the system, and he emphatically asked – can men who sustain such a system as this be Christian?

Mr. James Baffan [sic] also addressed the meeting on the same subject. Mr. R. D. Webb and Mr. James Haughton accompanied their American friends, and the public have their guarantee for the full respectability of the parties, whose object in visiting this country is to enlist Irish sympathy on behalf of the oppressed.

Anti-Slavery Meeting
Lecturer: Frederick Douglass
Date: Friday, 12 September 1845
Location: Friends' Meeting House, Dublin
Publication: *Dublin Evening Packet and Correspondent*
Date of Publication: Tuesday, 16 September 1845
Title: 'Slavery'.

Another very large anti-slavery meeting was held on Friday evening, in the Friends' Meeting House. The large house was quite insufficient to contain all who assembled, many had to go away for want of even standing room. Nor are we surprised at this anxiety, for Mr Frederick Douglass, the coloured man, who was a slave only seven years ago, is a man of extraordinary natural powers. His eloquence is surprising, and he uses chaste and eloquent language. He is a striking evidence that God has not placed the black man in a grade below the whites in the scale of creation, and that it is monstrous for the latter to hold the former in bondage on any such pretence. In his last lecture, Mr Douglass, alluded in forcible language, to the anti-Christian nature of slavery, and he denied the Christian name to slave-holders. He explained the nature of the system, and put his audience in full possession of it, by illustrations taken from his own personal experience, and by reading some extracts of newspapers published in the slaveholding states, which proved in a convincing manner the horrible nature of the system. He then emphatically asked, can men who sustain such a system be Christians? Can the man who ties up men and women, and even girls not more than seventeen years of age, who lashes them until the blood streams down their backs – who brands them with red hot irons hissing into their flesh – who cuts off their ears – who puts iron collars around their necks, and heavy chains upon their bodies – who hunts them with bloodhounds trained for the purpose, and who shoots them mercilessly when they refuse to surrender, (all of which horrifying charges can be proved in the clearest manner) – can these monsters be Christians? Even in a place of worship the audience had much trouble in retraining their feelings, as Mr Douglass presented to them these truths in glowing and eloquent words. He called upon the people of Ireland to demand of every American landing on our shores, are you an abolitionist? Are you prepared to vote for the immediate freedom of 2,800,000 of your brethren held in bondage, and to reject the social or Christian fellowship of all who could not answer in the affirmative? My friends, said Mr Douglass, we need your help in this matter; the churches in my country are against us; they torture the Bible in support of slavery. Public opinion is against us; it sanctions whipping, branding, and shooting slaves, it allows the father to be torn from his wife and children; it permits the sundering of the marriage tie; it sustains all manner of inequity in regard to the coloured man. We want your assistance and you can assist us effectually. My countrymen are very sensitive to the public opinion of the people of this land; they cannot stand your scorching rebukes, if you be honest. Tell the pro-slavery clergymen, or him who excuses slavery, that you won't listen to his preaching, and let all Christian churches do this, for they are all guilty in my country. Let Americans be made to FEEL, on landing in Ireland, that Irishmen and Irishwomen are all in earnest, and you will do good, real good, to the cause of freedom.

Mr James Buffum also addressed the meeting for some time, and the interest of the meeting was sustained for over two hours.

We recommend our fellow citizens who have not heard Mr Douglass to avail themselves of any opportunity they may have of doing so. If a small charge were made for admittance, it might prevent the over-crowding of any room in which he spoke; but of course this plan could not be adopted in a place of worship.

Mr R. D. Webb and Mr James Haughton accompanied their American friends; and the public have their guarantees for the perfect integrity of the parties, whose object in visiting this country is to enlist Irish sympathy on behalf of the oppressed, in which object we trust they should not be disappointed.

Anti-Slavery Meeting
Lecturer: Frederick Douglass
Date of Lecture: Friday, 12 September 1845
Location: Friends' Meeting House, Dublin
Publication: *Tipperary Free Press*
Date of Publication: Wednesday, 17 September 1845
Title: 'Anti-Slavery Meeting'.

Another very numerously attended Anti-Slavery meeting was held on yesterday evening in the Friends' Meeting House to hear a lecture on the horrors of slavery by Mr Frederick Douglas [sic], a man of colour who was formerly a slave himself.

In his lecture of last night, Mr Douglas alluded in forcible language to the Anti-Christian nature of slavery, and he denied the Christian name to slave-holders. He described the nature of the system, and put his audience in full possession by illustrations, taken from his own personal experiences while in bondage, and by reading some extracts from papers in the slave-holding states of his country – which proved in a clear and convincing manner, the horrible nature of the system, and then he emphatically asked, Can men who sustain a system such as this be Christians?

Mr James Buffan [sic] also addressed the meeting on the same subject.

Mr R. D. Webb and Mr James Haughton accompanied their American friends, and the public have their full guarantee for the respectability of the parties, whose object in visiting this county is to enlist Irish sympathy on behalf of the oppressed. *Dublin Evening Post.*

Editorial
Publication: *Pilot* (from the *Waterford Freeman*)
Date of Publication: Friday, 12 September 1845
Title: 'Ireland and American Slavery'.

IRELAND AND AMERICAN SLAVERY. (From the *WATERFORD FREEMAN* of 10 September 1845.)

We detest slavery, be the victim of its crushing rule the black man or the white. But we question the effect which the reclamation of a nation of white slaves may produce on the condition of their black brother-serfs in a hemisphere distant four thousand miles. We are not so selfish as to recommend the principle of 'charity begins at home,' though we fear that in this case the erratic benevolence of the white slaves of Ireland has done more harm than good for the objects of its solicitude. We know we tread on delicate ground. We say again that we abominate slavery in whatever guise it may appear; but, in our present helplessness, if we do more than exclaim against it, our exclamations may as well not be accompanied with ingratitude or insult. A nation in bondage has a right to obtain all legitimate aid – evil men may be made in the hands of Providence the instrument of good: a people in serfdom cannot afford to make new enemies, especially when they are begetting new hostility for themselves without benefitting the clients whose cause they advocate.

We have made these remarks in consequence of reading certain speeches at anti-slavery lectures lately held in the metropolis. It is unnecessary to re-state our feelings to slavery, but we regret that the language lately held in Ireland is embittering, if anything, the condition of the slave, whilst raising a hostile sentiment against our country. We wish with our whole heart that the abolitionists in America would agitate the Union, and make a simultaneous call upon the government of that Republic to commence doing what the English did – buy up the manumission of the negroes, or pass a law enabling the slave to purchase his freedom. The enlightened slaveholders of England did not give up *their* interest in their human cattle without them being well paid, and it is a sad consideration, yet a natural event, that the uncouth and lawless slave breeders and traders of the southern States of America should not be less selfish than the aristocrats of Britain. Yet such is human nature. *Free* Ireland, at all events, liberated, unprovincialised, would send forth a stronger and more persuasive voice upon this as well as other matters, than can now be expected. In this we are glad to see our honest and sensible contemporary, the *Tipperary Free Press*, agree with us:

"When we are ourselves free, let us then engage in any struggle to erase the sin of slavery from every land. But, until then, our own liberation is that for which we should take counsel and work steadily."

Editorial
Publication: *Southern Reporter and Cork Commercial Courier*
Date of Publication: Saturday, 13 September 1845
Title: 'Compendium'.

Mr. Frederick Douglas [sic], a young man of colour, who was formerly a slave in the United States, is in Dublin delivering lectures on the condition of those with whom, fortunately for himself, he no longer is classed. He narrated several personal adventures and denounced strongly the cruel system and the bitterness of which he had himself experienced. His address was listened to with uninterrupted attention.

Advertisement
Publication: *Freeman's Journal*
Date of Publication: Wednesday, 17 September 1845
Title: 'American Slavery'.

AMERICAN SLAVERY. TO give the Public an opportunity of hearing an Address on American Slavery, from Frederick DOUGLAS [sic], recently a Slave in the United States, the Hibernian Anti-Slavery Society has engaged the MUSIC HALL,[38] LOWER ABBEY-STREET, for THIS EVENING (Wednesday), the 17th inst.[39] Doors to be open at half-past Seven o'clock. Proceedings to commence at

Eight. This step has been taken in consequence of the inconveniently crowded state of the Royal Exchange Room, last Wednesday evening. To defray the expenses, the admission will be by Tickets, to be had at the door – 4*d.* each to the body of the house, and 2*d.* to the gallery.

Anti-Slavery Meeting
Lecturer: Frederick Douglass
Date of Lecture: Wednesday, 17 September 1845
Location: Music Hall, Dublin
Publication: *Freeman's Journal*
Date of Publication: Thursday, 18 September 1845
Title: 'Anti-Slavery Meeting'.

Last night a meeting was held in the Music Hall, Abbey-street, for the purpose of hearing an address on American slavery from Mr. Frederick Douglas [sic], a runaway slave. The chair was taken by Mr. Haughton, who, in a neat speech, bore testimony to the credulity of the refugee who was about to occupy their attention.

Mr. Douglas, who was loudly cheered on coming forward, entered on an elaborate and eloquent narrative of his late bondage. He had not, he said, been the worst treated of the American slaves, and yet his back had been mangled with the lash. The relation of master and slave as it existed in the United States was that of inexorable dominion on the one hand, and entire degradation on the other. The slave was a vendible article, and was ranked as an implement among his masters' goods. There were three millions of these slaves in America, notwithstanding the declaration of American independence, and they were habitually submitted to punishments alike inhuman and degrading. The speaker here entered into a long and horrifying description of their punishments, substantiating his statements by reading advertisements from the American newspapers. He likewise exhibited, amid great sensation, several instruments of torture in common use in the slave states.

Having resumed, he repudiated the opinion that the slave holder treated his slave kindly as regarded his moral or physical condition. In America public opinion was in favour of slavery; the public writer, and the minister of religion, sanctioned and supported it. The word of God had been profaned, then, to the purposes of slavery, and the clergyman justified the flogging of the negro, by quoting from Holy Writ – "He who knoweth his master's will, and doeth it not, shall be beaten with many stripes." Yet in that country there was a powerful church: there were many sects, differing in points of faith and discipline, but agreeing in principles of human oppression. The Methodists in America supported slavery, and when he exposed their conduct the other night to their friends in Dublin, he had the door of the meeting house closed against him, and he was denied any further sanction from their body. But whatever he might incur from them, he would not sacrifice his friends now in chains, and perhaps writhing under the lash while he spoke, to any fear of personal inconvenience (loud cheers). While he lived, he would plead for those whom he left behind him in bondage, and if the Methodists of Dublin closed their doors against him, it showed that they dreaded his disclosures about the members of their body in America (cheers).[40] He loved religion – that religion founded by Him whose commands were of love, and peace, and mercy, but he hated with his whole heart a slave-supporting religion (tremendous cheers). He wanted the friends of freedom in this country to test and question the American Methodists or other Christians [when they came to Ireland] as to whether they supported slavery at home. That was a fair and plain question to put to them, and the worth of their religious professions, would be proved by their answers, supported by their acts. After some further observations Mr. Douglas resumed his seat amid great cheering.

Mr Buffon [sic], an American gentleman, addressed the meeting in corroboration of the statements of the last speaker.

Mr Haughton announced that it was the intention of the opponents of slavery in any shape to hold another meeting like the present in a few days, and he trusted that all who had the interests of human liberty at heart would aid in diffusing it over the whole world.

Advertisement
Publication: *Nation*
Date of Publication: Saturday, 20 September 1845
Title: 'American Slavery'.

American Slavery. – Frederick Douglass, recently a slave in the United States, intends to deliver another lecture, in the Music Hall, Lower Abbey street, on Tuesday evening next, 23d instant, at 8 o'clock. Doors to be open at half-past seven o'clock. Admission, by tickets, to be had at the door. Promenade – four pence. Gallery, two pence.

Temperance Meeting
Date of Meeting: Sunday, 21 September 1845
Location: Broadstone, Dublin
Publication: *Dublin Weekly Register*
Date of Publication: Saturday, 27 September 1845
Title: 'Meeting at Broadstone'.

Pursuant to public notice, one of the largest meetings which Dr Spratt [41] has held within the last twelve months took place on Sunday evening with all the wanted éclat and spirit stirring display, at the Canal Harbour, Broadstone. The crowds were immense, and the bands numerous; the streets leading to the place of the meeting were thronged by all classes of the population. The lovers of temperance and domestic happiness looked on with pleasure and enthusiasm, and the congregated thousands were addressed by the Very Rev. Dr Spratt, Messrs Haughton, Webb, Douglas [sic], an American, and Barry. Twelve hundred persons took the total abstinence pledge. The meeting separated at 7. o'clock.

Temperance Meeting
Date of Meeting: Sunday, 21 September 1845
Location: Broadstone, Dublin
Publication: *Nation*
Date of Publication: Saturday, 27 September 1845
Title: 'Progress of Temperance in Dublin'.

On Sunday evening last, at four o'clock, an open-air meeting – one of the largest which Dr. Spratt has had for the last twelve months – took place at the canal harbour, Broadstone. The directors of the Royal Canal kindly opened the gates of the harbour, and erected a large platform for the occasion. The assembled thousands were addressed by the very Rev. Dr. Spratt, Messrs. Haughton, Webb, Douglas [sic] (an American), and Barry. It was computed that about twelve hundred persons took the 'total abstinence pledge' on the occasion at the hands of the Rev. Dr. Spratt. Several bands played lively airs during the evening, and all separated quietly about seven o'clock. Such continuous success in the good work to which he so strenuously devotes himself must be very gratifying to Dr. Spratt; and to every right-thinking Irishman it is a proud reflection that the cause of temperance is progressing steadily and surely.

Temperance Meeting
Date of Meeting: Sunday, 21 September 1845
Publication: *Tablet* [42]
Date of Publication: Saturday, 27 September 1845
Title: 'TEMPERANCE'.

PROGRESS OF TOTAL ABSTINENCE. – (From our Dublin Correspondent.) – On Sunday evening last, at four o'clock, one of the largest and most effective Temperance meetings in or near Dublin for many years was held at the Royal Canal Harbour, Broadstone. The assembled crowd was immense, and the ladies and gentlemen expressed their opinion that this was a spectacle truly delightful to behold, a scene the most charming and the most captivating, to witness thousands of human beings assembled for the purpose of promoting the glory of God and the happiness of mortals! The Directors of the Royal Canal kindly opened the gates of the harbour, and erected a large platform for the reception of the Very Rev. Dr. Spratt and his friends, the Temperance advocates. At four o'clock the Very Rev. Dr. Spratt arrived amidst great cheering, accompanied by Messrs. Houghton [sic], Webb, Douglass, Barry, &c., &c., and several bands playing lively and national airs. Dr. Spratt addressed the assembly in strong, clear, and energetic terms, on the cheering prospect of the good cause. He was followed by Mr. Houghton [sic], who spoke long and pathetically on the grateful theme. The first batch was then formed and pledged, making about five hundred. Subsequently Messrs. Barry, Webb, and Douglas [sic], addressed the meeting, and other batches were pledged, making in all about twelve hundred who thus became disciples of Father Mathew. About seven o'clock the masses returned home delighted with the enlivening scene, and looking with pride and pleasure on the happy fruits of this happy meeting.

Advertisement
Publication: *Nation*
Date of Publication: Saturday, 20 September 1845
Title: 'American Slavery'.

FREDERICK DOUGLASS, recently a Slave in the United States, intends to deliver ANOTHER LECTURE, in the Music-Hall, Lower Abbey-street, TUESDAY evening next, 23rd instant, at Eight o'clock.

Doors to be open at Half-past Seven o'clock.

Admission by tickets to be had at the door.

Promenade – Fourpence. Gallery – Twopence.

Advertisement
Publication: *Freeman's Journal*
Date of Publication: Saturday, 20 September 1845
Title: 'Recently a Slave in the United States'.

Frederick Douglass intends, at the request of the Hibernian Anti-Slavery Society, to deliver a fourth Lecture on American *Slavery* in the MUSIC HALL on THIS EVENING (Tuesday) the 23d instant, at Eight o'clock.

The Right Hon. the LORD MAYOR has kindly consented to take the Chair.

Doors to open at Half past Seven.

To defray the expenses, admission will be by tickets, to be had at the door. Promenade, 4*d*., Gallery, 2*d*.

Anti-Slavery Meeting
Lecturer: Frederick Douglass
Date of Lecture: Tuesday, 23 September 1845
Location: Music Hall, Dublin
Publication: *Freeman's Journal*
Date of Publication: Wednesday, 24 September 1845
Title: 'Anti-Slavery Society'.

Last night, an Anti-Slavery meeting was held in the Music Hall, Abbey Street. The chair was taken by the Lord Mayor who, on coming to the platform was greeted with long and continued cheers.

Mr Haughton introduced to the meeting the American vocalists, Messrs Hutch-inson who, he said, had volunteered their professional services on the present occasion in aid of abolitionist principles. These young gentlemen, accompanied by their sister, then sang an anti-slavery song in excellent style and were loudly applauded.

Mr Haughton said he felt the full force of a beautiful sentence once uttered by Mr Gregg at a meeting held to promote Irish manufactures. It was this, 'I am glad to be at this noble meeting, for every meeting of my fellow man is noble'. Assem-bled as they were to vindicate the rights of humanity, and to put down oppression, they would have the approval of the honest and the just, and meetings with this object might be looked upon by the angels with delight (cheers).

Mr Douglass then came forward and was received in a very enthusiastic manner. He made a long and powerful speech on the evils of slavery, and was frequently applauded throughout. He showed the fallacy of the argument so fre-quently resorted to by slave-holders, that the negro race were unfit for freedom, owing to their mental inferiority to the European nation. Admitting for the sake of argument that the negroes were an inferior race, he would ask by what philosophy could anyone justify himself for enslaving them? The scriptures told the strong to endure the weak, not to oppress them; and no man therefore could obey the word of God and sanction slavery. It was objected that the negro was ignorant and thereby incapable of participating in the advantages of social and political equal-ity. But those who charged them with being ignorant and degraded condemned themselves in that charge, for they had made education penal, and darkened the understanding of the slave. The Americans had generally conspired against the negro, and they had sought a justification for oppression in the roots of the oppres-sion. Even the Northern States sanctioned slavery, for they assented in Congress to the enactment and continuance of those bloody laws by which three millions of the population of America were held in brutal bondage by men professing Christi-anity (hear, hear). The Society of Friends, with other sects, had conspired to keep them in degrading subjugation, and had refused to admit them on equal terms into that house of God who is no respecter of persons. But the Roman Catholics never denied to them the privileges of the Christian faith, and the offices of brotherly love, but had opened to them their churches without any distinction (tremendous cheering). For fourteen years past there has been in America a strong opinion in favour of doing justice to the negro, and many of the grievances under which they had groaned were abolished, or but partially put in practice (hear, hear). But the slave was still a slave, submitted to the tyranny and caprice of his master, and no true justice could be extended to him until he was liberated (cheers). He would never ask of the white man to educate the black, or give him office – all he asked was to do the black man justice, to leave him to advance himself (cheers). Mr Douglass then detailed many of the circumstances relating to his own captiv-ity, which were given in a late number of the FREEMAN, and after paying a high compliment to the Messrs Hutchinson for their uniform resistance to slavery, concluded amid great cheering by thanking the Lord Mayor for the honourable part he had taken in the proceedings of the evening.

Mr Haughton said, in addressing the meeting at first, he forgot to mention the name of one of the greatest enemies of slavery – he meant Mr O'Connell (tremendous cheers, which were continued for some minutes). It could not be said of him (Mr O'Connell) that in advocating the rights of the American slave, he forgot his poor countryman at home (cheers).

Mr Webb and Mr Buffum spoke in favour of abolition principles, after which Mr Haughton begged in the name of the Anti-Slavery Society, to thank their excellent chairman, with all the sincerity of his heart, for his conduct in the chair; and for the generous manner in which he had come forward to associate himself with their proceedings (cheers).

The Lord Mayor who, on rising, was hailed with deafening plaudits, returned thanks. He declared that he was not only gratified but delighted with the whole proceedings. He was not at all times opposed to slavery (cheers), but after what he had heard that night he was a complete convert to abolitionist principles, and he would do all in his power to diffuse and support them (great cheering). He had heard that there was a requisition in course of signature to get up a great public meeting in Dublin to aid in abolishing slavery. The requisition originated in the accounts published relative to the American frigate *Missouri*, which was burned in the bay of Gibraltar, having on board manacles and instruments of torture for the purpose of slavery. He would give his ardent support to any undertaken having for its object the suppression of that cruel and degrading system (cheers).

3

DOUGLASS MEETS DANIEL O'CONNELL

Repeal Meeting
Lecturer: Frederick Douglass
Date of Lecture: Monday, 29 September 1845
Location: Conciliation Hall, Dublin
Publication: *Dublin Evening Post*
Date of Publication: Tuesday, 30 September 1845
Title: 'The Repeal Movement'.

The Liberator introduced to the meeting Mr. Douglas [sic], who had been an American slave. Mr. Douglas said he would not be expected to speak of Repeal as a political question, but he felt bound to say that the expressions of sympathy which he had just heard for his enslaved countrymen, had stirred feelings within him which he could not express. He had often heard of the Liberator when he was a slave in a way that was dear to his heart; he had heard of him in the curses of his masters, and thus he was taught to love him (loud cheers). O'Connell was denounced by the slaveholders in America, as he was denounced by those in this country who hated Repeal. The poor trampled slave of Carolina had heard the name of the Liberator with joy and hope, and he himself had heard the wish that some black O'Connell would yet rise up amongst his countrymen, and cry "Agitate, agitate, agitate." He had stopped in this country for a month hoping to see the Liberator, and when he heard of his approach in the streets to-day, he rushed forward to catch a sight of him who had ever befriended the poor negro (cheers). He never had such feelings in the whole course of his life as he looked on that meeting with freedom for its object, and thought that seven years ago he was a slave whose back had been mangled with the scourge (sensation). The spirit that animated those whom he then addressed had a kindred spirit in America, and thousands there who hated slavery were devoted to the cause of Ireland (cheers). They said that they would be Repealers if they were in Ireland (hear). There was a great bluster and noise in the United States when O'Connell denounced slavery; but he (Mr. Douglas) was happy to assure them that his words produced great effect among the Americans (hear, hear). Mr. Douglas resumed his seat amid applause.

142

The Liberator – I have now great pleasure in announcing the Repeal rent for this week 600*l* 3*s* 5*d* (cheering).

Major Lidwell was then moved from the chair, and Sir Simon Bradstreet, Bart., called thereto, when thanks were voted to the prior Chairman and the meeting separated.[43] (from Freeman's Journal).

Repeal Meeting
Lecturers: Daniel O'Connell; Frederick Douglass
Date of Lecture: Monday, 29 September 1845
Location: Conciliation Hall, Dublin
Publication: *London Standard*
Date of Publication: Wednesday, 1 October 1845
Title: 'THE REPEAL ASSOCIATION'.

DUBLIN, Sept. 29. Owing to the first appearance of the leading star in the Repeal force a full audience was attracted to the Conciliation Hall this day. On the motion of Mr. O'Connell, Major Lidwell was called to the chair. He assured the meeting there was not a warmer advocate for the repeal of the accursed union than the humble individual who had the honour to preside over them (cheers).

Mr. O'Connell said he had to move that the name of the Right Rev. Dr. Hely, Catholic Bishop of Kildare and Leighlin, be appended to the protest against the Colleges Bill,[44] which had been recently published by 19 of the prelates of the Catholic Church, and that that important document be inserted in the minutes (hear, hear). That official declaration pronounced the Colleges Bill dangerous to the faith and morals of the people; and the minority of the prelates remaining silent as to its merits, he (Mr. O'Connell) had no doubt the public would at once submit to the opinion of the great majority, and reject the act with scorn and contempt (hear, hear). Some of the newspapers said the bill had been materially amended in the last session, so as to meet many of the objections to it. Now, he could tell them the bill was not amended in any one respect for which the bishops condemned it. They condemned it on account of the absence of religious instruction – they condemned it on account of the power it gave the government over the colleges, and the total absence of control of the bishops. These were the grounds on which the bishops protested against the act, and so far from the amendments removing them they actually fortified all the objectionable powers. As the bill originally stood a parent might place his son with any person he pleased to select. But by the amendments he should have the approval of the president, who was to be appointed by government and removable at pleasure.

A gentleman called on him yesterday, and asked him (Mr. O'Connell) whether he did not prefer Armagh to Belfast for the Ulster College. He replied, neither (hear, hear). His friend's reason was a curious one. The boys, said he, might reside in Belfast, and by the aid of all the railways projected from that town they might go to college in the morning and return in the evening. Taking the cost of

143

travelling at 1s. a day, that would make 367*l*. 10*s*. a year – a sum more than equal to the support of the boy. No, no, said he (Mr. O Connell), I will have nothing at all to do with this new system of railway education (laughter). The motion was then put and carried.

Mr. O'Connell next said that he had to make to the association a communication from Wm. Smith O'Brien, Esq.[45] (cheers.) Anything coming from that most respectable and exalted public individual would of course be received with that respect which was its due, but it was generally enhanced by the contents of the letter itself. He then read the following letter from Mr. O'Brien, with the subjoined communication from Mr. Lloyd.

To John O'Connell, Esq.[46]

"Cahirmoyle, Sept. 25, 1845. My dear O'Connell, – The kind feeling which you have exhibited with reference to our much-regretted friend Davis,[47] makes me sensible that I was guilty of an impropriety in seeking to usurp to myself the melancholy satisfaction of proposing in Conciliation Hall that the association should procure a marble bust of him, with a view to its being hereafter placed in the senate-house of his emancipated country. You have left me without a claim to precedency in the execution of this mournful duty; and as there is no reason why it should be delayed, I trust that you will, upon Monday next, with the sanction of the committee, give notice of a motion upon the subject. I am disposed to think that he would have selected Moore[48] in preference to any other sculptor, as he appears to have added much personal regard for him to admiration of his abilities as an artist. I hope that we shall be able to induce the '82 Club[49] to request Mr. Burton[50] to paint for the club a portrait of his friend and admirer. These memorials will recall to us his connection with the cause to which he was so enthusiastically devoted; but those friends who have not yet learned to sympathise in all his patriotic aspirations will also desire the opportunity of recording their admiration of his genius and of his virtue. Grief quells every other passion. Party strife is hushed now in the tomb; and the erection of a monument seems to be an undertaking in the performance of which all who loved and honoured him may unite their efforts. If a subscription list should be opened for this purpose, I beg to offer my humble contribution of 1*l*.[51]

Believe me, very sincerely yours, "WILLIAM S. O'BRIEN."

Mr. O'Connell then said, that he had to hand in a pound as the monthly subscription of Mr. O'Brien, and 5*l*. as that of Mr. Lloyd. Since Mr. S. O'Brien himself joined them they had not had such glorious news. He was a Protestant of large fortune, of high education, of great talent, of strong Protestant religious feeling: he was one of those who discussed in a temperate manner the condition of Ireland – he said, notwithstanding the flimsy report of Lord Devon,[52] and even the reports of that miserable "gutter commissioner" of the *Times* (a laugh), that no country can be well governed which had not its own legislature under its control; and that legislation by England was a degradation to Irishmen. He (Mr. O'Connell) had the honour of knowing his father; he travelled the same circuit with him for upwards of 20 years, and a more excellent, accomplished, polished gentleman it was never his fate or fortune to have met with. He was a strong advocate for Catholic Emancipation; he went into parliament for his native county, and continued to represent it to his death, and always voted for everything which would prove advantageous to Ireland – particularly the emancipation of his Catholic fellow-countrymen.

He (Mr. O'Connell) had great pleasure in moving that Thos. Lloyd, Esq., be admitted by acclamation, – and that the secretary be directed to inform him of their heartfelt gratitude to him for his having sacrificed everything at the shrine of patriotism, and that they (the Repealers of Ireland) asked for no religious ascendancy or temporal advantage whatever, – and were determined never to allow a superiority to exist among themselves which they despised and hated, and abhorred in others. The motion was then carried by acclamation.

Mr. John O'Connell gave notice, on behalf of Mr. S. O'Brien, for a national testimony to the late Mr. Davis. Mr. O'Connell seconded the motion, and would have, he said, proceeded at once with the subject himself, but that he understood it was determined to raise a testimonial to the memory of that excellent Irishman by persons of all sects and persuasions; and he did not, therefore, wish to make it purely a repeal proceeding, but one as extensive as the Irish nation, and as warm as once were the throbbings of his own heart. Mr. John O'Connell then read the following letter, said to be addressed to him by the *Times'* commissioner in Ireland: –

"Halesworth, Sept. 25, 1845. "Sir, – I have this moment seen in the 'Times' of yesterday your dirty and unmanly remarks concerning the *Times'* Commissioner, and I do not lose one moment to tell you that you are a liar and a blackguard. "I am, Sir, your obedient servant," THOMAS FOSTER.[53] To John O'Connell, Esq., M.P."

That letter, Mr. O'Connell proceeded to say, was dated from England, and he should like to know if those communications, addressed to the *Times* from this country, with regard to the tenant right in Ulster, and other subjects which were published in the same paper, were not written in the same country. He (Mr. J. O'Connell) did nothing to offend the civil – he would not call him the handsome – gentleman, for he understood he was called "ugly always" in the country, except to combat the statements he put forward with respect to the county Donegal. When the new infidel colleges were established we hoped the gentleman would be appointed a professor of politeness (laughter). Mr. O'Connell said that it was such a specimen of English politeness, he would, for the benefit of the education of the Irish people, move that it be inserted on their minutes (a laugh).

He (Mr. O'Connell) saw by chance two English respectable persons in the gallery, who shook their heads at that declaration; he would, therefore, withdraw the assertion that it was a specimen of English courtesy, and attribute it solely to the blackguard himself (cheers). Now that individual ought to get his proper name. Formerly, when elections were carried by means of money exclusively, there were appointed persons from head down to gutter agents. So it was then with commissioners, for they had them from the commissioners of the great seal down to the "gutter commissioner" of the *Times* (a laugh). He (Mr. O'Connell) trusted he had influence enough with the press to have that person called in future the "gutter commissioner." Did they know what he said? He said the Irish women were ugly (great laughter). Oh! (pointing to the ladies' gallery) how ugly they are! (cheers). He was beginning to wish the fellow was there, but he would not, for may he never have the happiness of seeing such a sight as they saw there (cheers). He was done for the present with the "gutter commissioner," except to move that his letter be inserted on their minutes (cheers).

LOTS OF CASH. Mr. O'Connell rose again, and handed in several sums of money from the county of Tipperary, and which were announced at the Thurles dinner, on Thursday. He also handed in £100, remitted by the Catholic bishop of Waterford, contributed by 99 of his priests. As the letter of the worthy bishop contained a goodly amount of soft sawder[54] for the Liberator, it was read with peculiar care and all due emphasis. Of course his lordship got a receipt in full for his sweet epistle. The following is a copy: –

Waterford, September 23, 1815. "My Dear Mr. O'Connell, – I am requested by the Roman Catholic clergy of these united dioceses to transmit the annexed letter of credit for £100, being the amount of their contributions and my own to the Repeal rent for the current year. It is not necessary for me to repeat my firm conviction, again – that of the Roman Catholic clergy of these dioceses, that nothing short of a repeal of the Act of Union will raise Ireland to the dignity of a nation, consolidate her connection with Great Britain, and thus place on an immovable basis the power and prosperity of the United Kingdom. You, illustrious Liberator! are devoting the energies of your great mind, with untiring zeal to the accomplishment of that great end, and you are doing it by means which must have the approval of every good man and loyal subject. While you denounce crime of every kind, you preach charity, peace, loyalty to the Sovereign, and obedience to the laws. Persevere in this course, as I am sure you will, and you will be sustained by the Roman Catholic hierarchy and clergy of Ireland. That you may live to see the sacrifices you have made, and the toils you have endured for the regeneration of your country, crowned with success, is the ardent wish of Your devoted friend, NICHOLAS FORAN, Roman Catholic Bishop of Waterford and Lismore. To Daniel O'Connell, Esq., M.P."

MORE DINNERS. Mr. O'Connell considered it right to announce that on this day week he would be in the county Kerry at a monster procession and banquet. The following day there would be a regatta on the Lake of Killarney, and those who wished to see that lovely district could not select a better time for the purpose than next week. If the repeal demonstration had not sufficient attraction, the regatta on the lake and the fine weather which might be calculated upon, ought to have some weight.

On the following Sunday, the 12th, he was to attend another monster procession and dinner at Castlebar; and he had an invitation from Sligo under consideration.

RIBBONISM.[55] Mr. O'Connell next denounced the Ribbon conspiracy. He declared that nothing gave him so much pain as that horrible, wicked, and foolish system. It had no definite plan – no fixed scheme – no intelligible object.

The people seduced to join this conspiracy were sworn to obey all orders given by the leaders, and they rarely knew who they were – they might thus be engaged in the commission of murder; in short, there was no crime that might not be committed by that brotherhood. He called upon every man who regarded his liberty, who loved his country, to inform at once on the wretch who solicited him to take a ribbon oath. The fellows engaged in this abominable system generally came from England. The two men who swore in no less than 700 in Belfast had come from England. What interest could such persons have in Ireland? Oh! it was a brutal system, that ought to be denounced by every true Irishman.

THE SPEECH FOR THE DAY. Mr. O'Connell rose again, and began his speech by a laudatory account of the Thurles meeting, which he calculated to have amounted to 500,000 persons, 15,000 of whom were on horseback. That was a great national demonstration, and showed the spirit of the people – their determination to have legislative independence – but by legal and constitutional means. He had no doubt that in a short time their fondest expectations would be realised (cheers). Let them look to the condition of the several nations of Europe – ay, and America – and ask whether the times were not pregnant with anxiety and convulsion. But the people of Ireland had nothing to dread from this, but much to gain; and England could rest satisfied of her own safety against all enemies if she did full justice to the people of Ireland (cheers). Look to the state of Europe. France and England seem to be on very good terms with each other, but they were exceeding each other in the examination of the coasts at one side and the other. The Prince de Joinville[56] had recently examined the coasts and roadsteads of England, while the French themselves were fortifying every assailable point on their coasts, and the English were doing the same thing. Let them, however, give Ireland to the Irish, and they need not fear any enemy that appeared. He (Mr. O'Connell) would not rear a rampart of stone, but he would raise a rampart of men (cheers). At the present moment no cause of quarrel appeared between France and England, and no subject of difference was likely soon to arise; but what was the reason both sides were making preparations for war? Did it not bespeak a foregone conclusion – that danger was scented afar – the seeds of strife were in the wild winds of heaven? It was morally impossible that the present state of things could long continue. Passing from France to Spain and Portugal – there, the elements of quiet were scarcely in existence at all. Revolution followed revolution, violent changes followed violent changes, until no one knew where they would stop. Portugal was certainly tranquil at that period, but they knew not how soon a change would take place. Spain was struggling with contending parties to obtain power, and was then comparatively peaceable; but who would venture to assert that tranquility would long remain in those unhappy countries.

Proceed, then, to Germany, where the spirit of Jacobinism threatened states and powers and principalities, seeking by convulsion and wild anarchy to risk life and property, and everything that was valuable. He need not refer to the monster who ruled the empire of Russia – the most base and besotted tyrant that ever disgraced human nature – a Dioclesian in religion,[57] a Nero in civil government, as fanatical and brutal a tyrant as ever disgraced humanity. Fortunately, by a species of insanity which possessed him, he was wasting his strength in endeavouring to crush the brave mountaineers of the Caucasian regions; and, oh! where was the breast that did not throb at the bravery of those brave sons of the mountains, who turn back the hordes of the Russian hosts and their most famous general with discomfiture and disgrace? (cheers). Yes, they had the bravery of the Caucasians to protect the rest of Europe from the schemes and ambition of the monster of Russia. And even in his own dominions the throes of despotism were beginning to show themselves, and a struggle by the Poles and other Russian subjects must occur sooner or later to throw off the tyrant's yoke.

Coming, then, to the other side of the Atlantic, let them behold the position of America. It was quite clear that if England did not submit to abandon the Oregon territory, or if America did not insist on retaining it, eternal disgrace would befall her for her absurd vapouring, when she declared that England should not have it. They would see if the quarrel turned out to be a quarrel of words, or was likely to end in blows. While the canker of negro slavery eats the heart's core of America, she can never be strong; while that remains a plague spot on her institutions, Heaven forbids that any country should prosper which was tainted with that infernal system; but, nevertheless, England had to fear the commencement of such a struggle. They would, however, retain their position – they were determined to carry the repeal alone by peaceable means; but they were, nevertheless, on the watch for the difficulties of England, for the moment that period arrived, their freedom was certain (cheers). That, he contended, was a legitimate speculation of an Irishman who loved his country. Let them look, then, at the affairs of England. She was no doubt at that moment in a condition of great internal prosperity; within his memory she was never more so; but was it lasting – could it be calculated on? (cheers). In the time of the Whigs it seemed as if nature herself was playing a game against them, for in the last four or five years while they were in office there was a constant recurrence of bad harvests, and consequently high prices; all the manufacturing towns were in a state of the greatest distress, and consequently disaffection – the people were idle, unemployed, and starving, and consequently in a state of great excitement. The cycle of years went round, and since the Tories came into power trade has improved, the wages in the district of Lancashire increased in amount to one hundred and fifty thousand pounds a week more than was paid three years ago; the quantity of productive labour has increased, the labouring classes are happy, and abundance and tranquility reign throughout the country. But when the cycle is changed – when bad harvests occur, and they had had a narrow escape within the present year – when trade became bad and famine again stalked through the land, England would want their hands and hearts; and she should have Ireland cheap and at the price only of doing them justice. But while he alluded to these things, let them see what was achieved already. They were then in an infinitely prouder position than when the Whigs were in office; the spirit of Repeal was more consistent, it was better organised – better developed – than within his recollection. When the present administration came into office, they did so with a decided hostility to Ireland. There was a double basis on which their supporters rallied together – two prin-ciples which instigated them – one, religious bigotry and hatred to the Catholic religion, the other on hostility to the great body of the people. These were the true principles on which that government came into office. One million five hun-dred thousand pounds were expended to bribe the present parliament, which was procured by the most arrant bigotry and the most atrocious bribery (cheers). The hon. and learned gentleman then referred to the prosecution instituted against them by the government and its ultimate failure, and proceeded. The prime min-ister declared in his place in the House of Commons that it was impossible to put down the Repeal agitation by force. He did at one time contemplate such a proceeding. He did not, however, persevere, and woe to him had he done so (cheers). Five hundred thousand men met in Tipperary on Thursday last, which was security quite enough for them, that no such course would be attempted. What then remains? Bribery and corruption. And what chance, he asked, was there of bribing the Irish people (cheers). They began with the Maynooth grant; they gave it, certainly, handsomely, kindly, and justly; but the Right Rev. Dr. Higgins, the Bishop of Ardagh, calculated that the sum so given made exactly three farthings a year (a laugh).[58] Now he (Mr. O'Connell) submitted that it was not worthwhile to be bribed for that sum, nay even if they doubled it. The Irish had a deep interest in the difficulties of England, for they never got justice but at moments of danger. They spoke of calling out the Irish militia; that could not be done without an act of parliament; but if they did, would it be found quite wise just now? The Irish militia were not unaware of the injustice under which their country was suffering, and when the union would be repealed, they would be found useful in protecting the public peace during the transition from degrada-tion to national independence.

After a long flourish about the part he had taken in reference to American slavery, and another declaration in favour of abolition, he resumed his repeal address. He repeated the old story of the way the union was carried, the state of the English debt and the Irish debt at that period – of all he said and wrote him-self against the union, and finally shot off to Lord Devon's report – a synopsis of which he gave for the fiftieth time. Let, said he, the Repeal wardens be called upon to bestir themselves for the enrolment of members, and let them call upon every man competent to register a vote to do so, and if every man in Ireland who was entitled to register claimed his franchise, he (Mr. O'Connell) would have 70 members pledged to the repeal, aiding him in Conciliation Hall. Let every man endeavour to put down Ribbonism. Let every parish send forth a petition for the repeal of the Union; and thus Ireland would speak in a voice of thunder, not to be misunderstood, and not to be despised by the government. Let the draft of all such bills as are required be presented to the House of Commons. He had the draft of a bill for the repeal of the Union almost completely ready (cheers). This bill would recognise the prerogative of the British Crown in as full a form as it existed prior to the union. It would re-establish the Houses of Peers and Commons, and it would contain a declaration that no power on earth should make laws to bind the Irish people but the Queen, Lords, and Commons of Ireland (cheers). The hon. and learned Liberator concluded by calling upon the repeal wardens to execute with fidelity and dispatch the trifling little commissions this day issued to them (cheers).

THE CORPORATION.

Mr. O'Connell rose again and observed, that he would not bring on his motion respecting the corporation, as Mr. Reynolds was not present; but he would take care to let him have notice of the next day of meeting. This much he would say, that there never was anything so necessary for the repeal as supporting the corporation (cheers).

Mr. O'Connell next introduced a black gentleman, named Douglas [sic], who had been a slave. Mr. Douglas thanked the "Liberator" for the kind part he had ever acted towards his down-trodden countrymen. When he was a slave he heard the name of "The Liberator" through the curses of his master. After more of the same kind of matter, he said, but seven years ago he was a slave – one of those whipped ones – one of those chained ones – one of those bought and sold ones – and he could not but feel the deepest gratitude at being present at such a meeting. They were like those often held in his own country in the midst of mobs, he was sorry to say, and at an imminent risk to life and property; but such was not the case in Ireland. While the Liberator shook the chains of the people of Ireland in that hall, he was also knocking the chains from off the slaves in America, and paralysing the arm of the cruel flagellator of the human race. He had to apologise for addressing them; he was an uneducated man; he had never been a day at school, and when his mistress had humanely undertaken to teach him his alphabet her husband interfered, and said, that if he learned to read he would learn to write; that the consequence would be that he (Mr. Douglas) would write passes; that he would be discontented, and his value would be considerably deteriorated.

One of the first books which came into his possession after he learned to read was a speech of Mr. Sheridan's, an Irishman,[59] which certainly made him discontented, as his master had predicted. Shortly after that he fell in with a party of Irishmen employed as labourers, and having assisted them, he was asked by one if he were a slave. He (Mr. Douglas) said he was, and from what occurred between them he first contemplated his escape, which he accomplished a short time after. He fled and went to Massachusetts, where he had been in his own humble way endeavouring to advocate the cause of his country. He thanked them for the courtesy with which they had heard him, and would no longer trespass on their attention.

The Repeal rent was then announced to be 600*l*. 3*s*. 10*d*.; after which Sir Simon Bradstreet was called to the chair, and the meeting adjourned.

Repeal Meeting
Lecturer: Frederick Douglass
Date of Lecture: Monday, 29 September 1845
Location: Conciliation Hall, Dublin
Publication: *Dublin Evening Mail*
Date of Publication: Wednesday, 1 October 1845
Title: 'Repeal Association'.

The usual weekly meeting of the above association was held on Monday in the Conciliation Hall . . . Shortly before one o'clock Mr. O'Connell entered the hall and was greeted with loud cheers . . . FREDERICK DOUGLAS [sic], who was recently a slave in the United States, having been introduced to the meeting, detailed the manner in which he had escaped from slavery, the means by which he got a partial education, and his gratitude and that of his countrymen for the part which Mr. O'Connell had always taken to liberate the slave. He had heard of Mr. O'Connell frequently; he had heard of him through the curses of his master, which had made him love him, and he admired him because he had heard him condemned and denounced by those who oppressed the slave. He had waited in Dublin a month to see Mr. O'Connell; and on Sunday, when crossing the Liffey, he heard a parcel of little boys scream out 'There's O'Connell', and he rushed among them to see the man who had so nobly denounced slavery, and so bravely defended the rights of the poor negro. His desire to obtain his freedom was awakened by his reading a speech of Mr. Sheridan's, which he found in the *Columbian Orator;* and he was stimulated to escape to Massachusetts by some Irishmen whom he met upon a wharf at Baltimore, one of whom asked him if he never thought about running away. He did not dare disclose at the time what was passing in his mind lest those to whom he spoke might be the spies of his tyrant taskmasters; but he took the hint and fled from oppression – (cheers).

Sir Simon Bradstreet was then called to the chair, and the repeal rent for the week was announced to be 600*l* 3*s*. 5*d*., after which the meeting adjourned.

Repeal Meeting
Lecturer: Frederick Douglass
Date of Lecture: Monday, 29 September 1845
Location: Conciliation Hall, Dublin
Publication: *Tipperary Free Press*
Date of Publication: Wednesday, 1 October 1845
Title: 'Conciliation Hall – Monday'.

From our own reporter. The Loyal National Repeal Association met today in Conciliation Hall which, in consequence of Mr. O'Connell's arrival in Dublin on Saturday evening, was crowded to excess. Mr. O'Connell requested the meeting not to separate for a moment a Mr. Frederick Douglas [sic], who had been once a slave, wished to address them.

Mr. Douglas then addressed the association, thanking them and Mr. O'Connell on behalf of his brethren of the negro race, for their sympathy. He was loudly cheered.

Sir Simon Bradstreet took the chair.

Repeal Meeting
Lecturer: Frederick Douglass
Date of Lecture: Monday, 29 September 1845
Location: Conciliation Hall, Dublin
Publication: *Waterford Chronicle*
Date of Publication: Wednesday, 1 October 1845
Title: 'Loyal National Repeal Association'.

. . . Mr. O'Connell requested the meeting not to separate for a moment, as there was a person of the name of Mr. Douglas [sic], one who had been a slave, and who would address them. Mr. Douglas addressed the association, speaking of the gratitude which he and all of his negro brethren owed to Mr O'Connell. He spoke well, and was loudly cheered. Sir Simon Bradstreet was then moved to the chair, and the thanks of the association given to Major Lidwell.

Repeal Meeting
Lecturer: Frederick Douglass
Date of Lecture: Monday, 29 September 1845
Location: Conciliation Hall, Dublin
Publication: *Dublin Weekly Register*
Date of Publication: Saturday, 4 October 1845
Title: 'Repeal Meeting'.

. . . The LIBERATOR introduced to the meeting Mr. Douglas [sic] who had been an American slave.

Mr. Douglas said that having been brought unexpectedly before the attention of that assembly, he had no speech to make; but he could not resist the opportunity so kindly afforded to him of expressing his approval of the spirit of freedom and conciliation which pervaded the whole proceedings. He would not be expected to speak of Repeal as a political question, but he felt bound to say that the expressions of sympathy which he had just heard for his enslaved countrymen, had stirred feelings in him which he could not express. He had often heard of the Liberator when he was a slave, in a way that was dear to his heart; he had heard of him in the curses of his masters; and thus he was taught to love him (cheers). O'Connell was denounced by the slave-holders of America, and he was denounced by those in this country who hated Repeal. The poor trampled slave of Carolina had heard the name of O'Connell with joy and hope; and he himself had heard the wish that some black O'Connell would rise up amongst his countrymen and cry 'Agitate, agitate. Agitate'. He had stopped in this country for a month to see the Liberator, and when he heard of his approach in the street to-day, he rushed forward to catch a sight of him who had befriended the poor negro (cheers). He never had such feelings in the whole course of his life as while he looked on that meeting, with freedom for its object, and thought that seven years ago he was a slave whose back had been mangled with the scourge (sensation). The spirit that animated those whom he then addressed had a kindred spirit in America; and thousands there who hated slavery were devoted to the cause of Ireland. They said that they would be Repealers if they were in Ireland. There was great bluster and noise in the United States when O'Connell denounced slavery, but he (Mr. Douglas) was happy to assure them that his words produced great effect among the Americans (hear, hear). For, while with one arm the Liberator was bursting the fetters of Irishmen, with the other he was striking off the literal chains from the limbs of the negro (cheers). After some further observation of a general nature, Mr. Douglas resumed his seat amid a very great applause.

The Liberator: I now have great pleasure in announcing the Repeal Rent for this week as SIX HUNDRED POUNDS THREE SHILLINGS AND FIVE PENCE (tremendous cheering).

Major Lidwell was then moved from the chair, and Sir Simon Bradstreet, Bart., called thereto, when, on the motion of the Liberator, the marked thanks of the meeting were voted to the prior chairman, and the meeting separated.

Repeal Meeting
Lecturer: Frederick Douglass
Date of Lecture: Monday, 29 September 1845
Location: Conciliation Hall, Dublin
Publication: *Liverpool Mail* [60]
Date of Publication: Saturday, 4 October 1845
Title: 'The Repeal Association'.

The government having hitherto neglected their duty of suppressing the illegal meetings of this illegal body, the Great Agitator attended on Monday, at the Dublin Intimidation Hall, and attracted numerous auditory. Major Lidwell presided. After some declamation condemnatory of the new Irish Colleges Act, a little blarneying of Mr. Smith O'Brien and a Mr. Lloyd, who has just joined the association, and a talk about the erection of a monument to the late Mr. Davis, to be placed in the senate house of his emancipated country, Mr. John O'Connell read the following letter, said to be addressed to him by the *Times* commissioner in Ireland. When the infidel colleges were established he hoped the gentleman would be appointed a professor of politeness. . .

Mr. O'Connell next introduced a black gentleman named Douglas [sic], who had been a slave. Mr. Douglas thanked the Liberator for the kind part he had ever acted towards his down-trodden countrymen. When he was a slave he heard the name of "The Liberator" through the curses of his master. After more of the same kind of matter, he said, but seven years ago he was a slave – one of those whipped ones – one of those chained ones – one of those bought and sold ones – and could not but feel the deepest gratitude at being present at such a meeting. They were like those often held in his own country in the midst of mobs, he was sorry to say, and at imminent risk to life and property; but such was not the case in Ireland. While the Liberator shook the chains off the people of Ireland in that hall, he was also knocking the chains from off the slaves in America, and paralysing the arm of the cruel flagellator of the human race.

The rent was announced to be £600 3s. 10d.

Repeal Meeting
Lecturer: Daniel O'Connell
Date of Lecture: Monday, 29 September 1845
Location: Conciliation Hall, Dublin
Publication: *Liberator*
Date: Friday, 24 October 1845
Title: 'ANOTHER PEAL FROM O'CONNELL'S BUGLE'.

In the letter of Frederick Douglass, (of whose health and success we rejoice to hear,) is a reference to a powerful speech delivered by the Irish Liberator before the Repeal Association in Dublin, in the course of which he renewed his faithful and glorious testimony against American slavery and all its foul abettors. Fresh thanks and honors be given to this disinterested and undaunted friend of emancipation. In the *Dublin Evening Post* of Sept. 30, the speech of Mr. O'Connell is reported at considerable length, from which we take the following extract:

It is quite true that from many parts of America, we refused sympathy, because the evidence of that sympathy was accompanied by principles that we could not adopt (cheers.) We could take no sympathy and no assistance inconsistent with our allegiance to the Sovereign, and unworthy of our duty to our native land (cheers.) I have been assailed for attacking the American institution, as it is called – negro slavery (hear, hear.) I am not ashamed of that attack – I do not shrink from it. I am the advocate of civil and religious liberty all over the globe, and wherever tyranny exists, I am the foe of the tyrant: wherever oppression shows itself, I am the foe of the oppressor: wherever slavery rears its head, I am the enemy of the system, or the institution, call it by what name you will. (great cheering.) It has been said, what business has O'Connell in interfering with American slavery? Why, do not the Americans show us their sympathy for our struggles, and why should we not show a sympathy in efforts for liberty amongst themselves? (cheers.) But I confess I have another strong reason for desiring to abolish slavery in America. In no monarchy on the face of the earth is there such a thing as domestic slavery; 'tis true in some colonies belonging to monarchies, slavery exists; but in no European country is there slavery at all – for the Russian serf is far different from the slave of America; and, therefore, I do not wish that any lover of liberty should be able to draw a contrast between the democratic republic of America and the despotic States of Europe, (hear, hear.) I am in favor of the democratic spirit, and I wish to relieve it from the horror of slavery, (cheers.) I do not wish to visit America with force and violence – I would be the last man in the world to consent to it; I would not be for making war to free the negro – at least, not for the war of strife, and lash, and sword; but I would be for the moral warfare – I would be for the arms of argument and humanity to procure the extinction of tyranny, and to hurl contempt and indignation on those who call themselves freemen, and yet keep others in slavery. I would bring elements of that kind to bear upon the system until the very name of slavery should be regarded with horror in the Republics of America, (cheers.) I was much amazed to see a North American Review attributing to me motives on this head. It is *Brownson's Quarterly Review*, and is published at Boston. I quote from an extract in the *Tablet* of the 16th instant: 'Men do and will estimate Mr. O'Connell differently, according to the different points of view from which they contemplate him; nor is a man to be regarded as wanting in devotion to the interests of Ireland, even in case he cannot feel towards him as do the warm-hearted and enthusiastic Irish. We protest in advance against making the idolatrous worship of any man the test of one's devotion to the cause with which that man may be identified. For ourselves, as American citizens and patriots, we may have had our feelings wounded, our prejudices aroused, and even our judgments warped by Mr. O'Connell's unprovoked attacks on our country; for we are as sensitive to the interests, to the honor and glory of America, as Irishmen are to those of Ireland, and we are as quick to resent any attack upon them, come it from what quarter it may.' I never attacked their country – I wholly deny it – but I attacked slavery in America, and I attacked it equally in every other country on the face of the earth, (cheers.) The article goes on to speak of me in the most favorable manner, and then adds: – 'Nevertheless, we think Mr. O'Connell has, in his speeches, made remarks, with regard to this country, which are hard to justify or even palliate.' Now, I will never be driven from my course by insinuations. I never asserted anything of American slavery that I had not documents within my reach to prove, and before I sit down, with the consent of the Association, I will read a document quite conclusive as regards the matters and things which I have stated. Now for the insinuations of this writer: – 'We have strong reasons for believing that these remarks do not accord with his own private views and feelings, and that they are made mainly for the purpose of conciliating friends, or silencing enemies in England and Scotland.' There never was a man yet, more capable of concealing his thoughts, than I am. I have made more speeches than any human being, three to one; and the American reviewer has no right to say, that while I speak one thing, I think another, (hear, hear.) It is a foul insinuation – mind what he says, 'for the purpose of conciliating friends, or silencing enemies in England and Scotland.' – What a notion they have of me! (loud cheer.) – Again, we have: – 'Mr. O'Connell is better informed as to the state of things here than his public speeches would indicate. But, he appears to judge it important for his success to conciliate, and, as far as possible, to enlist the

Abolitionists in Great Britain on his side, and to have it clearly and distinctly understood by the British Government, and people, that however ardently he may desire Repeal, he is not prepared to carry it by courting or accepting any foreign alliance or sympathy. Thus, he repelled the proffered sympathy of the French Liberals, and thus he has repelled, in some measure, the proffered sympathy of American citizens.' Now, that is an accusation of being a base hypocrite – an accusation of affecting to be the friend of negro emancipation, merely to concili- ate the Abolitionists in England. In the year '25, when I left my profession,[61] and went over to England, there was an Anti-Slavery meeting, at which I attended, and spoke; and afterwards, when I went to parliament, another meeting was appointed, greater in magnitude – the West India interest was 27 strong in the House of Com- mons – the Algerine Bill was carried through the house by a majority of 19 – therefore, the Emancipation Bill was in the power of the West India interest; but when they sent a respected friend of mine – the Knight of Kerry – to me, to ask why I did not take a certain course with regard to it, what was my answer? I rep- resent the Irish people here, and I will act as the Irish people would sanction – come liberty, come slavery, to myself, I will never countenance slavery at home nor abroad. (cheers.) I said I came here on principle; the Irish people sent me here to carry out their principles; their principles are an abhorrence of slavery, and, therefore, I will take my part at that anti-slavery meeting, and though it should be a blow against Ireland, it is a blow in favor of human liberty, and I will strike that blow, (cheers.) So far was I from cultivating the slavery interest, that I adopted that course, though I regretted to lose their votes. But I must do them the credit to say that I did not lose them. They acted nobly, and said they would not revenge upon Ireland my attack upon them. (cheers.) But I believe no person can say that I was courting the anti-slavery party. Let me remind the Association, that at a later period, in the year '38 or '39, Mr. Fowell Buxton[62] and the anti-slavery party called a meeting in Exeter hall, for the civilization of the interior of Africa. I attended: but they determined that I should not take a part in the meeting. They arranged that I should not be heard.[63] – The people that attended the meeting were kind enough to be impatient to hear me, but they voted the chairman out of the chair, and got up a tune on the organ lest I should speak to the people. (laughter.) That was the way I conciliated the anti-slavery party. And when the howl was raised in England against the Maynooth Bill, who were the most active in raising that howl? The anti-slavery party. (hear.) Many of them, to be sure, wrote to me, apologizing for taking the part they did, and attributing their opposition to the grant to their attachment to the voluntary principle. I scorned that excuse. (cheers.) I said to them publicly, 'how can you say it is the voluntary principle you are going upon?' The Presbyterians receive 26,000*l*. a-year by annual votes – you never opposed the Presbyterian grant; it is equally obnoxious to the voluntary principle; but when a grant is proposed to be given to the Catholics, you oppose it. (hear, hear.) But have I traduced the Americans, when I talked of the horrors of domestic slavery?

I happened to receive a New Orleans paper, published in the centre of domestic slavery – it is called the *Jeffersonian Republic*, and I shall read an extract from it. By that I perceive that, in connection with the institution of slavery in New Orleans – for I find that in America they call it an institution – there are public whipping places – men are licensed to keep shambles of torture,[64] (hear, hear,) – the master sends his slave to those shambles, there to get one hundred lashes, and the man gets the hundred lashes, or whatever degree of punishment his master desires. (hear, hear.) There are actually shambles kept there for the torture of slaves, and there are persons who earn a livelihood – what a hideous livelihood – by flogging human beings at the instance of those who are called their masters. (hear, hear.) Am I to blame if I attack a system of that kind (hear, hear!) Male or female – young or old – whipped at the discretion of a man whose only limit is not actually killing the individual. (hear, hear.) They would thus make the slave declare whether he is guilty of a theft or not. Are they, I ask, Christian men who endure to see those scenes going on around them? (hear, hear). Recollect that this is not the statement of a calumniator, or a libeller, or foreign emissary, but it is the statement published in the darkest hole of slavery, New Orleans itself. (hear, hear.) Let them blame me – let me be execrated by them – let their support be taken from Ireland – slavery, I denounce you, wherever you are. (loud cheers.) Come freedom – come oppression to Ireland – let Ireland be as she may, I have my conscience clear before my God. (continued cheers.) I abhor the tyranny of man, and its demoralizing, brutalizing, torturing practice. (cheers.) It is not I who calumniate the Americans, if they be calumniated – but the American who writes this document, and publishes it. I speak only the words of that writer, and come good or evil, I am the enemy of slavery in every form. (cheers.)

4

DUBLIN CONT.

Advertisement
Publication: *Freeman's Journal*
Date of Publication: Wednesday, 1 October 1845
Title: 'AMERICAN SLAVERY'.

FREDERICK DOUGLAS [sic], at the request of the Hibernian Anti-Slavery Society, intends to deliver his Fifth Lecture in the MUSIC HALL, on THIS EVENING (Wednesday), the 1st of October, at Eight o'clock.

Doors to be open at half-past Seven.

To defray expenses admission will be by tickets, to be had at the door. Promenade, Four pence; Gallery, Two pence.

Anti-Slavery Meeting
Lecturer: Frederick Douglass
Date of Lecture: Wednesday, 1 October 1845
Publication: *Freeman's Journal*
Date of Publication: Saturday, 4 October 1845
Title: 'American Slavery'.

AMERICAN SLAVERY. At a Meeting held in the Music Hall on Wednesday Evening, Oct. 1, JAMES Haughton Esq., in the Chair, for the purpose of hearing a lecture from Frederick Douglass, recently a Slave in the United States, the following resolutions were unanimously adopted:

Moved by Mr. Allen;[65] seconded by Mr. J. H. Webb:

Resolved – That this meeting views with abhorrence the system of chattel Slavery which exists in the United States, as brought before our view by Frederick Douglass, once a victim of that "institution," and that they call upon all the friends of Christianity and impartial liberty to express their sense of the atrocity of this system by refusing their countenance to American Slaveholders and their abettors, and by holding out the right hand of fellowship to that noble band in the United States who have devoted their lives to the overthrow of Slavery.

Moved by Mr. Richard D. Webb; seconded by Mr. Shortt:

Resolved – That we learn with the most painful feelings that the system of slavery is mainly supported by the sanction given to it by professing Christians of the United States, many of whom participate in its crimes or refuse to aid in the righteous cause of abolition; and that we call upon all religious bodies in these countries to do their duty in the matter by persevering remonstrances with their fellow professors in America, and by endeavours to promote amongst their members and intelligent acquaintances with the anti-slavery cause, with a view to its diligent and energetic promotion. JAMES HAUGHTON, Chairman.

Anti-Slavery Meeting
Lecturer: Frederick Douglass
Date of Lecture: Wednesday, 1 October 1845
Location: Music Hall, Dublin
Publication: *Freeman's Journal*
Date: Friday, 3 October 1845 [66]
Title: 'ANTI-SLAVERY MEETING'. [67]

On Wednesday evening, a large and respectable audience assembled in the Music-hall, to hear Mr. Frederick Douglass deliver his fifth and last lecture on American Slavery. Mr. JAMES HAUGHTON was called to the chair. He stated that some misconception of Mr. Douglass's views of the various professing Christian Churches in America prevailed, which it might be well to do away with. It was undeniable that every section of the Church was guilty of the sin of upholding slavery, but that among them all, many noble-minded individuals were to be found, who were anxious to purge their Church from this vile stain. Such men were worthy of all honour; but those who sustained slavery, and by so doing practically overthrew Christianity, should be held up to the condemnation of mankind. This was all that Mr. Douglass meant to convey, and as he was there to tell them the truth, the people of Ireland should gladly hear him, in order that, knowing the truth, they might be prepared to apply a remedy. The sentiments of the chairman met a warm response from the audience.

Mr. DOUGLASS then came forward, and for an hour and a half he riveted the attention of his hearers by his eloquent appeals on behalf of his outraged coloured brethren. Recently a slave himself, and still liable, by the laws of his country, to be seized and carried back into bondage, he appealed to an Irish audience for help to break the chains which bound the black man in America. What the chairman had stated respecting the churches of America was true. They were all implicated more or less in the sin of maintaining the infernal slave system – of placing their brethren in chains like these, and flogging them with whips like this – (holding up to the audience some of the horrible instruments of torture used by the slaveholders.) It is with such a Church as this that I ask you to hold no Christian intercourse. Be faithful, friends, in your Christian testimony against such profanation of Christianity as this. I love religion – I love the religion of Jesus, which is pure and peaceable, and easy to be entreated. I ask you all to love this religion;

but I hate a religion which, in the name of the Savior, and which prostitutes his blessed precepts to the vile purposes of slavery, ruthlessly sunders all the ties of nature, which tears the wife from the husband – which separates the child from its parent – which covers the backs of men and women with bloody scars – which promotes all manner of licentiousness. I hate such a religion as this, for it is not Christianity – it is of the devil. I ask you to hate it too, and to assist me in putting in its place the religion of Jesus. Let the Methodist minister, the Presbyterian minister, the Baptist minister, the Unitarian minister, the Catholic clergyman, and the Protestant Clergyman – let the Society of Friends – let all, of every denomination in Ireland, be faithful to their Savior, and slavery in America will soon fall to the ground. For they are all in connection with churches in America, to whom they can send out faithful remonstrances. Public opinion in America boasts that it is almost omnipotent, and to a great extent this is true; it makes and unmakes laws – it establishes and overturns the customs of society; and while our people claim to be the most enlightened, and the most civilized, and the freest upon the earth, and while they are vain of their institutions, they are sensitive in the extreme to the opinions entertained of them in European countries, particularly in England and Scotland and Ireland. Friends of the poor slave, be therefore firm and faithful in your remonstrances with Americans; let your press teem with denunciations; let your pulpits proclaim to the world that Christianity disowns all fellowship with man stealers; let your social circles all talk on the subject as one of deep importance to the interests of humanity; let your entire community be filled with anti-slavery sentiment; so that when slaveholders or apologists of the system visit your country, they may feel that they breathe in an atmosphere too pure to be contaminated by them. Do this my friends, and you will render good service to the oppressed. I ask you in the name of humanity; I ask you in the name of Christianity; I ask you in the name of God; I ask you in the name of all you hold dear on earth or in Heaven, to be in earnest in this holy cause. I am the representative of three millions of bleeding slaves. I have felt the lash myself; my back is scarred with it; I know what they suffer, and I implore you to bring the weight of that powerful public opinion which you can make so effective, to bear on the hearts and consciences of the slaveholders of my country. Tell them they must give up their vile practices, or continue to be held in contempt by the whole civilized world.

(We have given but a faint outline of Mr. Douglass's eloquent and manly speech. He is a speaker of great ability, well calculated to interest the feelings and convince the judgment of his hearers. He read copious extracts from the laws of the slave States, proving that a grinding despotism exists in them, and that great pains are taken to keep the colored man in a condition of the most brutal degradation. He was loudly cheered throughout his long and most interesting discourse.)

At the close of it, the Hutchinson family, those most sweet and delicious warblers, came forward and sang one of their delightful songs, descriptive of the desolation of a slave mother when torn from her child at the auction block. Those who have not heard these sweetly harmonious songsters should do so on the first opportunity. There is a fine elevating tone in their performance, which should create for them the sympathy, and ensure the support of the virtuous and the good.

Two resolutions were passed by the meeting with much enthusiasm.

The first was moved by Mr. RICHARD ALLEN, in a short but appropriate speech, in which he eulogized the noble conduct of those slaves who, amid unheard-of difficulties, made their way to freedom. Thousands of them are now living in Canada, under the protection of the British law. Frederick Douglass was a living witness before them of the courage and talent of the coloured race.

The resolution was seconded by Mr. J. H. WEBB. Before putting it, The CHAIRMAN said he wished to mention one circumstance which was omitted by Mr. Douglass. By the laws of the slaveholders, it was made to appear that some care was taken to protect the slave from brutal cruelty; but this was only an ingenious fraud on the civilized world, as their framers took good care to make all such humane, or apparently humane, provisions of no value, by declaring that in no case should the evidence of a coloured man be taken against a white man.

The next resolution was moved by Mr. RICHARD D. WEBB, in a speech of great ability. He bore testimony to the truthfulness of all the statements of Frederick Douglass, and said it would be impossible for him to give a full and true account of the atrocious nature of slavery in America, which was characterized by every villainy, and should excite the indignation of mankind. He said it was a sin and a shame for our learned men, for our young men in college, to devote all their time to Greek and Latin, and so totally as they do, neglect the claims of humanity. Turning to the galleries, he said there are many men there who know more of the horrible details of slavery, thanks to their attendance on the monthly lectures in the Royal Exchange, by the committee of the Hibernian Anti-Slavery Society, than the students of Trinity College, whose apathy on the subject is disgraceful to our country. (Mr. Webb is a clever and a popular speaker; he created much amusement by his allusions to the sensitiveness of some religious bodies in our city, who closed their doors against Frederick Douglass, because of their delinquent brethren in America). What sort of a foundation has that Christianity in the heart, which seeks to cover up all the faults of its professors, and to make slaveholders and their abettors feel easy in the perpetration of enormities such as human nature, to say nothing of Christianity, shudders at.

Mr. Webb was loudly cheered throughout his speech.

The meeting separated soon after ten o'clock, the Chairman informed all present that Mr. Douglass intends to leave town in a few days, and to visit Wexford, Waterford, Cork, and other places in the south, previous to his return to Dublin, and begging of all who had friends in the south to prepare a hearty reception for Mr. Douglass during his visit to it, and for the Hutchinson family, whenever they go there. These devoted friends of humanity will, he doubted not, meet kind and warm-hearted friends all over our country. – (Cheers.)

5

THE SOUTH – WEXFORD AND WATERFORD

Advertisement
Publication: *Wexford Independent*
Date of Publication: Wednesday, 8 October 1845
Title: 'American Slavery'.

FREDERICK DOUGLASS, Recently a slave in the United States, intends to deliver a lecture on American Slavery in the ASSEMBLY ROOMS (which have been kindly granted for that purpose by the Mayor)[68] on WEDNESDAY EVENING the 8th inst. at eight o'clock.

Doors open at half past seven o'clock.

Admission tickets to the body of the House – tickets to reserved seats, 4*d.* each can be obtained at the door.

Anti-Slavery Meetings
Lecturer: Frederick Douglass
Location: Assembly Rooms, Wexford
Dates of Lectures: Tuesday, 7 October 1845; Wednesday, 8 October 1845
Publication: *Waterford Chronicle* [69]
Date of Publication: Saturday, 11 October 1845
Title: 'ANTI-SLAVERY MEETING IN WEXFORD'.

On Tuesday and Wednesday evenings Mr. F. Douglas [sic], who lately escaped from slavery, delivered two very interesting lectures in the Assembly rooms of this town. He said he loved O'Connell because Mr. O'C. befriended him when in the grasp of his tyrant slaveholders. At the mention of the Liberator's name the audience rose and cheered vehemently. I understand that the lecturer will be in Waterford in few days. Mr. Dudley and Mr. Buffon [sic], of America, also spoke. A resolution denouncing slavery was then moved and carried.

Letter: Joseph Poole to the Editor of the *Wexford Independent*
Publication: *Wexford Independent*
Date of Publication: Saturday, 11 October 1845
Title: 'American Slavery'.

To the Editor of the Independent.

Mr. Editor – You are without doubt an anti-slavery man, and will take pleasure in informing your readers who may be unware of the fact, that the execrable system of American slavery has a most competent exposure in our good town of Wexford, at the hands of one of its fugitive victims, and most eloquent and determined opponents, Frederick Douglas [sic] of Lynn, Massachusetts, recently a slave in Maryland, and now threatened in his life and his liberty for his courageous denunciation of its iniquities, and who has been driven thereby from the land of stars and stripes – the land of freedom and equality – the land of religion and civilization, the United States of America, to seek protection from the pitiless grip of his master in the bosom of the Green Island, in the heart and beneath the sheltering arm of the liberty-loving sons of old Ireland.

This Frederick Douglas [sic], this chattel, this thing, this article of property worth 1,000 dollars at the auction block of the capital of America, proclaimed aloud in the Assembly Room on Wednesday evening, his manhood and the manhood of his race and its identity with the whole brotherhood of man. 'I am your brother' said Douglas [sic], and the assent of his hearers was proclaimed in such a universal shout of approbation that the old walls shook to hear. Three millions of our brothers and sisters still languish in bondage of the most hideous description in the Southern States of America – but the day we doubt not is near when through the instrumentality of such advocates as Douglas [sic], in disseminating a thorough knowledge of the system, and before the contempt and abhorrence of civilized nations, surrounding them like a wall of fire upon all sides, the tyrants of the oppressed must at last be shunned or terrified into breaking every yoke and letting the oppressed go free.

Will you through the medium of your paper help forward the good cause by making known the feeling of a large assembly of your fellow townsmen, expressed in the following resolution which passed the meetings without a single dissenting voice:

Proposed by Joseph Poole seconded by William Whitney,

Resolved – that we have listened with interest to the development of horrors of American slave holding in the US, by Frederick Douglas [sic] (recently a slave in that country) and that we were filled with the greatest disgust and loathing at the horrible inconsistency between the profession and practice of those who – calling themselves *Christians, Republicans and Democrats* hold men women and children in the most degrading bondage, and we hereby register our remonstrance against all such, and declare that, as lovers of liberty – as Irish men having human hearts and human sympathies, we utter our solemn conviction that no Slaveholder can be Christian any more than Pirates and Robbers can be honest men; and we hereby repudiate all such as the enemies of true religion and the worst enemies of the human race and the rights of man.

Accounts of such meetings and such resolutions taking place or being passed in Ireland or England finding their way into American papers are well known to be influential in affecting public opinion in America, in disheartening those stealers of men, American slaveholders, and in strengthening the hands of those devoted friends of the slave and human freedom the world over, who are now exerting every faculty which God has given them, in their endeavour to wipe off this plague spot from their land.

You may perhaps aid the cause of the slave by giving a place to the above expression of opinion. I need not say that you would much oblige the subscriber.

Joseph Poole.[70]

Anti-Slavery Meeting
Lecturer: Frederick Douglass
Date of Lecture: Thursday, 9 October 1845
Location: Town Hall, Waterford
Publication: *Wexford Independent*
Date of Publication: Wednesday, 15 October 1845
Title: 'American Slavery'.

On Thursday evening a discourse was delivered at the large room in the town hall, on the subject of slavery in the United States by Frederick Douglas [sic] who had been recently a slave in the state of Maryland. The attendance was by no means large. Mr. Douglas [sic] detailed to the meeting the horrors of slavery, and the relative position of the slave owner to the slave. He showed clearly the fallacy of the argument which is made to us by many persons in this country, who enquire what good could result to the slave from their agitation of the question? Mr. Douglas [sic] speaks the English language fluently, and has rather a good delivery. During his address he dealt some extremely hard hits to freedom loving! republican and democratic Brother Jonathan, which we admit are richly deserved by the slave holding states of the union. It is a monstrous profanation to hear the cry of 'liberty' come from the lips of monsters who violate its most sacred principles. The system of slavery existing in America is an abomination that should call forth the indignant reprehension of every man professing Christianity. (from the *Waterford Freeman)*

Editorial
Publication: *Waterford Mail* [71]
Date of Publication: Saturday, 11 October 1845
Title: 'Mr Douglass. Anti-Slavery Lecture'.

On Thursday evening, Mr. Douglass, who, as our readers have already been informed, was but recently an American slave, and who is even now liable, should he come within the jurisdiction of his former masters, or their confreres in guilt, to be again subjected to their tender mercies – the fetter, and the lash, delivered a lecture on the subject of slavery, in the large room of the Town Hall. Notwith-standing the unfavourable state of the weather, and the short notice which the pub-lic had received of the intended meeting, Mr. Douglass, whose manner is highly prepossessing, delivered himself with energy and feeling, and was listened to with marked attention by his auditory, whose sympathies he excited by his faithful recital of the black man's sufferings, and the black man's wrongs. We regret being unable to give any portion of the able lecture of Mr. Douglass. The cause he so ably advocates deserves the support of every friend to humanity – of every Chris-tian, no matter of what denomination.

Article
Publication: *Wexford Conservative*
Date of Publication: Saturday, 18 October 1845
No Title.

Lately a Creole, of the name Douglas [sic] lectured in Wexford on Slavery as it exists in the United States of America. He had been himself a slave for many years. A short time ago, when traveling in that country, two gentlemen took their seats in the coach at the place where they were changing their horses. It was late in the evening, Douglas joined in their conversation and maintained it so well that he was Sir'd and Sir'd repeatedly. He felt, he could not tell how, as he had never been addressed in such way before, and he had a painful sensation in the reflection that when the morning's light should come, his consequence should vanish. As soon as the light broke in upon them, one of the gentlemen peeped under the hat of Douglas, then suddenly throwing himself back, he stirred his companion and whispered to him, 'Egad, it's a nigger!'. Yes, the light of truth shows everything in its correct character, colour, and proportions. The two men were prejudiced against the mere tincture of the poor Creole's skin; but they had only looked upon the surface. Had they turned their eyes upon their own 'Above all things deceitful' and 'desperately wicked' hearts they would have seen real blackness in them, not superficially, but throughout all their recesses.

Article
Publication: *Kerry Evening Post* [72] (from the *Cork Constitution*)
Date of Publication: Saturday, 18 October 1845
No Title.

The "pursuit of knowledge under difficulties" has formed the subject of some instructive volumes; but the experience of an American, named Frederick Douglas [sic], formerly a slave in one of the Southern States, but now an escaped freeman, might furnish materials for an enlargement. Our readers are aware that, in "the land of freedom" letters are forbidden to a slave – that it is penal to instruct him, and that Lynch-law is the *only* law of which the offender would be likely to enjoy the benefit. How, then, did Douglas learn? At a meeting in the Music Hall, Lower Abbey-street, Dublin (in which city, by the way, those into whose hands he fell would not be content without hawking him to Conciliation Hall) he explains the mystery:

"He would tell them how he had learned to read and write during the period of his bondage. He belonged to a Mr. Anthony, who lived in the south of the State of Maryland, and at seven years of age was transferred by him to a brother-in-law, whose wife was a benevolent woman, and began to take as much interest in him as her own children. She taught him spelling as far as words of four letters, being ignorant that the procedure was a crime according to the law of the land, but was soon caused to desist by her husband, who told her that it would not do to be teaching a slave. Upon this he (Mr. Douglas) possessed of himself a little book, and when he used to be sent on errands he contrived, by making extraordinary speed on part of the way to have time to pick up instruction from little boys whom he fell in with, who had no prejudice against colour, were ignorant of the law, and looked on him as a little playmate. When he learned to read in this manner he desired to learn how to write, and being placed by his master in a ship-yard, he began to notice that the timber which was prepared for putting on board the vessels was marked with different letters according to the parts of the hold in which it was intended to be stowed. He asked the carpenters the names of the letters and when they told him, good-naturedly and innocently, he took the chalk and learned to imitate them, and thus became familiar with four letters of the alphabet, commonly employed in marking the logs. (hear.) Then as soon as he had an opportunity of meeting in the streets little white boys who could read and write; he told them that he was able to write, and to satisfy their incredulity would make a letter on the flags: one of them, in a spirit of competition, would take the chalk from him and write a much finer capital, and so he had a fine copy before him at once. (hear, and cheers.) In this way he learned reading and writing; and when his mistress used to leave him at home to mind the house, he read by stealth the Bible, Clarke's Commentaries,[73] and other works, and as soon as he was at liberty, he recited what he remembered of his studies to the trees, to the pigs when he fed them, to animate and inanimate objects indiscriminately. (laughter.) Thus he acquired the little knowledge with which he appeared before them".

An advertisement announces that Mr. Douglas has arrived in Cork and is to lecture to-day at the City Court House.

Editorial
Publication: *Waterford Chronicle*
Date of Publication: Saturday, 18 October 1845
Title: 'AMERICAN SLAVERY'.

The *Boston Pilot* is vexed at our remarks regarding American Slavery, and the part Hiberno-Irishmen take in that inhuman Institution. Our writing is called weak at the same time that it brings into existence two columns of considerable spleen against us for honestly saying what was the belief of the majority of Irishmen in reference to the inhabitants of America, and that "Institution." And these columns do give us corroborating statements to our own, of the unfortunate state of American Society.

It is boasted in this country that the Irish in America are *free* – listen to the apology made by the American journal for the Irishmen in that country being silent on, or defending, the horrible traffic in human beings: "The Irish in America are in a minority to the native born of about one to eight. They are in most states in a *dependent* condition, earning a living from men whose opinions and predelictions, they are coerced by their necessities to *respect*."

Just as we remarked, "they learn the slave cant of the *free* land – they love what the Yankee loves, and they hate what he hates; evil communication corrupts good manners and Ireland being out of sight, she is called presumptuous and offensive, for reminding the heretofore sons of her bogs, her mountains, her valleys, that they are going on in an unnatural career." It is acknowledged by the sensitive *Boston Pilot* that the Irish are but *dependent* in America (has it come to this?) and that they are forced to respect by necessity the opinions of their master natives!

And is this the prosperity of America? Is this the position of those who would make the foreign Eagle lift up in her fierce beak the drooping harp of Erin? Ah, it is but an exchange of masters – or of one kind of master for a worse; because in Ireland the Irishman does not respect the opinions of those who tyranise over him, or to whom he is dependent. Did we not write accurately of American society?

In endeavouring to bully us (for the article is really offensive, especially to us who wrote most kindly of the correspondent of the *Nation*) the *Pilot* makes some sad (to him) admissions. In fact he concedes everything that we could wish. He admits, besides what is contained in the above extract, the following opinions which we number:

1. – That the Irishman carries the course [sic] of Swift, for being born in Ireland, and that the marks of the chains are still on his back.
2. – That the Irishmen coming to the United States finds slavery there, but that it is not so hard as represented in Ireland.
3. – That the Irishmen "know indeed, that a gross, horrible system prevails in some Southern places in the breeding and rearing of up [sic] those slaves, at which every moral feeling revolts."
4. – That, although Southern States slavery separates man and wife, child and parent, British slavery does the same amongst the Irish people, by the extirpation of parent or child.
5. – That the Irishman feels all of this, but that he is too *new* in the country to resist it.
6. – That it is more the business of *native* philanthropists than *wandering* adventurers to endeavour to "reform" these things.

6.   [sic] – That the Irishmen there "eats the bread of America, and breathes her air," and for these things they will be abused by the Irish at home.
7.   – That American money and sympathy helped Ireland heretofore in her struggles for Emancipation.

Now if the Irishman is made to feel the curse of Swift in America, how can he be a free citizen? How can his eagle pull up his fainting harp? Is this the land of freedom? For all the proud boasts and all the inflated oratory, and all the magnificent promises of the Irish Americans are empty sounds. No wonder that we receive no money – those *dependent* on natives must always be respecting the opinions of the natives. Does the land lie in this way, honest slave in Alleghania?[74] Whilst you escape from the Irish branch of Puritanism must you go forth to Massachusetts to be under the yoke of a much worse branch of Puritanism? Do not chafe in your chains expatriated Irishman; you grew by degrees to *love your enemies*: you endured, pitied and embraced, and we forgive you.

But, be just to your brethren in Ireland – how dare you vex the Orangemen who lord it over us – how dare you reproach wish [sic] your bitter taunts the men who have us in their power – the British government, its army, its navy, and its Irish supporters. You say that the Irish endure unknown sufferings in America, upon each new outburst of wrath poured out in the Conciliation Hall – have you no compassion for the Irish in Ireland, lest they be afflicted with the "unknown sufferings" by your attacks on the Irish and English oligarchy? Fair play, good Hiberno-American! And now would not the full measure of our most brutal slavery be filled up if *we the Repealers* cared about what you Americans said to our givers of the living? When you, the *Boston Pilot*, come out with your bitter attacks on the British government, and on Lord Morpeth, and even in the article on what we are commenting, what would you think if we cowered and waxed sullen, lest our rulers should hear of your attack, and visit us with vengeance? You would think we were the veriest of slaves! And yet we would be no greater slaves to the British than you are to the miscalled "natives".

We ask you, as you are an Irishman, to ponder on what Ireland would be now, if the people of Ireland, being *dependent*, had continued to *respect* the Irishmen who, to use your own words, applied to Native Americans, "filled the best positions in a commercial, agricultural and political sense?" And your "one to eight" in population will not save you. The Irish had against them every influence, every power – the army (as we said before), the navy, the land, the commerce, every thing – why should not the British opinions be respected still? And why should not Irishmen be still dependent? And WHY, ON YOUR PRINCIPLE, does not the Catholic Irishman VOLUNTEER his offensive indignation against you for daring to interfere with the British "Institutions". Behold your position! Thank God this is a freer land, with all its faults, than yours!

The Irishman, or the Boston paper for him, saw that the slaves were better off than *they* used to be in Ireland, and he admits the crying and horrible sin of southern slavery – that is, that because the Irish suffered – the coloured race should suffer; certainly a learned mode of reasoning; but he has not a word to say for the southern States; this is a bloody stain that sophism, prejudice and *dependency* can not obliterate. Again, the balancing system – because British slavery separates free emigrants from relatives, New Orleans must be allowed to tear and rend asunder the ties of Nature, by forcibly separating wife, child and husband from each other! "Weak" reasoning, indeed, and a reasoning which to some men ought to make use of.

The Irishman is *new*, and he is a "wandering adventurer", compared with the native philanthropist"! This from the *Boston Pilot*! Ah, wear your collar, "wandering" and tongue-tied "adventurer". You are weekly combatting the Natives and yet you fall into their very views, and give utterance to their very sentiments. Why one would say that a "new" and a wandering person could not feel such interest for settled "institutions" as you give expression to.

The Irishman "eats the bread and breathes the air of America!" Indeed, we thought the Irishman was not a-begging there. We thought he earned his bread as a freeman, and not by being thankful to "Americans" for it. And the air too – Pity it was not hermetically sealed for the Irishman, and only let out of the bottle occasionally by the Church burners of Philadelphia.[75] Truly there is something more that the marks of the chain in the flesh of the American Irishman. Why if the *natives* "can hide the sun in a blanket, and put the moon in their pockets" let the American Irish pay tribute to them. But who are the natives? The fugitive Indians we say.

As to the former support given by the Americans, we, as Irishmen, are grateful to them for it; the more so as it is enhanced by the circumstances of its coming from men who are so divided that they are tremblingly afraid of one another to express their opinions.

We conclude by promising to give the article by the *Boston Pilot* in our next (as, rather harshly, requested to do so), although our American contemporary did not insert with the article from the *Chronicle;* and by extracting for the present the following paragraph, in which the eating of the American bread occurs, and which we think is more calculated to confer honour on us than otherwise:

> There are bad Irishmen abroad as well as at home. We should be heartily indisposed to defend them, but we wish to relieve "Irishmen of America" so far as our influence extends, from the sweeping anathema of the *CHRONICLE*. We believe it is the first Irish journal that has ventured to attack them, but we presume we shall soon hear of a general attack from our friends across the Atlantic, in which, because we eat the bread and breathe the air of America, we shall be denounced.

Editorial
Publication: *Waterford Chronicle*
Date of Publication: Wednesday, 22 October 1845
Title: 'Frederick Douglas [sic]. The American'.

There was somebody in the *Mail* rhyming about the poor reception the "Slave" got in this city and blaming the citizens for not cheering him on; but the fact is, nobody heard of him. He did not come to the right place. If he had given intimidation of his coming at the *Chronicle* office, we should have made the city hear of him.

Editorial
Publication: *Waterford Chronicle* (from the *Boston Pilot*, Sept. 27.)
Date of Publication: Saturday, 25 October 1845
Title: 'American SLAVERY AND REPEAL'.

This is the heading of an article in the *Waterford Chronicle* of the 29 August. The writer undertakes to censure the Irishmen in America for a complication of crimes. He charges that they are not true to the Repeal cause, nor to the great principle of civil liberty! and he attempts to sustain the first by showing that their subscriptions to the Conciliation Hall have fallen off, and the second, by inferring that they sanction the immorality of southern slavery by an apathetic or an acquiescing silence in reference to it.

Now hear us in reply, and give your readers all our words.

Irishmen come to America to obtain a living by their industry, which they cannot find at home; they are strangers and wanderers in this new continent. The best positions, in a commercial, agricultural, or political sense, are already occupied by men of another race and another religion. The Irish emigrant comes in among the descendants of prejudiced Englishmen – among those whose fathers hated the very name of Catholic Ireland. He carries with him the course [sic] of Swift, the being *born in Ireland*; and has to hew out his way in America by sheer labour.

The Irishmen of the United States are in a minority to the native born, about one to eight. They are, in most of the states, generally in a *dependent* condition, earning a living from men whose opinions and predilections they are coerced by their necessities to respect. Before they leave their native land for this, they are aware that slavery exists in the Southern states; but they are also aware that more than half, the bigger, better, much richer half of the Union, is free. They take the United States, with all their faults, for better and for worse, as their future country; they find on their arrival that those slaves about whom they heard many pathetic appeals, are a far sight better fed, better clothed, better housed, and less worked than *they* used to be while in Ireland. They find that the 'whip' and the 'lash,' and all that, which finished the periods of popular orators in Ireland, are what they commonly understand, by the vulgar term *Collywest*.[76] They know, indeed, that a gross, a horrible system prevails in some Southern places in the breeding and rearing up of those slaves, at which every moral feeling revolts; and they find through the free states, that an active public hatred exists towards it. They have heard, too, that Southern American slavery separates man and wife, child and parent, but *they* know too well, also, that British slavery produces the self-same effect upon them and theirs; for who, that quits Ireland for home here, but quits also for ever some dear parent or dear child, whose hearts break and whose salt tears stream on separation which must, like the fiat of a cursed aristocracy, be final and death-like?

Byron describes better than any other, the Irish emigrant's feelings on quitting his relatives for ever.

"Look down the beach where the emigrant stands.
He takes a last look at his home and his hearth;
Tears drop from his chains as they fall from his hands,
For the dungeon he quits is the place of his birth."

True, it is a dungeon; but not all dungeon as it is nothing but the fear of positive starvation drives him from it; for it is the tomb of his ancestors, and the garden of his nativity and youth. Yet his separation is hidden "by act of parliament," and the monsters at home who are guilty of this "separation," scarcely ever receive a lash from those who make it the chief object of their lives to lacerate the Southern planters.

The Irishman in exile sees and feels all this; and although in his soul he hates slavery and tyranny be believes himself too humble and too new in the country to lead American sentiment in reform, which, though it be the business and duty of every living being, yet is more peculiarly the business of the *native* philanthropists, than of the *wandering adventurers*.

Nor is the American-Irishman the worst enemy of the negro race, although Lord Morpeth has said it, and the *Chronicle* believes it. Lord Morpeth, though what in Ireland is termed a "good fellow",[77] mixed when on his travels through America, with Englishmen chiefly, who are ever ready enough, the wealthy and cruel of them, to fling out a hard word upon the poor Irishman. No Englishman's testimony ought to be taken unqualifiedly against an Irishman. Though his Lordship's administration was highly relished by the Irish place-hunters during the "Experiment," we believe that it can and will be proved that during all this time he was picking open O'Connell's letters, and keeping in his pay a battalion of spies and "detectors," who made rebel Ribbonmen for the purpose of catching them, as in the good old days of Major Sirr and Castlereagh.

There are bad Irishmen abroad as well as at home. We should be heartily indisposed to defend them, but we wish to relieve "the Irishmen of America," so far as our influence extends, from the sweeping anathemas of the *Chronicle*. We believe it is the first Irish journal that has ventured to attack them, but we presume we shall sooner hear of a general attack from our friends across the Atlantic, in which, because we breathe the air and eat the bread of America, we shall be denounced.

But the expatriated Irishmen of America do not, and have not neglected their native land in any and every struggling in which they engaged with her oppressor.

They have stronger motives to urge them to this duty than the spur or the praise of any newspaper. They felt the chains while they wore them, and the marks are *yet in their flesh*; yes, the iron touched their soul. Their first aspiration, after the emotions which belong to Religion, was the Freedom of Ireland; and the prayer for her deliverance was frequently mingled with the prayer for their own salvation.

When Ireland battled for her religious rights in '25, the Irishmen in America, from Maine to New Orleans, associated on her behalf, and sustained her peaceful struggle with noble gifts. Had it been a physical contest, they were prepared to plunge into it on the wave and on the land, as they are at present with ten-fold resolution. On this head, *The Chronicle* may consult his townsman, Mr. Wyse, who in his history of the Catholic Association testifies in significant language his sense of the importance of that aid which the Irishmen of America rendered the Catholic agitators; and without troubling the editor to seek the passage, we will supply it:

[Here follows extract from Wyse's history of the Catholic Association, showing the value of American support, previous to Emancipation.]

All these symptoms, Mr. Wyse proceeds to show, operated on the Wellington-Peel ministry, and conspired, with other circumstances, to compel them to yield.

Such was the nature of Hiberno-American sympathy in the days of the Catholic struggle. There were more slaves in comparison with the white population, then in the United States than there are present. The Catholic agitators did not stop to expostulate with the slave-holders of America; they accepted their aid, and thanked them for it, and because they battled for one thing at a time, they succeeded. Again, when the standard of Repeal was raised in '32, and the Whigs brought in the Coercion Bill in '33, the Irishmen of America were at the back of Ireland in money and sympathy. When the great leader in his wisdom rolled in the flag of Repeal, in the hope of getting justice for Ireland, the friends of Ireland held aloof, patiently watching the issue. – And when in 1840 the flag was again unfurled, with a vehement earnestness they assembled in their cities and hamlets, and poured forth their sympathies across the ocean, in streams of gold, so much so, that O'Connell boasted that he could not walk three steps in any direction, without being congratulated upon the aid which America was sending them. American statesmen of every party joined in the holy association; the court-houses and senate-houses of America echoed with the shouts of sympathizing friends in Ireland, and Ireland, from her peerage her peasantry felt the electric influence of American sympathy. Presidents, and vice-presidents, and ex-presidents, and governors, and senators in the American Republic, were enrolled in our ranks. England trembled, Ireland raised her hand, and Europe was astonished.

All this was done in good faith, and in sincerity. By one effort more we could have identified Congress in the struggle, could have obtained a vote of sympathy from the grand council of the nation. With this at our back, and Canada struggling to get away, we would be nearer the Repeal than we are now.

These, and many more, which we could urge, are the reasons for the apathy which pervades our ranks, and which have their origin not with us, but with the other side of the Atlantic.

6

CORK

Article
Lecturer: Frederick Douglas
Date of Lecture: Friday, 12 October 1845
Location: Temperance Hall, Globe Lane, Cork[78]
Publication: *Cork Examiner*
Date of Publication: Monday Evening, 13 October 1845
Title: 'Slavery. Mr. Frederick Douglas [sic]'.

SLAVERY – MR. FREDERICK DOUGLAS. We beg to refer our readers to the advertisement of the Anti-Slavery Meeting, to be held in the Courthouse tomorrow.

Mr. Douglas, to hear whom the meeting has been called, is a most eloquent and effective speaker. We heard him last evening at the Festival in Globe Lane Temperance Hall, in honour of the Very Rev. Theobald Mathew, and were delighted with his calm, forcible manner, and his frequent bursts of fervid eloquence; and as we have no doubt he is as effective on the subject of slavery as on that of temperance, we can promise our citizens a happy intellectual treat. Never, we do think, was the assertion more signally disproved than on last evening, that the taint of African blood necessarily produces inferiority, either of body or mind; and the feeling that such a man should ever have been held the property of another, his noble frame tasked, flogged, and fettered, and his active, intelligent and expressive mind cramped and darkened, without a solitary chance of having its energies awakened, causes a loathing of the slave system which should be sufficient to enlist all our sympathies.

We are indebted to the circumstance of Mr. Douglas having published a narrative of his life, and his experience of the horrors of slavery for his present visit –. The sensation caused by the publication of his book rendered his stay in America unsafe, until the excitement dies away, as he is still liable to be captured, and taken back bondage.

Soirée
Date of Soirée: Sunday, 12 October 1845
Publication: *Cork Examiner*
Date of Publication: Monday, 20 October 1845
Title: 'Tea Festival at the Globe Lane Festival Hall'.

On Sunday evening week, the excellent members of this spacious Hall, celebrated the commemoration of the birth of their illustrious President,[79] by a Festival, which, notwithstanding the severity of the weather, was numerously and respectably attended. Amongst the guests we noticed Ald.[80] Roche (Mayor Elect), Mr. William Martin, Capt. O'Sullivan, Messrs. Frederick Douglas [sic] and Buffum, Teetotallers from America; J. Varian, Bernard Alcock &c., &c. The numbers of well-dressed females who were present, principally comprising the wives and daughters of Tradesmen, formed an interesting and spirited scene; and if evidence were wanting of the blessed effects resulting from Total Abstinence, the happiness which beamed on every countenance at this festive scene was sufficient testimony. The decorations were, if possible, more gay and effective than on any other occasion; festoons of laurels and flowers were most tastefully arranged; a very good Bust of Father Mathew occupied a prominent position, and at either end of the Hall were placed two beautifully executed stars. The one had printed in gold letters, a small star and the year which first gave birth to him who has been under Divine Providence, a blessing to the whole human family – under the large star was inscribed the 10th of October, 1845, the anniversary of that day, shewing that the Apostle has already spent 56 years of usefulness and charity amongst the people. The performances of the band attached to this Hall, are too well known to require our eulogy: it is sufficient to say that they formed the principal feature in the evening's entertainments.

After the company partaking of tea and sweet bread &c., Capt. O'Sullivan was moved to the Chair. The usual loyal sentiments were proposed and enthusiastically received. The sentiment of the evening "Father Mathew, and may he long live to diffuse the blessing of Temperance, Peace, and Happiness to his followers" was eloquently responded to by Mr. Bernard Alcock. The next sentiment "Temperance all over the world" was ably spoken to by Mr. John Bluett, who took occasion to read an address agreed to by his brother members, and presented to one of their most active officers, Mr. Edward Flaherty, with a beautiful Silver Medal and Chain, as a testimonial of the esteem and regard in which his services were held and appreciated.

The Chairman next gave "The guests," when Mr. Douglas of America, made a most brilliant speech.

"The Ladies" was replied to by Ald. Roche, (Major Elect) when the Chairman was moved from the chair and Mr. Wm. Martin called thereto, when the thanks of the meeting were most cordially awarded to Capt. O'Sullivan for his very proper and dignified conduct in the Chair. Dancing then commenced, and was kept up with animation until the serving out of Coffee and Cake, &c., after which the company separated highly delighted with the evening's entertainments.

Advertisement
Publication: *Cork Examiner*
Date of Publication: Monday, 13 October 1845
Title: 'APPEAL FOR LIBERTY'.

3,000,000 slaves
 FREDERICK DOUGLASS, a fugitive slave, will speak on the subject of AMERICAN SLAVERY at two o'clock on TUESDAY next, 14 inst. at the CITY COURT HOUSE.
 RICHARD DOWDEN[81] (R) will preside.
 The gallery will be reserved for Ladies.
 The committees of the Ladies and Gentlemen's Anti-Slavery societies will breakfast at LLOYD'S HOTEL, at half past eight o'clock on TUESDAY morning, to receive Mr. DOUGLASS. Any friends of the cause are invited to attend.

Anti-Slavery Breakfast
Lecturer: Frederick Douglass
Date of Breakfast: Tuesday, 14 October 1845
Location: Lloyds Hotel, Cork
Publication: *Cork Examiner*
Date of Publication: Wednesday, 15 October 1845
Title: 'Anti-slavery Breakfast'.

A breakfast was given at Lloyds' Hotel, yesterday morning, by several of the friends and advocates of Negro emancipation, to meet a Mr. Douglas [sic], a self-emancipated slave from one of the Southern States of America, and a Mr. Buffan [sic], an American gentleman, a friend of Mr. Douglas, and an ardent abolitionist. Among those present were the Mayor, Alderman Lyons, Mr. Mannix, Mr. R. Jennings, Mr. W. Martin, Mr. R. Martin, Messrs. Varian, Mr. W. Dowden, Mr. Abraham Beale,[82] Mr. W. Harvey, Mr. Logan, Rev. Mr. Whitlegge, Mr. W. Kelleher, Mr. John F. Maguire, (Barrister), Messrs. Scott, Mr. T. Dunscombe, &c. Among the ladies present were Mrs. Dowden, Mrs. Roche, the Misses Jennings, Miss Dowden, Miss M'Intosh, &c.
 Alderman Lyons, presided.
 Mr. R. Varian alluded to the exertions of the friends of Abolition in Cork, and the contributions forwarded by those who took an interest in the great work of humanity to the Boston Bazaar, which contributions expressed in a convincing manner the feeling of abhorrence which slavery awakened in the minds of the people of Ireland. He and Mr. Wm. Martin had been active in getting contributions towards the Annual Anti-Slavery Bazaar, in Cork; but on hearing that they were to be favoured with the visit of Mr. Douglas [sic] and Mr. Buffan [sic], whose presence would effect great good, and whose details of the evils and horrors of slavery would excite considerable interest, they thought it better to pause for a while, and take advantage of the impression which they calculated would be produced by the addresses of these gentlemen (hear, hear).

The Mayor, after alluding in general terms to the evils of the iniquitous system, and representing how forcible an instrument was public opinion, requested on the part of the company, that Mr. Douglas would favour them by a short address, which he had no doubt would create very considerable interest, and much advance the object they had in view, of exciting a strong sympathy against the abominable traffic in human beings by their fellow men (hear, hear).

Mr. Douglas rose in compliance with the wishes of the company, and proceeded to address them with the ease and grace of a gentleman – a gentleman of nature and society. Evidently, from his colour and conformation, he is descended from parents of different race, his appearance is singularly pleasing and agreeable. The hue of his face and hands rather a yellow brown or bronze, while there is little, if anything, in his features of that peculiar prominence of lower face, thickness of lips, and flatness of nose, which peculiarly characterize the true Negro type. His voice is well toned and musical, his selection of language most happy, and his manner easy and graceful. He said that it afforded him great pleasure to meet the ladies and gentlemen by whom he was surrounded, and who cheered him by their presence that morning. He occupied a position for which he was unprepared, the habits and customs of his previous life having quite unsuited him for that position in which he found himself placed by a combination of unforeseen circumstances. However, he would in simple terms state the objects and aim of his visit. He then continued – First, you will remember that I was a slave, that I am still a slave, that I am still a slave according to the law of the State from which I ran, and according to the general government of the States of North America. About seven years ago, I was spoken of as a slave, and was considered in the same light as beast or a creeping thing – I was the same as a chattle [sic], a thing of household property, to be bought and sold, or used according to the will of my master. I was subject to all the evils and horrors of slavery – to the lash, the chain, the thumb-screw; and even as I stand here before you I bear on my back the marks of the lash (sensation). Mr. Douglas then related how he attempted to escape from bondage, and aided by the hand of God, how he succeeded in reaching a State where slavery had been abolished. But even there he was not free from the danger of pursuit; for all States of the Union, even though slavery does not exist within them, concede to the Slave States the right of coming to their soil, and taking run-a-way slaves wherever they find them. When he saw how liable he was to be arrested – how the bloodhound might be placed upon his track – when this danger prevented his speaking openly of the place from whence he came, and of the name of his master, and other details, he avoided disclosing them. He remained in the State of Massachusetts for the last five years, where, from the tone of public feeling upon the question of Slave-abolition, it would be difficult to take him, that is, at least, by any open means; for where legal proceedings are adopted to recover a slave, he is generally either let off, or liberated by purchase.

For the last four years he (Mr Douglas) had lectured there on slavery, thinking himself safe. At the same time, from concealing the place, his master and his name, as well as other particulars, suspicion was aroused, and mistrust created in many minds; for many supposed that he had not been a slave, he was so different from all the notions of what a slave was supposed to be. Had he given those particulars, some meanly-disposed person might have written to his master, disclosing to him his whereabouts; and the result would have been his capture by someone of the many means put in force by slave owners, when he would be doomed to an interminable and cruel bondage. However, to free himself from the suspicion which was most painful, he resolved on publishing a little narrative, in which he exposed the place of his slavery, the name of his master, the crime of slavery, and all the circumstances of its perpetration. By this means he silenced the doubt; but his danger increased, and on the advice of friends he undertook a mission to Great Britain, so that he might be enabled to arouse that horror of slavery which would have a great effect on the public mind of America. Mr. Douglas, after some other observations, concluded by alluding to Mr. Buffan, as a gentleman who had been a consistent advocate of freedom, and who had been subjected to much personal indignity and injury on account of his zeal in the cause of the suffering Negro. Mr. Buffan did not come on any mission; he came for the purpose of improving his mind by Foreign contact, and was ready to bear his testimony on the subject of Slavery. Mr. Douglas sat down amidst applause.

Mr. Logan, on the part of the company, desired to have the advantage of Mr. Buffan's sentiments regarding the real state of public opinion in the Slave States; for it was upon that the Abolitionists of this country chiefly rested their hopes.

Mr. Buffan rose to comply with the request, and in the course of a pretty long address presented a vivid description of the difficulties against which the abolitionists had to struggle in the beginning – the outrages and indignities to which they were exposed, and which, for the sake of their God-like cause, they heroically endured. He illustrated, by a number of attractive anecdotes, the contempt in which the black and coloured population were held – the rigid exclusion practised towards them – how they were neither associated nor travelled with in a steamboat or carriage, and were even separated in houses of religious worship from the white population. I may here state that it was admitted by Mr. Buffan as well as by Mr. Douglas, that the only Churches in which Black pews did not exist, were Roman Catholic Churches – where no difference was made between the black and the white man. After some other addresses had been delivered, and a deserved compliment passed on Messrs. Beale and Martin, the company separated.

Anti-Slavery Meeting
Lecturer: Frederick Douglass
Date of Lecture: Tuesday, 14 October 1845
Location: City Court-House, Cork
Publication: *Cork Examiner*
Date of Publication: Wednesday, 15 October 1845
Title: 'Anti-Slavery Meeting'.

At a CROWDED MEETING of the CITIZENS, held in the CITY COURT HOUSE, on TUESDAY, the 14 Instant. RICHARD DOWDEN (R.), Esq., Mayor, in the Chair.

The following Resolutions were proposed, and carried by acclamation:

Proposed by Mr. William Martin, seconded by the Rev. Wm. Whitelegge, and unanimously adopted –

That we extend our cordial greetings to Frederick Douglass, on his escape from American Bondage; and J. N. Buffum, Esq., the American Freeman, who has nobly volunteered to suffer for the slave; and with warm hearts and open hands welcome them to our Native Land.

Proposed by J. N. Buffum, Esq., seconded by J. Besnard, Esq., and unanimously adopted – That it is the bounden duty of the people of this country to bring their moral influence to bear on the American Nation, to arouse its inhabitants from their criminal apathy as to the condition of three millions of their fellow countrymen, whom they hold in bondage. Proposed by J. F. Maguire, Esq., Barrister, seconded by Frederick Douglass, and adopted unanimously –

Resolved – That the system of slavery, as it exists in America, is of so extensive and hideous a character, that it influences and promotes Slave-holding, and Slave-trading in any country where they may unhappily exist. That therefore, our duty to injured Africa, and our abhorrence of the Slave system in every land – calls upon all people, however poor, however distressed, to give time, thought, and labour to the best means of exterminating a system that demoralizes the Slave, demonizes the Master, and is a degradation to the whole human family.

The Mayor having vacated the Chair, Thomas Lyons. Esq., Alderman, was moved thereto, and the thanks of the Meeting were proposed by Andrew F. Roche, Esq., Alderman; seconded by Mr. William Martin, and carried by acclamation, to the Mayor, for his very efficient conduct on the occasion.

Anti-Slavery Meeting
Lecturer: Frederick Douglass
Date of Lecture: Tuesday, 14 October 1845
Location: City Court-House, Cork
Publication: *Cork Examiner*
Date of Publication: Wednesday, 15 October 1845
Title: 'Public meeting'.

A meeting was held yesterday in the City Courthouse for the same excellent object as the above. It was attended by over 100 ladies, and a large audience of respectable gentlemen and citizens generally.

The Mayor presided.

After some resolutions had been proposed and seconded by Mr. Martin, Rev. Mr. Whitelegge,[83] Mr. John Besnard,[84] Mr. Buffum, and Mr. J. F. Maguire (Barrister).[85]

Mr. Douglas [sic] came forward to second the resolution proposed by Mr. Maguire, and was received with the heartiest applause. Mr. Douglas [sic] then delivered one of the most eloquent and impressive discourses ever heard, in which he detailed, more fully than at the breakfast, the sufferings of his early years, the horrors and inhumanities arising from the iniquitous traffic in human beings, that system of slavery which strips a man not of one right, of one privilege, but, by the laws of the land, deprives a man of his own body, and delivers him up to the unlimited control of an irresponsible master, to deal with as he would with his meanest chattel. Mr. Douglas expressed the surprise and embarrassment which his reception in Ireland had caused him – he who had been accustomed to regard white men as a superior and different race of beings, and who had never before been looked on himself by white men with such complacency as by the audiences he had addressed in the Emerald Isle. When a child, he had been taught to acknowledge the white man as his master, and to bend the obsequious knee before him; and even then he had not overcome this feeling of self-abasement, for there were so many in America who would remind him of his colour, and the difference of skin which placed him and the white man apart. He described how at an early age he had dreams after liberty, how his young mind revolted from his condition, and how, after self-questioning to the reason and right of his slavery and his master's authority, felt that he was not born to slave, and that no right, either human or divine, or based upon the law of God, authorized a fellow-creature to hold him in bondage. He had been given to a little boy as his slave, who, when he was fretted or annoyed at anything, was told by his good mamma to "kick Freddy." He alluded to the marks of the lash which he bore on his back, which he would carry with him to the grave; but he said that they were not the most degrading marks of his bondage, for he bore them on his soul, debasing his humanity, and often crushing down his spirit to the very darkest depths of shame and degradation (great sensation).

He then referred to the atrocious laws of the slave states, amidst expressions of the deepest execration. For losing a boat from its chain, the penalty was, *the loss of an ear*, for the second offence! and he saw men and even women nailed by the ear to wooden posts! For carrying a club, 39 lashes – for travelling in any but the most general and frequented road, 40 lashes – for being out at night, 40 lashes – for being found in any other plantation, 40 lashes – for hunting with dogs, 30 lashes – for riding a horse in the day time, to whipped, cropped (ears cut off) and branded on the cheek with the letter " R," the initial for rogue; and he had seen the slave flung down on his back, his hands and feet tied, and the hardhearted master coolly applying the branding iron the cheek, and holding it there until it burned into the quivering flesh! These and other details produced a feeling and expression of horror impossible to describe. He then tore the mask off the religious cant of those dealers in human flesh, the Wesleyans and Episcopalians of America, particularly the former, who preached from their pulpits the most atrocious doctrines justifying the system of slavery, and perverted the sacred word of God to the base purpose human oppression. One quotation used by these canting scoundrels to defend the brutal torture inflicted on the slave, is – "He that knoweth his master's will, and doeth it not, shall be punished with many stripes." This infamous system, like all other evil systems, is upheld by ignorance – the mental and moral darkness of its victims; and by the laws of some of the States, it is death to teach a slave his letters. Mr. Douglas then dwelt on the glorious services of Mr. O'Connell to the cause of the slave – how his mighty voice had shaken slavery to the centre, and paralysed the soul of the slave-dealer. He eloquently concluded by a splendid burst of soul-stirring oratory, and sat down amidst enthusiastic cheers. The above is but a mere outline of speech which occupied over two hours in delivery.

Mr. R. Varian moved a vote of thanks to Mr. Wm. Martin for his services in the cause of abolition and for having been the means of procuring the visit of Mr. Douglas and Mr. Buffan [sic].

Mr. Logan said – in seconding a resolution of thanks to William Martin, I feel there can be no difficulty in passing such a resolution in a meeting of the citizens of Cork. There are two grounds for adopting this resolution; William Martin is a member of that community which mainly effected the abolition of one of the greatest evils the world ever witnessed[86] – West India Slavery (cheers). We are asked what have we to do with American Slavery? the claims upon our benevolence at home are too numerous and too urgent to permit our attention to foreign objects. William Martin, we all know, is not the man who shews no regard or compassion for the sufferings of his fellow countrymen, or the evils which afflict his own country; but we always find the men who are alive to the claims of humanity in every clime and in every country, are the men of the most active benevolence at home (cheers). We are to thank William Martin for bringing to our city Frederick Douglas and James Buffan (hear). It was only necessary to bring such men before us to awaken Irish feeling and the expression of Irish sympathy on this great question. We should ask why such a man as Frederick Douglas should have been a slave? such a specimen of our common humanity, and we must feel the injustice and cruelty of slavery more than ever. There are millions of such men still in slavery. Did you ever hear a more eloquent description of freedom than that which came from his lips? Could the sacred and inalienable rights of man be more distinctly asserted? Did you ever hear the horrors of slavery more forcibly or justly depicted? The fact is, the arrival of these men on our shores should be a great epoch in our history on this great question; the liberties of the world are not safe whilst three millions of men in the freest country in the world are in slavery. I have heard at the great Anti-slavery Meeting in London, year after year, those indignant denunciations against American Slavery which you have heard have been wafted across the Atlantic, and have made the conscience of the Slaveholder to tremble; but notwithstanding their effect on England and upon America they have never yet awakened in Ireland an adequate expression of feeling and sympathy for those who are suffering all the horrors of slavery in America. We see the power of public opinion on political injustice or legislation at home; let it be exerted for the removal of personal slavery abroad, and it will be omnipotent (cheers).

Mr. Martin returned thanks, but was surprised that any merit should have been attributed to him, for having merely done his duty. He had an abhorrence of slavery for the last years (cheers). The Mayor being called from the chair, and Alderman Lyons thereto, and a vote of thanks having been given to him for his conduct, the meeting separated.

Anti-Slavery Meeting
Lecturer: Frederick Douglass
Date of Lecture: Tuesday, 14 October 1845
Location: City Court House, Cork
Publication: *Southern Reporter and Cork Commercial Courier*
Date of Publication: Thursday, 16 October 1845
Title: 'INTERESTING NARRATIVE OF FUGITIVE SLAVE'. [87]

(From our REPORTER.)

On Tuesday an influential and numerously attended meeting of the citizens was held in the City Court House to hear the statement Mr. Frederick Douglas [sic], himself a fugitive slave, relative to slavery in America, and also to give expression to public opinion, against that atrocious and cruel system.

The meeting was announced for two o'clock, but long before that hour the Court House was densely crowded in every part. The Grand Jury Gallery was thronged with ladies, who seemed to take the liveliest interest in the proceeding. His Worship the Mayor entered the Court a little after two o'clock, accompanied Mr. Buffum, an American gentleman and Mr. Frederick Douglas, who certainly appeared a noble specimen of the race to which he belonged. The oratorical powers possessed by Mr. Douglas were a matter of admiration, nay astonishment during the progress of the speech he delivered. To facility and power of expression he joined the most impressive and energetic delivery, with the most humorous method of exposing the hypocrisy and duplicity of some of the American slaveholders. In fact his powers in this latter respect literally kept the meeting in a roar.

The Mayor, on taking the chair, explained the object for which the meeting had been convened. The cause of human liberty should not be limited to any country or clime, and he was sure it would readily be taken up by an Irish audience. Whatever might be the condition of men who were badly fed, and badly paid, still they stood intellectually and in every other way higher than those who were made mere chattel goods, and beaten without mercy or consideration. (Cheers) They had many things to do to elevate their own country, but they had not to get rid of the lash, and the privilege they enjoyed of personal freedom they should strive to extend to all mankind. (Loud Cheering) They were only asked to extend to the American continent the exertions and influence which worked so much good in their own islands. His Worship here alluded to the exertions of Mr O'Connell in the cause of freedom, observing that it must be gratifying to him to reflect that these exertions had been attended with many and signal triumphs. (Loud Cheering) He, the speaker, held it to be spurious philosophy and worse morals to suppose that he, into whom the Deity had breathed a living soul, should be less than a man simply because of the darkness of his skin. They had many instances to show that however they differed outwardly in colour, the soul was of one colour and that it was bright and noble (Loud Applause).

Mr Martin proposed the first resolution (See our advertising columns).

Rev. Mr Whitlegge seconded it. He wished to express the pleasure he felt in attending such a meeting. It was said if they went abroad to look for grievances they would be neglectful of their duties at home, but facts disproved the assertion for among the most strenuous advocates of freedom abroad were to be found the most untiring supporters of liberty and peace at home (cheers).

Mr Buffum proposed the next resolution. The kind and sympathetic manner in which he was received in Cork more than compensated for him for all he suffered for the Anti-Slavery cause. He was mobbed, his life was in danger, but what of that, he felt a glory to mingle in the strife (Applause) – to take part in the emancipation of his countrymen in bonds. The cause of freedom in one country was intimately connected with the same cause in another, and if they contributed to break off the shackle of American Slavery, the latter country would then be better able assist them in turn (Cheers). How could America labour for the elevation of any class of people while she had in her own bosom three millions of Slaves? The Speaker here observed that Frederick Douglas, who had been twenty years in slavery, and had experienced its horrors, would address the meeting, so that it would not be necessary for him to trespass on them any further.

Mr Besnard said that justice was so fully understood by a Cork audience that he would say no more than merely second the proposed resolution.

Councillor Maguire proposed the third resolution. It was a matter of record that in spite of the renown of America (Cheers) her slavery system made her the most degraded country on the face of the earth. The boasted free institutions of America, were only a mockery and a scorn, because they were tainted with slavery at the heart's core.

Mr. FREDERICK DOUGLAS (sic) then came forward amid loud cheering. He said –

Sir, I never more than at present lacked words to express my feelings. The cordial and manly reception I have met with, and the spirit of freedom that seems to animate the bosoms of the entire audience have filled my heart with feelings I am incapable of expressing. I stand before you in the most extraordinary position that one human being ever stood before his race – a slave. A slave not in the ordinary sense of the term, not in a political sense, but in its real and intrinsic meaning. I have not been stripped of one of my rights and privileges, but of all. By the laws of the country whence I came, I was deprived of myself – of my own body, soul, and spirit, and I am free only because I succeeded in escaping the clutches of the man who claimed me as his property. There are fourteen Slave States in America, and I was sold as a slave at a very early age, little more than seven years, in the southern part of Maryland. While there I conceived the idea of escaping into one of the Free States, which I eventually succeeded in accomplishing. On the 3rd Sept., 1838, I made my escape into Massachusetts, a free state, and it is a pleasing coincidence that just seven years after I stood up in the Royal Exchange in Dublin, to unfold to the people of that good City the wrongs and sufferings to which my race in America were exposed. (Applause.) On escaping into Massachusetts, I went to work on the quays, rolling oil casks, to get a livelihood, and in about three years after having been induced to attend an anti-slavery meeting at Nantucket, it was there announced that I should go from town to town to expose their nefarious system. For four years I was then engaged in discussing the slavery question, and during that time I had opportunities of arranging my thoughts and language. It was at last doubted if I had ever been a slave, and this doubt being used in injure the anti-slavery cause, I was induced to set the matter at rest by publishing the narrative of my life. A person undertaking to write a book without learning will appear rather novel, but such as it was I gave it to the public. (Hear, Hear.) The excitement at last increased so much that it was thought better for me to get out of the way lest my master might use some stratagem to get me back into his clutches. I am here then in order to avoid the scent of the blood hounds of America, and of spreading light on the subject of her slave system. There is nothing slavery dislikes half so much as the light. It is a gigantic system of iniquity, that feeds and lives in darkness, and, like a tree with its roots turned to the sun, it perishes when exposed to the light. (Loud cheering.) We want to arouse public indignation against the system of slavery and to bring the concentrated execrations of the civilized world to bear on it like a thunderbolt. (Loud cheering.) The relation of master and slave in America should be clearly understood. The master is allowed by law to hold his slave as his possession and property, which means the right of one man to hold property in his fellow. The master can buy, sell, bequeath his slave as well as any other property, nay, he shall decide what the poor slave is to eat, what he is to drink, where and when he shall speak. He also decides for his affections, when and whom he is to marry, and, what is more enormous, how long that marriage covenant is to endure. The slaveholder exercises the bloody power of tearing asunder those whom God has joined together – of separating husband from wife, parent from child, and of leaving the hut vacant, and the hearth desolate. (Sensation.) The slaveholders of America resort to every species of cruelty, but they can never reduce the slave to a willing obedience. The natural elasticity of the human soul repels the slightest attempt to enslave it. The black slaves of America are not wholly without that elasticity; they are men, and, being so, they do not submit readily to the yoke. (Great cheering.) It is easy to keep a brute in the position of a brute, but when you undertake to place a man in the same state, believe me you must build your fences higher, and your doors firmer than before. A brute you may molest sometimes with impunity, but never a man. Men – the black slaves of America – are capable of resenting an insult, of revenging an outrage, and of looking defiance at their masters. (Applause.) Oftentimes, when the poor slave, after recovering from the application of the scourge and the branding iron, looks at his master with a face indicating dissatisfaction, he is subject to fresh punishment. That cross look must be at once repulsed, and the master whips, as he says, "the d – l out of him;" for when a slave looks dissatisfied with his condition, according to his cruel taskmaster's idea, it looks as if he had the devil in him, and it must be whipped out. (Oh, oh.) The state of slavery is one of perpetual cruelty. When very young, as I stated, I was sold into slavery, and was placed under the control of a little boy who had orders to kick me when he liked, whenever the little boy got cross, his mother used to say, "Go and whip Freddy." I however, soon began to reason upon the matter, and found that I had as good a right to kick Tommy, as Tommy had me. (Loud laughter and cheering.) My dissatisfaction with my condition soon appeared, and I was most brutally treated. I stand before you with the marks of the slave-driver's whip, that will go down with me to my grave; but, what is worse, I feel the scourge of slavery itself piercing into my heart, crushing my feelings, and sinking me into the depths of moral and intellectual degradation. (Loud cheering.) In the South, the laws are exceedingly cruel, more so than in the Northern States. The most cruel feature of the system in the Northern States is the slave trade. The domestic slave trade of America is now in the height of its prosperity from the Annexation of Texas to our Union. In the Northern States they actually breed slaves, and rear them for the Southern markets; and the constant dread of being sold is often more terrible than the reality itself. Here the speaker proceeded to comment upon the law of America relative to the punishment of slaves, and read the following:

"If more than seven slaves are found together in any road, without a white person – *twenty lashes* a piece. For visiting a plantation without a written pass – *ten lashes*. For letting loose a boat from where it is made fast – *thirty nine lashes;* and for the second offence, shall have his ear cut off. For having an article for sale without a ticket from his master – *ten lashes*. For being on horseback without the written permission of his master – *twenty five lashes*."

I saw one poor woman (continued the speaker) who had her ear nailed to a post, for attempting to run away, but the agony she endured was so great, that she tore away, and left her ear behind. (Great sensation.) This is the law of America after her Declaration of Independence – the land in which are millions of professed Christians, and which supports their religion at a cost of 20 million dollars annually, and yet she has three millions of human beings the subjects of the hellish laws I have read. We would not ask you to interfere with the politics of America, or invoke your military aid to put down American slavery. No, we only demand your moral and religious influence on the slave holder in question, and believe me the effects of that influence will be overwhelming. (Cheers.)

We want to awaken the slave holder to a sense of the iniquity of his position, and to draw him from his nefarious habits. We want to encircle America with a girdle of Anti-slavery fire, that will reflect light upon the darkness of the slave institutions, and alarm their guilty upholders – (great applause). It must also be stated that the American pulpit is on the side of slavery, and the Bible is blasphemously quoted in support of it. The Ministers of religion actually quoted scripture in support of the most cruel and bloody outrages on the slaves. My own master was a Methodist class leader (Laughter, and "Oh"), and he bared the neck of a young woman, in my presence, and he cut her with a cow skin. He then went away, and when he returned to complete the castigation, he quoted the passage, "He that knoweth his master's will and doeth it not, shall be beaten with many stripes." (Laughter.) The preachers say to the slaves they should obey their masters, because God commands it, and because their happiness depended on it. (A laugh.) Here the Speaker assumed the attitude and drawling manner so characteristic of the American preachers, amid the laughter of all present, and continued – Thus do these hypocrites cant. They also tell the slaves there is no happiness but in obedience, and wherever you see poverty and misery, be sure it results from disobedience. (Laughter.) In order to illustrate this they tell a story of a slave having been sent to work, and when his master came up, he found poor *Sambo* asleep. Picture the feelings, they say, of that pious master, his authority thrown off, and his work not done. The master then goes to the law and the testimony, and he there read the passage I have already quoted, and *Sambo* is lashed so that he cannot work for a week after. "You servants," continued the preacher, "To what was this whipping traceable, to disobedience, and if you would not be whipped, and if you would bask in the sunshine of your master's favour, let me exhort you to obedience. You should also be grateful that God in his mercy brought you from Africa to this Christian land." (Great laughter.) They also tell the wretched slaves that God made them to do the working, and the white men the thinking. And such is the ignorance in which the slaves are held that some of them go home and say, "Me hear a good sermon today, de Minister make everything so clear, white man above a Nigger any day." (Roars of laughter.) It is punishable with death for the second attempt to teach a slave his letters in America (Loud expression of disgust), and in that Protestant country the slave is denied the privilege of learning the name of the God that made him. Slavery with all its bloody paraphernalia is upheld by the church of the country. We want them to have the Methodists of Ireland speak to those of America, and say, "While your hands are red with blood, while the thumb screws and gags and whips are wrapped up in the pontifical robes of your Church, we will have no fellowship with you, or acknowledge you (as) Christians." (Great applause.) There are men who come here and preach, whose robes are yet red with blood, but these things should not be. – Let these American Christians know their hands are too red to be grasped by Irishmen. Presbyterians, Episcopalians, Congregationalists, and Roman Catholics, stand forth to the world and declare to the American Church, that until she puts away slavery, you can have no sympathy or fellowship with them – (Applause). For myself I believe in Christianity. I love it. I love that religion which is from above, without partiality or hypocrisy – that religion based upon that broad, that world-embracing principle, "That whatever you would that men should do to you, do ye even so to them." (Loud cheering). – In America Bibles and slave-holders go hand in hand. The Church and the slave prison stand together, and while you hear the chanting of psalms in one, you hear the clanking of chains in the other. The man who wields the cow hide during the week, fills the pulpit on Sunday – here we have robbery and religion united – devils dressed in angels' garments. The man who whipped me in the week used to attend to show me the way of life on the Sabbath.

I cannot proceed without alluding to a man who did much to abolish slavery, I mean Daniel O'Connell. (Tremendous cheers.) I feel grateful to him, for his voice has made American slavery shake to its centre. – I am determined wherever I go, and whatever position I may fill, to speak with grateful emotions of Mr. O'Connell's labours. (Cheering.) I heard his denunciation of slavery, I heard my master curse him, and therefore I loved him. (Great cheering.) In London, Mr. O'Connell tore off the mask of hypocrisy from the slave-holders, and branded them as the vilest of the vile, and the most execrable of the execrable, for no man can put words together stronger than Mr. O'Connell. (Laughter and cheering.) The speaker proceeded at some length, and related amusing anecdotes connected with his history in the United States. In one instance he was travelling to Vermont, and having arrived at a stage, they took in five new passengers. It being dark at the time, they did not know the colour of his (the Speaker's) skin, and he was treated with all manner of respect. In fact he could not help thinking at the time that he would be a great man if perpetual darkness would only take the place of day. (Laughter.) Scarcely however had the light gilded the green mountains of Vermont than he saw one of the chaps in the coach take a sly peep at him, and whisper to another "Egad after all 'tis a nigger." (Great laughter.) He had black looks for the remainder of the way, and disrespect. That feeling of prejudice had now changed, and he could now walk through Boston in the most refined company. The speaker concluded by saying that he would again address them during his stay in Cork.

Anti-Slavery Meeting
Lecturer: Frederick Douglass
Date of Lecture: Tuesday, 14 October 1845
Location: City Court-House, Cork
Publication: *Liberator*
Date of Publication: Friday, 7 November 1845
Title: 'PUBLIC MEETING'.

A meeting was held yesterday in the City Court-house for the same excellent object as above. It was attended by over one hundred ladies, and a large audience of respectable gentlemen and citizens generally. The MAYOR presided.

After some resolutions had been proposed and seconded by Mr. Martin, Rev. Mr. Whitelegge, Mr. John Besnard, Mr. Buffum, and Mr. J. F. Maguire, (Barrister,) Mr. Douglass came forward to second the resolution proposed by Mr. Maguire, and was received with the heartiest applause. Mr. Douglass then delivered one of the most eloquent and impressive discourses we ever heard, in which he detailed more fully than at the breakfast, the sufferings of his early years, the horrors and inhumanities arising from the iniquitous traffic in human beings, of that system of slavery which strips a man, not of one, or of one privilege, but, by the laws of the Land, deprives a man of his own body, and delivers up to the unlimited control of a master, to deal with as he would with his chattel. Mr. Douglass expressed the surprise and embarrassment which his reception in Ireland caused him – he who had been accustomed to regard white men as a superior and different race of beings, and who had never before been looked on himself by white men with such complacency as by the audiences he had addressed in the Emerald Isle. When a child, he had been taught to acknowledge the white man as his master, and to bend the obsequious knee before him; and even then he had not overcome this feeling of self-abasement, for there were so many in America who would remind him of his colour, and the difference of skin which placed him and the white man apart. He described how at an early age he had dreams after liberty, how his young mind revolted from his condition, and how, after self-questioning as to the reason and right of his slavery, and his master's authority, he felt that he was not born to be a slave, and that no right, either human or divine, or based upon the law of God, authorized a fellow-creature to hold him in bondage. He had been given to a little boy as his slave, who, when he was fretted or annoyed at anything, was told by his good mamma to 'kick Freddy.' He alluded to the marks of the lash which he bore on his back, which he would carry with him to the grave; but he said that they were not the most degrading marks of his bondage, for he bore them on his soul, debasing his humanity, and often crushing down his spirit to the very darkest depths of shame and degradation, (great sensation.) He then referred to the atrocious laws of the slave States, amidst expressions of the deepest execration. For losing a boat from its chain, the penalty was, the *loss of an ear* for the second offence! and he saw men and even women nailed by the ear to wooden posts! For carrying a club, 39 lashes – for travelling in any but the most frequented road, 40 lashes – for being out at night, 40 lashes – for being found in any other plantation, 40 lashes – for hunting with dogs, 30 lashes – for riding a horse in the day time, to be *whipped, cropped,* (ears cut off,) and *branded* on the cheek with the letter 'R,' the initial for rogue; and he had seen the slave flung down on his back, his hands and feet tied, and the hard-hearted master coolly applying the branding iron to the cheek, and holding it there until it burned into the quivering flesh! These and other details produced a feeling and expression of horror impossible to describe. He then tore the mask off the religious cant of those dealers in human flesh, the Wesleyans and Episcopalians of America, particularly the former, who preached from their pulpits the most atrocious doctrines justifying the system of slavery, and perverted the sacred word of God to the base purpose of human oppression. One quotation used by these canting scoundrels to defend the brutal torture inflicted on the slave, is – 'He that knoweth his master's will, and doeth it not, shall be punished with many stripes.' This infamous system, like all other evil systems, is upheld by ignorance – the mental and moral darkness of its victims; and by the laws of some of the States, it is death to teach a slave his letters. Mr. Douglass then dwelt on the glorious services of Mr. O'Connell to the cause of the slave – how his mighty voice had shaken slavery to the centre, and paralyzed the soul of the slave-dealer. He eloquently concluded by a splendid burst of soul-stirring oratory, and sat down amidst enthusiastic cheers. The above is but a mere outline of a speech which occupied over two hours in delivery.

Mr. R. Varian moved a vote of thanks to Mr. Wm. Martin for his services in the cause of Abolition, and for having been the means of procuring the visit of Mr. Douglass and Mr. Buffum. Mr. Logan said – In seconding a resolution of thanks to William Martin, I feel there can be no difficulty in passing such a resolution in a meeting of the citizens of Cork. There are two grounds for adopting this resolution; William Martin is a member of that community which mainly effected the abolition of one of the greatest evils the world ever witnessed – West India Slavery, (cheers.) We are asked what have we to do with *American* slavery? the claims upon our benevolence at home are too numerous and too urgent to permit our attention to foreign objects. William Martin, we all know, is not the man who shows no regard or compassion for the sufferings of his fellow-countrymen, or the evils which afflict his own country; but we always find the men who are alive to the claims of humanity in every clime and in every country, are the men of the most active benevolence at home, (cheers.) We are to thank William Martin for bringing to our city Frederick Douglass and James Buffum, (hear.) It was only necessary to bring such men before us to awaken Irish feeling and the expression of Irish sympathy on this great question. We should ask why such a man as Frederick Douglass should have been a slave? such a specimen of our common humanity, and we must feel the injustice and cruelty of slavery more than ever. There are millions of such men still in slavery. Did you ever hear a more elegant description of freedom than that which came from his lips? Could the sacred and inalienable rights of man be more distinctly asserted? Did you ever hear the horrors of slavery more forcibly or justly depicted? The fact is, the arrival of these men on our shores should be a great epoch in our history on this great question; the liberties of the world are not safe whilst three millions of men in the freest country in the world are in slavery. I have heard at the great Anti-Slavery Meeting in London, year after year, those indignant denunciations against American slavery which you have heard have been wafted across the Atlantic, and have made the conscience of the slaveholder to tremble; but notwithstanding their effect on England and upon America, they have never yet awakened in Ireland an adequate expression of feeling and sympathy for those who are suffering all the horrors of slavery in America. We see the power of public opinion on political injustice or legislation at home; let it be exerted for the removal of personal slavery abroad, and it will be omnipotent, (cheers.)

Mr. Martin returned thanks, but was surprised that any merit should have been attributed to him, for merely having done his duty. He had had an abhorrence of slavery for the last 50 years, (cheers.)

The Mayor being called from the chair, and Alderman Lyons thereto, and a vote of thanks having been given to him for his conduct, the meeting separated.

Breakfast and Anti-Slavery Meeting
Lecturer: Frederick Douglass
Date of Lectures: Tuesday, 14 October 1845
Location: City Court House, Cork
Publication: *Cork Constitution*
Date of Publication: Thursday, 16 October 1845
Title: 'AMERICAN SLAVERY'.

About fifty ladies and gentlemen, members of the Cork Anti-Slavery Society, entertained at breakfast, at Lloyd's Hotel, on Tuesday, two American advocates of Abolition—one an escaped negro, named FREDERICK DOUGLAS [sic], the other, his patron and friend, Mr. BUFFUM, who detailed the progress of the abolition cause in the United States.

At two o'clock, a public meeting was held in the City Court-house, at which the Mayor presided, which was numerously attended by the working classes, and several ladies occupied the Grand Jury gallery. FREDERICK DOUGLAS again addressed the meeting in a speech displaying considerable cleverness and humour. He is a fine young negro, with expressive features, and speaks English with ease and correctness. He gave a history of his escape from Maryland seven years since, and drew a striking contract between the treatment he received in the boasted land of freedom and equality, and that he received since he landed on the British soil. He stated that the cause of abolition was advancing in America, and exhorted everyone to use his influence in the only legitimate way, by bringing public opinion to bear on the American people, until they should be shamed into justice and humanity.

Resolutions exhibiting these sentiments were proposed and seconded by Ald. T. Lyons, Messrs. W.C. Logan, J.P. Maguire, W. Whitelegge, Buffum and Douglas, after which the meeting separated.

Anti-Slavery Meeting
Lecturer: Frederick Douglass
Date of Lecture: Friday, 17 October 1845
Location: Wesleyan Chapel, Cork
Publication: *Southern Reporter and Cork Commercial Courier*
Date of Publication: Saturday, 18 October 1845
Title: 'ANTI-SLAVERY MEETING'.

The eloquent advocate of the abolition of Slavery, Frederick Douglas [sic], released some time since from the yoke of the American task-master, attended yesterday the Wesleyan Chapel,[88] where a large company had assembled to hear his statement upon the subject of American Slavery.

The Mayor presided – and said that the meeting was held for the purpose of hearing the subject of liberty to the slave in America conversed upon. It was not the first time upon which freedom of thought for mankind was discussed in that building, and, no doubt, the spirit which had heretofore animated the abolitionists who had assembled there, still remained and would be found as active ever (Cheers). He would leave the subject to be dealt with in the masterly and affecting manner which Mr. Douglas, who was about to address them, was so well capable of treating it. The object hoped for was to arouse their sympathies into action – to make thought the source of action – and to see that action worked for the benefit of mankind.

Mr Douglas then came forward amidst loud applause. He said it was his purpose that day to speak of the evils growing out of the Institution of slavery – the first evil, no doubt, was the cruelty endured by the poor slave – but by far the greatest was, the corrupting influences which it exercised over the inhabitants of the Country where it existed – and the people living in the immediate vicinity (Hear, hear). No nation upon the face of the globe furnished a stronger illustration of this fact than America. There, the institution of slavery spread its dark cloud over the intellect of the nation – corrupting the channels of morality, poisoning the fountains of religion, and perverting the objects of Government (Hear). America started from the highest point of freedom – she proclaimed that all men were created free and equal, and were entitled to liberty in the pursuit of happiness, and in the vindication those principles, she swore by high Heaven to persevere at the sacrifice even of life and fortune. But how had she lived up to these principles? The corrupting influences of slavery were not to be seen more clearly than in the religious organizations of the land. The Society of Friends, distinguished heretofore for its opposition to slavery in America, had, nevertheless, been to some extent influenced, injured, and corrupted by the institution of slavery – and was even complimented and spoken of as being an excellent, peaceable, quite [sic] body by the slave holders. The Methodist Episcopal Church in that Country, also, the great founder of which proclaimed that "Slavery was the compendium of all crimes," and who regarded the slave holders in the light of men stealers, was also no friend to the abolitionists. The slave holders had in fact wound themselves around the heart of the Church, and had succeeded in removing some of the noblest sentiments of humanity (hear.) In 1780, indeed, one their conferences bore testimony against the laws of slavery – but the moment the ministers' salary was made to depend on the slave-holder, that moment the ardour of the pulpit against slavery ceased. The conference eased off, and little or nothing was heard on the subject of slavery till they were roused from their lethargy for a time in 1836 by a handful of abolitionists. The number of slaves held by the ministers, members, and class leaders in the American Episcopal Church was estimated at 250,000 (Oh! oh!) – and standing upon the minutes of their proceedings were the words "we have no right, *no wish*, to disturb the relations of master and slave." Bishop Andrews, one head of this Church, when some steps had ostensibly been taken to discontinue the practice of slave-holding by the church, was requested by the conference to suspend his labours till he got rid of his "impediment." The Presbyterian denomination exercised also a wide influence on the subject of Slavery, were equally destitute of principle in regard to the rights of slaves – and held amongst the Ministers and Members of their Church 90,000 Slaves. The Baptist Church, extending from one end of America to another, were also Slaveholders. On the death of one of their Bishops, the following Notice appeared in the Papers:

NOTICE. On the first Monday February next, will be put up for public auction before the Court house, the following property belonging to the estate of the late Rev. Dr. Furman,[89] viz:

A plantation or tract land on and in this Wateree swamp. A tract of the first quality of fine land on the waters of Black River. A lot of land in the town of Camden. A library of miscellaneous character, *chiefly theological*.

27 negroes, some of them very prime. Two mules, one horse and an old wagon.

This Advertisement reminded him of the description of him (Mr. Douglas) in one of the Cork Newspapers – that he was "a good specimen of a young negro". He could not believe that a Newspaper in all Ireland could be found to speak so contemptuously of a human being. It looked to him very like an Advertisement for a good prime negro but he was assured that the overwhelming public opinion was against any such contemptible allusions.

Mr. Martin – Mr. Douglas is alluding to the *Constitution*. I not see any Reporter from that Office here now.

Mr. Douglas then proceeded to advert to the avowed barbarities of the Slaveholders in their Advertisements for the recovery of absconded slaves – enough to make humanity blush even at this distance. The following are a few of the Notices referred to:

Committed to jail as a runaway, a negro woman named Martha, 17 or 18 years of age, has numerous scars of the whip on her back.

J. Dudd. Jailor. Davidson County Tenn.

Lodged in Jail a mulatto boy, having large marks of the whip on his shoulders and other parts of his body.

M. J. Garcia, Sherriff of the County Jefferson.

Committed a mulatto fellow – *his back shows lasting impressions of the whip*, and leaves no doubt of his being slave. J. Watson, Rockville. Montgomery County.

Was committed to jail a yellow boy named Jim – *had a large lock chain around his neck*. W. Toler. Sheriff of Simpson Co.

Detained at the Police station, Nina, has several marks of lashing and has irons on her feet. P. Bayhi, Captain of Police.

Ran away a negro woman and two children – a few days before she ran off – *I burned her with a hot iron on the side of her face. I tried to make the letter M.* Micagan Ricks, Nash Co. NC.

Ran away, Sam – he was shot a short time since through the hand and has *several shots in his left arm and side*. O. W. Lain. Ark.

Ran away, my negro man Denis – said negro has been shot in the left arm between the shoulder and the elbow, which has paralysed the left hand. R. W. Sizer. Mi.

Ran away a negro girl called Mary – has a small scar over her eye, a good many teeth missing – the letter A is branded on her check and forehead.

Run away, Anthony – one of his ears is cut off, and his left hand cut with an axe.

Even the liberty of the Press had been availed of, as an engine for the perpetuation of slavery – as the following extracts would show; –

(From the *Charleston Gazette*)

We protest against the assumption, the unwarrantable assumption, that slavery is ultimately to be extirpated from the Southern states.

(From the *Washington Telegraph*)

As a man, a Christian, and a citizen, we believe that slavery is right – and slave holding the best existing organization of civil society.

(From the *Augusta (Georgia) Chronicle*)

He (Amos Dresser)[90] should have been hung up as high as Haman, to rot upon the gibbet, until the wind whistled through his bones. The cry of the whole South should be, death, instant death, to the abolitionist, wherever he is caught.

Three millions of these poor people were deprived of the light of the Gospel, and the common rights of human nature; were subjected to the grossest outrages – and the poor bondsman rattled his chain, and clanked his fetters calling upon the Christianity of the world to relieve him. There was a wide field in America for missionary operations (Hear). Let them not therefore whisper as heretofore, but speak as the tempest did, sterner and stronger (Hear.) Let their importunities in this country be such as to give the slave-holder no peace while his hands were besmeared with human blood. Let them do this and tears of gratitude would be their reward, and the smiles of a merciful God would lavish upon them. (Cheers)

The Rev. Mr. Heely then addressed the meeting at some length, contending that the Methodists in this country had ever been prominent in the cause of anti-slavery – and commented upon the circumstance of Mr. Douglas omitting to speak of the Roman Catholics while he adverted with much asperity to the Methodists. There was no identity of sympathy between the Methodists of this country and those of America on the slave Question.

The Rev. Mr. M – – then addressed the meeting, and said that some offence had been taken by the Methodists, that at the meeting in the Court House, that body should have been strongly spoken of by Mr. Douglas, while the Roman Catholics, of whom his audience was principally composed, had not been adverted to. It was therefore the manner that was objected to in which the cause was pleaded before people who perhaps needed little excitement to induce them to cast reproach upon the Methodists. He would therefore suggest to Mr. Douglas, that when he made statements against the American Episcopal Church, he should state that the Methodists of this country had remonstrated against the slave-holding system in America.

Mr. Douglas said with reference to the meeting at the Court-house, that he was a fallible man and probably did not always order his words in the best direction, and might give offence, where probably a more judicious person would not – but he would tell the gentlemen who advised him, that it was not to be expected that he would know of what religious denomination his audience was composed. It was not to be expected he could tell a Methodist by looking him in the face. (Laughter.) And if the fact was, as stated, that his audience were principally Roman Catholics, it proved one thing, and that was, that Roman Catholics had taken more to the subject than the other sects (hear, hear.) It was not his fault that his audience was composed chiefly of Roman Catholics – and if he addressed himself to Methodists and they were not there, he was not to blame. He happened himself to have been the Slave of the Methodist Church Leader, and he knew a good deal about the Methodist Church. He said this is not to cast reproach upon the Methodists in this Country – but they were not to get along by defending the Methodists of America. In making these observations he did not mean to feed the Roman Catholics, or any other denomination, with the means of ridiculing each other. He would now say what he had not ventured to say before in public, that he observed over-sensitiveness among the individuals of some sects, when he alluded to the denominations the same class to his own country.

Mr. R. D. Webb, of Dublin, then made a few observations, after which thanks were returned to the Mayor, and the meeting separated.

Anti-Slavery Meeting
Lecturer: Frederick Douglass
Date of Lecture: Friday, 17 October 1845
Location: Wesleyan Chapel, Patrick-street, Cork
Publication: *Cork Examiner*
Date of Publication: Monday Evening, 20 October 1845
Title: 'ANTI-SLAVERY MEETING – Friday'.

A meeting was held on Friday last, in the Wesleyan Chapel, Patrick-Street, for the purpose of hearing Mr. Frederick Douglas [sic] detail the horrors of American slavery, and also to enter into such measures as may lead to the abolition of the tyrannical, unnatural, and anti-Christian system. The house was well filled, and on the platform were several Methodist clergymen, members of the Society of Friends, and other friends of humanity.

The MAYOR presided.

Mr. Douglas addressed the meeting in a speech of some two hours duration, in which he graphically described the horrors of American slavery. He said the first evil that presented itself to the mind's eye, growing out of Slavery, was its cruelty to the unhappy slave; but although it was the first, yet it was not the paramount evil of the infamous institution. One of its greatest and most potent evils was its corrupting influence not alone on the institutions of the society in which the bond-master moved, but also on all that came in contact with it, or even in its vicinity; and there was no nation on the face of the earth that more faithfully illustrated such than did America (hear, hear, hear). There, in that *soi dissant* "land of liberty" it spread a dark cloud over the intellect of the nation, corrupting the channels of morality, poisoning the fountains of religion and perverting the beneficial objects of government. And this was the more to be wondered at, as America had started on the highest, noblest principle that ever actuated a nation – the principle of universal freedom (hear, hear). Yes, she started and proclaimed to the world that all mankind were created freeborn; and for the maintenance of that principle she solemnly swore before high Heaven that she would vindicate and uphold it by force, at expense, at the sacrifice of life, and everything that was dear to honour and integrity. But alas! how had she carried out her pledge: what was the condition of slavery there? Did they not see it disregarding the rights of property, outraging the laws of God and nature, and setting decency and morality at nought (hear, hear)? But in no case did they see its corrupting influences more dreadfully portrayed than in the religious organization of the country. The Society of Friends at one period strenuously opposed the system of slavery, and made it a religious obligation on every member of their communion to discountenance the slave dealers, who then detested them; but he regretted that of late they were influenced and corrupted by the upholders of the system; and instead of being detested, as they formerly were by the inhuman traffickers, they were at present speaking of them as being "an excellent body". The Methodists of the Episcopal church had also started on the high principle of opposition to the slavery system, and, the words of their great founder, proclaimed it the "perfection of all infamy." They stood by the principle for years, but of late they had also become influenced. [The speaker here read several extracts from American Journals justifying the infamous system of slavery by more infamous perversions and misapplications of texts from the sacred Scriptures, and then continued]. In the Southern States it was impossible to raise one's voice against slavery, and whoever attempted it did so at the risk of being hanged, or shot, or having his tongue cut out, and – as one of the journals of that "land of freedom" required – cast on a dung hill!! As regarded the Episcopalian church, though he had suffered much at the hands of its members – and at that moment was the property of one of its members – and though had been subjected to every possible indignity, yet he would say nothing of them but what truth, justice, and honesty admitted him. In the year 1780, four years before the church had been organised, the conference published a declaration that slavery was contrary to the laws of God and religion, on the principle of "doing unto others as you would they should do unto you" and they resolved on expelling from their communion all slave holders. Whilst their body was in its infancy it adhered scrupulously to the principle, but when it extended itself, and when slave holders intermarried with its members they succeeded in rooting out the noble sentiments of humanity, and the moment the clergyman's salary became dependent on the voice of the slave holder, eked by him from the toil and sweat of the bondsman, that moment their pulpits became silent; and at that moment, there were no less than 250,000 slaves in the possession of ministers and members of the Episcopal Methodist Church of America (oh). How unlike the conduct of their great founder, John Wesley, who denounced the system as "the compendium of all crime and the *summum bonum* of all villainy"[91] (hear, hear). In South Carolina the Episcopalian Conference decided that slave holding was not sinful, nor contrary to religion (oh, oh). Bishop Andrews having married a woman, who had large property in slaves, was called on by several members of his church to emancipate them, on pain of being superseded from his functions, five other bishops interfered and merely recommended Bishop Andrews to get rid of his impediment (the slaves), get rid of them perhaps by selling or transferring them (oh, oh); and he was finally restored. The Presbyterian body also had done as much in upholding the slavery system as the Episcopalian. Indeed they went farther, for they justified it by reference to Abraham and the other patriarchs of antiquity who held slaves, and particularly instanced the act of St. Paul, who caused a runaway slave to be sent back his master (oh, oh). And yet these men, who scourged and branded feeble women until they were saturated in their own blood, and who plundered the cradles of helpless infancy, these were the men who sent out missionaries to evangelise the world, and who turned their eyes to heaven to thank their God that they lived in a land of religion (great cries oh, oh, and deep sensation). It was calculated that the Presbyterians in America held 90,300 slaves (oh, oh). The Baptist church, which extended from end to end of America, equally supported and countenanced the system. They at their triennial conference appointed slave holders missionaries to preach the Gospel of Christ. At their last meeting in Baltimore Dr. Johnson, a man-thief, preached the sermon, whilst another man-thief read the prayers, and then the congregation of slave-holders, women and cradle-plunderers all sang – "Lord what a pleasing sight; we brothers all agree" (laughter). On the occasion of the death of the Rev. Dr. Firman [sic] of South Carolina, his executor or legal representative advertised his property for sale in the following terms in the public journals: – 'On Monday next will be sold the property of the late Dr. Firman, [sic] consisting of a plantation of land in a watery swamp on the banks of the Black River; a choice Library; *Twenty-seven Negroes, in prime condition*; one horse and old wagon' (oh, oh!) Let them mark that – 'in prime condition'; or, as a paper in Cork said of himself, 'an excellent specimen of the Negro.' He was familiar with such epithets in America, and cared little for what their public journals said; but in Cork, in a place of enlightenment, he was not prepared for such language from a public journal: it looked like a good advertisement from a slave trader.

Mr. William Martin – I see a Reporter present from that journal (cries of 'The *Constitution.*') Yes, it was the *Constitution* that wrote it; and I felt so disgusted on reading it, that I instantly gave up my subscription – (loud applause.)

Mr. Douglas said he would not dwell on the consideration of the matter; it was too contemptible – (hear, hear.) He (Mr. Douglass) loved and cherished the sacred principles of Christianity; but he despised the man-trapping, woman-whipping, slave-branding and cradle-robbing Christianity of America; for the minister who held forth once a week, to enlighten them and lead them to eternal salvation, was paid and clothed, his very hat, boots and watch being purchased out of the sweat and groans of the oppressed slave, who was lashed and manacled, and weekly robbed of the earnings of his hard toil. Methodists, Baptists, Roman Catholics and Protestants, all were engaged in the infamous traffic of their fellow-men. The speaker next proceeded to read several advertisements of an atrocious character, inserted at the instance of American slave-masters, and offering rewards for runaway slaves, whom they described to the world as being branded on the cheek or forehead, or bearing lacerations from the lash, and concluded by a forcible appeal to the sympathy and humanity of his audience to unite for the abolition of the soul-benighting, inhuman and infamous system of American slavery. He resumed his seat amid loud applause.

The Rev. Mr. Riley rose and said, that though he loved freedom and detested tyranny, everywhere and in every shape, yet he could not but observe that an animus was evident in the language of Mr. Douglas not at all favorable to the Methodists. Now it was well known that the Methodists did everything in their power, and never ceased till they banished slavery from the British colonies – (hear, hear.) The Reverend gentleman then proceeded to read lengthy correspondence which passed between clergymen at home and on the foreign mission, at the period of the agitation for the abolition of slavery in the British colonies, in proof of his statements, and concluded by enumerating the important services rendered by that sect to Mr. Wilberforce, who so effectively conducted the measure through the House of Commons.

Mr. W. Martin said he was one of the five hundred delegates to the 'World's Convention,' which went to London some years ago; and at that meeting the American delegates were most anxious that the agitation should be taken up in England. He knew Mr. Douglas very well, and he was firmly convinced that he meant no offence to the Methodists of England, Ireland or Scotland – (hear.)

Mr. Douglas begged to say that the church of these countries had not been put on trial that day, as he was merely speaking of the church in his own country – (hear.)

The Rev. Mr. Mackay should say that he felt offended at the language used by Mr. Douglass, at the meeting in the Court-House, as it was calculated to cast opprobrium on Methodists in particular, whilst the Roman Catholic and other sects were passed by; and he need scarcely remark that the majority of the audience at that meeting was composed of persons who required but little incentive to induce them to cast opprobrium on their sect – (partial cries of 'hear.')

Mr. Douglass, in reply, would say that he was a fallible man; and it would be requiring too much that he should know men's religion by their faces. He meant no offence, in anything he said, to any sect or religion; but he should say that, if the majority of the persons at the meeting in the Court-House were Roman Catholics, it showed that they felt more sympathy with the slave than did the other sects – (hear, hear, and applause.) He was a Methodist himself; but he cautioned his fellow-religionists how they defended their brethren of America, for in doing so, they would be defending the men who scourged his (Mr. Douglas's) female cousin until she was crimsoned with her own blood from her head to the floor – (hear, and oh, oh.) He again cautioned them how they defended the American church; and he would then say what he did not say before in public, that there was an over-sensitiveness on the part of some persons, which induced them to curl up when any charge was laid to their co-religionists of another country, which decidedly was the result of a bad state of things; but it would not be so when the hearts of such few individuals were saturated with the sacred love of the cause, and not of the sect – (hear, hear, and loud applause.)

Mr. Webb, of Dublin, next addressed the meeting, and stated that Mr. Douglass wanted nothing from the meeting in a pecuniary point of view. His auto-biography, which would be found very interesting, could be had for half a crown, and on the profits of which he maintained himself without seeking pecuniary aid from any assemblage.

After some few further observations, the speaker concluded, and the meeting adjourned at five o'clock.

Anti-Slavery Meeting
Lecturer: Frederick Douglass
Date of Lecture: Friday, 17 October 1845
Location: Wesleyan Chapel, Patrick St, Cork
Publication: *Liberator*
Date of Publication: Friday, 28 November 1845
Title: 'From the *Cork Examiner* of October 20. Anti-Slavery Meeting'.

Frederick Douglass in Ireland. For the gratification of our anti-slavery readers, we lay before them fresh evidence of the hearty and generous reception which has been given to Mr. Douglass in Ireland.

This preceded the report of Douglass's lecture in Cork, reprinted above.

Editorial
Publication: *Cork Constitution*
Date of Publication: Monday Evening, 20 October 1845
No Title.

The following appears to have occurred at a meeting in Wesley Chapel on Friday. The speaker is the Mr. Douglas [sic], an escaped slave, whom we some days ago mentioned. Our extract is from last night's Examiner:'On the occasion of the death of the Rev. Dr. Firman, of South Carolina, his executor or legal representative, advertised his property for sale in the following terms in the public journals: - 'On Monday next will be sold the property of the late Dr. Firman, consisting of a plantation of land in a watery swamp on the banks of the Black River; a choice Library; twenty-seven negroes, in prime condition; one horse and old wagon (Oh, oh!). Let them mark that, 'in prime condition', or, as a paper in Cork said of himself – 'an excellent specimen of the Negro'. He was familiar with such epithets in America, and cared little for what their public journals said, but in Cork, in a place of enlightenment, he was not prepared for such language from a public journal, it looked like a good advertisement from a slave journal.Mr. William Morris – I see a Reporter present from that journal. (Cries of, the *Constitution*.) Yes, it was the *Constitution* that wrote it; and I felt so disgusted at reading it that I instantly gave up my subscription – (Loud applause.)Mr. Douglas said he would not dwell on the consideration of the matter; it was too contemptible. (hear, hear.)'.

Now there is not, we believe, in the city a person less included to speak slightingly of another than the gentleman who acted as our Reporter on the occasion which furnished the spark for this unexpected explosion, and when we quote his words (which are not the words that Mr. Douglas palmed on the meeting) the reader will be disposed to marvel at the face with which the speaker attempted to manufacture a grievance from them. We don't wish to insinuate anything to the discredit of Mr. Douglas's slavery sentiments, but when we find him misquoting so near home, we should be unwilling to rely on every thing he says of things afar off. Here is what our Reporter wrote:

'Frederick Douglas again addressed the meeting in a speech displaying considerable cleverness and humour. He is a fine young negro, with expressive features, and speaks English with ease and correctness'.

Well ladies! is there anything uncomplimentary in that? Mr Douglas may have felt his dignity disparaged by being described as a 'negro,' but in a man of his mission that would be a queer subject of complaint, yet that is the only thing he has to catch at, for as to the 'excellent specimen', it is altogether a creation of his own imagination. The scene, on behalf of all of the performers, was an exceedingly silly one (by the way, the Mayor was in the Chair), and not calculated to do good to any cause that was to be advanced by temper and intelligence and truth. If the persons who are parading their 'lion' from platform to platform and from tea-party to breakfast party would teach him (having first taken the trouble to acquire it themselves) to cultivate somewhat more sense and less sensitiveness, they would do him a service. It seems, however, that he has a habit of giving offence as well as of taking it, for we find the very Ministers of the Chapel with which he was accommodated driven to complain. Thus:

'The Very Rev. Mr. Reily rose and said, that although he loved freedom and detested tyranny everywhere and in every shape, yet, he could not but observe that an animus was evident in the language of Mr. Douglas not at all favourable to the Methodists. Now it was well known that the Methodists did everything in their power. And never ceased until they banished slavery from the British Colonies. (Hear, hear.)

Mr. W. Martin knew Mr. Douglas very well, and he was firmly convinced that he meant no offence to the Methodists of England, Ireland, or Scotland. (Hear.)

Mr. Douglas begged to say that the Church of these countries had not been put on trial that day, as he was merely speaking of the Church of his own country. (Hear.)

The Rev. Mr. Mackey should say that he felt offended at the language used by Mr. Douglas at the meeting in the Court house, as it was calculated to cast opprobrium on Methodists in particular, whilst the Roman Catholic and other sects were passed by; and he need scarcely remark that the majority of the audience at that meeting was composed of persons who required but little incentive to induce them to cast opprobrium on their sect. (Partial cries of 'hear'.)

Mr. Douglas, in reply, should say that he was a fallible man: and it would be requiring too much that he should know men's religion on their faces. He meant no offence in anything he said to any sect or religion; but he should say that, if the majority of the persons at the meeting in the Court-house were Roman Catholics, it showed they felt more sympathy with the slave than did the other sects. (Hear, hear, and applause.)

Advertisement
Publication: *Cork Southern Reporter*
Date of Publication: Tuesday, 21 October 1845
Title: 'NARRATIVE OF FREDERICK DOUGLASS. WRITTEN BY HIMSELF'.

We refer our readers to our advertising columns for notices from the American press, of this work. We are sure that no honest man can arise from its perusal without defending convictions of the power which true men everywhere possess of triumphing over the most formidable obstacles – nor without the belief, that it is his bounden duty to omit no means, however great or small, which opportunity affords, of aiding the African people to escape from a worse than Egyptian bondage, and of cheering on their devoted friends, the abolitionists of America. It appears from the advertisement that Mr. Douglass will deliver an address on Thursday evening next at the Imperial Hotel.[92] Those who are desirous to see nature's nobleman, and hear the native eloquence of a self-educated man, ought to avail themselves of this opportunity to hear Mr. Douglass.

Advertisement
Publication: *Southern Reporter and Cork Commercial Courier*
Date of Publication: Tuesday, 21 October 1845
Title: 'FREDERICK DOUGLASS'.

Frederick Douglass, an eloquent fugitive slave, will deliver an address on American Slavery, at the Imperial Hotel, on Thursday next, the 23 inst. at the hour of 2.00 o'clock. Attendance 6*d*. each.

Narrative of the life of Frederick Douglass. An American Slave. Written by himself.

To be had of Messrs. Bradford and Co., Messrs Purcell and Co., Messrs Varian, and of Mr William Martin, Patrick Street. Price 2*s*. 6*d*.[93]

Critical Notices etc. of the American Press.

'Frederick Douglass – we observe this self-emancipated man has lately sent forth from the Press a sketch of his life. Everybody should read it. It is an exceedingly interesting as well as ably written work' – *Philadelphia Elevator*.

'Frederick Douglass has been for some time a prominent member of the Abolition party. He has had the courage to name the persons, time, and places, thus exposing himself to obvious danger, and setting the seal on his deep convictions as to the religious need of speaking the whole truth. Considered merely as a narrative, we have never read one more simple, true, coherent, and warm with genuine feeling' – *New York Tribune*.

Narrative of Frederick Douglass. This admirable volume is just out. It will doubtless prove a valuable auxiliary to the cause of abolition. Frederick Douglass is a strong man and will not fail to arouse the sympathy of his readers on behalf of the oppressed. May he long live with his burning eloquence to pour truth on the wicked conscience of this wicked nation – *Practical Christian*.

The Cork Anti-Slavery Societie [sic] beg to acquaint the public that the profits arising from the sale of this moderately priced and excellent Anti-Slavery work are the means by which Mr Douglass is sustained in his noble efforts while in these countries.

The Cork Ladies' Anti-Slavery Society beg to inform all friends who intend to contribute to the Boston Anti-Slavery Bazaar, that if the articles are ready by 23rd of next Month, they will be in sufficient time.

Cork, October 22, 1845.

Advertisement
Publication: *Southern Reporter and Cork Commercial Courier*
Date of Publication: Tuesday, 21 October 1845
Title: 'NARRATIVE FREDERICK DOUGLAS. WRITTEN BY HIMSELF'.

We refer our readers to our Advertising Columns for notices from the American Press, of this work. We are sure that no honest man can arise from its perusal without deepened convictions of the power which true men everywhere possess of triumphing over the most formidable obstacles – nor without the belief, that it is his bounden duty to omit no means, however great or small, which opportunity affords, of aiding the African people to escape from worse than Egyptian bondage, and of cheering on their devoted friends, the Abolitionists of America. It appears from the Advertisement that Mr. Douglas will deliver an address on Thursday evening next at the Imperial Hotel. Those who are desirous to see nature's nobleman, and hear the native eloquence of a self-educated man, ought to avail themselves of this opportunity to hear Mr. Douglas.

Advertisement
Publication: *Cork Examiner*
Date of Publication: Wednesday, 22 October 1845

Our readers will perceive by our advertising columns, that this eloquent Anti-Slavery Advocate will deliver an address tomorrow, at the Imperial Hotel. He is undoubtedly a man of genius – a man of high mental gifts – whose mental and physical powers are harmoniously developed. All who wish to see how the gifts of nature can triumph over the most disheartening circumstances, ought to avail themselves of the opportunity which tomorrow offers. FREDERICK DOUGLASS has published a Narrative of his Life, of which the American press, as will be seen in our advertisement, speak in the strongest terms of commendation. It gives an insight into the workings of the slave system in America, which cannot elsewhere be obtained in so concise and interesting a form and should be in everyone's possession – especially as the profits arising from its sale will sustain Mr. DOUGLASS in his career of usefulness in these countries.

Advertisement
Publication: *Cork Examiner*
Date of Publication: Wednesday, 22 October 1845
Title: 'Frederick Douglass'.

THE Eloquent FUGITIVE SLAVE will deliver an Address on American Slavery, at the IMPERIAL HOTEL, THURSDAY Next on the twenty-third Inst., at the hour of Two o'clock. Admittance 6*d*. each.

NARRATIVE OF THE LIFE OF FREDERICK DOUGLASS, An American Slave, Written by Himself, TO BE HAD of Messrs. PURCELL & CO., Messrs BRADFORD & CO., and Mr. WILLIAM MARTIN, Patrick Street. – Price 2*s*. 6*d*.

CRITICAL NOTICES OF THE AMERICAN PRESS. "Frederick Douglass – We observe that this self-emancipated man has lately sent forth from the press a sketch of his life. Every body should read it. It an exceedingly interesting well ably written work." – *Philadelphia Elevator*. "Frederick Douglass has been for some time a prominent member of the Abolition party. He has had the courage to name the persons, time and places, thus exposing himself to obvious danger, and setting his seal on his deep convictions as to the religious need of speaking the whole truth. Considered merely as a narrative, we have never read one more simple, true, coherent, and warm with genuine feeling." – *New York Tribune*.

"Narrative of Frederick Douglas. – This admirable little volume just out. It will doubtless prove a valuable auxiliary to the cause of Abolition. Frederick Douglass is a strong man and will not fail to arouse the sympathies of his readers in behalf of the oppressed. May he long live with his burning eloquence, to pour truth on the naked conscience of this wicked nation." *Practical Christian*.

THE CORK ANTI-SLAVERY SOCIETIES Beg to acquaint the Public, that the profits arising from the sale of this moderately priced and excellent Anti-Slavery work, are the means by which Mr. Douglass is sustained in his noble efforts while in these countries.

The Cork Ladies' Anti-Slavery Society beg to inform all friends who intend contributing to the Boston Bazaar, that if the Articles are ready the 23d of November next, they will be in sufficient time.

October 22, 1845.

Temperance Meeting
Lecturer: Frederick Douglass
Date of Lecture: Monday, 20 October 1845
Location: Temperance Institute, Cork
Publication: *Truth Seeker* [94]
Date of Publication: November 1845 [95]
Title: 'Intemperance and Slavery'.

Mr. Frederick Douglass said: – 'Ladies and Gentlemen, – The first sentiment that presses for utterance, is that of gratitude. I feel exceedingly grateful to my honored friend, the president, for affording me an opportunity of meeting with so many highly intelligent and influential people as I see before me. I feel grateful also for the distinguished honour conferred upon me by having been invited by him to a seat by his side in your distinguished presence. I know not why 'tis so, I know not why I am humbled, when I reflect on what I have been, and what I now am. When I think of the situation I once filled, and of the one I now fill, I can scarcely believe my own identity. I was not a slave to intemperance, but a slave to my fellow-men. From deprivation of the ordinary facilities of addressing bodies like the present, you will naturally infer, that I feel embarrassment in my present situation, as one entirely beyond anything I ever expected. But seven years ago I was ranked among the beasts and creeping things; to-night I am here held as a man and a brother. I don't know what to say. That I am a teetotaler is most true. I have been a staunch one for some years. I shall forget for a moment that I ever was a slave. If I can forget it, I think I could move as a man among you. If I can but forget the position in which I once was, I can turn my attention to teetotalism, and shall be able to speak as a man for a few moments.

1   Mr. President, – Teetotalism has been an interesting subject to me. We have a large class of free people of colour in America; that class has, through the influence of intemperance, done much to retard the progress of the anti-slavery movement – that is, they have furnished arguments to the oppressors for oppressing us; they have pointed to the drunkards among the free coloured population, and asked us the question, tauntingly – "What better would you be if you were in their situation?" This of course was a great grievance to me. I set my voice against intemperance. I lectured against it, and talked against it, in the street, in the wayside, at the fire-side; wherever I went during the last seven years, my voice has been against intemperance. But notwithstanding my efforts, and those of others, intemperance stalks abroad among the coloured people of my country. Still I am pleased to be able to say, that the change in their situation, with regard to intemperance, has been great in the last seven years. Take Philadelphia, for example: there are 1,500 coloured people there, and there are now not less than 80 Temperance Societies among that class. In the constitution of these societies are incorporated rules to look after their sick, and to bury members that may die. They have been enabled to contribute a sufficient sum to the treasury to take care of their own poor.

2   But we have had difficulties in struggling out of our drunkenness. No longer ago than 1842, on the 1st day of August – the day, Mr. President, on which the slaves in the West Indies were emancipated. It is common in our country among abolitionists to celebrate that day. Well, a large number of coloured people in Philadelphia attempted to celebrate that day by forming themselves into a temperance procession, and walking through the streets, with appropriate banners, and thus to make a temperance impression on their fellow brethren who had not yet joined their ranks. They had also 'freedom' inscribed upon their banner. Well, such was the feeling in this slave-holding city, that the display of the banner brought upon these poor coloured people an infuriated mob! Their houses were burnt down in different parts of the city, and their churches were burned to the earth, themselves turned out of the city, and the city authorities and police did nothing to prevent it!

3   We have great difficulty in becoming virtuous men in our country; this feeling, as developed thus, is not felt as much in the New England States. About three years ago it was not common to see a coloured person in a temperance meeting in New England even, because it was understood they were unacceptable people. Though rum would degrade them in common with white people, they were excluded by what is called prejudice against colour! True, the white and the black could wallow in their degradation in the same mire, but when the white man became sober, he had no idea of the black man coming up by his side, sober. But this state of things has much altered, and

a little before my leaving Massachusetts, I received several invitations from white temperance societies to lecture to them upon temperance. And in the last procession in Boston, some 16,000 teetotalers passed on, mingling with them, – you might see the sons and daughters of Ethiopia in common with the whites. The consequence has been, the coloured people of New England have gradually advanced out of their degradation. I have great reason to rejoice at the temperance movement.

4   Temperance in our Country has made rapid advances from time to time. I have heard of the advance of temperance in this country. I have heard also of the interest having decreased very much. The enemies of temperance represent the good cause to be waning here; – they say that the temperance movement is going down! You may thus hear in all directions those who are desirous to throw – not cold water, but rum and brandy, over the temperance ranks! Well, I am glad to have been in Ireland, and to be able to answer their charges, to the utter chagrin of the enemies of this cause in my own country. If meeting with thousands of beings who are taking the pledge with every sincere expression of delight, then is the temperance movement on the wane. We may answer the objection as a man once answered it in America. He said – "Twas going down – going gloriously down – going down east, down west, down north, down to every point of the compass – going into every family – spreading peace and comfort and gladness over the entire community." It may be said to be so going down in Ireland. (Great applause.)

5   I am deeply engaged in the anti-slavery cause. I am deeply engaged in attempting to get my coloured brethren out of slavery. I believe, Mr. President, that if we could but make the world sober, we would have no slavery. Mankind has been drunk. I believe that if the slaveholder would be sober for a moment, Would consider the sinfulness of his position – hard-hearted as he is, I believe there is humanity enough if we could get him sober – we could get a public opinion sufficiently strong to break the relation of master and slave. All great reforms go together. Whatever tends to elevate, whatever tends to exalt humanity in one portion of the world, tends to exalt it in another part; the same feeling that warms the heart of the philanthropist here, animates that of the lover of humanity in every country.

6   I have some experience in this matter. When first I landed in Dublin, the warmest reception that I received any where, at home or abroad, was in a temperance meeting, where thousands had congregated to receive the pledge from the Rev. Doctor Spratt.

7   I feel glad to speak to you. All that I wanted was to shew you that I loved the temperance cause; and I love emancipation. DON'T FORGET THE BONDSMAN. I can talk a little better upon that subject than upon temperance. I have a wonderful sight of facts on the question of slavery to throw before the people of Ireland. My words, feeble as they are when spoken at home, will wax stronger in proportion to the distance I go from home, as a lever gains power by its distance from the fulcrum.

Temperance Meeting
Lecturer: Frederick Douglass
Date of Meeting: Tuesday, 21 October 1845
Location: Temperance Institute, Cork
Publication: *Cork Examiner*
Date of Publication: Friday, 24 October 1845
Title: 'Festival at the Temperance Institute'.

Tuesday Evening, the Rev. Fr. Mathew and the members of the Institute held a Festival. It was given to compliment Mr. Douglas [sic], the American Slave, and eloquent denouncer of American Slavery. There were upwards of 260 ladies and gentlemen present. The decorations of the room were admirable and picturesque, and the supply of confectionary and fruit most tempting and abundant. When Mr. Douglas [sic] was introduced by the Rev. President he was received with great applause. He addressed the assembly with his usual animation and eloquence on the subject of Slavery, and the great beneficial effects of temperance. His address was much cheered. He subsequently sang a Nigger song. Music and dancing were the concluding recreations of the evening, after which the company retired, highly delighted with the social and festive scene.

Article
Lecturer: Frederick Douglass
Date of Lecture: Thursday, 23 October 1845
Location: Imperial Hotel, Cork
Publication: *Cork Examiner*
Date of Publication: Monday, 27 October 1845
Title: 'Frederick Douglass in Cork'.

ANTI-SLAVERY MEETING AT THE IMPERIAL HOTEL. Mr. M'Dowell's Great Room was thronged,[96] on Thursday, last, with a most respectable and attentive audience. Thomas Lyons, Esq. Ald. occupied the Chair. The Rev. Mr. O'Regan, John Besnard, Esq. Jr., Mr. W. Martin, &c. were on the platform.

Mr. Douglass being introduced to the meeting, it commenced – Mr. President, Ladies and Gentlemen – There is perhaps, no argument more frequently resorted to by the slaveholders, in support of the slave system, than the inferiority of the slave. This is the burden of all in their defence of the institution of Slavery, "the negro is degraded – he is ignorant, he is inferior – and therefore 'tis right to enslave him" A distinguished divine lately travelled in these countries – stung to shame for the humanity of his country, instead of confessing its sin before God, and the Universe, adduced the pitiful argument for Slavery of "inferiority of our race." What if we are inferior? Is it a valid reason for making slaves of us? For robbing us of our dearest rights? Can there be any reason found in moral or religious philosophy, justifying the enslaving of any class of beings, merely on the ground of their inferiority – intellectual, moral, or religious? If we search the words of inspired wisdom, we shall find that the strong are to bear the infirmities of the weak, – teaching the wise the duty of instructing the ignorant; and if we consult the better feelings of humanity, we find all hearts on the side of the weak, the feeble, the distressed, and the outraged.

In no sound philosophy can Slavery be justified. 'Tis at war with the best feelings of the human heart. 'Tis at war with Christianity. Wherever we find an individual justify Slavery on such a pretext, you will find him also justifying the slavery of any human beings on the earth. 'Tis the old argument on the part of tyrants. Tyrants have ever justified their tyranny by arguing on the inferiority of their victims. The slavery of only part or portion of the human family, is a matter of interest to every member of the human family; Slavery being the enemy of all mankind. I wish it distinctly to be understood that this is no feeling of merely intellectual interest, but 'Tis also a matter of moral interest to you; since the morals it produces affect all men alike. I speak to Christian men, and Christian women. The glory of Christianity is to be defended, to be maintained, but how, Mr. President, I ask, is Christianity to be defended and maintained, if its professors – if those who stand forth as its advocates – are found with their hands dripping with the blood of their brethren? Why is Christianity to be maintained, if Christians stand by and see men, made in the image of God, considered as things – mere pieces of property?

In the name of Christianity, I demand that the people of these countries be interested in the question of Slavery! In vain may the slave-owner tell you it is no concern of yours. Mr. President, it belongs to the whole nation of America; and to the Irishmen, not because they are Irish, *but because they are* MEN. Slavery is so gigantic that it cannot be coped with by one nation. Hence I would have the intelligence and humanity of the entire people of Ireland against that infamous system.

I plead here for man. Notwithstanding our inferiority, we have all the feelings common to humanity. I will grant frankly, I must grant, that the negroes in America are inferior to the whites. But why are they so, is another question – and a question to which I will call your attention for a few moments. The people of America deprive us of every privilege – they turn round and taunt us with our inferiority! – they stand upon our necks, they impudently taunt us, and ask the question, why we don't stand up erect? They tie our feet, and ask us why we don't run? That is the position of America at the present time; the laws forbid education, the mother must not teach her child the letters of the Lord's prayer; and then, while this unfortunate state of things exist, they turn round and ask, why we are not moral and intelligent; and tell us, because we are not, that they have the right to enslave. Now let me read a few of the laws of that Democratic country, not that I have anything against Democracy. I am not here to call in question the propriety or impropriety of a Democratic Government, or to say anything in favour of any kind of Government. I am here but to urge the right of every man to his own body, to his own hand, and to his own heart. (Applause.)

Mr. President, I shall give you a few specimens of these laws. In South Carolina, in 1770, this law was passed. "Whereas the teaching of slaves to write is sometimes connected with inconvenience, be it enacted that every person who shall teach a slave to write, for every such offence shall forfeit the penalty of £100." Mark, we are an inferior race, morally and intellectually. – Hence 'Tis right to enslave us. The same hypocrites make laws to prevent our improvement. In Georgia, in 1770, similar laws were passed; and Virginia, and South Carolina, in 1800, passed the following – that the assemblage of slaves and mulattoes for the purpose of instruction may be dissolved. In Louisiana the penalty of teaching a black in a Sunday-school, is, for the first offence, five hundred dollars fine, for the second, death. This is in America, a Christian country, a democratic, a republican country, the land of the free, the home of the brave – the nation that waged the seven years' warfare to get rid of a three-penny tea-tax, and pledged itself to the declaration that all men are born free and equal, making it at the same time a penalty, punishable with death, for the second offence to teach a slave his letters.

Now I will briefly tell you what passed during my voyage to this country, which will illustrate the feelings of our people towards the black man. In taking up one of your papers this morning I saw an extract from the *New-York Herald* by Gordon Bennett, one of the greatest slave-haters in the world. It relates that a remarkable occurrence took place in the *Cambria* during its passage to England: – "A colored slave named Douglass is said to have spoken on Anti-Slavery, and that a row took place in consequence." You may have occasion to hear more of the New-York Herald. The editor was over here some time ago, at the Conciliation-hall, and Mr. O'Connell denounced him in round terms.

Now the circumstance to which this refers is as follows – I took passage at Boston, or rather my friend Mr. Buffum, the gentleman who lived in the same town with me, went to Boston from Linn [sic] to learn if I could have a cabin passage on board the vessel. He was answered that I could not, that it would give offence to the majority of the American passengers. Well, I was compelled to take a steerage passage, good enough for me. I suffered no inconvenience from the place – I kept myself in the forecastle cabin, and walked about on the forward deck. Walking about there from day to day my presence soon excited the interest of the persons on the quarter deck, and my character and situation were made known to several gentlemen of distinction on board, some of whom became interested in me.

In four or five days I was very well known to the passengers, and there was quite a curiosity to hear me speak on the subject of Slavery – I did not feel at liberty to go on the quarter-deck – the Captain at last invited me to address the passengers on Slavery. I consented – commenced – but soon observed a determination on the part of some half-a-dozen to prevent my speaking, who, I found, were slave-owners. I had not uttered more than a sentence before up started a man from Connecticut, and said "that's a lie." I proceeded without taking notice of him, then shaking his fist, he said, again – "that's a lie." Some said I should not speak, others that I should – I wanted to inform the English, Scotch, and Irish on board on Slavery – I told them blacks were not considered human beings in America. Up started a slave-owner from Cuba – "Oh," said he, "I wish I had you in Cuba." – Well, said I, ladies and gentlemen, since what I have said has been pronounced lies, I will read, not what I have written, but what the Southern legislators themselves have written – I mean the law. I proceeded to read – this raised a general clamor, for they did not wish the laws exposed. They hated facts, they knew that the people of these countries who were on the deck would draw their own inferences from them. Here a general flurry ensued – "Down with the nigger," said one – "he shan't speak" said another. I sat with my arms folded, feeling no way anxious for my fate. I never saw a more barefaced attempt to put down the freedom of speech than upon this occasion. Now came the Captain – he was met by one of the other party, who put out his fist at him – the Captain knocked him down – instead of his bowie, the fallen man drew out his card crying, "I'll meet you at Liverpool." Well, said the Captain, "and I'll meet you." The Captain restored order, and proceeded to speak. "I have done all I could from the commencement of the voyage to make the voyage agreeable to all. We have had a little of everything on board. We have had all sorts of discussions, religious, moral, and political, we have had singing and dancing, everything that we could have, except an Anti-Slavery speech, and since there was a number of ladies and gentlemen interested in Mr. Douglass, I requested him to speak. Now, those who are not desirous to hear him, let them go to another part of the vessel. Gentlemen," he said, "you have behaved derogatory to the character of gentlemen and Christians. Mr. Douglass," said he, "go on, pitch into them like bricks!" (laughter.) However, the excitement was such that I was not allowed to go on. The agitation, however, did not cease, for the question was discussed, to the moment we landed at Liverpool. The Captain threatened the disturbers with putting them in irons if they did not become quiet – these men disliked the irons – were quieted by the threat; yet this infamous class have put the irons on the black. [Mr. Douglass showed the slave-irons to the meeting.]

Now that I am alluding to papers, allow me to say that there has been a little misunderstanding between myself and the reporter of one of your papers. I am glad to have an opportunity of making an explanation respecting the matter. I believe the name of the paper is the *Constitution*. The first meeting, which was held in the Court-house, was reported, and the reporter took occasion to speak of me as a fine young negro. – Well, that is the mode of advertising in our country a slave for sale. I took occasion to allude to the apparent sweeping manner in which I was spoken of; but I find from information which I have received that the gentleman who wrote it had no intention to sneer or speak slightingly of me or the negro race at all. I am glad to know it.

This simple meeting gathered together to-day, may do something towards freeing the bondsman. Every true word spoken, every right aim levelled against Slavery in this land will effect wonders in the destiny of the black slave in America. They will be free only by the combined influence of the Christian world. They can't be free otherwise. America has not sufficient moral stamina in herself to emancipate the slave, unassisted by the world.

My friends, you yourselves can cheer the heart of the slave by making every pro-slavery man feel the strength of your opposition to Slavery. I have had an excellent illustration of this put into my hands by a friend recently – a letter from Mr. Haughton, of Dublin, in which he exposes the conduct of a minister of the

Unitarian denomination, who ventured across here, the Rev. F. Parkman.[97] That gentleman wished an introduction to Mr Haughton, and sought an interview with him, but Mr. Haughton first inquired, "was he an Abolitionist?" – "I am not an Abolitionist in the sense of the term that is understood in our country. Abolitionism is a party-name, and I am not one in the party sense." "Sir, would you preach against Slavery in your pulpit?" – "No, Sir, I would not, it would injure my influence with my congregation, 'twould offend some of my members. I am bound not to introduce anything that would be offensive," – that is, in other words, I am not sent by God to preach, I am sent by my congregation.

My friends, there are charges brought against coloured men not alone of intellectual inferiority, but of want of affection for each other. I do know that their affections are exceedingly strong. Why, but a short time ago we had a glorious illustration of affection in the heart of a black man – Madison Washington,[98] he has made some noise in the world by that act of his; it has been made the ground of some diplomacy: – he fled from Virginia for his freedom – he ran from American Republican Slavery, to Monarchical Liberty, and preferred the one decidedly to the other – he left his wife and little ones in Slavery – he made up his mind to leave them, for he felt that in Virginia he was always subject to be removed from them; he ran off to Canada, he was there for two years, but there in misery; for his wife was perpetually before him. He said within himself – I can't be free while my wife's a slave. He left Canada, to make an effort to save his wife and children; he arrived at Troy, where he met with Mr. Garnett, a highly intellectual black man, who admonished him not to go, it would be perfectly fruitless. He went on, however, to Virginia, where he was immediately taken, put with a gang of slaves on board the brig *Creole*, destined for Southern America. After being out nine days, he could sometimes see the iron-hearted owners contemplating joyfully the amount of money they should gain by reaching the market before it was glutted.

On the 9th day Madison Washington succeeded in getting off his irons; and reaching his head above the hatchway, he seemed inspired with the love of freedom, with the determination to get it or die in the attempt. As he came to the resolution he darted out of the hatchway, seized a handspike, felled the Captain – and found himself, with his companions, masters of the ship. He saved a sufficient number of the lives of those who governed the ship to reach the British Islands, where they were emancipated. This soon was found out at the other side of the Atlantic, and our Congress was thrown into an uproar, that Madison Washington had, in imitation of George Washington, gained liberty. They branded him as being a thief, robber, and murderer; they insisted on the British Government giving him back. The British Lion refused to send the bonds men back. They did send Lord Ashburton as politely as possible to tell them that they were not to be the mere watchdogs of American slave-owners; and Washington, with his 130 brethren, are free. We are branded as not loving our brother and race. Why did Madison Washington leave Canada, where he might be free, and run the risk of going to Virginia? It has been said that it is none but those persons who have a mixture of European blood who distinguish themselves. This is not true. I know that the most intellectual and moral coloured man that is now in our country, is a man in whose veins no European blood courses – 'tis the Rev. Mr. Garnett; and there is the Rev. Theodore Wright [99] – people who have no taint of European blood, yet they are as respectable and intelligent, they possess as elegant manners as I see among almost any class of people. Indeed, my friends, those very Americans are indebted to us for their own liberty at the present time, the first blood that gushed at Lexington, at the battle-field of Worcester, and Bunker Hill, (applause.) Gen. Jackson has to own that he owes his farm on the banks of the Mobile to the strong hand of the negro. I could read you Gen. Jackson's own account of the services of the blacks to him, and after having done this, the base ingrates enslave us. Mr. Douglass here sat down amidst the warmest applause of the meeting.

Mr. Douglass again rose, and said – I ought to have stated that there is held annually in the city of Boston, an Anti-Slavery Bazaar, the proceeds of which are appropriated to printing Anti-Slavery truth – sending the light of Anti-Slavery truth into the community; and that there are ladies, English, Irish, and Scotch, who are interested in that bazaar, and send annual contributions to it in the shape of needle-work, painting, &c. Any such contributions will be thankfully received. Whatever is done, every stitch that is taken – every motion made with the paint brush, has a treble value on our side of the Atlantic. We are made to know that there are hearts beating in unison with our own. We hold up those little works of art that are presented at the fair, as incentives to industry on the part of our own people. True to their noble nature as women, they ask –

> 'While woman's heart is bleeding,
> Shall woman's voice be hushed.'

I wish just to say to persons desirous of contributing to this Bazaar in Cork, that they can do so by forwarding their contributions to the Misses Jennings, Brown street, before the 23d of next month.

Editorial
Publication: *Nenagh Guardian* [100]
Date of Publication: Saturday, 25 October 1845
Title: 'THE ANTI-SLAVERY CAUSE'.

There is at present an extraordinary man in Cork – a self-liberated American slave – one who, strong in his aspirations for liberty, braved the dangers of the blood-hound – the slaveholders' rifle – and the perils of fatigue and famine; and, following the north star, reached a free State in safety. For some time after his escape, he supported himself in honest respectability by the labour of his hands; but, having been at length prevailed on to speak on the anti-slavery platform, he has since travelled through various parts of America, exposing the wrongs and sufferings of his enslaved brethren. Several advocates of the colonial race, both here and in America, having judged it might be useful for him to visit these countries, he crossed the Atlantic last month, and has held a series of meetings in Dublin with excellent effect. From thence he proceeded to Wexford and Water-ford – at both of which places he held meetings before visiting Cork. Frederick Douglas [sic] is truly a specimen of nature's nobility – tall and erect in figure, and commanding in appearance; he feels that he has regained his manhood, and is now no longer a CHATTEL, but one of nature's great human family, as his father was a white man (very probably his master). He has not the black colour, although he has the black hair of the negro, – as a speaker, he is strong, forcible, and inert, convincing his audience that he is speaking the truth and the whole truth. He has also published a short account of his life – it is a striking narrative, and we may probably allude to it on some future occasion. He has excited much interest, and is still attracting large audiences in Cork.

Advertisement
Publication: *Cork Examiner*
Date of Publication: Friday, 24 October 1845

THE Friends of the Anti-Slavery Cause in this City intend entertaining Frederick Douglass, the eloquent Fugitive Slave, at SAINT PATRICK'S HALL (which has been kindly placed at their disposal for the purpose,) on TUESDAY EVENING, the 28th Inst. JOHN BESNARD, Esq, Jun., will Preside. Chair taken at 7.30 o'clock.
   Tickets 2*s*. Each. Oct. 25 1845.

Advertisement
Publication: *Southern Reporter and Cork Commercial Courier*
Date of Publication: Saturday, 25 October 1845
Title: 'SOIRÉE TO FREDERICK DOUGLAS [sic]'.

THE FRIENDS of the ANTI-Slavery Cause in this City, intend Entertaining Fred-erick Douglas, the eloquent Fugitive Slave, at SAINT PATRICK'S HALL (which has been kindly placed at their disposal for the purpose); on TUESDAY EVEN-ING, the 28th inst. JOHN BESNARD, Esq., Jun. will preside. Chair taken at 7½ o'clock. – Tickets 2*s*. each. Oct. 25. 1845.

Temperance Festival
Date of Festival: Tuesday, 21 October 1845
Publication: *Wexford Independent*
Date of Publication: Saturday, 25 October 1845
Title: 'Festival at the Temperance Institute, Cork'.

On last evening, a festival on a very splendid scale was given the Very Rev. Mr. Mathew, at the above Institute, the object of which was to compliment Mr. Fred-erick Douglas [sic].
   At eight o'clock the Chair was taken by the Very Rev. President – on his right, Mr. Douglas, supported by his Worship, the Mayor. To say that the festival was

the largest and most respectably attended yet, is quite true; in fact, no less than 260 ladies and gentlemen were present. Indeed, the hall was crowded to inconvenience, and it was much desired that the accommodation in that respect was more than it was. I will not, Mr. Editor, encroach on your columns, by detailing its proceedings at length. However, I cannot refrain from remarking upon the admirable, superior, and tasteful arrangement of the Hall of the Institute, which can be equally said of the refreshment room, which, under the skilful management of Mr. Russell, our Secretary, was all that could be wished for, and afforded everything that the most fastidious could desire – confectionary, apples, pears, &c., with an abundance of grapes, which last was considered a very great treat.

The proceedings of the night were opened by the Very Rev. Mr. Mathew, thanking the ladies and gentlemen who attended at his invitation to compliment Mr. Douglas, whom he introduced to the assembly, and who was received with the most marked demonstrations of applause.

Mr. Douglas spoke at considerable length on the abject and degrading state of slavery, and of the good and beneficial results of temperance. His discourse was listened to with the greatest attention throughout. He was much admired as a speaker, possessing as he does, a fine soft, mellow, and sonorous voice. On resuming his seat he was greeted with the warmest plaudits.

Mr. Douglas again got up and gave an original Yankee Temperance song, to the air of "Old Dan Tucker," which was received with the most unbounded applause – so much so, that he was 'encored' again and again, which he was kind enough to comply with. The admirable Band of the South Main-street Harmonic Society attended and played during the evening in first-rate style, as also for dancing. And as we speak of dancing we greatly admired its opening rustic jig, by our worthy Mayor, followed Mr. Captain Lockyer, and Captain Sullivan, which was the admiration of all present, but of none more so than Mr. Douglas, who never before saw a national Irish dance. The members of the Temperance Institute have to thank the Rev. Mr. Mathew for thus affording them and their Temperance friends of Cork a great treat as that which last evening took place at the Temperance Institute. The members also have to thank the very efficient Secretary, Mr. Russell, for the admirable manner in which the 'tout ensemble' of the evening's proceedings were so successfully conducted; as also, the gentlemen stewards, who kindly attended on the occasion. Yours, Mr. Editor, A Correspondent, and a Member of the Cork Institute.

Editorial
Publication: *Cork Examiner*
Date of Publication: Monday, 27 October 1845
Title: 'FREDERICK DOUGLASS'.

We are highly gratified to find that another anti-slavery meeting will be held in the Independent Chapel, on this (Monday) evening. We are glad that the people will have another opportunity of listening to a man, – who is as amiable and interesting in private and social life, as he is original and eloquent in his capacity of public lecturer. As an able public denouncer of the slave system in his own country, he has been long known to the friends of freedom here. These four years back, they have been aware of the sensation which he created in America among the abolitionists of that country, and their enemies – the palliators and promoters of the most horrible system of slavery that ever degraded a people making any pretensions to civilization. We are glad of the interest evinced by our people on this question. It shows their love of freedom most sincere – not bounded by country, clime, or colour – not merely selfish in its character, but embracing all. How this gives the lie to the cowardly palliators of American slavery when they spoke of O'Connell's denunciations of the abominable hypocrisy of shouting for freedom on the one hand, while tightening the slave chain and welding the slave whip, on the other – as not participated in by the people of Ireland – a fanatic they called him, who should not prevent their sympathy from being extended to the suffering people of this country! But thanks be to God! our suffering poor are not to be thus deluded. Now we have them thronging to listen to exposures of the American slave system, by one who has in his own person suffered under its iniquities. They can recognize that slavery – and such slavery as America inflicts upon her victims – is an evil of a magnitude that outweighs the most object poverty. We are glad that our people can spare a portion, from their abundant sympathies, to the distressed and suffering poor of other lands. The people are always benefitted and strengthened by an awakening of their generous nature, for the poorest of the poor,

'Long for some moments in a weary life
When they may feel that they have been the meters
And the dealers out of some small blessings –
Have been kind to such as needed kindness –
For this simple cause, that we have all of us ONE HUMAN HEART.'

Advertisement
Publication: *Cork Examiner*
Date of Publication: Monday, 27 October 1845

An Anti-Slavery entertainment will be given to Frederick Douglass tomorrow evening, at St Patrick's Hall. From the arrangements which are being made, as to appropriate music, decorations etc. We feel confident that this will be a most successful Soirée.

Soirée
Date of Soirée: Tuesday, 28 October 1845
Location: St Patrick's Temperance Hall, Cork
Publication: *Cork Examiner*
Date of Publication: Wednesday, 29 October 1845
Title: 'ENTERTAINMENT TO FREDERICK DOUGLASS AT ST PATRICK'S TEMPERANCE HALL'.

This compliment to Frederick Douglass and manifestation of feeling to the Abolition movement, projected by John Besnard Esq., Jun. assisted by several of the Anti-Slavery friends, experienced in such affairs, was one of the pleasantest social gatherings we ever witnessed, or had the happiness to be present at. Shortly after the hour announced the room was filled by the most respectable company. The Mayor, Mayor Elect, Rev. Mr Whitelegge, Messrs Varian, John F. Maguire, etc. etc. Mrs and Miss Dowden, the Misses Jennings, the Misses Connell etc. etc. were present. The Very Rev. Theobald Mathew was unable to attend, from great fatigue in the country, where he had that day been administering the pledge, and sent an intimation to that effect to the friends from whom he had accepted the invitation.

Mr Bernard being moved to the chair, in a few complimentary well-chosen sentences introduced Mr Douglass, the guest, with whom they had all met to honour.

Mr Douglass gave an animated sketch of the Abolition movement in the United States – shewed how every civilized country had a concern in the destruction of the slave system there – pointed out the efficient course of action for all to adopt, and concluded by producing United States Abolition statistics, of a most cheering character. Mr Douglass was cheered throughout, and sat down amidst enthusiastic applause.

The Chairman called on Mr John Donovan, the well-known and respected member of St Patrick's Hall – for a song, which he intimated had been composed expressly for the occasion. The song gave great satisfaction – the words being a welcome to Mr Douglass adapted to one of the Negro melodies. Mr D. himself, was so moved that he sang unsolicited with great effect, and power, a noble *Abolition* song. The company with one effect caught up the chorus, and swelled the notes of freedom after every verse. Mr Besnard, Mr Hackett, Mr Ladd, Mr Amos, and Mr William Varian, in the course of the evening, delighted the company with several delightful glees and duets and songs.

We cannot conclude our short notice of this happy evening without some allusion to the decorations of the room – these were of a very tasteful character – wreaths and festoons of flowers as abundant and fresh, as if summer had not departed – the well-known verse of our National poet, rendered familiar to the most unlettered, by our Liberators reiterated quotation – 'Oh where's the slave so lowly" etc. wrought in gold, hung from the walls; at either side were other appropriate mottos.

The Chairman having moved a vote of thanks, which was carried by acclamation – to the members of St Patrick's Hall – the company separated at 12 o'clock.

Soirée
Date: Tuesday, 28 October 1845
Location: St Patrick's Temperance Hall
Publication: *Southern Reporter and Cork Commercial Courier*
Date of Publication: Thursday, 30 October 1845
Title: 'ENTERTAINMENT TO FREDERICK DOUGLASS AT. PATRICK'S TEMPERANCE HALL'.

Mr. Frederick Douglass, the eloquent fugitive Slave, was entertained on Tuesday evening at the St Patrick's Temperance Hall. The attendance was most numerous and highly respectable. The Hall itself was tastefully fitted up for the occasion, several beautify drawings were hung up, illustrative of the benefits of Total Abstinence, and around them were formed wreaths of flowers, which had an exceedingly pretty and striking effect. Nor was the guest forgotten in the decorations of the place. The words "Ceade Mille Failthe [sic] to the Stranger" were posted up in conspicuous parts of the room, and also the following verse:

Oh where is the slave so lowly,
Condemned to chains unholy.
Who could he burst his bonds at first,
Would pine beneath them slowly.

There was a Pianoforte in the room, at which Mr. W. Hackett jun. presided.

The occasion on the whole was highly creditable to the members and friends of the St. Patrick's Temperance Hall.

The chair was taken by John Besnard Esq., who said he was proud of the high position in which he was placed. He would shortly introduce to their notice the man whom they had set out to compliment, Mr. Frederick Douglass. To those who had already heard him, he need say nothing: but to those who had not, he would just say that they would be instructed, and entertained in a manner, they probably had never before witnessed (Hear. hear.) They beheld in their friend a dark man, but with a bright and glorious soul, and with an intellect as pure and clear as the stream that flowed from the riven rock. He believed that if Frederick Douglass had had quarter the advantages of others, he would have been able to fill any situation which fortune or Providence might have called him (Applause). It was monstrous to think for a moment, that the Creator of the universe, who gave life and impulse to all creatures, and who breathed into man's nostrils the breath of life and intelligence, could ever have intended that such a man as Frederick Douglass should have been a slave (Loud Applause).

Mr. Douglass then rose and was received with acclamation. He said his words were insipid on that occasion, when summoned to express the gratitude he felt. Those to whom he felt that gratitude should however take the will for the expression. He confessed that he had not contemplated such respect at the hands the Irish people as he received since he landed in this country. He was prepared, it was true, for much feeling and sympathy in this country on behalf of the oppressed, because he knew that Ireland had known something of oppression herself, but he confessed his expectations were more than realized. On the present occasion he intended to give a short history of the Anti-Slavery movement in America, which he would do with the permission of the meeting (Hear, hear.) It was asked what had the Abolitionists done in America, for slavery still existed there? People said triumphantly. "Oh, the Abolitionists have done nothing – they have laboured for fifteen years, and there are as many slaves now as a hundred years ago." That was the language of some persons, but they took a partial view of the great movement on behalf of humanity. They also forgot the obstacles that had to be removed, and the labour that had to be undergone. They had not only to abolish slavery, but they had also a great deal of preparatory work, which was too often overlooked (Hear, hear.) The first thing they had to establish was the right of speech – a right that tyrants of all ages endeavoured to destroy. (Loud cheering). William Lloyd Garrisson [sic] stood up for the right of speech, the combined interests of the country joined to crush him. There was first the commercial interest who felt they would suffer if slavery was freely denounced. Then there was the social interest – people in the Northern States had relations in the South who were linked with the slave Institutions, and they did not wish to encourage free discussion of slavery. The ecclesiastical interest was also opposed to the 'right of speech,' for it was thought that if the discussion of the slave question was tolerated, it would produce a rupture in the Church, some of the professing members of the different religious denominations being slaveholders. It was believed that the interests of the several sects would suffer if prayer was sent up to the God of the Universe, that he would be pleased to break the bonds of those pining in slavery and misery. (Loud cheering). The two great political interests, "Whig and Democratic," were also opposed to the right of free speech on the slave question. The Legislature of the South called the Executive of the North, to adopt such measures as would effectually suppress free discussion on the question of slavery. Mr. Everett was the person who actually recommended that proposition to the Legislature of Massachusetts. But they were not able to carry it. The indignation of the people was kindled against the legislatures; their voice broke upon them, and startled them into sobriety, and despite of all their efforts, the right of speech eventually triumphed. No nation gained its freedom without the right of speech. (Cheering). The right of speech was established in Massachusetts, and here he should observe that that was the great theatre of the recent anti-slavery movement – a movement which differed from all previous ones, as it demanded justice and freedom immediate and unconditional. Some persons had been advocating a gradual abolition of slavery, but under that doctrine slavery continued to progress. Mr. Lloyd Garrisson, however, seeing that the slaves had a right to their liberty, and that having that right, that they had it at the present moment, he proclaimed emancipation immediate and unconditional. The slave-holders at once saw they were in danger, and that this movement must be crushed. They rallied the mobs to put down every man who advocated the free discussion of the slave question. In 1835 the Abolitionists literally passed through a sea of blood; their houses were burned, their property confiscated, and in some instances even their lives were sacrificed. Truth however triumphed. The Legislature who endeavoured to make an indictable offence having freedom of speech on the slave question, in 1840 adopted every principle contended for by the Abolitionists. In 1837 the Anti-Slavery Society of Massachusetts was obliged to assemble in a stable, for the purpose of holding their meeting, so unpopular was their cause, but in 1840 the spacious State House threw open its doors to receive them. That great change was produced by the untiring exertions of a few individuals, who devoted themselves zealously and perseveringly to the cause of abolition. Formerly the children of the Blacks were denied common education, and subjected to every insult; and the trades and schools were closed against them. That state of things was, however, changed. The schools were thrown open to them, and now side by side might be seen the little white and the black child, both drinking from the same fountain of education, (Cheers.) They also removed the proscription from the railroads and stage coaches, and enabled the coloured man to travel without molestation. Here the speaker referred to the conduct of the Free Church of Scotland, in first collecting money from the slaveholders, and through the preaching and exertions of Mr. Wright of Philadelphia, who showed them slavery in its true colours, consenting to return the unhallowed gain toils to its original owners. The Abolitionists of America, aided by Old Ireland, and other countries, had done much. In 1829 they had not a single Anti-slave paper in the States; but in 1839 the number of such had increased to l00. That showed the progress of the Anti-slavery movement. In 1829 if a man opened his lips against slavery in the Southern States, he was in danger of being hung to a lamp-post or burnt. Now they found the papers did not hesitate to execrate and denounce the system of slave-holding as being a cancer eating into the vitals of the American institutions. There were also three or four antislavery Reporters on the foot of the House of Congress, to take down and publish the sayings of the pro-slavery reptiles (Cheers, and laughter.) In 1829 they had not a single Anti-slavery society, and now they had thousands of them (Cheers.) All that was accomplished, but they had yet to establish the right of the fugitive slave to his freedom – to carry out the great principle of the Bible, which laid down that the fugitive should not be returned to his master. That principle was trampled under foot in America, and it was a lasting disgrace to that country that there was not a spot in it on which a coloured man can stand free. Mr. Douglas continued to enforce upon the meeting the necessity of renewed efforts in the cause of abolition, and returned to his seat amid the plaudits of the company.

Refreshments, consisting of fruit and confectionery, were then served round by the stewards who certainly were most active and attentive.

The Chairman called on Mr. Donovan to sing a song, to which that gentleman readily responded, and sung the following in a capital style.

Cead Mille Failte TO THE STRANGER
by Dan Casey Esq. *Sung to the air of 'Old Dan Tucker'*

Stranger – from a distant Nation,
We welcome thee with acclamation,
And, as a brother, warmly greet thee,
Rejoiced in Erin's Isle to meet thee.
    (Chorus) Then 'Cead Mille Failte' to the Stranger,
        Free from bondage – chains and danger.
        'Cead Mille Failthe' [sic] to the Stranger,
        Free from bondage – chains and danger.

Who could have heard thy hapless story,
Of Tyrants canting, base, and gory,
Whose heart throbbed not with deep pulsation,
For the trampled slave's emancipation?
         (*Chorus*) Then 'Cead Mille Failthe [sic]'

Oh! why should different hue, or feature
Prevent the sacred laws of nature,
And every tie of feeling sever –
The voice of Nature thunders – 'Never!'
         (*Chorus*) Then 'Cead Mille Failthe [sic]'

And borne o'e th' Atlantic waters,
The cry of Erin's sons and daughters,
For Freedom, shall henceforth be blended,
Till Slavery's hellish reign be ended.
         (*Chorus*) Then 'Cead Mille Failthe [sic]' etc.

Mr. Douglas also sung a song in favour of abolition, to the air of 'Old Dan Tucker,' to the infinite amusement of the company.

The evening's amusement closed with dancing which was kept up to a late hour.

Poem: Read at Soirée to celebrate Frederick Douglass
Date of Soirée: Tuesday, 28 October 1845
Location of Soirée: St Patrick's Hall, Cork
Author: Daniel Casey [101]
Location: St Patrick's Hall, Cork
Date of Event: Saturday, 25 October 1845 [102]
No Title.[103]

Stranger, from a distant nation,
We welcome thee with acclamation,
And as a brother, warmly greet thee –
Rejoiced in Erin's isle to meet thee.

Then *Cead Mille Failthe [sic][104] **to the Stranger.**
Free from bondage, chains and danger.

Who could have heard thy hapless story
Of tyrants canting, base and gory;
Whose heart throbbed not with deep pulsation,
For the trampled slaves emancipation.

Oh! Why should different hue or feature
Pervert the sacred laws of Nature,
And every tie of feeling sever,
The voice of Nature thunders, 'Never!'

Then bring o'er the Atlantic waters,
The cry of Erin's sons and daughters,
For freedom shall henceforth be blended,
Till Slavery's hellish reign be ended.

*Gaelic, literal translation: one hundred thousand welcomes.

Anti-Slavery Meeting
Lecturer: Frederick Douglass
Date: Monday, 3 November 1845
Publication: *Cork Examiner*
Date of Publication: Friday, 7 November 1845
Title: 'Anti-Slavery Meeting at the Independent Chapel'.[105]

Monday night the Independent Chapel was crowded by a most respectable audience. The platform was occupied by men of influence of our City.

The Mayor, being called to the chair, began by saying that it was unnecessary to tell the people of Cork *what* Mr. Douglass had done – they are already fully aware of it. The citizens of Cork were always ready in everything of this kind. In this instance they had to deal with a question not so much their own – but as good Christians ought – they have made the work of every part of the world their own. Now, there are one or two matters of duty to proceed with before Mr. Douglass addresses you. We have a duty of thanks to perform. I will begin with the press. We know it is a mighty engine; and when we find it engaged on the side of humanity, we are glad to give it our full testimony of thanks – their giving us a *corner* at all might well be considered a compliment, instead of this they have given us *columns*. The Anti-Slavery Societies of Cork are deeply indebted to the *Examiner* and *Reporter* papers in giving publicity to the Anti-Slavery efforts.

The resolutions were here proposed and carried, which will be found in our advertising columns. Mr. Ralph Varian[106] stated that he had been requested to read to the meeting, and present to Mr. Douglass, the following address, which was adopted unanimously, at a meeting of the Ladies' and Gentleman's Anti-Slavery Societies of Cork, held on Monday morning, the 3rd instant, at the Committee-Room of the Royal Cork Institution.

The Mayor in the chair, read

ADDRESS TO FREDERICK DOUGLASS, FROM THE ANTI-SLAVERY SOCIETY OF CORK.

Dear Sir: –

Allow us to express our sense of the advantages that the cause by which we are bound together as societies has derived from your labours in Cork, during your short visit here; and to request you to transmit to the Abolitionists of America, our estimation of their services to the holy cause in which we are engaged. By your labours here we have been stirred up to renewed and active life for the deliverance of the captive. We feel that if not associated with him by the ties of a common government, we are bound to his relief by the higher and holier claim, the revealed and universal truth of a common humanity and a common origin. Seeds of truth – which can never be eradicated – have been disseminated by you, in numerous public assemblies here; and sent far and wide through the instrumentality of a liberal public press. By your addresses the mass of the people have had an opportunity – which they eagerly embraced – of gaining knowledge. Their best sympathies have been aroused in behalf of those suffering under an evil of greater magnitude than the most abject poverty. They have been benefited by being made aware how they too might do something to hasten the emancipation of the American slave from his debasing bondage – simply by forming a portion of the public sentiment of the world – which must finally awaken the American Government and people to a sense of the degraded position in which their support of a hideous slave system, places them amongst the civilized nations of the earth.

The Anti-Slavery press of the United States, and our letters from the Abolitionists of America, led us to anticipate many good results from your visit to our city – but our anticipations have been more than realized. In the happy hours of social intercourse which we have enjoyed in your society, a further opportunity has been afforded us of becoming acquainted with the details of that abominable system of savage law, and degraded public sentiment, by which three millions of human beings are held in bodily and mental bondage, yoked to the car of American Freedom! Never were we so impressed with the horrors of the system, as while listening to one, who was himself born subject to the lash and fetter – who, in his own person, endured their infliction; yet who is so gifted, as he to whom we dedicate this address, with high moral, intellectual, and spiritual power, together with so much refinement of mind and manners.

Allow us to say that in estimating the pleasures and advantages which your visit has conferred upon us – we value highly those derivable from your excellent Anti-Slavery work – the unpretending memoir of your escape from chattled bondage to the liberty and light of a moral and intellectual being. While perusing it, we have been charmed to the end by the power of simple truth, and warm and genuine feeling.

We beg of you to transmit to the Abolitionists of America expressions of our regard and admiration. Even previous to your visit we deeply felt their services to humanity. To their cry for "*immediate, unconditional emancipation, the right of the slave, and the duty of the master!*" raised by William Lloyd Garrison, so as to startle an unwilling people from their criminal apathy – we have responded. In the establishment of that seminary of Freedom – "*The Oberlin Institute,*" we felt deeply interested.[107] While the persecutions to which the Abolitionists were subjected – calumnies – injuries of property and person – arouse our indignation. And the death of the martyred Lovejoy, stirred the deepest feelings of our souls.

Especially would we be affectionately remembered to that intrepid female band, who – scorning all petty feeling, and false sentiment at the call of duty, rallied to the heavenly work of delivering the captive; directing him to those possessions which are rightfully his – knowledge, liberty, and power.

The mode in which the Abolitionists of America conduct their Great Annual Bazaars calls for expressions of our thorough approbation. The exertions necessary to send our mite in appropriate articles to the Boston Fair – we have felt as a relief to our feelings, a pleasure to our hearts. We could wish that this sentiment was more generally participated in here, that the claims of our neighbours, the coloured population of America, who have fallen among thieves – were better understood, so that all might regard their prostrate condition, and afford them aid. In the funds raised at these Bazaars we recognize a means of sustaining a noble missionary labour, – that of opening the prison doors, and letting the oppressed go free; that of pouring light upon the mental sight, so that he who stole should steal no more, but make restitution to the captive of his plundered property in his limbs, head, and heart, in his children, and his home. When the preachers of glad tidings to the oppressed; and of warning and stern rebuke to oppressors and abettors; when the educators of a people are reared in the land where they teach, and among the people they volunteer to elevate; there is, in this, assuredly, a great facility to the work of redemption. Such teachers and labourers are the Abolitionists of America: as such we would willingly sustain, support, and cheer them on to live and die for the happy consummation of the glorious work they have in hands.

We have not forgotten the visit to our shores of Charles Lenox Remond.[108] His labours here were fruitful. He is still affectionately remembered.

In conclusion, we beg of you to present our respectful and kind remembrances to your friend and fellow-traveler, J. N. Buffum, Esq. whose property, and powers of mind and body have been long devoted to the aid of those labouring for the slaves' emancipation in his native country. And let us hope that the intercourse which your visit, and that of Mr. Buffum has established between us – may not be severed by land or sea, but may continue, based on the foundation of united labors for oppressed, down-trodden, and bleeding humanity.

We are, dear Sir, your friends and fellow-laborers. Signed on behalf of the Anti-Slavery Societies of Cork,

Richard Dowden, Esq. Mayor, Chairman.
Mary Mannix, Isabel Jennings, Secretaries,
Ralph Varian, Secretary, Pro. Tem.[109]

The votes of thanks and the reading of the address were loudly applauded by the meeting.

Mr. Douglass arose and was received with enthusiastic cheering. When it subsided, he said – The sentiments of gratitude expressed by the meeting are in perfect unison with my own. Never was I held under greater obligations to the press, and to the proprietors of public buildings, than I have been since in Cork, and I express my sincere gratitude for it in behalf of the bondsmen. Particularly am I indebted to the press for their freedom in copying the few feeble words I have been able to say in this city, that they may return to my land, and sound terribly in the ears of the oppressors of my countrymen. Mr. President, the address which has been read, I certainly was not expecting. I expected to go through the length and breadth of your country preaching to those who are ready to hear the groans of the oppressed. I did not expect the high position that I enjoy during my stay in the city of Cork, and not only there, but in Dublin. The object which we have met to consider is the Annexation of Texas to the United States. You have perhaps heard that in America when an individual has absented himself unaccountably for any time, such a person is said to have gone to Texas, few knowing where it is. Texas is that part of Mexico, bounded on the north by the United States, on the south side by the Gulf of Mexico. The extent of this country is not correctly known. It is as large as France – a most prolific soil – climate most salubrious. The facilities for commercial and agricultural proceedings are unsurpassed anywhere. A Mr. Austin obtained a grant of the Royal Government, to settle three hundred families in Texas, with an understanding that such families should obey the laws then existing, and also, that they should be members of the Roman Catholic religion. He succeeded in introducing thirty families. His son took up the business, and introduced three hundred families. Before he succeeded, the revolution in Mexico severed the Mexican provinces from the crown, and the contract was rendered void. He made application to the new Government, and obtained a similar contract. Other men in the West made similar applications to the Mexican Government. Among the rest were Irishmen, and they were among the few who fulfilled their contracts.

The consequence of making the Catholic religion a necessary qualification to settle in Texas afforded opportunity for hypocrisy. A number of persons of Catholic persuasion entered the territory and made complaints. They succeeded in fomenting a revolt against the Mexican Government. Soon after the Texans managed to lodge complaints of oppression against it. Under these pretences they declared for religious freedom, applied to the United States for sympathy, for religious liberty. After getting the property under conditions of submission, they turn round for sympathy in a revolt in behalf of religious toleration. Mexico came forward nobly and abolished Slavery in Texas. In open violation of this, slaves were introduced. Mexico, outraged at this violation of her laws, attempted to compel obedience – this resulted in the revolution. Texas applied to the United States for assistance. Here came the deed that ought to bring down on the United States the *united* execration of the world. She pretended to be in friendly relation with Mexico. Her Congress looked with indifference on the raising of troops to aid the slaveholding Texans in wresting from the Mexicans, Texas. Indeed they encouraged it. Texans succeeded in holding at bay, the Mexican Government. The United States with an indecent haste recognized the independence of Texas. This was the preparatory step to the consummation of Annexation to the Union. The object was that of making Texas the market for the surplus slaves of the North American States.

The Middle States of the United States are slave-raising States. In 1837 you might meet in Virginia, hundreds of slaves handcuffed and chained together, driving southward to be sold. The Southern States were formerly these where the slaves brought the highest price, but at present they are fully supplied with slaves; and there is a consequent reduction in the price of human flesh and bones. In 1836 slaves brought from $1,000 to $1,500; but a year ago the price was reduced to $600. The slaveholders saw the necessity of opening a new country where there would be a demand for slaves. Americans should be considered a band of plunderers for the worst purposes. T. Coke is the leader of the Whig party in America,[110] he declared his intention not only to annex Texas, but Oregon. When he heard the British lion growl at this, he allowed that he considered it an open question. It was well he did, for the Americans ought to dread a war. – Should they go to war with three millions of slaves in their bosom, only looking for the first favorable opportunity of lifting their arms in open rebellion? – American statesmen are aware of this. The reasons they give for the annexation of Texas not only prove them to be rotten at heart, but a band of dastards. They say that Mexico is not able to go to war, therefore we can take their country. I dare the Americans to reach their arms to Canada. The conduct of America in this particular instance has not been sufficiently dwelt upon by the British press. England should not have stood by and seen a feeble people robbed without raising a note of remonstrance.

I have done with the question of Texas – let me proceed to the general question. I will read you the laws of a part of the American States regarding the relation of master and slave, the laws which created the row in the steamship *Cambria*, not because they are the worst I could select, but because I desire to have them remain upon your memory. – If more than seven slaves are found together without a white person, twenty lashes a piece; for letting loose a boat from where 'tis moored, thirty-nine lashes, for the first, and for the second offence the loss of an ear. For having an article for sale without a ticket from his master, ten lashes. For travelling in the night without a pass, forty lashes. Found in another person's quarters, forty lashes. For being on horseback without a written permission, three lashes; or riding without leave a slave may be whipped, cropped, or branded with the letter A, in the cheek. The laws may be found in Heywood's manual,[111] and several other works. These laws will be the laws of Texas. How sound these laws, Irishmen, and Irish women, in your ears? These laws, as you are aware, are not the worst, for one law in North Carolina makes it a crime punishable with death for the second offence, to teach a slave to read. My friends, I would wish to allude to another matter in relation to the religious denominations of Cork. My friends, all I have said respecting their brethren in America has been prompted by a regard for the bondman. I know what Slavery is by experience. I know what my experience has been at the hands of religionists. The Baptist, or Presbyterian that would desire me not to tell the truth, is a man who loves his sect more than he loves his God. (Cheers). To you who have a missionary spirit, I say there is no better field than America. The slave is on his knees asking for light; slaves who not only want the Bible, but someone to teach them to read its contents. (Hear, hear.) Their cries come across the Atlantic this evening appealing to you! lift up your voices against this giant sin. (Loud cheers.) Mr. President, I am glad to learn that the simple reading of my narrative by a minister in your town, was the cause of his preaching last Sabbath an able Anti-Slavery discourse. (Hear, hear.) My friends, labour on in this good work, for hearts on the other side of the Atlantic have long been cheered by your efforts. When England with one effort wiped from her West Indies the stain of Slavery, turning eight hundred thousand *things* into eight hundred thousand beings, from that time the bondmen in our country looked with more ardent hope to the day when their chains would be broken, and they be permitted to enjoy that liberty in a Republic, which was now enjoyed under the mild rule of a Monarchical Government. This infused amongst us a spirit of hope, of faith, of liberty. Thus you have done much, but *don't feel your power cease here.* – ONLY SPEAK THE TRUE WORD – BREATHE THE RIGHT PRAYER – TRUST IN THE TRUE GOD – and your influence will be powerful against all wrong! (Loud and continued applause.)

Your land is now being travelled over by men from our country, their whole code of justice is based on the changing basis of the colour of a man's skin; for in Virginia there are but three crimes for which a white man is hung, but in the same State there are seventy-three crimes for which the black suffers death. I want the Americans to know that in the good city of Cork I ridiculed their nation – I attempted to excite the utter contempt of the people here upon them. O, that America were freed from Slavery! her brightness would then dazzle the Eastern world. The oppressed of all nations might flock to her as an asylum from monarchical or other despotic rulers. (Applause.) I do believe that America has the elements for becoming a great and glorious nation. Those three millions of foes might be converted into three millions of friends – but I am not going to say anything in her favour – I am an outlaw there – and 'tis time to bid you farewell! Mr. Douglass sat down amidst the most enthusiastic applause, which was again and again repeated.

Editorial
Publication: *Southern Reporter and Cork Commercial Courier*
Date of Publication: Tuesday, 4 November 1845
Title: 'Mr. Douglas [sic], the Anti-Slavery Lecturer'.

We have often thought that perhaps the most potent eloquence that could be enlisted in the anti-slavery cause would be the simple and unadorned narrative of the suffering and ignomies of slavery, told with all the thrilling earnestness of conscious injury by an emancipated slave. But if to this could be super-added the universal influence over the human mind possessed by a striking person, rich, full-toned voice, great natural eloquence, under the command of good taste, guided and directed by sound judgement and a fair amount of education, it would be difficult to over-rate the efforts of such a theme, so discoursed upon by such a man, before any audience of freemen, lovers of liberty and of their kind. Such a man, we are assured, has recently left the shores of America for the purpose of lecturing on slavery in the United Kingdom. He is now in Ireland where he is attracting and riveting the attention of large and increasing auditories; and we believe he intends, ere long, to visit Liverpool and Manchester in the prosecution of his object. Meantime we may mention one or two things connected with him that do not appear to be known, or respecting which very imperfect accounts have as yet appeared in the papers. Mr Douglas is a man of colour, born in slavery, his white master being his father. After twenty years of slavery he effected his escape; immediately upon reaching the New England states he married, and has for some time been a resident of Lynn, near Boston, Massachusetts, where his wife and four children are now living. He received his education from the Methodists, by whom he was encouraged to preach; but his mission is clearly that of an anti-slavery lecturer. He came over in the Cambria mail steamer, and such is the intensity of American prejudice against people of his colour that the agents of the vessel in Boston would not receive him as a cabin passenger and he was consequently compelled to take a berth in the steerage. During the voyage a citizen from Lynn, well-acquainted with Mr Douglas, finding much enquiry amongst the passengers as to his life and profession, lent them copies of a brief memoir of his life which has been printed. This led to numerous requests that he would deliver an anti-slavery lecture on board, Mr Douglas declined, stating that he would not do so unless he was invited by the captain. A number of passengers then went to Captain Judkins and asked him to make a request to Mr Douglas, and ultimately on the last day the vessel was at sea, the Captain asked Mr Douglas if he could be prepared to give a lecture on slavery at five minutes' notice in the saloon deck. Mr Douglas assented; the passengers were convened by sound of a bell, and the captain introduced the lecturer to his passengers generally. Mr Douglas commenced and made some statements as to slavery as he had seen it in the southern states, when he was repeatedly interrupted by several persons, who were subsequently ascertained to be planters, who called out at the end of every statement, 'that's a lie'. Mr Douglas bore this patiently for some time, but these unmanly interruptions being continued, he at length pulled out of his pocket a book, and said he would read something he knew they could not deny, being in fact the laws enacted against slaves in states which he named. He was reading these when the rage of the planters burst into ebullitions of wrath, which had very nearly led to bloodshed. One of them threatened to pitch Mr Douglas overboard, and offered more insulting language to the captain for permitting such a man to lecture on board his ship. An Irish gentleman, a passenger on hearing the threat, went to the planter and told him that if he attempted to lay hands on Mr Douglas he would find that more persons than one could play at throwing overboard. The altercation grew warmer; the belligerents began to allay themselves into hostile parties; and the requests of the captain that the gentlemen would behave peaceably were met by a challenge to fight a duel on the part of one of the planters who thrust his card before the captain, and who also intimated that if Captain Judkins would not fight aboard his own ship, he would give him a hostile meeting in Liverpool, immediately after the vessel's arrival there.

This made matters worse and had the captain not displayed the greatest firmness and resolution there would, in all probability, have been a serious termination to the affair. Finding that the remonstrances were of no avail against the gasconading and braggadocio he, at length, ordered three sets of irons to be brought and declared that he would put the first man in irons who took any steps to break the peace. This had the desired effect, the rage of the discomfited planters subsided into angry murmurs, and they slunk away, declaring that the captain should hear of it again when he returned to Boston. Peace was re-established and the passengers separated on the following day upon their reaching Liverpool, without any further hostile manifestation on the part of the planters. We may add that it is possible it may be a month or two before Douglas reaches Manchester.

Anti-Slavery Meeting
Lecturer: Frederick Douglass
Date: Tuesday, 14 October 1845
Publication: *Hampshire Advertiser* (from the *Cork Southern Reporter*)
Date of Publication: Saturday, 8 November 1845
Title: 'AMERICAN SLAVERY'.

INTERESTING NARRATIVE OF A FUGITIVE SLAVE. The Cork Southern Reporter gives an account of an influential and numerously attended meeting on Tuesday, in the City Court-house, to hear the statement of Mr. Frederick Douglas, himself a 'fugitive slave,' relative to slavery in America, and also to give expression to public opinion against that atrocious and cruel system. The meeting was announced for two o'clock, but long before that hour the Court-house was densely crowded in every part. The grand jury gallery was thronged with ladies, who seemed to take the liveliest interest in the proceedings. The Mayor entered the Court a little after two o'clock, accompanied by an American gentleman, and Mr. Frederick Douglas, who certainly appeared a noble specimen of the negro race. The oratorical powers possessed by Mr. Douglas were a matter of admiration during the progress of the speech he delivered. To facility and power of expression he joined a most impressive and energetic delivery, with the most humorous method of exposing the hypocrisy and duplicity of some of the American slaveholders. The Mayor, on taking the chair, explained the object for which the meeting was convened.

After some well-expressed resolutions had been put and carried,

Mr. Frederick Douglas came forward amid loud cheering. He said – Sir, I never more than at present lacked words to express my feelings. The cordial and manly reception I have met with, and the spirit of freedom that seems to animate the bosoms of the entire audience, have filled my heart with feelings I am incapable of expressing. I stand before you in the most extraordinary position that one human being ever stood before his race – a slave; a slave not in the ordinary sense of the term, not in a political sense, but in its real and intrinsic meaning. I have not been stripped of one of my rights and privileges, but of all. By the laws of the country whence I came, I was deprived of myself – of my own body, soul, and spirit;

and I am free only because I succeeded in escaping the clutches of the man who claimed me as his property. There are fourteen slave states in America, and I was sold as a slave at a very early age, little more than seven years, in the southern part of Maryland. While there I conceived the idea of escaping into one of the free states, which I eventually succeeded in accomplishing. On the 3rd September, 1838, I made my escape into Massachusetts, a free state. I there went to work on the quays, rolling oil casks to get a livelihood, and in about three years after, having been induced to attend an anti-slavery meeting at Nantucket, it was there announced that I should go from town to town to expose their nefarious system. For four years I was then engaged in discussing the slavery question, and during that time I had opportunities of arranging my thoughts and language. I was at times doubted if I had ever been a slave, and this doubt being used to injure the anti-slavery cause, I was induced to set the matter at rest by publishing the narrative of my life. A person undertaking to write a book without learning, will appear rather novel, but such as it was I gave it to the public – (hear, hear). The excitement at last increased so much that it was thought better for me to get out of the way, lest my master might use some stratagem to get me back into his clutches. I am here then in order to avoid the scent of the bloodhounds of America, and of spreading a light on the subject of her slave system. There is nothing slavery dislikes half so much as the light.

The relation of master and slave in America should be clearly understood. The master is allowed by law to hold his slave as his possession and property; the master can buy, sell, bequeath his slave as well as any other property: nay, he shall decide what the poor slave is to eat, what he is to drink, where and when he shall speak. He also decides for his affections, when and whom he is to marry, and, what is more enormous, how long that marriage covenant is to endure. The slave-holder exercises the bloody power of tearing asunder those whom God had joined together – of separating husband from wife, parent from child, and of leaving the hut vacant, and the hearth desolate – (sensation). The slaveholders of America resort to every species of cruelty, but they can never reduce the slave to a willing obedience. The natural elasticity of the human soul repels the slightest attempt to enslave it. The black slaves of America are not wholly without that elasticity; they are men, and, being so, they do not submit readily to the yoke – (great cheering). Oftentimes, when the poor slave, after recovering from the application of the scourge and the branding iron, looks at his master with a face indicating dissatisfaction, he is subjected to fresh punishment. That cross look must be at once repulsed, and the master whips, as he says, 'the devil out of him'; for when a slave looks dissatisfied with his condition, according to his cruel taskmaster's idea, he looks as if he had the devil in him, and it must be whipped out – (oh, oh).

The state of slavery is one of perpetual cruelty. When very young, as I stated, I was sold into slavery, and was placed under the control of a little boy who had orders to kick me when he liked; whenever the little boy got cross, his mother used to say, 'Go and whip Freddy'. I, however, soon began to reason upon the matter, and found that I had as good a right to kick Tommy as he had me – (loud laughter and cheering). My dissatisfaction with my condition soon appeared, and I was most brutally treated. I stand before you with the marks of the slave-driver's whip, that will go down with me to my grave; but, what is worse, I feel the scourge of slavery itself piercing into my heart, crushing my feelings, and sinking me into the depths of moral and intellectual degradation (loud cheering).

In the South, the laws are exceedingly cruel, more so than in the northern States. The most cruel feature of the system in the northern States is the slave trade. The domestic slave trade of America is now in the height of its prosperity from the annexation of Texas to our Union. In the northern States they actually breed slaves, and rear them for the southern markets; and the constant dread of being sold is often more terrible than the reality itself.

He then proceeded to comment upon the law of America relative to the punishment of slaves. This is the law of America after her declaration of independence – the land in which are millions of professed Christians, and which supports their religion at a cost of twenty millions dollars annually, and yet she has three millions of human beings the subjects of the hellish laws I have read. We would not ask you to interfere with the politics of America, or involve your military aid to put down American slavery. No, we only demand your moral and religious influence on the slavery question, and believe me the effects of that influence will be overwhelming – (cheers). We want to awaken the slaveholder to a sense of the iniquity of his position, and to draw him from his nefarious habits. It must also be stated that the American pulpit is on the side of slavery, and the Bible is blasphemously quoted in support of it. The ministers of religion actually quoted Scripture in support of the most cruel and bloody outrages on the slaves. My own master was a Methodist class-leader – (laughter, and 'Oh') – and he bared the neck of a young woman, in my presence, and he cut her with a cow skin. He then went away, and when he returned to complete the castigation, he quoted the passage: 'He that knoweth his master's will and doeth it not, shall be beaten with many stripes' – (laughter). The preachers say to the slaves they should obey their masters, because God commands it, and because their happiness depended on it – (a laugh). It is punishable with death for a second attempt to teach a slave his letters in America – (loud expressions of disgust) – and in that Protestant country the slave is denied the privilege of learning the name of the God that made him. Slavery, with all its bloody paraphernalia, is upheld by the church of the country.

The speaker proceeded to say, that the feeling of prejudice against colour had now changed, and he could walk through Boston in the most refined company. The speaker concluded by saying that he would again address them during his stay in Cork. The other proceedings were ended by a vote of thanks, carried by acclamation, and the meeting adjourned.

Editorial
Publication: *Liberator*
Date of Publication: Friday, 28 November 1845
Title: 'FREDERICK DOUGLASS IN IRELAND'.

On our first page, we have given from Cork papers some account of the public reception of Mr. Douglass in that city. In the course of his speech, delivered in the Wesleyan Chapel, Patrick-street, Mr. Douglass referred to an allusion made to himself by the editor of 'The Constitution,' as 'an excellent specimen of the negro' – and treated it as an intentional insult; though, at a subsequent meeting, he stated that the editor had disavowed any such intention. Had our friend Douglass understood the world-wide difference that there is, in meaning and in spirit, in the use of the term 'negro' on that and on this side of the Atlantic, he would not have had any occasion for manifesting so much sensitiveness. In this country, the term is almost as odious to our coloured population, as the idea of slavery, because it is generally used in a contemptuous and vile manner; but across the Atlantic, the term conveys no idea of scorn, but is used with all possible respect. Below is another very interesting epistle from Mr. Douglass. The manner in which the great apostle of Temperance, Father MATHEW, received him, will exalt that great benefactor of the human race still more highly in the estimation of all those whose good opinion it is desirable to possess. To Douglass, this transition from slavery-cursed America to the Emerald Isle must be thrilling indeed: – 'Tis somewhat like the burst from death to life, From the grave's cerements to the robes of heaven.'

7

LIMERICK

Anti-Slavery Meeting
Lecturer: Frederick Douglass
Date of Lecture: Monday, 10 November 1845
Location: Independent Chapel, Bedford Row, Limerick
Publication: *Limerick Reporter*
Date of Publication: Tuesday, 11 November 1845
Title: 'Frederick Douglass'.

Last evening, at the Independent Chapel, Bedford Row,[112] at eight o'clock, a lecture was given upon the horrors and cruelty of negro slavery by a fugitive slave, who afforded in his own person a striking refutation of one of the grounds upon which the slaveholder upholds his diabolical traffic – namely, the inferiority of the intellect of the negro race, for so clever a speaker it has rarely fallen to our lot to hear; and certainly in his exterior manner, he is far superior to the majority of slave holders as he is in intellectual endowments.

The building was crowded in every part, and by all classes and parties. There was a large number of females present.

The Chair having been taken by Mr. Fisher of the Society of Friends,[113] who introduced the lecturer to the audience.

Mr. Douglas [sic] (for that is his name) proceeded to address them. He said slavery was a question in which every human being ought to feel a deep interest. It aimed at, and accomplished, the destruction of all the rights of men. It was an enemy of the entire human family. The principle that enslaved the black would enthrall the white, and the spirit of tyranny that for the last 300 years made the children of Africa its victims, would devote every one whom he now addressed to its cruel altar. It was a strange contradiction that in human character, that in a country that boasts to be the freest in the world, slavery exists in its worst and most aggravated forms – a country that threw off the yoke of colonial bondage for a three-penny tax on tea, proceeding upon the principle that all men were equal, and yet was the propagator of the heinous crime of slavery. It was to slavery, as it existed in the United States, he alluded, and he thought he might be permitted to speak of it, having himself endured its woes, and felt the bloody lash.

He had been met with the objection that slavery existed in Ireland, and that therefore there was no necessity for describing its character as found in another country (hear, hear). His answer was, that if slavery existed here, it ought to be put down, and the generous in the land ought to rise and scatter its fragments to the winds (loud cheers). – But there was nothing like American slavery on the soil on which he now stood. Negro-slavery consisted not in taking away a man's property, but in making property of him, and in destroying his identity – in treating him as the beasts and creeping things. GOD had given the negro a conscience and a will, but his conscience was no monitor to him, for he had no power to exercise his will – his master decided for him not only what he should eat and what he should drink, what he should wear, when and to whom he should speak, how much he should work, how much and by whom he is to be punished – he not only decided all these things, but what is morally right and wrong. The slave must not even choose his wife, must marry and unmarry at the will of his tyrant, for the slave-holder had no compunction in separating man and wife, and thus putting asunder what GOD had joined together. Could the most inferior person in this country be so treated by the highest? If any man exists in Ireland who would so treat another, may the combined execrations of humanity fall upon him, and may he be excluded from the pale of human sympathy!

There was a feeling in some quarters that the descriptions given in this country of negro-slavery were all exaggerations. He had seen a sketch by a geologist, Doctor or Professor Lyell,[114] who had gone from England on a tour to America, and returned from it apparently under the impression that the negro's lot was not an unenviable one. If this individual be only as loose in his reasoning, and as fallacious in his premises in geological matters, his theories were of little value. It was but eleven days' sail to America, and there was, therefore a great intercourse between the two counties. Tourists were constantly going over. Professor Lyell was a geologist, and when he visited the south where he saw slavery, he was taken by the hand by the slave-holding geologists – he walked with their daughters, dined at their tables; in fact, lived with them. It was from these he received all his impressions of slavery, and was it not to be presumed that the wolf would say that the lamb loved to be eaten up by him (laugher, and cheers). Thus, even geologists were led astray. He said that slaves laughed and sung, and were, therefore, happy. This man was not the geologist for him. But he would not attack his geology, but his slaveology. And it was important that a slave who struck off his fetters should come forth and proclaim to the world what he experienced in his own person.

He would, in the first place, proceed to show them some of the laws and the implements under which the bondsmen luxuriated. – (There were here loud cries of "hear, hear, hear.") The speaker then said that in America they were not accustomed to much applause at public meetings, and without any wish to alter the customs of this country, or introduce American customs, he begged respectfully to say that he had no desire for any demonstrations of applause, and, considering the sacred character of the building in which they were assembled, he would prefer being allowed to proceed without them, as he was anxious not to give offence, or

231

have it given to those who might have any objection to cheers. Mr. Douglas(s) then proceeded to read extracts from the laws of the slave holding states, from which it appeared that a slave was liable to be whipped severely, and have his ear cut off for the most trivial offence, such as riding a horse without the written permission of his master. There were now 14 slaveholding states, Florida having been lately added to the union, and Texas was about to be added, which would make 15 slave-holding to 13 free states. Now, he charged the American nation with being emphatically responsible for slavery in the whole of the country. It was not peculiar to the Southern States, for all the states were united under one constitution, and that constitution protected and supported slavery – for instance there was no one spot in all America upon which he could stand free.

Though God had said, "thou shalt not deliver up the slave to his master," the constitution of the United States said differently. He was an outlaw in America, and he could be hunted back again to his master, if identified. Yet their liberty caps were striking the clouds (there were here loud cries of "hear, hear," when the speaker again said that these demonstrations rather disconcerted than aided him. He proceeded) – The Americans were most anxious to have it understood, that all the country was not implicated in slavery, and accordingly when one of them came to this country he was sure to say that he was from a free state; but unless he came as an out-and-out abolitionist he came stained with robbery and human blood – a participator in the law of the land, that the slave must be a slave or die. To carry out this law the judges and the other officers of the state solemnly swore every year. Even the battle places could not protect the slave. If he (Mr. Douglas[s]) should go to Bunker's Hill, and there seizing the monument erected to liberty, and claim the freedom for which his fathers shed their blood (for it was a negro who shed the first blood, and fired the first gun on that battle field), yet there would be no liberty for him there. Even when that monument was dedicated, and Daniel Webster, the great American orator, was eloquent upon human liberty, boasting of the deeds achieved by their ancestors, and their throwing off the British yoke, John Tyler, the man-slaver, was there – John Tyler who had even sold his own children as slaves, *he* was present with a slave holding an umbrella over his head (hear, hear).

Yes; the Americans, as a nation, were guilty of the foul crime of slavery, whatever might be their hypocritical vaunts of freedom. It was not his wish to condemn republicanism, but the slavery that was identified with it; but it was not a true democracy, but a bastard republicanism that enslaved one-sixth of the population. – They were free booters who wished to be free to plunder everyone within their reach – stretching their long, bony fingers into Mexico, and appropriating her territory to themselves in order to make it a hot bed of negro slavery. Mexico with all her barbarism and darkness had wiped away the stain of slavery from her dominions, and now the enlightened, Christian United States had stained again what was washed. He wanted them to know, and if there was a reporter present they would know, that a slave had stood up in Limerick and ridiculed their democracy and their liberty.

One of the reasons why he was there to-night was that he was not to be a fugitive from a nation of men-stealers. He did not say there were not so many good men in America, but the majority of the country and the legislature were stained with blood. About 7 years ago he escaped from his master Thomas Auld, in Maryland, into Massachusetts, the freest of the free states. He lived there till within the last 3 months, and his family were there still. He escaped on the 3d of December [September], 1838, and came to New Bedford. He got his livelihood by rolling oil casks, and the labour was sweet to him, for it was voluntary, and he received his own earnings which were filched from him before by his master.

About 3 years after his escape some gentlemen hearing of his addressing meetings of the black population on the subject of slavery induced him to go about lecturing through that state, concealing his name and the place from which he escaped, for had these been made known, some Judas or Lago would have betrayed him. Having thus lectured for 4 years a number of persons began to doubt if he ever were a slave. He did not answer the Jim Crow description which was given of negroes at New York, and in theatres in this country. He was sorry to find that one of these apes of the negro had been recently encouraged in Limerick, but the reptile was only supported by those of his own kind. The people of the free state of Massachusetts thought from the description they had seen given of negroes, and from the fact of his having an education, the conclusion was come to by many – that he was not a slave. This led him to publish a narrative of his life, in which he detailed the crimes of the slaveholders, and mentioned their names. That settled the question, but it endangered his safety. There were 6500 copies of the work sold from the time of its publication in May last till the first of August.

Not deeming it safe to remain in America, he embarked at Boston, on the 16th of August, in the *Cambria*, for this country; and he could not illustrate slavery better than by stating what took place on board the ship. The slaveholders got up a regular mob, and threatened to throw him over board. They first manifested their feeling when they found he took a cabin passage, and insisted that he should go to the steerage, for it is the law of the skin aristocracy at the other side of the waters, that a negro should not go in the cabin with whites. He had therefore, to change to the steerage, and he was content with it particularly when he reflected that every wave brought him further from the bloody and persecuting prejudice that drove him out of his country. A gentleman asked him where he was going, and he soon found out that he was a fugitive slave; considerable interest was excited on board, and there was a wish among the Scotch, English, and Irish passengers that he should address them and give a narrative of his case. He well knew that he could not do so without the permission of the Captain, and he accordingly declined. Some gentlemen however made interest with Captain Judkins, who gave the permission when they got in sight of Ireland. He little thought that he had American democrats on board. – The meeting was announced on the saloon or quarter deck, among the rest the slaveholders made their appearance and would not allow him to speak; but the Hudson [sic][115] family being on board, and being American abolitionists, they sung one of their beautiful songs, and drowned the uproar. At the conclusion of it the Captain took advantage of the silence, and introducing him begged them to hear what he had to say. He had not uttered an entire sentence when one of the slaveholders said "that is a lie." When he got into the middle of another sentence, another slaveholder said "that is a lie" in true American fashion. Well said he (Mr. Douglas) if everything he had stated upon his authority was a lie, he would read for them what they would admit was not a lie.

He then took up a book and quoted from it the laws of the slaveholding states. A spark of fire thrown into a magazine could not have produced a greater explosion. They could not bear to have the iniquities of slavery exposed, and they reared up against him like demons. One said, shaking his fist at him (Mr. D.) he wished he had him at Cuba. Another little creature, that he wished he had him at New Orleans; and a third, if he had him at Savannah how he would "use him up;" he would be *one* of the number to throw him overboard. How very courageous, one of the indefinite number to throw one man overboard (laughter).

There happened to be an Irishman present from Dublin whose name was Gough; he was so tall that he (Mr. Douglas(s)) had to look up to him. It was remarkable, that not a man of the slaveholders wished to have him (Mr. Douglas(s)) in Ireland, for they knew that he would get fair play there (hear, and cheers), and when the fellow threatened to throw him overboard, he was told by the Irishman that two might play at that game (enthusiastic cheering). He (Mr. Douglas(s)) then called for three cheers for old Ireland. Mr. Gough had stood up with such a calm dignity, over-looking these little creatures, that he awed them into silence. Afterwards, however, they cursed and swore, and raved, as only slaveholders can. The Captain called them to order, and told them their conduct was derogatory to the character of gentlemen, of Christians, and of men. He had, at the request of a number of the passengers, permitted Mr. Douglas(s) to address them; and if there were any there who did not wish to hear him, let them go to another part of the ship. The Captain then said, "Douglas(s), pitch into them like bricks" (loud laughter). He did his best to comply with the Captain's order, when a New Orleans man ran at him. The Captain, who was a powerful man, pushed the little fellow aside, when he put his hand into his breast, and he (Mr. Douglas(s) thought he was now about to draw a bowie knife to stab the Captain, but behold he showed him his card, and told him he would meet him in Liverpool. "Very well," said the Captain, "I will meet you there," a reply which caused the slaveholder to slink away in silence, and he afterwards seemed to have totally forgotten the challenge (hear, and laughter).

The Captain then desired the mate to bring irons to put these gentlemen into who were so fond of putting others in irons. This silenced them. And these were the friends of free speech! So much did they hate discussion on the subject of slavery, that if any man stood up on that assembly and defended it against him (Mr. D), they would be anything but obliged to him. It was upon this feeling of slaveholders that he wished to operate, and his words would be borne on the wings of the press beyond the Atlantic wave. They would fly up and down through the regions of the north – they would cross the line of the slave-holding south – they would reverberate through the valley of the Mississippi, and there was no part of the land into which they would not penetrate.

Mr. Douglas(s) then proceeded to exhibit some of the implements used in torturing the slaves, among which was an iron collar taken from the neck of a young woman who had escaped from Mobile. It had so worn into her neck that her blood and flesh were found on it (sensation). After showing the fetters used in chaining the feet of two slaves together, he exhibited a pair of hand-cuffs taken from a fugitive slave who escaped from Maryland into Pennsylvania. He knew the man well. He was being brought in custody to his master by a constable – he saw a sharp rock before him, and with one mighty effort he raised his hands, and, striking the hand-cuffs against the stone, broke them and at the same time his left wrist (sensation). He fled and was overtaken but with the unbroken hand he drew a dirk from his breast, and cut down his pursuer (cries of "bravo"). He escaped to Canada where alone on the American Continent he could be safe, and there he enjoyed that liberty under a monarchical government which he looked for in vain in his own land under a boasted democracy.

So true was it that the slave must leave his native soil to be free. In the language of Curran,[116] their own orator – "I speak in the spirit of the British law which makes liberty commensurate with, and inseparable from British soil; which proclaims even to the stranger and sojourner, the moment he sets his foot on British earth, that the ground upon which he treads is holy, and consecrated by the genius of *universal emancipation*. No matter in what language his doom may have been pronounced; – no matter in what complexion incompatible with freedom, an Indian or an African sun may have been cloven down – no matter with what solemnities he may have been devoted upon the altar of slavery; the first moment he touches the sacred soil of Britain, the altar and the God sink together in the dust; his soul walks abroad in her own majesty – his body swells beyond the measure of his chains, that burst from around him, and he stands redeemed, regenerated and is enthralled by the irresistible genius of *universal emancipation*" (applause).

If an American ever came among them speaking of the liberty of his country, let them make his cheek crimson by telling him that there is not a single spot in all his land where the sable man can stand free. Mr. Douglas(s) then went on to exhibit a horrid whip which was made of cow hide, and whose lashes were as hard as horn. They were clotted with blood when he first got them. He saw his master tie up a young woman eighteen years of age, and beat her with that identical whip until the blood ran down her back. – And the wretch accompanied the whipping with a quotation from Scripture, "He that knew his master's will and did it not obey shall receive many strips" (cries of "horrible"). This man was Thomas Auld, of St. Michael(s). He would proceed further in his exposure of slavery, but it was now too late, being half-past nine o'clock, and he would therefore reserve what he had to say till Wednesday evening, when he would give another lecture of the series he intended to deliver.

Editorial
Publication: *Limerick Reporter*
Date of Publication: Tuesday, 11 November 1845
Title: 'American Slavery'.

In another column we publish an admirable lecture delivered last night on American slavery by one who had himself, in his own person, experienced its human cruelties. There was no man who listened to his eloquent and touching statement that did not burn with indignation against the atrocious system which makes chattel property of men made in the image of God, and only 'guilty of sin not coloured' like that of their white tyrants. Every word spoken by this persecuted son of Africa bears the impress of truth, and for ourselves we must say that we were never before so fully convinced of the necessity of Mr O'Connell's denunciations of the abominable traffic. So far from his ever having exaggerated its iniquities, even his peerless eloquence could not paint in colours sufficiently glaring. It would be impossible to exaggerate its infamy, to feel too strongly against it, or to give expression to that feeling in words too burning. It deserves no quarter and admits of no compromise. We trust it shall receive none in Ireland, but that on the contrary such a spirit will be excited against it that the slaveholders must at length give way before the irresistible tide of public opinion. It is a melancholy consideration that in a country which liberty seemed to mark out as her own favoured land, where she loved to dwell and where she found an asylum when banished from the rest of the world, a majority of the confederated states should nurture negro slavery in its worst forms, and that there is not a single spot in any state of America, even the most free, upon which the slave can put his foot and say, 'the ground whereon I tread is holy'. As a nation, therefore, the American people are guilty of a foul conspiracy against the rights of man.

In common with our fellow-countrymen we feel grateful for the sympathy of many Americans in our own struggle for freedom; they have contributed their money to sustain our national league. But we trust no slaver-holders polluted dollars ever found its way in the sacred fund of our Repeal Association. If any such dared to make us the medium of his contribution, we would have no hesitation in throwing it in his face, and saying in the language of PETER to ANNANTAS [sic] and SAPHIRA [sic], when they laid a part of their unholy gain at his feet, 'Thy money perish with thee'. Every coin produced by the slave is stained with human blood, and until 'the damned spot' is washed away by abolition of the accursed thing, neither the slaveholder nor his money ought to have part or lot in our glorious struggle for redemption.

In reference to the lecture last night there are two things we regret – first, that it should be delivered in a place of worship, thus giving a sectarian appearance to a cause that equally belongs to all. Secondly, that Mr Douglass attacked Mr Bateman – the Comedian – so bitterly.[117] We do not think he deserved the language applied to him. Mr Bateman is a clever actor, and his representation of a particular negro character, debased by his white despot, is no more to be considered as a description of negros generally than the representation of *Macbeath* in the 'Beggar's Opera' can be regarded as a delineation of the character of Englishmen, or any of the Irish buffoons represented by LEONARD or MISS HERON can be viewed as types of Irish character. But there is every allowance to be made for the outraged feelings of humanity in the person of Mr Douglass. We are not disposed, however, to make the same allowance for him or his friends in selecting the Independent Chapel as the place for delivering his very interesting lectures. He might have seen the impropriety of it himself from the fact that the demonstration of applause which he wished to be repressed burst their barriers. Why should not the lectures be given at the Northumberland Rooms, or some other public and unsectarian building? The error, however, may have been unconsciously committed, and it is not yet too late to rectify it. We have no doubt that these observations will be received in the same kind spirit in which they are given, and that the citizens of Limerick at large will be permitted the opportunity of identifying themselves with the cause of the slave.

Anti-Slavery Meeting
Lecturer: Frederick Douglass
Date of Lecture: Wednesday, 12 November 1845
Location: Independent Chapel, Limerick
Publication: *Limerick Reporter*
Date of publication: Friday, *14 November 1845*
Title: 'Negro Slavery – Second lecture of Mr Douglass'.

On Wednesday evening Mr Douglas [sic], once a slave, delivered to a crowded and highly respectable audience, his second lecture, at the Independent Chapel, on the atrocities of American Slavery. He shewed that it was the Churches of America, the bishops and the clergy, that sustained it, and that were it not for those, it would have been long since abolished by the people. He shewed from the newspapers of the day, that Churches, in their corporate capacity, were Slaveholders, and so were the Bishops and Clergymen. The clergy too, were supported by the Slaveholders, and they were afraid to denounce them. He particularly mentioned the Methodists, Independents and Presbyterians, as guilty of the crime. The Catholic was less guilty, for though, as individuals, many of them were slave-holders, they were not as a body, and they alone of all other religions put the slave and his master on the same level at the communion table, and in the house of worship. – Mr Douglas gave a description of a sermon preached by one of the Country Knaves upon the text, "Servants Obey Your Own Masters", which they interpreted "Slaves obey your own masters". His intimation of the manners of these preachers kept the audience in roars of laughter. He said his object was not to deride Christianity or its teachers, for it was upon Christianity he relied for victory, but to gain the sympathy of the people of every religious denomination in this country, and to induce them to hold no fellowship with their co-religionists in America, till they washed away the foul stain of blood from their hands. Mr Douglas then described the manner in which he learned to read. When he was seven years old he was sent by his master to his father-in-law whose wife was a good woman and taught him his letters, and then to speak words of three and four letters. The crowded state of our columns obliges us to decline further observation.

Anti-Slavery Meeting
Lecturer: Frederick Douglass
Date of Lecture: Friday, 21 November 1845
Location: Philosophical Rooms, Limerick
Publication: *Limerick Reporter*
Date of Publication: Tuesday, 25 November 1845
Title: 'Mr Douglas [sic]. The American Slave'.

On Friday evening last, an Anti-Slavery Soiree was held in the Philosophical Rooms, Upper Glentworth street,[118] given to Mr. *Frederick Douglas*, the American slave.

The attendance was numerous and most respectable. On a raised platform we noticed the following gentlemen: – The Mayor,[119] Francis P. Russell, Esq., Rev. Mr. Brahan, P. P., Rev. Mr. Quin, P. P., Rev. Mr. Egan, R. C. C., Rev. Mr. Williams, Independent Minister, Wm. Lee, Esq., J. J. Fisher, Esq., Mr. O'Neill, Mr. Caldwell, Dr. Gore, Henry Woodburne, Esq., Captain Brady, &c.

On the motion of Mr. J. J. Fisher, the Mayor was moved to the chair amidst loud applause.

The company having partaken of tea, and St. John's Temperance Band having played several beautiful airs, the Chairman rose and said: – In the course of the past twelve months he had the honour of presiding at soirees of his fellow-citizens, and he never felt such pleasure as at the present one. They met together, as men of the same soil, to do honour to a man that came among them from America, and who was once a slave, but who is now a freeman. His worship concluded by proposing the health of "The Queen." Air – God save the Queen.

After a short space of time, the Chairman again rose, and said he would give them, without preface, the health of their guest – "Mr. *Frederick Douglass*."

The toast was received with vehement cheering.

Mr. Douglass then rose, and was received with loud cheers. He said he felt grateful for the honour that had been done him, and gratified for the sake of the great and glorious cause which he came to advocate. He was frequently in the habit of meeting in such assemblies as this, and he assured them that he was never more delighted than at the present moment. (Cheers.) In the West Indies there had been 800,000 slaves, and the people of this country had done something for them. There were two millions and a half of slaves in America that cried, "come and help us." If he was now in America he would be his master's property, and be liable to be sold as a piece of merchandize. Thank GOD, it was not so in this land. (Cheers.) When he attempted to return gratitude for liberty, he failed, for his heart rose to such a pitch of happiness that he was rendered utterly unable to give utterance to his feelings. Seven years ago he was a slave – an object of merchandize – dragged and ranked with beasts to be sold in the market or auction mart. He was happy to see that not only the humble classes of Limerick recognized him, but its wealth and respectability. Oh, what a transition it was to be changed from the state of a slave to that of a freeman! Really, when he thought of his former condition and his present, he was puzzled to know whether *Frederick Douglass* then was the same *Frederick Douglass* now. (Laughter.) He could hardly believe how his proud spirit could be ever bound in chains. If he returned to the United States, he would be taken and bound in slave chains. He must plant himself, therefore, under the protection of the Irish and British people. He was not there to denounce the American Government, but, indeed, he could not say much in favour of it. He would just relate an act of that Government. In South Carolina, the law goes so far as to take coloured seamen when they arrive there in different vessels, and put them in prison until the vessels are about to leave; and if the captain of the vessel did not go and pay jail fees, the unfortunate coloured seaman would be sold in the market to the highest bidder. This the British Government denounced, and were by treaty promised that no coloured seaman in the employment of British vessels, should be touched. The law of South Carolina was accordingly modified, but not changed. Some short time back, a white gentleman had occasion to visit South Carolina, and was attended by a black servant. The authorities were about to enforce their law, but the gentleman remonstrated about his servant, and they told him the only way he could keep his servant was to place him in a British vessel which lay in the port. This was done, and the American authorities dreaded to go near him, because he was under the British flag. The reason that this law was in force was, that they considered a free coloured man as an incendiary among the slaves, lest they should be struck with the thought of freedom. So that a coloured freeman is liable in his own country, and under the American flag, to be dragged to prison, but not under the British flag. (Cheers.) Again he said he was not there to speak against the American Government, but to bring under their notice American Slavery, and to try to make America like any other Christian country in the world. It was the only nation on earth in which the African Slave-Trade was allowed to be carried on. When this is washed away, the American escutcheon will be cleansed, and not till then. (Hear, hear.) When England and France wanted to crush Slavery on the high seas, America gave all the opposition in her power, and afforded every protection to the slavers. He then adverted to the annexation of Texas, and denounced the conduct of America in wresting Texas from Mexico as that of a bully whose only right was that of the strongest. He then alluded to the various battles won for America by negro blood, and depicted in glowing colors, the base ingratitude with which they were rewarded. He would not trespass further upon them. He found freedom and a welcome to speak against Slavery in Dublin, Wexford, Waterford, and Cork, and though last not least in Limerick, (cheers). Whether home or abroad he would never forget the very kind manner he was received in Limerick, Mr. Douglass resumed his seat amidst loud cheers.

After Mr. Parry sung "The battle and the breeze,"[120]
Mr. Douglass again rose, and gave the health of the Mayor.
The toast was received with loud cheers.

The Mayor then rose and thanked them for the kind manner in which the toast just given was received. He said that this, the country of his birth, was always for freedom, and he knew of no country so opposed to slavery as Ireland (cheers).

The Rev. Mr. Brahan, P. P., in giving the health of the Stewards, said he had not the pleasure of hearing Mr. Douglass until this evening, when he was much gratified.[121] When he looked around him, he could see many persons of various denominations, and he also saw some of his own creed, all engaged in denouncing slavery. They had been slaves themselves, they were no longer slaves; but, they sympathized with the enslaved of every creed, and clime, and hue. (cheers.)

Mr. Argles, on the part of the Stewards, responded.

Mr. Douglass then sang a beautiful sentimental air.

The Rev. Mr. Williams, (Independent Minister) then rose, and addressed the meeting at some length. He said that Mr. Douglass spoke of the different religious denominations in America, favoring slavery; but, Mr. Douglass never spoke against Christianity. In the course of his lectures he spoke of the denomination to which he had the honour to belong. Now, the members of his church in Wales and Scotland, sent to the professors of the same church in America, and told them, they would not recognize them as belonging to their church if they countenanced slavery. (cheers.)

Master Dartnell and Mr. Parry sung a few songs to the gratification of all present, and the Mayor having been moved from the chair, and Mr. F. P. Russell called thereto, thanks were voted to the prior chairman for the kind and dignified manner in which he presided over them, and the meeting separated, it being then 11 o'clock.

Anti-Slavery Meeting
Lecturer: Frederick Douglass
Date of Lecture: Friday, 21 November 1845
Location: Philosophical Rooms, Limerick
Publication: *Liberator*
Date of Publication: Friday, 26 December 1845
Title: 'From the *Limerick Reporter* of November 25. Anti-Slavery Soiree'.

Here is another gratifying instance of Irish hospitality, urbanity and respect, extended to one who, in this country is registered as a thing, but in Ireland is treated as a 'man and a brother'. It will make some sensation down South, among the haughty slave-mongers. We should like to look at them while they are reading the account.

The paper then reprinted the report provided above.

8

BELFAST

Advertisement
Publication: *Belfast News-Letter* [122]
Date: Friday, 28 November 1845
Title: 'MR FREDERICK DOUGLASS'.

A GENTLEMAN OF COLOUR, FORMERLY A SLAVE IN THE UNITED STATES OF AMERICA, is expected next week in Belfast, having LECTURED on AMERICAN SLAVERY for several nights in Dublin, Waterford, Cork, and Limerick, to large assemblies, who were delighted at the powerful eloquence displayed by the talented lecturer.

In a subsequent Advertisement, the Belfast Anti-Slavery Society will announce the night of Mr. Douglass's first Lecture, the Hour and Place of Meeting.

Belfast. 28th Nov., 1845.

Advertisement
Publication: *Belfast Vindicator* [123]
Date: Saturday, 29 November 1845
Title: 'MR FREDERICK DOUGLASS'.

A Gentleman of Colour
Formerly a Slave in the United States of America

Is expected next week in Belfast, having lectured on American slavery for several nights in Dublin, Waterford, Cork and Limerick, to large assemblies, who were delighted at the powerful eloquence displayed by the talented Lecturer.

In a future advertisement the Belfast Anti-Slavery Society will announce the night of Mr Douglass's *first* lecture, the hour and place of meeting.

Belfast. 28 November 1845.

241

Advertisement
Publication: *Northern Whig* [124]
Date of Publication: Saturday, 29 November 1845
Title: 'MR. FREDERICK DOUGLASS'.

A GENTLEMAN OF COLOUR. FORMERLY a Slave in the United States of America, is expected next week in Belfast, having LECTURED on AMERICAN SLAVERY, for several nights, in Dublin, Waterford, Cork, and Limerick, to large assemblies, who were delighted at the powerful eloquence displayed the talented Lecturer. In a subsequent Advertisement, the Belfast Anti-Slavery Society will announce the night of Mr. Douglas's First Lecture, the Hour and Place of Meeting.
Belfast, 28 November 1845.

Advertisement
Publication: *Belfast News-Letter and General Advertiser* (hereafter *Belfast News-Letter)*
Date: Friday, 5 December 1845
Title: 'Important Meeting'.

THE MEMBERS and FRIENDS of the BELFAST ANTI-SLAVERY SOCI-ETY will hold a PUBLIC MEETING THIS EVENING, in the INDEPENDENT CHURCH, DONEGALL-STREET, at which the Mayor, ANDREW MULHOL-LAND, Esq., will preside.[125] Mr. FREDERICK DOUGLAS [sic], a Gentleman of Colour, formerly a Slave in America, will address the Assembly, and depict the horrors of that iniquitous system, under which he suffered long. Chair to be taken at half-past Seven o'clock. Belfast. Friday Morning. 5th December, 1845.

Anti-Slavery Meeting
Lecturer: Frederick Douglass
Date of Lecture: Friday, 5 December 1845
Publication: *Northern Whig*
Date of Publication: Saturday, 6 December 1845
Title: 'Belfast Anti-Slavery Society'.

Last night, the members and friends of this Society held a meeting in the Independent Church, Donegall-street, the Mayor in the Chair. Mr Frederick Douglass (formerly slave) addressed the meeting at considerable length, and was received with the warmest applause. He gave an interesting account of his struggles in the cause of freedom, and the difficulties he was forced to encounter in freeing himself from the bondage in which had been held – shewing the tortures which the unfortunate slave was subjected to by his unfeeling taskmaster, who, not satisfied with taking from his fellow-man the liberty he should enjoy, inflicts upon him the most horrible and revolting cruelties. The meeting was largely and respectably attended.

Anti-Slavery Meeting
Lecturer: Frederick Douglass
Date of Lecture: Friday, 5 December 1845
Location: Independent Chapel, Donegall Street, Belfast
Publication: *Banner of Ulster* (Belfast)[126]
Date of Publication: Tuesday, 9 December 1845
Title: 'MR. FREDERICK DOUGLASS'S ADDRESS'.[127]

On Friday evening last, a meeting was held in the Independent Chapel, Donegall Street, under the auspices of the Belfast Anti-Slavery Society for the purpose of hearing an address on the subject of slavery, from Mr. Frederick Douglass, a man of colour. The attendance was numerous and respectable. On the motion of Mr. James Standfield, the Mayor of Belfast was called to the Chair. The Chair having briefly addressed the meeting, Mr. Douglass was introduced to it, in an appropriate speech, by Mr. Standfield.[128]

Mr. Douglass then came forward and was received with loud applause. He said he had pleasure in seeing so many kind and respectable people there assembled, in order to hear an account of the system of slavery from one who had experienced what it was to be a slave. He felt considerable embarrassment in thus standing before intelligent people, for the purpose of instructing them. Slavery was a poor school for acquiring moral, religious or intellectual improvement. He had never had the advantage of attending a day school, and all that he knew of literature had been obtained by stealth, for in the country whence he came, it was considered a crime to teach a slave to read; and there the coloured child was not even allowed to learn to spell the name of the God that made him. On this account, they were not to expect that he should entertain them after the manner of learned men, but they would listen to his simple narrative of the arguments he might advance against slavery, with those allowances which the peculiarity of his case required. (Cheers) He ought, perhaps, before entering on the subject of slavery, to state how he came there, and why he was in their midst, and he could not do this better than by giving a narrative of the escape he had made from slavery. Having been extensively known by the testimony he had long made against slavery, the narrative was eagerly sought after, so that in the period of three months, 6500 of it were sold. He was apprehensive that some plan would be formed for his re-enslavement, and to get rid of the kidnapper and his galling fetters, he ventured across the wave to tread the sacred soil of the Emerald Isle. (Enthusiastic cheering.) The effect of the opposition (continued Mr. Douglass) given by the slaveholders to the abolitionists is always the reverse of what they wish. They want it covered up. Like all evil things, its element is darkness. The slaveholder would not have him go through the country apologizing for slavery. They want the subject shut out from light altogether. Their language is, 'Let us alone'. John C. Calhoun called on the lovers of American institutions (and these were synonymous with slavery) and American freedom to suppress the anti-slavery agitation: but it will not go down at his bidding. It was progressing in America, and the interest taken in the subject in Britain had a great effect upon its advancement in the States. And this was the reason he was there at present. It seemed strange that a slave should rise up in the midst of his brethren to proclaim the outrages that they had suffered, to counteract the prejudices under which many laboured, and to expose the false statements of the apologists of the accursed system of slavery. (Cheers) And he was glad to see the friendly manifestations of those present. When the slave-holder learnt that an anti-slavery meeting had been held in this town, so populous, thriving, and intellectual, that one of their churches had been thrown open to him, and that some of the most respectable of the inhabitants were there to hear him, and that they responded to his sentiments, he would be troubled in conscience, and a thrill of agony would convulse him, as he felt that his system could not continue when the morality and intellect of the civilized world were being arrayed against it. (Great Cheering.)

Since he had come to Ireland, he had been thus accosted – 'We are slaves here as well as your countrymen in America,' and his answer was, 'if you have slaves, they ought to be emancipated; if the people here are tyrannized over, they ought to be relieved from oppression; but let us inquire what slavery is, and see whether you are in that state.' The error which people who spoke in the way he had stated fell into was, that they did not sufficiently distinguish between certain forms of oppression and slavery. Slavery was not what took away any one right or property in man; it took man himself, and made him the property of his fellow. It was what unmans man, takes him from himself, dooms him as a degraded thing, ranks him with the bridled horse and muzzled ox, makes him a chattel, a personal, a market-able commodity, to be swayed by the caprice and sold at the will of his master. God had given the slave a conscience, and freedom of will, but the slaveholder took that from him, and said he should not be governed by conscience and his religious aspirations – he should not be able to say what he should eat, when he should eat, or how he should eat – when he should work, what he should work at, or how he should work – when he should speak – what he should speak, or how he should speak. All his rights were conveyed over to his master. The slave might not decide on anything pertaining to his own actions. It was his master who decided for him when he should marry, how long his marriage should continue, and what might cause its dissolution. The slaveholder might, at any time, when influenced by the accursed thirst for gain, tear asunder the render which bound the husband to the wife, and the children to the parent. (Hear, hear, hear.) These were the inseparable concomitants of slavery, and not the accidental circumstances sometimes accompanying it. The slave might not go to God openly, and pray for deliverance. He might not aspire to such a boon, and say, 'Grant me freedom ere I die,' without incurring the penalty of being hung up at the first lamp-post. (Hear, hear, hear.) Had they anything like this in Ireland? Ah, no! And he thanked God for being permitted to stand upon their soil. Well might John Philpot Cur-ran exclaim – 'I speak in the spirit of the British law, which makes liberty com-mensurate with, and inseparable from, British soil; which proclaims even to the stranger and sojourner the moment he sets his foot, where he stands is holy, and consecrated by the genius of Universal Emancipation. No matter in what language his doom may have been pronounced – no matter what complexion, incompatible with freedom, an Indian or an African sun may have burned upon him – no matter in what disastrous battle his liberty may have been cloven down – no matter with what solemnities he may have been devoted upon the altar of slavery – the first moment he touches the sacred soil of Britain, the altar and the god sink together in the dust; his soul walks abroad in her own majesty; his body swells above the measure of his chains that burst from around him; and he stands redeemed, regenerated and disenthralled, by the irresistible genius of Universal Emancipation.' (Loud cries of 'hear, hear,' and long continued applause.) To know the happiness which he felt in having this privilege, they must have been in the same condition as himself – they must have felt the ignominious lash, and worn the iron of the slave – fully to appreciate his feelings. Freed from the degrading paraphernalia of slavery, he stood there, at least for a time, acknowledged by man, possessed of human rights. (Applause.) The system of slavery which he had depicted could only be sustained by brute force. He knew that there were men in this country and in Scotland, who contended the slavery might exist apart from cruelty. They urged, 'We don't beat horses and cattle; it is unnatural to do that; and why should the slave be beaten?' But they should go a step farther, and say it was unnatural to keep him in bondage. God had given us dominion over the interior animals – the horse and the ass were in their place when labouring for man – 'the ox knoweth his owner, and the ass his master's crib,' but, whenever they put a man in a like condition – herding him with the beasts of the field – they would have trouble in keeping him there. It then became necessary to make him as like a beast as possible, in other respects – to darken his intellect – to put out the eyes of his mind – for it was impossible to keep any large number of human beings in slavery, while their moral and religious vision remained open to the influence of the truth. All these crimes were concomitants of slavery as it exists in America; and he would repeat, without physical force it could not continue. (Applause.) Guns, whips, and thumbscrews – the branding-iron and the bloody scourge – all these were its necessary accompaniments, without which its existence was impossible. (Cheers.)

His object in appearing among them was to get an expression of their detestation of slavery. He knew that they were in heart opposed to it, but he wished their opposition to be manifested. Their Wilberforces, and Clarksons, and Sturges had done much by their declarations against the system of slavery, and O'Connell's sturdy and wholesale denunciations had been followed by the best effects. (Cheers.) He did not pretend to speak of O'Connell in connexion with any other subject than that of the one before him, but he had heard his name denounced by the tyrants of America, and his efforts spoken of in such a manner as made the slave's heart leap for joy. (Cheers.) The influence of public opinion would do much for the slave; and though the Americans were in the habit of speaking contemptuously of Britain and her institutions, they were indebted to that country for their religious and judicial knowledge. English literature guided, to a great extent, the literature of America. They had much to do, therefore, in forming the social institutions in the United States; they could operate upon public opinions there;

and as the public opinion was an aggregate of private opinions, they might see how the opinions of a country could be changed.

Let the Americans, when they come here, feel that they are not looked upon as Christians, while they continue to trade so largely in the bodies of their fellow-men. He wanted the people here, and everywhere, to rise up, in indignant remonstrance, to tell the Americans to tear down their star-spangled banner, and, with its folds, bind up the bleeding wounds of the lacerated slaves. (Great cheering.) He might be told that they had already spoken – that the different religious bodies of this town had already recorded their opinions on slavery. He was there to thank them for doing so; but if they had whispered merely, let them whisper no more, but speak 'as the tempest does – sterner and stronger' – let them speak loud until every slaveholder heard their rebukes, and resolved to do justice to the down-trodden slave. (Great applause.)

Mr. Douglass concluded his eloquent address by giving an interesting statement of the difficulties he encountered in learning to read and write, and then stated that he intended to deliver a series of lectures on the subject of slavery, during his stay in Belfast.

The Rev. Dr. Drew was then called to the chair; and Mr. Standfield, in moving a vote thanks to the previous chairman, expressed his deep regret that his year of office, as Chief Magistrate, was so near terminated, as in his conduct as mayor he had reflected the greatest credit on the town and its municipal institutions, and given his countenance and support to every deserving object. Dr. Drew then pronounced the benediction, and the meeting terminated.

Anti-Slavery Meeting
Lecturer: Frederick Douglass
Date of Lecture: Friday, 5 December 1845
Location: Independent Church, Donegall-street
Publication: *Belfast News-Letter*
Date of Publication: Tuesday, 9 December 1845
Title: 'LECTURE ON SLAVERY'.

On Friday evening last, according to announcement, Mr. Frederick Douglass, a gentleman of colour, formerly a slave in Maryland, delivered the first of a series of lectures on slavery in this town, in the Independent Church, Donegall-street, at half-past seven o'clock. From an account of Mr. Douglass's life, written by himself, and published in America, we learn that he escaped from his master in the year 1838, and after working as a free labourer in the North Eastern States till 1841, was engaged by an American Anti-Slavery Society as an itinerant lecturer, an office for which he is admirably adapted. He is a Mulatto, and supposes his first owner was his father. At the age of six years, according to his best calculation, he was sent from the estate where he was born to wait upon his master's nephew in Baltimore; and while in the service of his new master he learned to read. For this he was mainly indebted to the kindness of his mistress – a lady who was free from all slave-holding prejudices – and who continued her instructions to the poor slave till forbidden by her husband. However, by dint of perseverance, and the assistance of white little boys, he made considerable progress, and to reading added cyphering. At the age of fifteen, he was taken from his service, and brought back to his former master, and was engaged, at field labour. He was in the employment of his third master, when he planned an escape with some fellow slaves, but being detected and imprisoned, was afterwards sent back to Baltimore, whence he managed to escape in reality. The lecture of Friday evening was merely a simple narrative of all the circumstances attending his escape from slavery, his first introduction into public life, and the manner in which he had been occupied during the last four years, pleading the cause of his oppressed brethren.

The lecture was well attended. ANDREW MULHOLLAND, Esq., Mayor of Belfast, occupied the chair.

The CHAIRMAN having read the advertisement convening the meeting, and stated the object for which they had assembled.

JAMES STANDFIELD, Esq., introduced Mr. Douglass to the meeting. Before doing so, however, he took occasion to deliver an eloquent address on the subject of the evening.

Mr. DOUGLASS then came forward, and was received with loud applause. Having apologised for his inability to address so large and respectable a meeting, he, as we have already mentioned, proceeded to say that he was born in Maryland, a state of America, and remained in slavery twenty years. About seven years ago he made his escape into Massachusetts, one of the free states, which place he made his home till within the last four months, and the four years past he had devoted to the advocacy of the cause of his enslaved brethren. In the town of New Bedford, to which he had gone after having made his escape, and where he laboured on the wharves as a labourer in rolling oil casks, and at other work. He attended an anti-slavery meeting, where he met with a white gentleman, who, knowing him to have been a slave, and that he had writhed under the lash of the tyrant, induced him to say a few words. He (Mr. Douglass) felt reluctance in coming before them, but being so persuaded he got up and addressed the meeting, and although he did so confusedly, they were all deeply affected at the details which he then presented. It was certainly a novel thing to see a slave addressing a New Bedford meeting. He was then called upon to tell his own experience of slavery, which he did. The Anti-Slavery Society then thought it right that he should be sent forth and so for a period of four years, – amid the smiles of friends and the frowns of foes, opposition extending even to blows, as, on one occasion, his right hand was broken by a ruthless mob in New England, he continued to speak and to plead on behalf of the down trodden slave, and to tell of the wrongs of his race. (Hear, hear, and loud applause.)

They then insinuated that he was not a slave at all, but a free negro, because he possessed a certain degree of intelligence more than might be expected; and it was on that account principally that he had been led to come to this country, because he found that any influence he could exercise would only be retarded by remaining there. The publication of his book set at rest the question as to his being really a slave. It told every circumstance of his life, so that there could be no mistake. That book, when published, was seized upon with avidity, and an immense number of copies were sold in Boston before he left. By the publication of that narrative he became known, and lest they might find out his whereabouts, and in order to get rid of the American kid-nappers, who would have hurled him back into interminable bondage, he ventured to tread upon the sacred soil of the "Emerald Isle." (Great applause.) But he was sorry to say his slavery had followed him over the Atlantic, and the customs of slavery had been practised even on the high seas. (Cries of "Shame.") In the steamer which brought him over there were also slave-holders, real republican, democratic, mobocratic apologists of slavery. (Laughter.) He left Boston on the 16th August, on the *Cambria*, and he had not been on board more than two days when he was subjected to annoyance. It was not customary or common to see a coloured man – he would not say a gentleman – a passenger, and he was accordingly regarded with some curiosity. What he had to complain of was, that slaveholding customs should be followed up and established even on board a British ship. He was not allowed to take a cabin passage on account of the colour of his skin and the crisp of his hair. (Cries of "Shame, shame.") This was in a British vessel, though he was bound to say Captain Judkins and his crew treated him with the greatest kindness, and he had reason to believe that the conduct of which he complained, was owing to the interference of the American agent in Boston. When the passengers on board learned he was a slave, and coming to England to tell the wrongs of his brethren, they wished him to tell something about the matter on board; but he refused to do so until the captain gave his free consent. His narrative was in the meantime sent among them, and when they came in sight of Ireland and were got into smooth water he felt that he was bound to obey the call made upon him, and from his knowledge of slavery to come forward and say something in favour of his brothers who were in bondage. Accordingly, being invited by the captain, and the bell being rung round the ship to announce that he would deliver a lecture, upon the saloon deck, an audience was convened but when he went on deck, he saw there was a party there that would not allow him to speak. He saw that they were slaveholders, and he heard them cursing and swearing. A hymn having been sung by an abolitionist family on board, he proceeded to deliver his lecture, but he had not uttered five words, when a slaveholder came forward, and shaking his fist in his face said, "That's a lie." I proceeded (continued the lecturer) notwithstanding his conduct, but was again interrupted in the same manner. I then said, as all I have told you has been pronounced a lie, I will read your own laws on the relation that exists between a slave and his master. I then read the following:- "If more than seven slaves are found together in any road, without a white person, twenty lashes a piece; for visiting a plantation without a written pass, ten lashes; for letting loose a boat from where it is made fast, thirty-nine lashes for the first offence, and for the second, shall have cut from off his head one ear; for keeping or carrying a club, thirty-nine lashes; for having any article for sale without a ticket from his master, ten lashes; for travelling in any other than the most usual and accustomed roads, when going alone to any place, forty lashes; for being found in another person's negro quarters, forty lashes; for hunting with dogs in the Woods, thirty lashes; for being on horseback without written permission of his master, twenty-five lashes; for riding or going abroad in the night, or riding horses in the day time, without leave, a slave may be whipped, cropped, or branded on the cheek with the letter R, or otherwise punished, not extending to life, or so as to render him unfit for labour".

The laws referred to may be found by consulting 2d Brevard's Digest, 228, 243, 246; Haywood's Manual, 78. chap. 13, page 518, 529; 1. Virginia Revised Code, 722–31; Prince's Digest, 454; 2. Missouri Laws, 741; Mississippi Revised Code, 371. Laws similar to these exist throughout the Southern Slave Code (Hear, hear.) This, as might be expected, caused the slaveholders to writhe in agony. They saw that these laws – their own laws – would do more harm to them than anything I could say. These laws were not intended for British eyes – they were not intended to be known but by slaves – nor to see the light, for to be abhorred, they need only be seen, but they were intended only for the darkness of slavery. The slaveholders, as I have said were in agony at hearing these things, and one cried out, "O, I wish I had you in Cuba;" another, – "O, I wish I had you in New Orleans;" another, "I wish I had you in Savannah;" but there were none of them wished they had me in Ireland, (Loud applause and laughter.) One of them said he would be "one of a number" to throw me overboard – recollect, my friends, he said, he would be only "one" of an indefinite number to throw me overboard. (Loud laughter and applause.) There was one gentleman on board – an Irishman – a Mr. Galt,[129] of Dublin – a tall, clever man, who looked over all our heads like a large Giraffe, and he hearing the little slave-holder speak so largely turned towards him and putting his glass to his eye said, in tones very significant, "Perhaps two could play at that game." (Laughter.) This had a good effect upon the slave holder, because the matter had never before been pressed upon his mind, till reminded of the possibility of it by the Irishman. (Renewed laughter.) The storm grew higher, till at length the Captain interfered, and said I should be heard, that it was by his permission I spoke, and that he would protect me. At this a little man walked up to the Captain and said I should not. The Captain, however, put him aside, and a ring-bolt laying in the way, the little fellow almost fell over it. (Laughter.) When he came to himself again he put his hand into his pocket – I thought he was feeling for his bowie knife, but at length he pulled it out again, and handed the Captain his card – (laughter) – saying "I will meet you in Liverpool." He meant that he was to fight a duel. (Laughter.) The Captain replied quite coolly – "Well, I'll be there." (The lecturer uttering these words in a sepulchral tone of voice, occasioned considerable merriment among the audience.) The Captain's reply cooled the slaveholder very considerably. The Captain then called the boatswain and ordered him to bring the irons. You see he was about to play the slave-holder over them in case they did not keep quiet, and being brought, they looked at them and sneaked off, and in a few minutes, if search had been made, they might have been found snugly stowed away in their berths. (Laughter.) This little circumstance has created great interest, and I have been considerably abused by the pro-slavery press in America for my alleged conduct on that occasion. Instead of the facts I have laid before you, they have stated that I intruded myself and that the Captain was imposed upon. I say this, that if any report of this evening's proceedings is taken, this reply to their charges may go as my answer. (Applause.)

Mr. Douglass, after making a passing remark upon the good effects which would result from the agitation of this question in England and Ireland, and expressing his heartfelt thanks for the friendly reception he had met in Belfast, proceeded to speak on the question of slavery as it at present exists in America, the horrors of which, although no new feature was exhibited, were depicted with much force and effect. He called attention to the wretched state of the slave, who was degraded to the level of a beast – pronounced incapable of judging for himself in any particular – denied the common rights of man – ranked among beasts and creeping things – compelled to associate with the neighbouring horse and the lowing ox – and made a marketable commodity at the will of his master. The slave is to have no power or will of his own as his master wills all for him – he must not decide for himself; his master decides how he is to speak, and when he is to speak and to whom he shall speak; when he is to work, and how much he is to perform – in fact, every act of his life is governed by his master. His master must decide when he shall marry and to whom he shall be married, and how long that shall be binding – how long the slave wife and the slave husband shall continue together, and when they shall be torn asunder – when the tender tie shall be broken and they be sent asunder. These, and many others, were the inseparable concomitants of slavery. These are the claims and the asserted rights of the slaveholders, although they pretend to the contrary when on this side of the Atlantic. Yes, the master is to determine when the slave shall be punished and how much punishment he ought to receive. The slave can of himself do nothing, he is denied the use of his reason and the exercise of those faculties which God has given him. He must not go to God in prayer and ask that his fetters may be broken off, and that he may obtain his freedom before he dies – should he presume to do so he would be taken up and hung upon the first lamp-post. [Here the lecturer erected himself to his full height, and in a tone of commanding eloquence exclaimed]. Oh! I thank God that I stand upon British soil. (Loud and protracted applause.) Well might John Philpott Curran exclaim "I speak in the spirit of the British law, which makes liberty commensurate with and inseparable from British soil, which proclaims even to the stranger and sojourner the moment he sets his foot on British earth that the ground on which he treads is holy and consecrated by the genius of universal emancipation. No matter in what language his doom may have been pronounced, no matter what complexion incompatible with freedom, an Indian or an African sun may have burned upon him – no matter in what disastrous battle his liberty may have been cloven down – no matter with what solemnities he may have been devoted upon the altar of slavery: the first moment he touches the sacred soil of Britain the altar and the god sink together in the dust; his soul walks abroad in her own majesty; his body swells beyond the measure of his chains that burst from around him, and he stands redeemed, regenerated, and disenthralled by the irresistible genius of Universal Emancipation." (Loud applause.) To know the happiness I now feel, you, my friends, must have been slaves also. You cannot – you cannot feel it. You must have felt the lash – you must have felt the fetter upon your bruised limbs – you must have been freed from the brutality of a tyrant master, and all the bloody paraphernalia of slavery, before you can judge of my feelings aright. (Applause.) I stand here after all this, an acknowledged man with human rights. Mr. Douglass next proceeded to show that slaves possessed those rights and feelings, in common with white men, quoting the beautiful lines of Cowper:-[130]

Fleecy locks and black complexion
Cannot forfeit nature's claim;
Skins may differ, but affection
Dwells in white and black the same.

After paying a tribute of thanks to several English and Irish orators who had raised their voices on behalf of the slave, he remarked that the people of America were to a great extent guided by British feeling – they were moulded in it, and the people of Great Britain had much to do in forming the moral feeling of America. They (the Americans) were indebted to the English people for their knowledge in various literature was guided by English, and for their judicial knowledge they had also to be indebted to England. It was, therefore, necessary that they should feel the full force of public opinion and he trusted that the expression of just indignation which would be given, by the British people, on the subject of slavery, would be productive of the best effects. He rejoiced to know that when on a late occasion in England, a follower of the meek and lowly Saviour – a minister from one of the slave-holding States of North America, presented himself at the Methodist Conference, to the credit of that body be it spoken, he was told to be "off" (laughter) – and when he returned to his own country and reported to his brethren how unkindly and ungraciously he had been received, they all set up a boo-ooing (laughter.) That was the way he (Mr. Douglass) wished the people of this country to serve them up when they came to this country; and then when they returned home and told how badly they had been received, they would also, no doubt, set up a similar boo-ooing, and that, he assured them, would be music in the ear of the slave. (Applause.) It was time, indeed, that one indignant remonstrance should be offered by the people of Great Britain. After some further remarks, Mr. Douglass concluded his eloquent and instructive address by promising that, on a future evening, he would enter still further into matters connected with the accursed system of slavery.

Mr. DOUGLASS again rose, and being requested, gave a most amusing narrative of his early life, and the singular manner in which he learned to read and write while in slavery. Having concluded,

JAMES STANDFIELD, Esq., proposed a vote of thanks to the Mayor, and in doing so, took occasion to pass upon his Worship a well-merited eulogium for his conduct during his year of office.

The motion was seconded by the Rev. Mr. Boyd, and having been put to the meeting by the Rev. Dr. DREW, it was passed unanimously. The second lecture was announced for this evening.

Anti-Slavery Meeting
Lecturer: Frederick Douglass
Date of Lecture: Friday, 5 December 1845
Location: Independent Meeting-house, Donegall-street
Publication: *Northern Whig*
Date of Publication: Tuesday, 9 December 1845
Title: 'Anti-Slavery Meeting in Belfast'.

Friday evening, a meeting of the members and friends of this Society was held in the Independent Meeting-house, Donegall-street, the Worshipful the Mayor of Belfast in the Chair.

Mr. Mulholland, on taking the Chair, said, that the meeting had been assembled by the members and friends of the Anti-Slavery Society, in Belfast, in order to give the public an opportunity of hearing a lecture on the condition of slaves in America. The system of slavery was now held in such abhorrence, and the sympathy excited by the sufferings of that portion of their fellow-men who were its unfortunate victims, was so general, and strong, that it was to be hoped, that those countries where it was still practised would be, if not from conviction of their error, at least from a sense of shame, soon forced to abandon it. Indeed, it was astonishing that a system so opposed to that benevolence, which was the fundamental principle to Christianity, should be so long permitted to exist. Such a state of society was wholly at variance with the Divine maxim, which enjoins them to love their neighbour as themselves. They all knew, however, that slavery did still continue, to great extent, and many particulars connected with that melancholy truth would be related to them by Mr. Frederick Douglass, who would now address them, and who, having, in his own person, experienced the horrors of slavery, could best describe the painful circumstances attendant on that degrading condition. (Hear, hear.)

Mr. Standfield then introduced to the meeting, in suitable terms, Mr. Frederick Douglass (formerly an American slave.) Mr. Douglass was a person who had, in his own person, experienced the horrors of slavery, and no one was better qualified to enter into a detail of the system than he. Nothing could exceed the barbarities practised by the slaveholders of America, whose liberty was only an empty and unmeaning boast. Mr. Douglass would enter into a detail of the system, and (Mr. Standfield) trusted that the people here, of every religious denomination, would avail themselves of the opportunity offered to them, by expressing their horror of those things, which were so much opposed to the laws and the Gospel of their Redeemer. (Hear, hear, and cheers.)

Mr. Frederick Douglass, formerly an American slave, rose and addressed the meeting. He said, that he felt great pleasure in seeing so many of the kind and intelligent people of Belfast before him, for the purpose of hearing the wrongs of his enslaved fellow-countrymen discoursed upon. He could not disguise the fact of his somewhat embarassment. The circumstances of his early life had gone far to disqualify him to stand before intelligent people, for the purpose of instructing them. Slavery was a poor school for morals, or religion, or intellectual improvement, he had never had the advantage of a day's schooling in his life. All that he knew of letters he obtained by stealth. It would not, therefore, be expected that he should be able to entertain them after the fashion of learned men. He was born in the State of Maryland, and remained a slave for nearly twenty-one years. About seven years ago, he, through the providence of God, effected his escape from his chains, and secured a partial freedom, getting into one of the Free States in the country – the State of Massachusetts – and there he had made his home, till within the last four months. The last four years he had devoted to advocating the cause of his enslaved brethren. When in Massachusetts, he had gone into the town of New Bedford, where he was employed in rolling oil casks, getting a subsistence for himself and his family. In the month of August, he had attended an anti-slavery meeting, where he met a white gentleman, who had heard him speak to some coloured people in New Bedford; and this gentleman induced him to say a word to the meeting, knowing that he bore on his back the scars inflicted by the lash of the tyrant. (Hear, hear, and loud cheers.) As he had been taught to look upon white people as his superiors, he felt, of course, reluctant in coming forward; but at last got up, and told the people that he had been a slave; and, although he spoke stammering, the audience seemed to be deeply interested in what he had to say. It was something extraordinary – something novel – to see a slave stand up, and hear him speak as he did and the Anti-Slavery Society thought it would be advantageous, and the other New England Societies, to have him to tell what he knew about slavery. For four years, he had laboured, in season and out of season, through the smiles of friends and the frowns of enemies; he had struggled with many difficulties, and he had had his right hand broken, when speaking of slavery, by a ruthless mob. It was said by some that it was impossible for such a man to have been a slave – that he was some educated Negro, and that he affected the slave for a given purpose. He found that his usefulness would be greatly impaired unless he silenced those rumours and he resolved to publish all the particulars connected with his history – he published his master's name, and the name the of State he belonged to, etc. (Hear, hear.) But, he could not tell the place from which he (Mr. Douglass) ran, lest he should be kidnapped, and hurled back into interminable bondage. (Loud cheers.) There was not a single spot of land in all the United States, upon which he could stand free. (Hear, hear.) He wrote and published a narrative of his former state, of which six thousand five hundred copies had been sold in three months, and the greater part of which were sold in Boston, before he left that place. Apprehensive, however, while in America, that some plan might devised, which might again be successful in depriving him of freedom, he left the place, and ventured to tread on the sacred sod of the 'Emerald Isle.' (Loud cheering.) But, the spirit of persecution and slavery travelled with him across the Atlantic. In the vessel in which he came over from America, there were slaveholders, apologists for slavery and democratic mobocrats. He took passage over in the *Cambria*, on the 16th of August, for Liverpool, and found that a deep interest and curiosity were excited among the passengers, in consequence of his appearance on board. It was a little strange for a coloured man to take his passage for England – it was, indeed, strange in slave-holding eyes; and on board that steamer, prejudices common to American slaveholders were established. (Cries of Shame.) He was not allowed to take a cabin passage; but, however, he would say, that the Captain, and his whole ship's company, treated him with the greatest kindness and cordiality. It was through the American agent, in Boston, that he was prevented from obtaining a cabin passage. There was a deep interest excited among the cabin passengers about him, knowing that he had been a slave, and that he had already spoken on the subject of slavery. They wished him to speak to them on the matter; but he would not do so unless the Captain of the vessel desired him. He had with him a number of copies of his narrative; and, through these, the greater number of the passengers soon became well acquainted with him. The Captain's leave was obtained for him to speak when they were in smooth water, near Ireland; and he asked him to deliver an address to the passengers on the subject of slavery. Soon, an audience was convened. When he went forward to the saloon-deck, to address them, there was one party which was resolved that he should not speak. He found them cursing and swearing, and uttering the most horrid sentiments with reference to him; but the Captain, after a hymn had been sung, introduced him to the kindly notice of the passengers assembled. He proceeded to address them, but had uttered hardly five words, when one of the slaveholders stepped up to him, shook his stick in his face, and said it was a lie. Three times, in succession, he pronounced what he said to be lies.

He (Mr. Douglass) then said to the audience that, since all he had said was pronounced to be lies, he would give them a few facts, in regard to slavery, as shadowed forth by their own Legislature. – And once the slaveholders knew he was about to expose them; for there was nothing they more dread or avoid than letting strangers know their laws with reference to the unfortunate creatures over whom they hold absolute sway and uncontrolled dominion. [Mr. Douglass then read a list of laws from the slaveholders' code of regulations with regard to the slave, in which the most cruel and barbarous punishments, such as lashings on the back, the cropping of ears, and other revolting disfigurements, were awarded for the most venial crimes, and even frequently when no crime whatever had been committed.] The reading of these before the audience caused the slaveholders, on the occasion, to writhe in utter agony – for those laws were not intended to be known by the Christian world, and they were crying out on every side, and shaking their fists at him. One would say, 'O! I wish I had you in Cuba!' Another, 'I wish I had you in New Orleans.' And another, 'I wish I had you in Savannah'. (Loud laughter.) But nobody said that they wished they had him in Ireland. (Renewed laughter, and loud cheers.) One of them said, that he would be part of a number to throw him overboard. What a discreet man that was. (Laughter.) He would be one of an indefinite number to throw him overboard! *and only one.* There happened to be on board an Irishman – a man of gigantic size – of the name Gough; and Mr. Gough, looking down upon this man with his glass in his eye, and coolly surveying the discreet gentleman who would be one of an indefinite number to throw him (Mr. Douglass) overboard, hinted that two might possibly play at that game – (loud cheers) – and that two might possibly be thrown overboard. (Cheers.) That had a very good and salutary effect upon the young man. Threats of the most bloody character were urged by the slaveholders against him (Mr. Douglass); but the Captain said, that he must have a respectful hearing, for he was the Captain of the ship, and he would see that order was maintained. (Cheers.) A little man, from New Orleans, said that he should not speak; but the Captain turned him round with a scarce perceptible motion of his hand, and the poor fellow had like to have fallen. The Captain, in sea phrase, could have broken every timber in his body. The little man got into a fearful rage, and he put his hand into his pocket, and felt about for something. He (Mr. Douglass) thought that he was going to draw out his bowie knife, or perhaps, his pistol. – But he pulled out his card, and handed it to the Captain, and cried, 'I will meet you – I will meet you – I will meet you in Liverpool' (In a sepulchral tone) – 'Very well,' said the Captain, 'I'll be there' (Loud cheers, and laughter.) – He heard but little more of him. Some of them were so outrageous in their conduct, that the Captain at last said, he would put them in irons – the irons were brought forward; and the slaveholders, who were going to fight, and who, the moment before, had been so brave and courageous, sneaked away to different parts of the ship. (Cheers.) John Bull had but to speak to them, and they were all quiet. (Loud cheers.) The slaveholders of America wanted to keep their system of slavery covered up – all they wanted was perfect quiet. And, when the slaveholders found, that, in Belfast – a place famed for its intellect and moral superiority – one of their spacious Meeting-houses was thrown open to Frederick Douglass, to expose the infamous system of slavery, it would cause a feeling of agony thrill through their hearts – but that system could not long continue, while the power, and moral rectitude, and religious influence of the civilized world were arrayed against it. (Loud cheers.) Slavery was that which took man from his proper position, and gave him a place among the beasts and creeping things of the field – that sold him in the marketplace, and constituted him a marketable commodity, to be bought and sold at the will or caprice of his master: for the slaveholder claimed absolute right and power over his slave. God had given the slave moral perception – he had given him his intellect, and the power of reason; but the slaveholder took it from him. He was entirely subjected to the control of his master – his master decided every thing he should do. He might tear him from his wife – he might tear asunder the pair whom God had joined together – he might tell him when to pray, and when to eat, and when to sleep, and exercise over him the most galling and persecuting tyranny – those were the inseparable concomitants slavery. (Hear, hear, and cheers.) Those were the results of slavery, although the slaveholder pretended to the contrary, on this side of the Atlantic. The poor slave had no right, moral, religious, or political – he might not even go to God openly, and ask for his chains to be broken, or express the great desire of his heart, 'Oh, give me freedom!' or he might be hanged at the first lamp-post. Such was the condition of the slave – had they anything like it here? (Loud cheers.) He for himself, thanked God that he had been permitted to stand on this soil of freedom. (Cheers.) Well might Curran exclaim, in his glowing, and oh! how eloquent, apostrophe to the spirit of liberty, – 'I speak in the spirit of the British law, which makes liberty commensurate with and inseparable from British soil – which proclaims even the stranger and sojourner, the moment he sets his foot on British earth, that the ground which he treads is holy and consecrated by the genius of universal emancipation. No matter in what language his doom may have been pronounced, no matter what complexion incompatible with freedom an Indian or African sun may have burned upon him – no matter in what disastrous battle his liberty may have been cloven down – no matter with what solemnities he may have been devoted to the altar of slavery, the first moment he touches the sacred soil of Britain, the altar and the god sink together in the dust – his soul walks abroad in her own majesty – his body swells beyond the measure of his chains that burst from around him, and he stands redeemed, regenerated, and disenthralled, by the irresistible genius of universal emancipation.' (Loud and pro-longed cheering.) One, to know the happiness that he (Mr. D.) then experienced, must have been born himself slave – must have had the lash on his back, as he had, and worn the irons, as had done, – all these things they must have done, to appre-ciate the blessings which he now enjoyed. (Cheers.) Freed from American chains and whips, he stood an acknowledged man with the human race. (Great cheering.)

Mr. Douglass then proceeded to pass a high eulogium on the conduct of Mr. Daniel O'Connell. He would not speak of him as a politician, or enter into those questions with which he was concerned – he would speak of him, merely, in connexion with slavery. In Dublin, some narrow-minded persons would not permit him to speak approvingly of him; but in Mr. O'Connell he would say, he had heard him cursed at by the slaveholders America – he had heard him denounced, and spoken of in such manner, as made the heart of the slave leap with joy. He (Mr. Douglass) would say, that, if they could only get the people to see and understand the system, in all its naked deformity, much good would be done. And it was time that the people of all countries should rise up in one indignant remonstrance against its cruel and barbarous iniquities. (Loud cheers.) Mr. Douglass then entered into an interesting account of the manner in which he had learned to read and write; and concluded his address, which was listened throughout with deep attention, by an appeal to the good feeling and sympathies of his hearers, on behalf the persecuted bondmen, who were once his brothers in misfortune.

It was announced that Mr. Douglass would deliver another lecture, on the subject slavery, this evening, an intimation which was received with loud cheers.

His Worship having been moved from the Chair, and the Rev. Dr. Drew called thereto, the thanks of the meeting were given to Mr. Mulholland, for his kindness in presiding upon the occasion. The meeting then separated.

Anti-Slavery Meeting
Lecturer: Frederick Douglass
Date of Lecture: Friday, 5 December 1845
Location: Independent Church, Donegall Street
Publication: *Belfast Vindicator*
Date of Publication: Wednesday, 10 December 1845
Title: 'BELFAST ANTI-SLAVERY MEETING'.

A public meeting of the friends of human freedom was held on Friday evening, in the Independent Church, Donegall Street, to hear Mr. Frederick Douglass's harrowing description of the sufferings of his enslaved brethren in America.

His Worship, the Mayor, having been called to the chair.

Mr. Standfield rose and said – Mr. Chairman, and gentlemen, we are met together this evening for the purpose of discharging a duty which, as members of the human family, we are bound to perform. (Hear, hear.) I need hardly remind you that we are here to offer our humble meed of sympathy to the oppressed of every clime, and to pour forth our honest and heartfelt denunciations of that inexorable tyranny which would, for its own base and selfish purposes, perpetuate the degradation of mankind. (Applause.) Although, Sir, it has been asserted that individual exertions for the abolition of slavery will be unavailing without the co-operation of government, still, I maintain, that if the vast majority of the people of these countries lend their assistance to their fellow-labourers in the good cause on the other side of the Atlantic, ultimate success is inevitable, despite the apathy of kings and legislatures. (Applause.) I hope, therefore, that men of all sects and subdivisions of political opinion will combine in one irresistible phalanx to overthrow the unsightly structure, within whose unhallowed precincts is offered homage to the arch-fiend – slavery. (Applause.) Public opinion is, Sir, in the present day, the all potent engine by which every great social amelioration is effected, and it is to its onward and unceasing progress that we are to look for the ultimate regeneration of man. (Hear, hear.) It has been my pride and honour to behold, on the other side of the Atlantic, the triumph of public opinion over prejudice and wrong. A slaveholder will not be admitted in communion with any of the various sects of religionists, nor will they permit any clergyman who is a slaveholder to ascend their pulpits. (Applause.) Thus much has the march of intellect effected; and it will go on triumphing in the sacred cause of liberty until, by incessant collision with the flinty hearts of the selfish and insensate, it shall have elicited a spark that will enkindle, even in the breasts of tyrants, respect and veneration for the inalienable rights of man. (Loud applause.) This, Sir, is no party or sectarian movement. We meet upon the high-ground of our common Christianity, to demand that the same franchises and immunities enjoyed by the white man shall be extended to his dusky brethren, and that none shall so outrage the immutable ordinances of heaven, as to arrogate to themselves, in virtue of their hue, an unwarrantable ascendancy over their fellow-men. (Applause.) Sir, it is a "bend sinister" on the escutcheon of the high and titled of this land that they are indifferent to the miseries of the wretched slave population of America. I trust, however, that the day is approaching when every baronial hall and lordly resilience in the empire shall have engraven on its portals the motto which the Earl of Buchan has caused to be inscribed over Dryburgh Abbey – "No slaveholder admitted here."[131] Gentlemen, as I know you are anxious to hear Mr. Douglass, I shall not trespass further upon your time, but at once introduce that gentleman to your notice.

Mr. Douglass, on coming forward to the front of the platform, was greeted with the warmest demonstrations of applause. He said – Mr. Chairman, ladies, and gentlemen, it were vain for me to attempt disguising from you the deep feeling of embarrassment under which I labour this moment. I do, I assure you, feel most acutely the awkwardness of the position in which capricious circumstances have placed me, when I find myself standing forth to speak in the presence of an influential and enlightened assembly; nor does my self possession receive any augmentation from the recollection of the fact, that never, in the whole course of my existence, did I obtain the advantage of day's education. In the country from which I came, it is accounted criminal for a slave child to learn to spell the name of the God who made him, and, therefore, whatever little knowledge I possess, I acquired by stealth. I hope, therefore, that you will allow this consideration to plead my apology if I am unable to entertain you after the manner of learned men. (Hear, hear.) Having promised thus much, gentlemen, it is necessary that I should now proceed to inform you by what means, and for what object, I have the honour of appearing before you this evening. I was born a slave in one of the states of America, and continued in that capacity for twenty-one years. About seven years ago, I obtained my freedom taking refuge in the state of Massachusetts, where I resided for a considerable period, during which I procured the necessaries of life by rolling oil casks on the wharf at New Bedford. Whilst attending a meeting of abolitionists, I was prevailed upon by a person who knew what were my sentiments on the subject, to address the audience, and such was the impression that my description of slavery made, that I imagined I could not do a more meritorious act than exert energies for the liberty of my brethren in bonds. In accordance with this determination, I have, during the last four years, laboured incessantly for the furtherance of that great object, on the attainment of which is centred the fondest wishes and aspirations of my heart. (Applause.) Slavery, Sir, like any other gigantic scheme of iniquity, grounds its tenure of existence on the condition of being allowed exemption from the test of free inquiry and impartial investigation; but the moment it is subjected to that ordeal, the flimsy veil with which its hideous aspect was concealed from the gaze of nations, is torn asunder, and the monster vanishes from the theatre of the universe amid the indignant denunciations of those whom apathy or ignorance had rendered insensible to its deformity. (Hear.) It upon this principle that we are to account for that anxiety evinced by the slaveholder to stifle the yearning voice of humanity. But, how vain the effort, how utterly abortive. The progress of man's regeneration resembles the mountain avalanche in all but its destructiveness. It gathering volume and velocity in its course, and will, ultimately, reach the level ground of perfect equality, triumphing over every difficulty, and surmounting every obstacle in its onward career. – (Applause.) Is it not then, my friends, most meet and expedient that I, a slave, should arise and promulgate, throughout the length and breadth of the land, the fiendish atrocities perpetrated under the name of slavery? Oh! it will be pain to the conscience and anguish the heart of the slaveholder, to hear that, in the sacred soil of the Emerald Isle, the inhabitants of the Irish Athens, the emporium of commerce and seat of enterprise, interested themselves on behalf of the poor persecuted negro. Since my arrival in these countries, the question has been put and reiterated, why endeavour to excite our sympathy towards the enslaved in America, when every sentiment of compatriotism demands that our first efforts should be directed to the disenthralment of the victims of tyranny in our own land. My answer is, if you have slaves at home, let them, by all means, be emancipated; if misrule has extended its iron influence over you, continue to impugn its sovereignly in firm and legitimate conflict, but do not contemplate your own wrongs with such an absorbing selfishness as to turn with indifference from the appeal made to your better feelings by millions of your fellow-men, with whom life is best:

'A heritage of service and woes
A blindfold bondage where their hire is blows.'

'Tis true misgovernment may partially deprive you of your just and indefeasible rights – it may wrest you from certain immunities, and withhold others; but, it is equally true, that you would never tolerate that complete deprivation of your birthright, which reduces man, the lord of creation, to an equality with the neighbouring horse and the lowing ox, or, in the expressive language of the law, 'a chattel, personal to all talents and purposes whatsoever'. (Hear) The bloody lash and galling shackles are the only restoratives administered by the savage taskmaster to the poor slave, whose racked and over-wrought frame sinks exhausted under the magnitude of the task imposed upon him. The slave is subjected, absolutely, to the whim and caprice of his master; he is not guided by his own moral perceptions of right and wrong – by his own religious aspirations. Every enduring bond and holiest tie is snapt asunder, and he is left to pine, unheeded, after the friends and home of his buoyant youth, when life itself was a fairy dream, and this sweet earth a perfect wilderness of enchantment. (Applause.) But, slavery is, Sir, an unnatural relation of men, and it requires extraordinary means to sustain it. The Americans say that the black man can prefer no legitimate claim to freedom, but such an assertion can only be mentioned in order to be execrated.

If the colour of our respective skins is to be admitted as the criterion of our merits, I think we may well claim a superiority over the white man in that particular. It has been said that the leopard cannot change his spots nor the Ethiopian his skin, and this is more than can be affirmed of any European, whose skin varies its hue with the varying climate. (Laughter.) I am persuaded, gentlemen, that I have said enough to apprize you that my object in coming to this country is to procure a manifestation of British sympathy on behalf of my poor unemancipated brethren in America. Your ancestors were the first that elevated into an institution the various commercial gains from the thews and sinews of their fellow-men, and it rests with you, subjects of the British empire, whether or not you will efface that foul blot upon your character, by endeavouring to redeem the errors of your race.

Many good and noble spirits have already been in the way of working for the alleviation of the born slaves' grievances. (Hear and applause.) – In England, the Wilberforces, the Broughams, and the Sturges, and in Ireland your own illustrious Daniel O'Connell, deserve undying fame by their generous condemnations of slavery. (Applause.) O'Connell is the idol of his countrymen, he is the willing and powerful advocate of freedom in every quarter of the globe; and wherever liberty is prized and oppression hated, there the talismanic name of O'Connell is loved, venerated, and worshipped. (Vehement applause.) It is true that I dissent from him in many respects, but still I honour him in my heart of hearts for his advocacy of our cause; and when the detestable slaveholders cursed and execrated O'Connell, the negro's heart mocked his wrath with its impulsive throbbings of delight. (Applause.) It is time, then, that the people of this country, that the people of every country, should rise up in one loud and universal remonstrance, proclaiming to America the degradation which she incurs in her attempts to perpetuate the diabolical system of human slavery. If you have been content to whisper truth hitherto, whisper it no longer. Let your voice, reverberating from shore to shore of your island, be wafted in accents of thunder across the broad bosom of the Atlantic, bringing terror to the slaveholder and joyous hopes of deliverance to his victims. Finally, tell America that though her eagle should soar through the farthest empyrean, there shall be a plague-spot upon her flag that shall make her the jest and by-word of the nations, until she shall enfranchise every bondsman in her dominions. In the language of one of the most eminent of your poets

"United States, your banner wears two emblems – one of fame;
Alas! the other but reminds us of your shame.
The white man's liberty stands blazoned in your stars;
But what's the meaning of your stripes?
They mean your negros' scars."

The speaker resumed his seat amid deafening applause.

His Worship having vacated the chair, and the best thanks of the meeting having been tendered to that gentleman for his dignified conduct therein, the meeting separated shortly after ten o'clock.

Anti-Slavery Meeting
Lecturer: Frederick Douglass
Date of Lecture: Tuesday, 9 December 1845
Location: Wesleyan Methodist Chapel, Donegall Square
Publication: *Belfast News-Letter*
Date of Publication: Friday, 12 December 1845
Title: 'LECTURE ON SLAVERY'.

Mr. Douglass delivered his second lecture on Slavery on Tuesday evening last, in the Wesleyan Methodist Chapel, Donegall Square.[132] At the hour appointed for commencing the lecture (half-past seven), the chapel was crowded in every part, so much that even standing room could not be had. Large numbers surrounded the doors endeavouring to get, if possible, within hearing of the speaker's voice, and hundreds were obliged to go away.

Professor STEVELLY, LL.D.,[133] was called to the chair, and after a few brief remarks on the object for which they were assembled, Mr Standfield read a letter from the Rev. Dr. Drew, apologising for his unavoidable absence from the meeting.

Mr. DOUGLASS then commenced his lecture by stating the relation of America with slavery in her civil polity. There were, he said, in the Union what were termed free states in contradistinction to slave-holding states, but, notwithstanding that some of them were called free states, inasmuch as persons residing in those states were not permitted to keep slaves, still those free states were implicated in the sin of slavery. Each state in the Union had a local legislature, and made its own laws in all local matters. The institution of slavery is one of those things which every state had the power in itself either to abolish or uphold. There were three things on which the state local governments could not legislate; these were the levying of taxes, the regulation of the commerce of the country, and the declaring of war. On these three things the Congress, or general Government, legislated for the whole Union. In the southern states slavery was an institution of the country, while in the northern, it did not exist but though that was the case, still he contended that the sin of slavery was chargeable against the free, as well as the slave-holding states, on the grounds that the General Government which represented all the states, free and otherwise, enforced the laws which were enacted by the local government, and consequently in the slave states carried into execution the law which held 3,000,000 of American subjects in cruel bondage. He was therefore prepared to maintain in the face of all opposition which might be offered to the statement, that America as a nation, with all her boasted freedom, was deeply implicated in the sin of slavery. (Hear, hear.) America had declared to the world that all men were born free, and while that great truth still remained in her declaration of independence, three millions of her sons were fast bound in chains, and forbidden even to ask for freedom, and if they did ask for it, it was in the eye of the law, looked upon as a crime that deserved the severest punishment. The lecturer then proceeded to show that the General Government could at any time abolish slavery, if it had the will. It was not, however, to the Government he looked for redress, but to the power of truth – to the moral feeling of the country. Religion exercised a powerful influence in America – everything might be said to receive its support from the pulpit, or to be put down by it; but he was sorry to say that, in America, with very few exceptions, the pulpits were occupied either by the avowed advocates of slavery or the apologists for it. The religion of Christ, both in its precepts and spirit was entirely at variance with slavery. The gospel had been preached in America for more than 200 years, and, not withstanding that, slavery still existed; and if he was asked how that came to pass, his answer would be, that those who preached it were not influenced by its spirit, and did not allow it to affect their conduct. He loved the religion taught in God's blessed word, which said to all men "Do unto others as you would they should do unto you". But in proportion as he loved that religion which taught him that God made of one blood all men that dwell on earth, he listed the religion of the American slaveholder, which allowed its votaries to trade in the bodies and souls of their fellow man, a religion which permitted of men selling babes to purchase bibles, and to support missions to the Heathen. The men who encouraged such blasphemy were the enemies of all religion. Mr. Douglass said he was determined to expose the different churches in America which were the abettors of slavery, and he would take the opportunity of speaking of the church which went by the name of the place in which he was delivering his lecture. When in a Presbyterian House he would expose the American Presbyterians, and when in an Independent House the Independents. As he was then in a Wesleyan place of worship he would allude to the connexion of the Wesleyans with slavery in America. He wished it to be understood that he did not speak of any church for the purpose of reflection on those connected with that church in this country. What he wanted was to expose slavery, and show the part the church had taken in upholding it, so as to prevent the people of this country holding any fellowship with those in whose skirts were the blood of the slave. He then proceeded to show the connexion of that body in America with slavery; and, after dwelling at great length on the sin which the church was guilty of which either supported or became the apologist of the system of slavery, he concluded his lecture with a powerful appeal to Christians of all Churches in the lands to hold no fellowship with those in America. Each were chargeable with the sin of slavery. This, he said, would produce an effect in America which nothing else could do.

The next lecture was announced for Thursday evening, in the Rev. Mr. Nelson's church, Donegall-street, after which Dr. Stevelly having left the chair, the Rev. R. G. Cather was called thereto, and the thanks of the meeting were voted to Dr. Stevelly. Mr. Cather then pronounced the benediction, and the meeting separated.

Anti-Slavery Meeting
Lecturer: Frederick Douglass
Date of Lecture: Thursday, 11 December 1845
Location: Presbyterian Meeting House, Donegall-street[134]
Publication: *Belfast News-Letter*
Date of Publication: Friday, 12 December 1845
Title: 'LECTURE ON SLAVERY'.

Mr. Douglass's third lecture took place yesterday evening, in Mr. Nelson's Meeting House, Donegall-street. The length at which we have given the proceedings of the Evangelical Alliance meeting precludes the possibility of our giving further notice of it at present.[135]

Editorial
Publication: *Belfast Protestant Journal* (from the *Manchester Guardian*)
Date of Publication: Saturday, 13 December 1845
Title: 'Mr Douglas, the Anti-Slavery Lecturer'.

We have often thought, that perhaps the most potent eloquence that could be enlisted in the anti-slavery cause would be the simple and unadorned narrative of the sufferings and ignomies of slavery, told with all the thrilling earnestness of conscious injury by an emancipated slave. But if to this could be superadded, the universal influence over the human mind possessed by a striking person, rich, full-toned voice, great natural eloquence, under the command of good taste, guided and directed by sound judgment and a fair amount of education, it would difficult to overrate the effect of such a theme, so discoursed upon by such a man, before any audience of freemen, lovers of liberty and of their kind. Such a man, we are assured, has recently left the shores of America, for the purpose of lecturing on slavery in the United Kingdom. He is now in Ireland, where he is attracting and riveting the attention of large and increasing auditories; and we believe he intends, ere long, to visit Liverpool and Manchester in the prosecution of his object. Meantime we may mention one or two things connected with him that do not appear to be known, or respecting which very imperfect accounts have as yet appeared in the papers. Mr. Douglas [sic] is a man of colour, born in slavery, his white master being his father. After twenty years of slavery he effected his escape: immediately on reaching the New England States he married, and has been for some time a resident of Lynn, near Boston, Massachussets, where his wife and four children are now living. He received his education from the Methodists, by whom he was encouraged to preach; but, indeed, his mission is clearly that of an anti-slavery lecturer. He came over in the *Cambria* mail steamer, and such is the intensity of American prejudice against people of his colour, that the agents of the vessel in Boston would not receive him as a cabin passenger, and he was consequently compelled to take a berth in the steerage. During the voyage, a citizen of Lynn, well acquainted with Mr. Douglas, finding much inquiry among the passengers as to his life and profession, lent them copies of a brief memoir of his life which has been printed. This led to numerous requests that he would deliver an anti-slavery lecture on board, but Mr. Douglass declined, stating that he would not do so without he was directly invited by the captain. A number of passengers then went to Captain Judkins, and asked him to make the request to Mr. Douglas, and ultimately, the last day the vessel was at sea, the captain asked Mr. Douglas, if he could be prepared to give a lecture on slavery at five minutes' notice on the saloon deck. Mr. Douglas assented; the passengers were convened by sound of a bell; and the captain introduced the lecturer to his passengers generally. Mr. Douglas commenced and made some statements as to slavery as he had seen it in the southern states, when he was repeatedly interrupted by several persons, who were subsequently ascertained to be planters, who called out at every statement 'That's a lie.' Mr. Douglas bore this patiently for some time; but these unmanly interruptions being continued, he at length pulled out of his pocket a book, and said he would read something which he knew they could not deny, being, in fact, the laws enacted against slaves in states which he named. He was reading these, when the rage of the planter burst into ebullitions of wrath, which had nearly ended in bloodshed. One of these threatened to pitch Mr. Douglas overboard, and offered some insulting language to the captain for permitting such a man to lecture on board his ship. An Irish gentleman, a passenger, on hearing the threat, went to the planter and told him that if he attempted to lay hands on Mr. Douglas, he would find that more than one person could play at throwing overboard. The altercation grew warmer; the belligerents arrayed themselves in hostile parties; and the request of the captain that the gentlemen would behave peaceably, was met by a challenge to fight a duel on the part of one of the planters, who thrust his card before the captain, and who also intimated that if Captain Judkins would not fight on board his own ship, he would give him a hostile meeting in Liverpool, on their arrival there. This made matters worse, and had not the captain displayed the greatest firmness and resolution, there would, in all probability, have been a serious termination to the affair. Finding that remonstrances were of no avail against the gasconading braggadocio of the slaveholders, he at length ordered three sets of irons to be brought, and declared that he would put the first man in irons who took any steps to break the peace. This had the desired effect; the rage of the discomfited planters subsided into angry murmurs and they slunk away declaring that the captain should hear it when he returned to Boston. Peace was re-established and the passengers separated the following day on their reaching Liverpool, without any further hostile manifestation on the part of the planters. (*Manchester Guardian*).

Anti-Slavery Meeting
Lecturer: Frederick Douglass
Date: Friday, 12 December 1845
Location: Presbyterian Church, Rosemary Street
Publication: *Banner of Ulster*
Date of Publication: Tuesday, 16 December 1845
Title: 'ANTI-SLAVERY MEETING'.

MR. FREDERICK DOUGLASS'S FOURTH ADDRESS.

On Friday evening last, Mr. Douglass delivered his fourth lecture on American slavery, in the Presbyterian Church, Rosemary Street, to a large audience –

Mr. John Clarke, ex-Mayor, was in the Chair. After few observations from the Chairman, suited to the occasion.

Mr. Douglass came forward, and was received with loud plaudits. He stated that it had often been attempted, by the slaveholder and those interested, to represent the Bible, and particularly the Old Testament, as countenancing slavery; but he was prepared to show that no part of the Sacred Scriptures gave the least encouragement to such a system as prevailed in America at the present time. It was necessary for them to consider what slavery is. It did not consist in taking a man's property from him, but taking himself. It had been contended, by some, that there were many other kinds of slavery in existence – that in the relations of husband and wife, parent and child, master and apprentice, were involved the principles of slavery. But arguments founded on such statements were entirely sophistical; for, in each of the cases, a voluntary agreement was entered into, and mutual benefit resulted from the relationship. (Hear, hear.) Slavery, as he had said, was the taking a man from himself – not robbing him of his property merely, but of his person – not merely of his acquirements, but of his identity with the human family. The fundamental principle of slavery, according to the laws laid down upon the subject, was, that the slave was not to be ranked among men, but herded with brutes, degraded to a chattel, for the use of his master. The Creator had given the slave moral and intellectual faculties, and religious aspirations; but the slaveholder stepped in and forbade their exercise. Now, the question which he had more particularly to consider was, did the Book of God sanction such an atrocious system? Let them look to the law as delivered on the Mount, for the answer. God gave the decalogue amid thunder and lightning, and other solemnities, to a people just emancipated themselves from bondage; and let them see what these said upon the subject. "Thou shall not steal" was a command which dealt death to the principle that slavery was a Divine institution. (Cheers.) The right which a man possessed to his own person was, perhaps, the only absolute right he had – all other rights grew out of that one; and if any one denied to his neighbour the possession of this right, by doing so he cancelled his own claim to it. (Cheers.) The slaveholder arrogated an absolute, unrestricted right over his slave, in spite of the commandment, 'Thou shall not steal.' Another commandment opposed to slavery was, 'Thou shall not covet' and no one could hold his fellow in bondage without directly violating this injunction. (Cheers.) Mr. Douglass proceeded to show, that not only were the positive precepts of Scripture condemnatory of slavery, but the whole scope and tendency of the New Testament were opposed to it. He then spoke of the proceedings of the Presbytery of South Carolina, and other Presbyteries in America, in connexion with slavery, in order to show that they, by the countenance which they had given slavery, were unworthy of being called Christians, and of enjoying fellowship with the Churches of Great Britain and Ireland. The South Carolina Presbytery – that body with which Dr. Chalmers was in correspondence – was stained with the sin of slavery; and in one of the resolutions passed by it, in reference to the subject, they justified themselves, on the plea that slavery had existed 'from the days of the good old slaveholders, the patriarchs Abraham, Isaac, and Jacob'. These men appealed to Holy Writ in defence of their practices, and pointed, with exultation, to Dr. Chalmers's opinion, as conveyed to them, that he was not prepared to say that the holding of slaves, in every case, was inconsistent with Christianity, or formed a ground, in itself, for Churches withdrawing their fellowship from those who did so. The Free Church of Scotland, on this view of the matter, retained communion and intercourse with the slaveholding Presbyterian Churches in America; and thus gave their support to a system which held 3,000,000 human beings in bondage. Alas that this should be so! – that a land which had emancipated her own West India slaves, and which had long been looked upon as one pre-eminently free, should thus act. But there was gold in the matter. The money of the slave-holder had assisted in building up the Free Church; but he trusted that she would see her error in this respect, and return the bribe stained with blood, and say to the slaveholder, 'Thy money perish with thee!' (Great cheering.) Was it too much to expect that the Free Church would do this, when Daniel O'Connell, the mere secular politician, disdained to accept pecuniary aid from the Americans, because he would not have a cause which he considered holy polluted with the price of blood? (Cheers.) Mr. Douglass, after some more remarks of a similar nature, stated that he meant to proceed to Scotland, in order to have an opportunity of confronting the apologists of slavery in the Free Church, and concluded his lecture by mentioning, that the Unitarian ministers, in America, to the number of nearly two hundred, had lately issued a protest against slavery, which absolved that body from the sin of giving it countenance.

Mr. James Standfield then said that their work was only half done. In order to complete it, the meeting would have several resolutions, bearing on the subject of the lecture, submitted to them.

The Rev. James Hodgens, Independent minister,[136] proposed the first resolution – [for which, and the others passed at the meeting, see advertisement.] In doing so, he stated that Mr. Douglass had not, in his lectures, charged the Congregational Churches in America as being implicated the crime of slavery; if they were so in any degree, however, the lecturer was welcome to the use of his place of worship, in order to expose them, he (Mr. Hodgens) wished to show that the body with which he was connected in this country had no sympathy with slaveholders, to whatever Church they might profess to belong. – (Cheers.)

The Rev. W. R. Wright, of the American Associate Reformed Church, in seconding the motion, stated that the body with which he was connected had long repudiated slavery. For himself, he considered it alike opposed to humanity and the moral government of God. (Cheers.)

The resolution was unanimously adopted.

The Rev. Isaac Nelson proposed the second resolution. He said he was convinced that many Churches now countenancing slavery only needed be made acquainted with its real character to renounce it as utterly opposed to Christianity.

He felt ashamed, as a Presbyterian and as a minister, that any encouragement should be given to such a system of Churches professing to be Christian. One of the most powerful addresses against slavery he had ever read had been sent to the American Synod by the Rev. Mr. Morgan – [A Voice – 'But that was four years ago.'] and, in 1844, the General Assembly of the Presbyterian Church in Ireland had sent a similar communication of the most decided kind; but there was another Church holding intercourse with theirs which had acted in a different way – he meant the Free Church of Scotland. He thought that that Church would have been the last, with the Bible in hand, to say a word in favour of slavery. The Rev. Dr. Cunningham, in apologising for the Americans, had said that the abolitionists were unable to sustain the Bible argument against slavery; but (Mr. N.), though not pretending to much learning, had a different opinion. The word "slave" was not to be found from Genesis to Revelations, as the Hebrew term *obed*, and the Greek *doulas*, expressed no such meaning as that attached to the term slave. It was not right for Dr. Cunningham to say that the abolitionists could not sustain the Bible argument against slavery; and, for himself, he would never again open his mouth in opposition to it, if the Bible could be shown to be on the side of the slaveholder, and opposed to the liberation of the bondsman. (Great cheering.) He did not say that money had anything to with the matter, as regarded the Free Church; he rather thought it was to save the honour of their deputation that they had consented to receive subscriptions from America. (Hear, hear.) He did know this much, however, that if he were deputed to the States, and to speak there about slavery, as he now did, he would not get a sixpence. (Cheers and laughter.) The apologists of slavery had challenged the opposers of it to the Word of God, and he would show them what were the opinions of men eminent in the Church in regard to slavery. Mr. Nelson here referred to the published sentiments of the Rev. Henry Grey, the Rev. J. Angel James, and, at considerable length, those of Rev. Mr. Brown, ex-Moderator of the Irish General Assembly, to show that their ideas on the subject were the same as his own. The ministers of Belfast had taken part together in forwarding a Christian union; but if, at the forthcoming meeting in London, to form the Evangelical Alliance, the representatives from the slaveholding Churches America were admitted, for one he would withdraw his name, and knew two or three more who would do the same. (Great cheering.) The rev. gentleman, after a few more observations, concluded proposing the resolution.

The Rev. Mr. Boyd, of the Secession Church, in seconding the resolution, alluded to what had been said by the previous speaker regarding the subscriptions collected by the Free Church deputations in America. He thought that Mr. Nelson had spoken too delicately on the subject. There was one thing which they ought to consider, "that a gift bridleth the tongue." Dr. Cunningham had received the utmost attention on his visit to America, from the slaveholders of that country. He lodged in their houses, sat at their tables, and shared their hospitality; and it would have been a very bad thing of him to say, "You are not Christian men" – it would have been exceedingly ungracious to return such favours by stating,

"You are unfit for Christian fellowship." (Loud cheers.) Mr. Boyd at considerable length went on to show the inconsistency which existed between Christianity and slave-holding, and concluded by an appeal to those present to increase their efforts for the liberation of the degraded bondsmen of America. The resolution was adopted.

Mr. James Standfield moved, and Mr. Boyd seconded, the next resolution, which was adopted. Dr. Stevelly having taken the chair, on the motion of the Rev. Dr. Coulter the cordial thanks of the meeting were voted to Mr. Clarke. The benediction was then pronounced, and the meeting terminated.

Meeting of the Belfast Anti-Slavery Society
Date of Meeting: Friday, 12 December 1845
Location: Rosemary-street Presbyterian Church, Belfast
Publication: *Belfast News-Letter*
Date of Publication: Tuesday, 16 December 1845
Title: 'Anti-Slavery Society'.

AT a large and highly-respectable meeting of the friends and supporters of the Anti-Slavery Association of Belfast, held in Rosemary Street Church,[137] on Friday, 12th December, JOHN CLARKE, Esq., in the Chair, the following Resolutions were unanimously adopted: Moved by the Rev. JAMES HODGENS, seconded by the Rev. Mr. WRIGHT, of the Associate Reformed Church, of America, –

1   That Christians of every denomination, are in duty bound solemnly to protest against the existence of slavery, as repugnant to the Word of God, contained in the Old and New Testaments.

Moved by the Rev. ISAAC NELSON,[138] and seconded by the Rev. JOHN BOYD,

2   That we trust the various Churches of Great Britain and Ireland will inform those of their own persuasion, in the United States of America, who retain slave-holders in their communion, that, if they continue to tolerate such iniquity, they are unworthy of being enrolled among the followers of Christ, as they act so contrary to the Spirit of his Gospel.

Moved by JAMES STANDFIELD, Esq., and seconded by John BOYD, Esq.

3   That the following gentlemen (with power to add to their number) – F. A. Calder,[139] James B. Ferguson, Robert J. Bell, John Arnold, Samuel Edgar, Edwin Blow, Maxwell Sanders, John Boyd, and Jas. Standfield, Esqs. – form a deputation, to wait on the several ministers for Belfast, to obtain their consent, by signature, to the resolutions passed at this meeting; and report the result of their application to a meeting to be held on the return of Mr. Frederick Douglass, from Birmingham.

JOHN CLARKE, Chairman.

Moved by the Rev. Dr. COULTER, that John Clarke, Esq., leave the chair, and John Stevelly, Esq., LL.D., be called thereto; when the thanks of the meeting, by acclamation, were returned to Mr. Clarke, for his dignified conduct in the chair.

JOHN STEVELLY, LL.D. Chairman.

Anti-Slavery Meeting
Lecturer: Frederick Douglass
Date of Lecture: Tuesday, 23 December 1845
Location: Independent Meeting House, Belfast
Publication: *Belfast News-Letter*
Date of Publication: Friday, 26 December 1845
Title: 'BELFAST-ANTI-SLAVERY SOCIETY'.

IMPORTANT PUBLIC MEETING

On Tuesday evening, a very numerous and respectable meeting was held in the Independent Meeting House, Donegall-Street, in furtherance of the objects of the above-named Association. The interest attaching to this meeting was greatly enhanced by a previous announcement, circulated by placards, that Mr. Frederick Douglass (who has returned to Belfast from England, where he has been, on his great mission, for a fortnight) would address the audience. At half-past seven, although the admission was not gratuitous, the Meeting House was crowded to excess, not a spare seat attainable. The platform was occupied by a large number of the clergy of the town, and of the influential laity who have evinced so creditable an interest in the Abolition of Slavery in the United States. The meeting having been constituted in the customary manner.

The Chair was taken by James Gibson, Esq., amidst loud cheering.[140]

When silence was restored, the learned Chairman then said – The times in which we live are distinguished, more than any, by the vast concentration of human thought and human energy which are now directed towards any subject in which our race is interested, whether as regards the present condition of our being, *or* the still more momentous considerations connected with our future destiny. Everywhere we behold around us, in active operation, widely extended combinations or rather confederacies of men, associated for some common enterprise, and bound together by one common principle, so that we are often tempted, in looking at the magnitude of the result proposed, and the multiplicity of the agents employed, to overlook the importance and the responsibility of individual effort. It is, however, a thought, full of the most ennobling emotion, that whilst by far the greatest number of these may be traced to the suggestion of the selfish principle of human nature, having for the objects of their realization, the promotion of superior power, or more enlarged enjoyment of those in which the sentiment of sympathy for the distressed, and a desire to discharge the duties of benevolence, constitute the moving power, are these which will occupy, if not the most conspicuous place in the world's regard, at least, the most prominent in the world's history. (Hear, hear.) Amongst those which must ever hold the highest rank in public estimation – inferior only to that which sends forth the light of the Gospel to the land of heathen darkness – is the association of which this meeting is an auxiliary – an association, whose efforts have struck off the fetters from the limb of every slave that once trod the soil or breathed the air of Britain's wide extended Empire, and which is pledged, whenever its voice can be heard, to testify against the oppressor, and, wherever its influence can reach, to break the chains of the oppressed. (Hear, hear.) It would be an unwarrantable waste of the time of the meeting to refer to the history of the efforts already made with such glorious results on behalf of the injured race of Africa – to trace the progress of the cause of humanity, from the time when Granville Thorpe established the law that slaves could not exist in England, until Clarkson and Wilberforce effected the total abolition of Slave Trade – down to later days, when the absolute emancipation of every slave, completed the full measure of its success in our colonies, and swept the last remnant of the horror of slavery from the domain of Britain. But the work of this Anti-Slavery Society has only been in part accomplished. It has yet to proclaim to the slaveholder so loudly, that the most unwilling shall be forced to hear – that, as the slave-trade is an act of outrage upon the rights of man, and those who are engaged in it the common enemies of their race, as slavery itself, in its form even the most modified, and under external circumstances the least oppressive, is opposed to every principle of Christian love and Christian duty, and at direct variance with the precepts of that Gospel, which enjoins us to 'do unto all men even as we would have them to do unto us,' that those who continue to hold their fellow creatures in bondage, using them as beasts of burden and chattels personal, to be bought or sold as caprice dictates, or as convenience may demand, whatever may be their profession as members of a Christian Church, yet are strangers so far to the power and spirit of the Gospel, and do thereby disentitle themselves to all claims to be regarded as members of that brotherhood whose bond of union is that of love to man and obedience to the law of Christ. (Hear.) Who will be found so bold as to say that the conduct of the slave-holder is consistent with the law of Christian love? What prescriptive right can be established to perpetuate the outrage which was originally committed again the slave? – to claim as his own the infant born of another – born with all the rights of man, rights which God has given, and rights which no other than he who gives has right to take away? What right to separate the husband from the wife – to part asunder those whom God has made one? What right to keep out from his mind the light of knowledge – to make it an offence to teach the slave to read – to deny him the power to peruse for himself the Scriptures of truth, which Christ himself has commanded us to search, and so far to debar him from access to the means of salvation? Yet these are the monstrous, the fearful rights which the system of slavery dares to assert and to enforce. (hear, hear.) It is in vain to attempt to justify such things – they cannot be justified. The violation of the law of God – that God, with whom is no respect of persons, in whose sight the soul of the black man is as precious as the soul of the white – will most assuredly draw down upon all concerned his righteous displeasure, unless restitution be made to the Injured, and confession of guilt to the Most High. For professing Christians to be silent against the continuance of such a system is, in the language of our old Puritan Divines, to homologate its guilt (Cheers.) They are commanded in any wise, to reprove their brother, and not to suffer sin upon him. Do they believe that slavery is repugnant to Christianity? If so, they can not, they dare not – directly or indirectly – either through fear of giving offence or any other consideration personal to the slave-holder, or to themselves, avoid protesting against the system in which the latter participates and whose existence he upholds. Under the present circumstances of the Christian world, the duty which was at all times incumbent is more than ever imperative. (Hear.)

Such was its declaration in the days of its faithfulness, when it might be presumed that the principles of the church of their fatherland still lived in the minds of its members. But the foul contagion of the system had blighted those principles, and their testimony was now expunged from its confession. (Hear, hear.) This abandonment of their testimony was a reproach to the name of Presbyterians; a reproach which would cling to every member of that church in the United States until, as a church, they returned to their former profession – and, till then, should exclude it from the fellow-ship of those who would else be delighted to call its members their brethren. (Hear.) It is only by the unequivocal expression of the opinion of the Christian people of these lands, that any reasonable hope can be indulged of inducing American slave-holders to consider it to be their duty to abandon the hateful practice. In the United States, the sentiment has to encounter such opposition that it is comparatively powerless; but in these countries there appears to be, in the arrangements of Providence, the opportunity afforded to hear such testimony against the sin and guilt of slave-holding – so critical in its juncture, and so influential in its character, that it would be the neglect of a most solemn responsibility, were that opportunity not made use of. When the Christian people of these lands meet together in the promotion of that Christian union, the desire for which is now so generally expressed, will they hold out the hand of Christian fellowship to those who are chargeable with the guilt of such a system? Will the voice of that Christian brotherhood not be upraised in friendly, but firm and faithful, ex-postulation against its inherent depravity? It would be indeed a glorious triumph of Christian principle, if the very first result of the movement towards the union of Evangelical Churches in those lands, would be to break asunder the bonds that have so long pressed upon the limbs of the American slave, and to force, by the expression of its faithfulness, even from the unwilling slave-holder, the deliverance of the oppressed. (Hear, hear.) The creation of this public opinion, or rather the utterance of the deep conviction, already existing, of the Christian people of those lands upon this subject, should be the first object of all friends of humanity – the responsibility of individual effort should be felt by everyone who desired to be considered a friend of his race – the current of honest indignation against the iniquity of the system – against the sinfulness of the practice – and its utter inconsistency with all sincere regard to the precepts of the Gospel, should be swelled by tributary streams from every Christian Church, from every faithful heart – until, like some mighty torrent, it would roll along resistless in its force breaking down before its way, every barrier which cold-hearted sophistry or calculating selfishness dared to erect against its progress, and sweep away every subterfuge under which the spirit of fearful compromise, or hateful hypocrisy sought to justify its guilt. (Hear).

FREDERICK DOUGLASS then presented himself and was received with loud plaudits. He spoke as follows. Ladies and gentlemen, one of the most painful duties I have been called on to perform in the advocacy of the Abolition of Slavery, has been to expose the corruption and sinful position of the American Churches with regard to that question. That was almost the only duty which, when I commenced the advocacy of this cause, I felt inclined to shrink from. Really, any attempt to expose the inconsistencies of the religious organisations of our land is the most painful undertaking. I have always looked upon these churches as possessing, in a superlative degree, the love of virtue and of justice – the love of humanity – the love of God. I had not supposed that they were capable of descending to the low and mean act of uphold and sustaining a system by which three millions of people have been divested of every right and privilege which they ought to enjoy. (Hear.) But, in examining into the character of these churches, I was led to see, that unless the deeds of these ministers were made known – unless the light of truth should be permitted to shine into their dark recesses, there will for ever be a stink of iniquity in the midst of them. The only way of purifying our church from the deep damnation into which she was plunging, was to expose her deeds to the light. But, in exposing these deeds, I do not wish to place myself in the position of an enemy. Let no man rank me among the enemies of the church, or of religion, because I dare to remove the mesh from her face, and give the nations of the earth a peep at her enormities. It is for her salvation and purification I do it, and for the redemption and disenthralment of my race. (Hear.)

I was exceedingly pleased to hear, at the meeting before the last, that the Minister who occupies the pulpit of this House (Mr Hodges)[141] welcomed me to this platform, within these walls – before these people, to expose the corruptions of the Church of America. It was a noble act, which must identify that Rev. gentleman with the friends of truth. It displayed a conscientiousness or innocence on his part, or, at least, an optimism and a magnanimity that are ever associated with innocence (hear, hear) – and a willingness for self-examination seldom displayed. Innocence, you know, lives in the sunlight – it rushes out to the day – it asks to be examined, and searched, and tried. (hear, hear, hear.) This is its language. You never hear it crying – Rocks, cover us, and Mountains, on us fall, and hide us from the face of Truth and Justice! This is the language of guilt – of those convinced of their own iniquity. Innocence never bolts and bars its meeting-house doors, to shut out the light, nor hides itself behind some 'important engagement'. (Hear, and laughter.) It never does any such thing as this. It rushes forth to be seen. Its element is the light. It opens its own eyes and is willing to have the eyes of the world opened on itself. It is glorious, and I love it. The nature of guilt was never set forth more clearly in a few words than by the Blessed Redeemer, when he said, that it hateth the light, neither cometh to the light, lest its deeds be revealed. Eighteen hundred years ago, as it is now, was the reason of this obvious – because God looks on sin with no degree of allowance; and truth will not hold that man Guiltless who, in the light of the nineteenth century, upholds American Slavery, in any shape or form whatever. (Cheers.)

Before entering on the subject of my discourse at large, I beg to say a few words as to my own position among you. One among the many means taken to destroy the influence of these lectures, has been that of circulating insidiously a suspicion, that I am not a really sincere person – that my character is not good. 'He may be an impostor', has been the word. I am not an impostor. If those who insinuate that I am one can prove it, I shall be as ready as anyone to give way. Besides, I would inform this audience that the story that I am here without credentials is absolutely false. I have any quantity of testimonials you may demand from the most distinguished Abolitionists of the day. I have no fears of being examined. I have been in Ireland four months, and have delivered upwards of fifty lectures in different parts of the country, and it was not until I reached Belfast, that I had been even asked for credentials. No enquiries were made of me in Dublin, for I had been known to the Abolitionists of that city for the last four years, through the American papers. They knew me, and understood me, and had heard all about me, and I had no need of showing to them even a letter of introduction. I had no need of one. But, what sensible people you are in Belfast! (Laughter.) How cautious lest they should make a mistake! How prudent they are, and how desirous of being placed on a sure footing, lest they should take into fellowship such characters as won't bear examination – especially how they receive a fugitive slave. But then the Free Church of Scotland is. . . (hear, hear.) Well, I won't say another word about them.

One of the prevalent apologies for the American slave-holders is, that the laws of the States, or at least of several of them, are such as to deprive the masters of the privilege of emancipating the slaves. This is the objection made by every apologiser for Christian union with the slave-holders. My motto is, "No union with the slave-holder." (Cheers.) Because, I believe there can be no union between light and darkness. You cannot serve God and Mammon. Justice can have no fellowship with injustice. Liberty can have no fellowship with slavery. But those who go for uniting with slave-holders, must always have some strong cause for their conduct. Such as this – there are, it appears, a number of good slave-holders in the States, whose breasts are overborne with sorrow on being placed in such an unhappy relation to their slaves (hear) and there are "circumstances over which they have no control," and so forth, and so forth. (Laughter at the droll manner in which the speaker intonated his words.) "Persons situated as these slave-holders are," and so forth – (laughter) "cannot be held accountable for the evil, when they cannot help themselves," and so forth; "but – they would very gladly get rid of it if the laws –, " and so forth. (Continued laughter.) I pronounce this apology to be a falsehood. There is not a slave-holder in any State, who may not, if he will, emancipate his slaves, by taking them across Mason's and Dixon's line, and all the apologies built upon this supposition – all the arguments founded upon it – must fall to the ground. When they presume to offer this excuse, tell them of Brisburn [sic] of South Carolina,[142] who, when he became sensible of the guilt of holding slaves, took them to Ohio, and went to work with his own hands, like an honest man. (Cheers.) If any other instances are required, take that of James G. Birnie, [sic][143] who emancipated his slaves, and a hundred of others. But, besides this, there are, in fact, only two or three of the States in which it is necessary to remove slaves which are emancipated. There are twelve States in which the master may emancipate his slaves on the spot. Another suggestion is, the slave-holder is responsible for the future maintenance of the emancipated slave. There is no such thing. It is not true; and they will tell you you ought to know better, for the facts are all on the other side. (Hear.) They are always glad to receive emancipated slaves in New England, and even if the Northern States were not disposed to take them, thank God, the British lion asserts dominion in the Western hemisphere. (Cheers.) Canada is open to them, and, I am sure, will not charge brother Jonathan with the expense of their keeping. So much for the story that these men cannot get rid of their slaves. Oh, what an easy amount of reasoning it takes to uphold a bad cause. Truth needs but little argument, and no long drawn out sophisticated detail to establish a position. There is something in the heart which instantly responds to its voice. You feel differently when even the term slavery is mentioned, from the way you feel when the word freedom salutes your ears! Freedom, the word produces a thrill of joy even in the bosom of the slave-holder himself – in the absence of his slaves. Then the term is musical to his ears, but when it is mentioned in the slaves' presence, then the slave-holder is stung to the very quick, and he behaves more like a demon than a man, Oh, yes – our hearts leap up to the very name of freedom, while we recoil with horror at the sound of slavery. We feel, then, that the slave-holder is a wrong doer, and we know that wrong-doers can have no fellow-ship with the meek and lowly Jesus.

It is said, we ought not to enter into people's motives. I don't want to do so. I only speak what I know. I may be told, "judge not, that you be not judged". I admit the truth of this part of Scripture, but those who read it to me, should read a little further, where it is said, "by their fruits ye shall know them." (Cheers.) I do not judge you when you cut me, if I cry out that you hurt me. (Hear.) It is not judging the state of your soul, when I tell you, that you have done me an injury, I know that, by injuring me, you are acting contrary to Christianity, and when you tell me that there are some Christian slave-holders in the States, I tell you, as well might you talk of sober drunkards. (Laughter.) Just as if the lash in the hands of a Christian is not as injurious to my back as it would be in the hands of a wicked man. (hear, hear.) As far as my experience goes, I should rather suffer under the hands of the latter; and, I tell you, as I have mentioned in my narrative, that next to being a slave, there is no greater calamity than being the slave of a Christian slave-holder. (Hear.) I say this from my own experience, and it is further proved by theory. There is a reason for it. When the finest – the most excellent bodies are decomposed, they become the most corrupt and offensive. So, when the most excellent element is perverted to a base use, it becomes the basest and most hateful in itself – so the religious element raises up and stamps man with the image of God, when pure, but, when perverted, it makes him a fallen angel and sinks him among demons. A man becomes the more cruel the more the religious element is perverted in him. It was so with my master.

Some persons have taken offence at my saying that slave-holders become worse after their conversion, and it was thought that I was hereby damaging the cause of religion; but I say this is the same principle upon which Christ denounced the Scribes and Pharisees, when he said that they showed compassion and kindness to make one proselyte, and after they had made him, he was ten times the Child of Hell than he was before. They do make proselytes, and convert men to what they call religion, but their converts are still in the gall of bitterness and in the bond of iniquity. Why is it, if this be not the case, that if they are women-whippers, cradle-plunderers, and man-stealers before their conversion, they are women-whippers, cradle-plunderers, and man-stealers after it (hear) – and that 'religion' is to them but an additional stimulant to re-enact these atrocious deeds? The religious slave-holder is a man from whom I have been myself happily delivered, so that I am not to be told it is a good thing to have a "religious" slave-holder for a master.

I beg now to introduce to your notice a little of the doings of one or two of the Churches of America, and I shall begin with the Baptist Church. (Hear.) This is congregational in its organization and government, but its congregations are united by what is called a 'Triennial Convention', the object of which is to spread the gospel among the heathen. At the last but one of these conventions, in the City of Baltimore, the Rev. Dr. Johnston, of South Carolina, presided, and he on this occasion asserted the doctrine that when any institution becomes established by law, a Christian man may innocently engage to uphold it. The president of the Baptist convention is a slaveholder himself. He is a man-stealer. (Hear.) The Secretary of the convention is another man-stealer, and the most of the other officer-bearers were man-stealers themselves. During the progress of the business, there was one man in one of the committees, who was found to be an Abolitionist – Elon Galusha.[144] This man is now, I trust, in Heaven. He dared to say that a slave was a man, and that slavery ought to be abolished. For this, the members of his church cut him off (Hear) though he was a man of talent and of unblemished character, and, as a minister of the gospel, unparalleled. Another great Baptist minister, the Rev. Lucius Bowles,[145] congratulated his brethren that there was a pleasing degree of unity among the Baptists through the land, for the southern brethren *were all slave-holders*. "Slave-holders! Oh, my friends, do not rank the slave-holder as a common criminal – as no worse than a sheep stealer or a horse stealer. The slave holder is not only a thiever of men, but he is a murderer; not a murderer of the body, but, what is infinitely worse, a murderer of the soul (hear, hear, hear) as far as a man can murder the soul of his fellow-creature, for he shuts out the light of salvation from his spirit".

Mr. Douglass then read an advertisement which appeared in the American papers, by the legal representatives of the Rev. Dr. Furman, another eminent

Baptist minister, who, in his lifetime, asserted that the Scriptures warranted the holding of slaves. The advertisement was to the effect, that, on a certain day, would be put up to auction the property of the late Dr. Firman, [sic] consisting of land to a certain extent, "together with twenty-seven negroes – *some of them very fine* – a library chiefly theological – two mules and an old waggon!" (The reading of this advertisement created considerable merriment). Mr. Douglass proceeded – O, my friends, instead of smiling and laughing at this, we should be sadly weeping to think that such a man ever lived as this Dr. Furman – this 'Doctor of Divinity' – to think that Christianity should be so degraded by one of its professing ministers. Yet, that man was reckoned among the pious of the earth, and would have been received among the Baptists here as a good Christian minister – What a shame! But I must hasten.

We have here a specimen of the Baptist Church of America in one quarter. I have now to speak of them in the State of Virginia, where men regularly enter into the raising or breeding of slaves, as a business, (hear), just as cattle are raised for the Smithfield market; and is here the marriage institution is set aside. In some cases it becomes in the interest of the slave holder to separate two slaves (male and female) already married. When the question was proposed to the Baptist Society there, whether parties thus separated might marry again, the answer was, that this Separation being tantamount to the *civil death* of either of the parties, to forward the second marriage in either case, would be to expose to Church censure those who did so for disobedience. (Great sensation). Here we find a deliberate setting aside of the Marriage Institution, and a deliberate sanction of a wholesale system of adultery and concubinage; and, yet the persons who authorised and enforced such wickedness call themselves Christians! (Hear, hear.) I might go on, giving fact after fact, relative to the doings of the Christian slaveholders in America; but, after what I have said, I wonder who will say in Belfast that a Christian can innocently associate with these men (Hear.)

Rev. Doctor S – [146] has been over here a few months. He is one of those who, like Dr. Chalmers, looks on slavery as an evil, that though wrong in itself, nevertheless, it is not sufficiently important to exclude persons from Christian Union. He finds it necessary to keep communion with slaveholders, because he gets not a little of his support from them. These people feel that they must live. George Bradburn tells an excellent thing illustrative of his apology.[147] Bradburn was very deaf, and one of these apologists said to him, "you seem to overlook the fact that ministers must live," said Dr Bradburn. Here the speaker imitated the nasal twang of the old mans, in a style curiously characteristic of the negro passion for mimicry. "I deny any such necessity. I dispute your premises. I deny that it is necessary for any man to live, unless he can live honestly". These slave-holders ever urge this overwhelming argument of necessity. But they are under a great mistake. What should render it necessary for a man to live by slavery? (Hear.) Why, the very watches in the pockets of these men – the very coats on their backs, are the price of blood. (Hear). And they know this. We understand their difficulty about getting rid of their slaves if it is all that they are afraid of is getting rid of their fat salaries.

(Hear.) And yet, it is my belief, that a minister will be better paid, when there are no slaves. (Cheers.) It is curious, that the higher we go in ecclesiastical rank, in the church, the colder we find the ministers in the cause of freedom. The most ardent friends of the slaveholders are in the highest grade of church office, while those in an inferior station, are invariably on the side of humanity and Christianity.

Mr. Douglass continued to address the meeting, for nearly an hour further, on the subject of the Church of Scotland, in reference to American Slavery, but we are obliged to curtail our reporter's notes of the remainder of his address, in order to make room for the important political issues which appear elsewhere.

After Mr. Douglass had sat down, the Chairman rose and said, that he felt constrained by the feelings excited by some allusions made by Mr Douglass to the Free Church of Scotland, towards the close of his speech, to interrupt the order of proceeding, lest the impression should go abroad that he (Mr. Gibson) concurred in the application to the Free Church of the illustration that had thus been introduced. He (Mr. Gibson) would feel most sorry to diminish, by a single particle, the sentiment of those observations with which Mr. Douglass had finally concluded his address. He regretted most sincerely that the deputation of the Free Church had visited the slave-holding states in America, and that the Free Church had consented to receive a single farthing of their money. It had been done, he believed, inadvertently. The Free Church had given to the world the most signal proof of its disinterested devotedness to the cause of Christ. Its ministers had surrendered all of their endowments and flung their own livelihood to the winds, rather than by obedience to the law of man disobey the law of Christ. They had thus placed themselves well beyond all possibility of suspicion of any selfish motive, with regard to this petty amount which they had received from the slave-holder. (Hear, hear, hear, and loud cheers.) Could his voice reach them, he would say, in the spirit of the most sincere Christian regard, and in the discharge of that duty which Christians owe to one another – Send away from you this money which, inadvertently, the deputation received; let not even the appearance of evil rest upon the bright Christian reputation of your body; let not one single stone of the Free Church fabric be contaminated by contact with the blood of the slave, or money obtained as the price of a human being. (Hear, hear.) He (Mr G.) believed that the language of brotherly love was that which would be always most heartily responded to, and was powerfully convincing. (Hear.) The men of the Free Church were right hearted men, but their judgment in this matter was, he believed, erroneous; let them be convinced as he trusted they would be, and none would be more ready than they to act on their conviction. As Mr. D. had observed, it would be indeed the bursting asunder of the shackles of the slave, as if by the lightening of heaven, the Free Church should yet come forth with a deliverance, acknowledging their inadvertency, and putting away from them the money of the slave-holder, and the act of which the slave now complained, as rivetting his fetters, could be thus overruled, by the interposition of Providence, to accelerate his freedom, and prostrate to the ground that fabric of oppression which it had been laid hold of to support. (Hear, hear.)

After the Chairman had concluded, remonstrances, on the part of the Baptist denomination in this town, and also, of the Independent Congregations of the Donegall-Street Meeting-House, addressed to the American churches of these denominations, were read. A letter, in answer to one signed 'Civis', in the *Banner of Ulster*, in which certain insinuations were thrown out as to the integrity of Mr Douglass, and the prudence of his supporters in this town, was also read, and commented upon by Mr. Standfield, in his usual eloquent and straight forward style.[148] Thanks were then voted to Mr. Standfield, and his excellent fellow-labourer, Lieut. Calder, after which, Counsellor Gibson was moved out of the Chair and appropriately thanked for the manner in which he had presided over the meeting. It was, lastly, announced, that a noon-day meeting on the subject of the Abolition of Slavery, would be held this day in Mr. Nelson's Church, Donegall-Street, when Mr. Douglass would deliver another address. The meeting then separated.

We much regret that the pressure of important political intelligence has compelled us to abridge, very materially, the latter portion of the proceedings of this meeting.

Anti-Slavery Meeting
Lecturer: Frederick Douglass
Date of Lecture: Tuesday, 23 December 1845
Location: Independent Chapel, Donegall-street
Publication: *Belfast Commercial Chronicle*
Date of Publication: Saturday, 27 December 1845
Title: 'AMERICAN SLAVERY'.

The following is a brief outline of the proceedings of the anti-slavery meeting, held in the Independent Chapel, on Tuesday last, James Gibson, Esq. in the chair.

Mr. Gibson, on taking the chair, said, that the occasion for which they were then met together was one of the most Interesting kind, and he felt that he should scarcely be doing justice to his own feelings, if he did not state what his convictions were, and which, he believed, were shared by a large portion of his fellow-townsmen. They saw everywhere the improvement on behalf of the slave making itself visible (hear, hear, and cheers) – and it was an ennobling thought to reflect, that, of all the movements which were going forward, that which was connected with the present meeting might be justly considered to occupy the most permanent place in the world's history, and was calculated to confer the largest amount of benefit to mankind at large, (hear, hear and cheers.) The work was only done in part, and theirs was the duty to sweep away every trace of slavery – that foul outrage on humanity. It was a sacred cause – one that was not confined within the narrow limits of time; for it spoke the language of universal man (Hear.) It yet remained for the Anti-Slavery Society, after having prevailed on mankind to treat, with common consent, the slave holder as the tyrant of his race, to go forward to those men who still persisted in holding slaves, and tell them that they held an unhallowed property – that they held a property which no man had a right to hold – that they were guilty, not of the original outrage which made man a slave, that most revolting of all human outrages – but that they were guilty of perpetuating the original wrong, and scenes of guilt and misery, from generation to generation (Cheers.) But the time he hoped, was fast approaching when the weight of public opinion would come down upon the slave-holder with such force, and such effect, that the Christian nations of Europe – that Great Britain and Ireland – would oblige them, by their reproaches, to abandon that system, which the high and holy principle of Christian love had not been able to induce them to forsake. (Hear, hear, and loud cheering.) He trusted they would give the people of America an opportunity of knowing how they felt on this subject – they should be bold, and faithful, and unflinching. (Hear, hear.) Mr. Gibson, after enlarging at some length on the evils of slavery, resumed his seat, loudly cheered.

Mr. Standfield, after a few introductory observations, introduced to the meeting Mr. Frederick Douglass, who was received with loud and prolonged cheering.

Mr. Douglass, in addressing the meeting, said – One of the most painful duties he had been called on to perform, in the way of his anti-slavery advocacy, had been that of expressing the corruption and sinful position of the American Churches, in regard to slavery (Hear, hear.) It was, indeed, when he first commenced that advocacy, one among the only duties that he felt anything like shrinking from. It was to him a most painful undertaking; but he had always looked upon it as possessing, in superlative degree, justice, love of humanity, and the love of God. He had not supposed they were capable of descending to the low and mean work of upholding and sustaining a system, by which three millions of people were divested of every right that belonged to humanity. (Cheers.) But, in examining into the character of the Churches of America, he was led to see, that, unless the Church was exposed, unless the deeds of her Ministers were made known and the light of truth permitted to shine into her dark recesses, they must have for ever a very sink of iniquity in the midst of the Church. (Hear, hear, and cheers.) The only way of proving her, and saving her from the deep damnation of which she was in danger, and into which she was plunging, would be, to expose her, and enlist all the energies of the good and the upright to reform her. (Cheers.) In exposing that Church, he did not place himself in the position of an enemy – let no man rank him among the enemies of the Church, or the enemies of religion, because to move the masses in his favour, to tear off the pontifical robes she wore, and give freedom to the oppressed. (Cheers.) It was for her salvation he did it – it was for her purification he did it – it was for the redemption and disenthralment of his race from the chains of slavery he did it. (Loud cheers.) He was exceedingly pleased, in the last meeting which he had held, to hear a Minister, who occupied that pulpit, welcome him (Mr. D.) to that platform – within those walls – before those people, who listened to him – to expose the corruption and evil which prevailed in the Congregational Churches of America; – it was an act which must identify that man, that Minister, within the friends of truth and freedom. He displayed an openness, a magnanimity, and willingness for self-examination, which argued innocence. Innocence, they knew, sought the light of God – it sought to be examined, searched, and tried. Truth would not hold that man guiltless, who, in the light of the nineteenth century, lent his sanction to the system of American slavery. (Hear, hear.) Having said so much, he begged permission to say a few words personal to himself. He was always unwilling to speak of himself, but it was imperative on that occasion that he should say a few words, attempts were being made to destroy his influence, insinuating that he was not what he pretended to be, and could not exhibit any credentials from persons of respectability – that he was not a reliable person, and might be an impostor. He was, however, no impostor, and those who made the charge ought not do so under the curtain, but in a public manner, and bring proofs to substantiate their allegations. He had letters of introduction to gentlemen of the highest respectability in this country, from well known abolitionists in America. But what appeared to him somewhat strange, was, that he had been four months in Ireland, and delivered about fifty lectures, and never till he came to Belfast had he been asked for credentials. What a sensible people the inhabitants of this town are! How cautious and how calculating, and what a prudent desire they evince for proceeding on sure grounds, lest they take a person void of respectability into their confidence How circumspect about the character of a slave! But how about the Free Church? (Laughter) Well, I won't say a word more on that point. The lecturer then proceeded to notice the statement which he said was sometimes made by the apologists of slavery, that the slaveholders were in some degree compelled by the circumstances of their position to continue the system. This statement, he said, was utterly false, and to prove that it was unfounded, he showed the facility with which slaves could be emancipated, and gave several instances in which this had been effected on a large scale. (Hear, hear.) Some persons were in the habit of saying that it was a fortunate circumstance that many of the slaveholders in America were Christians – Christian slaveholders! As well might they speak of sober drunkards. He here spoke the sentiments of his heart when he said that, next to being a slave, the greatest calamity which he knew was being the slave of a Christian slaveholder. He said this from experience; and it was accounted for on the principle that the most excellent bodies, when decomposed, emitted the most offensive odours. The religious element which stamped man with the image of God, when prostituted, changed him into a fallen angel, and sank him to the level of demons.

After showing at some length a great many of the Independent and Baptist Churches in America were implicated in the sin of slaveholding, either directly or indirectly, he referred to the opposition made by Mr. Jonathan Walker and Mr. John L. Brown to slavery and the punishment which they were sentenced to receive for aiding in the liberation of a number of slaves. Mr. Walker had been pilloried and branded in the arm, and Mr. Brown had sentence of death recorded against him; but the remonstrances of the British people were successful in getting the sentence revoked, and he was set at liberty. But the apologists of slavery might ask, was not John L. Brown guilty of violating the law in favouring the escape of runaway slaves? Yes, they would answer; and were not Daniel, and Shedrach, Meshach, and Abednego, equally guilty in violating the law of the governments under which they lived? He (Mr. Douglass) thought if some of the wise advisers which they had now had lived then, we should not have had those brilliant examples of faith recorded in Scripture. These prudent counsellors would have said to the three children, "You should be very cautious what you do. You are here in the midst of heathenish people, and if you violate the laws, what will be the consequence? You will lose your life, and then no ministers will be left to preach to these poor perishing heathens. They will then have to grope in the dark without your aid. But you should be wise serpents, and, instead of making a stand against the king's decree, the better way is to bow down to the image set up: but when you do so, you need not bow down with the intention of worshipping the image. While you appear to do this, you can be communing with the Lord all the time." (Cheers and laughter.) Such (continued Mr. Douglass) was the wisdom of the times – the wisdom which was actuating this moment with the Free Church of Scotland in reference to the slave-holding Churches in America. But he thanked God that a higher principle was operating among many. God had said he would bring to nought the wisdom of the wise. He was doing so at the present time, and he hoped the unanimous cry from Belfast and all the Churches would now be, "No terms with the American slave-holder," and that the next cry in sevenfold thunder, from this town to the Free Church, would be, "Send back the blood-stained money which you have received." (Great Cheering.) Was there ever such an opportunity of doing good enjoyed by any religions denomination as that which the Free Church now has? He believed they might be instrumental in breaking the chains of every bondsman if they were only to say, "We took this money without due consideration. We did not see how far such an act committed us to be upholding of slavery; but having examined it in the light of revelation, having offered up the petition, 'Lord, what wilt thou have us do?' we cannot deem ourselves safe any longer, unless we obey the Scripture precept. 'Touch not, taste not, handle not.' We will wash our hands in innocence, and compass the altar of our God. We cannot build up our churches at the expense of the blood and tears of the bondsmen. We would gladly commune with you in Christian fellowship, but God forbids it – the tears of the injured slave forbid it." Oh! If the Free Church would say this, she would give a deadly blow to slavery; at least among those religious bodies in America over which her influence prevailed. Mr. Douglass sat down amid cheering.

The Chairman rose and said – he trusted, from his heart and soul, that the Free Church of Scotland would send back contributions she had received from America; but, whilst he thus expressed himself, he hoped the meeting would permit him to say that he dissented from the manner in which Mr. Douglass had introduced his remarks on the Free Church. He could not approve of the parallel which had been drawn between those who might have urged Shadrach, Meshach, and Abednego, to an act of hypocrisy, and the course pursued by the Free Church towards the American Churches. (Hear, hear.) He thought the observation an unfortunate one; and believing, as he did, that the Free Church was right and sound at the heart – that, if ever noble self-denial had been evinced – if ever the force of

Christian principle had been manifested – it was assuredly by her members, when, at the call of conscience and duty, they threw every selfish consideration to the winds, and resolved, at whatever risk, to obey God rather than man – (prolonged cheering) – feeling this to be the case, he could not believe that, if the matter were rightly set before them, they would act in opposition to the course of duty. He would wish to adopt towards them the language of brotherly admonition, and say, "As you value your Christian character, which stands deservedly high – as you wish to act as those who have received a new name, and whose integrity and Judgment are not impeached, send back the money which you have received from the slaveholders, that it may not be said that any of the stones of your churches are cemented with the blood of the slave." (Cheers.) Speak to them as Christian should speak to Christian. Tell them that you cannot see their sin without beseeching them to put it away; and believing, as he did, that they were actuated by Christian principle, he was confident the desired result would be attained. (Cheers.) He believed in his heart that the Free Church had acted in the matter inadvertently; and if they were dealt with in the manner he had stated, it would be overruled by Providence for good, and the rejection of what they had received might act like the bolt of heaven to prostrate the whole fabric of tyranny and oppression, which many of the Churches in America upheld. He trusted that Mr. Douglass would not think he had said anything amiss; and he thought those around him would see that, as a member of the Presbyterian Church of Ireland, having all his sympathies and affections on the side of the Free Church, he could not keep silence when he heard it stated that a spirit of hypocrisy was actuating her members. The Chairman resumed his seat amid great applause.

Mr Keir read a letter of remonstrance from the Baptist church in this town, to the churches of the same denomination in America which countenanced slavery.

Mr. James Rose read a similar letter addressed by Independents to those of the same denomination in America.

Mr. James Standfield then called the attention of the meeting to a letter signed 'Civis' which had appeared in a recent number of the *Banner of Ulster*. He said the members of the Anti-slavery Society, in reading it, thought it should be answered, and some of their members had, accordingly, drawn up a reply to the letter. Two gentlemen had, on Monday, at the hour of one o'clock, taken the letter to the *Banner of Ulster* for the purpose of having it published on Tuesday. When they went there they were told the Editor was not in, but that if they would call at three o'clock they would get an answer; and when they returned they learned that the Editor had gone to Scotland, and taken the letter of reply with him in his pocket. (A laugh.) So that, instead of the answer to 'Civis' being in Tuesday's *Banner*, there appeared in the 'Notices to Correspondents' an intimation that it had arrived too late for that day's publication. But, fortunately, another copy of the letter was in their possession, and as it had met with the approval of the Anti-slavery Society, it would be read to the meeting as their answer to 'Civis' (Cheers.)

The Rev. Isaac Nelson then presented himself, for the purpose of reading the aforesaid reply; but, before doing so, he declared, as a member of the Anti-slavery

Society, that he had not been actuated by desire to give offence to any one when he at any time denounced slavery or its abettors. He had come to the conclusion that no slave-holder should be admitted to sit down at the table of the Lord, partake of sealing ordinances, and he was free to express this opinion, whatever might be thought of it by the Churches on the other side of the Atlantic, or those on this side of it, in George's-street. (Cheers.) Mr. Nelson then said he considered the *Banner* had acted unfairly in this matter. It was a shame that the reply which he was about to be read had not been permitted to come through the medium of the press; but he was thankful that they had a public platform from which to read it, and a public meeting from which they could appeal. (Cheers.) The Rev. gentleman then read the following letter:

AMERICAN SLAVERY, Sir, – I consider the letter of Civis cunning but inconsistent. A cursory reader would imagine that it was intended to oppose slavery, yet I suspect, if its writer be not an apologist for, he would not refuse Church fellowship to those who support it. However, we shall know more of his sentiments if he write again on the subject; and here I take the liberty to say, let him give his real signature, and I will give mine. If we only seek after truth, we have nothing to conceal and nothing of which to be ashamed, and let neither of us say anything unbecoming a Christian.

His first reason for the absence of the Presbyterian Ministers from the platform – namely, other important engagements, I dismiss, remarking, that the less said on the subject the better; it will not bear sifting. As to the support Mr. Wright received last year, Civis is wrong again, and it was ill-judged of him to refer to it all – the truth is, an attempt was made to put Mr Wright down because he referred to the Free Church as having come to a decision injurious to Anti-Slavery, and out of this have sprung many of the difficulties of the friends of the cause.

The main reason which kept Ministers from the meetings says Civis, is, 'a system of denunciation and pronouncing absolutely as to the spiritual condition and eternal destinies of every man in any way connected with American slavery, which has become the bane of the Belfast Anti-Slavery Committee's movements'. Is the writer of the above paragraph a Minister of the Gospel? If he be, let him read I. Corinth, v.5. Deliver such a one to Satan for the destruction of the flesh, that the spirit may be saved in the day of the Lord. Here the apostle Paul excluded men from the Church of Christ that their souls might be saved. Was this pronouncing on their eternal destinies? If Civis himself would exclude the fornicator, the perjurer, the robber, the adulterer, from the communion of the Lord's Supper, would this be denouncing such persons.

The Belfast Anti-Slavery Society has been pronounced indiscreet, because it believes and proclaims that slaveholding is a sin of such magnitude as to deserve exclusion from the table of the Lord. Will Civis be good enough to come forward under his real name, and say whether or not slaveholders should be admitted to the membership of the Church. Drs. Chalmers, Candlish, and Cunningham say they ought. The Rev. John Angell James, Rev. Mr. M'Beath, of the Free Church, Glasgow, and Dr. Brown, late Moderator of the Irish Assembly, declare they ought not. The Rev. James Morgan, four years ago, as Chairman of the Belfast Anti-Slavery Society wrote, that 'the Christians of Britain have felt themselves called upon to enter into a solemn compact to refuse the privileges of Christian fellowship to any members of the American Churches who may be participators in the crime of slavery, either by practising it themselves, or conniving at it in others.' Does Mr. Morgan continue to hold the same opinion? If he does, he is on the side of the Society, and joins in denouncing the abettors of slavery. If he has changed his mind, and would now admit slaveholders to the Lord's Table, let him say so frankly, but let not the Society be blamed for still asserting the same principle for which he then contended.

I pass over the remarks of Civis as to the impertinence of the resolutions; it is too bad for a person, under an assumed signature, to call the unanimous act of a large and highly-respectable meeting, impertinent. Civis was present, why did he not protest against the proceedings? Is it impertinent to ask the Ministers of Belfast, of every denomination, for a unanimous declaration on so plain a matter of duty? Did Civis now see the array of names attached to the resolutions, he would not call the errand of the deputation bootless.

I am, Sir, A Member of the Belfast Anti-Slavery Society. Belfast, 22d Dec. 1845.

After he had concluded, he recommended that the letter he had read, in order to get publicity, should be printed, together with that of Civis and extensively circulated. On the motion of Mr John Boyd, seconded by Mr. Edwin Blow, a very cordial vote of thanks was given to the Secretaries of the Auxiliary Society, Mr. James Standfield and Lieutenant Calder, for the very able manner in which they had always discharged their duties, and for the zeal they manifested on all occasions for the emancipation of the slave. A vote of thanks was then given to the Chairman, and the Rev. Dr. Paul having pronounced the benediction, the meeting separated.

Anti-Slavery Meeting
Lecturer: Frederick Douglass
Date of Lecture: Tuesday, 23 December 1845
Location: Independent Chapel, Donegall-street
Publication: *National Anti-Slavery Standard* (From Belfast *News-Letter*, 26 December 1845)
Date: Thursday, 5 February 1846
Title: 'Selections'.

On Tuesday evening last, Mr. Douglass delivered his fifth lecture, on the subject of Slavery, in the Independent Chapel, Donegall street, at the hour of half-past seven o'clock, to a large and respectable audience. James Gibson, Esq. in the chair.

Mr. Gibson, on taking the chair, said, that the occasion on which they were then met together was one of the most interesting kind, presenting features of no common interest. He should feel that it, certainly, it would be unnecessary for him to take up the time of the meeting by any lengthened observations, but he felt that he should scarcely be doing justice to his own feelings, if he did not state what his convictions were, and which, he believed, were shared by a large portion of his fellow-townsmen. They saw around them men associated in a kind of compact, or, if he might use the word, confederacy, to accomplish certain purposes, one with the other; in the effecting of which, their present condition, or their future hopes, were concerned. – They saw everywhere the movement on behalf of the slave making itself visible – (Hear, hear, and cheers) – and it was an ennobling thought to reflect, that, of all the movements which were going forward, that which was connected with the present meeting might be justly considered to occupy the most permanent place in the world's history, and was calculated to confer the largest amount of benefit on mankind at large. (Hear, hear, and cheers.) It would be nothing more than a waste of time to speak of the labors of the Anti-Slavery Association – of the labours of a Sharpe or of a Wilberforce, – although they called up some of the most hallowed recollections, and presented some of the most glorious achievements. But the work was only done in part, and theirs was the duty to sweep away every trace of slavery – that foul outrage on humanity. It was a sacred cause – one that was not confined within the narrow limits of time; for it spoke the language of universal man – (Cheers) – and, where-ever wrong was heaped by man on his fellow-man, there would the hand of relief reach, in sympathy, to the most degraded of the human race. (Hear, hear.) It yet remained for the Anti-Slavery Society, after having prevailed on mankind to treat, with common consent, the slaveholder as the tyrant of his race, to go forward to those men who still persisted in holding slaves, and tell them that they held an unhallowed property – that they held a property which no man had a right to hold – that they were guilty, not of the original outrage which made man a slave – that most revolting of all human outrages – but that they were guilty of perpetuating the original wrong, and scenes of guilt and misery, from generation to generation. (Cheers.) But the time, he hoped was fast approaching, when the weight of public opinion would come down upon the slaveholder with such force, and such an effect, that the Christian nations of Europe – that of Great Britain and Ireland – would oblige them, by their reproaches, to abandon that system, which the high and holy principle of Christian love had not been able to induce them to forsake. (Hear, hear, and loud cheering.) He trusted they would give the people of America an opportunity of knowing how they felt on this subject – they should be bold, and faithful, and unflinching – they should go forth with the Bible in their hands, and the love of God in their hearts, and endeavor, by the utmost exertions, to do away with the horrors of that nefarious system. (Hear, hear.) Mr. Gibson, after enlarging, at some length, on the evils of Slavery, resumed his seat, loudly cheered.

Mr. Standfield, after a few introductory observations, introduced to the meeting Mr. Frederick Douglass, who was received with loud and prolonged cheering.

Mr. Douglass, in addressing the meeting, said – One of the most painful duties he had been called on to perform, in the way of his Anti-Slavery advocacy, had been that of expressing the corruption and sinful position of the American churches, in regard to Slavery. (Hear, hear.) It was, indeed, when he first commenced that advocacy, one among the only duties that he felt anything like shrinking from. It was to him a most painful undertaking; but he had always looked upon it as possessing, in a superlative degree, justice, love of humanity, and the love of God. He had not supposed they were capable of descending to the low and mean work of upholding and sustaining a system, by which three millions of people were divested of every right that belonged to humanity. (Cheers.) But, in examining into the character of the churches of America, he was led to see, that, unless the Church was exposed, unless the deeds of her Ministers were made known, and the light of truth be permitted to shine into her dark recesses, they must have forever a very sink of iniquity in the midst of the Church. (Hear, hear, and cheers.) The only way of proving her, and saving her from the deep damnation of which she was in danger, and into which she was plunging, would be, to expose her, and enlist all the energies of the good and the upright to reform her. (Cheers.) In exposing that Church, he did not place himself in the position of an enemy – let no man rank him among the enemies of the Church, or the enemies of religion, because he dared to move the masses in his favor, to tear off the pontifical robes she wore, and give freedom to the oppressed. (Cheers.) It was for her salvation he did it – it was for her purification he did it – it was for the redemption and disenthralment of his race from the chains of Slavery he did it. (Loud cheers.) He was exceedingly pleased, in the last meeting which he had held, to hear a minister, who occupied that pulpit, welcome him (Mr. Douglass) to that platform – within those walls – before those people, who listened to him – to expose the corruption and evil which prevailed in the Congregational churches of America; – it was an act which must identify that man, that minister, with the friends of truth and freedom. He displayed an openness, magnanimity, and a willingness for self-examination, which argued innocence. Innocence, they knew, sought the light of God – it sought to be examined, searched, and tried. Truth would not hold that man guiltless, who, in the light of the nineteenth century, lent his sanction to the system of American Slavery. (Hear, hear.) He begged to be permitted to give utterance to a few words, with reference to his own person. (Applause.) Among the many means which had, unworthily, been employed to destroy the effect of those lectures which he was delivering, a foundationless and insidious assertion had been made, that he, Frederick Douglass, was not a reliable person – he might be an imposter. He only wished, in reply, to say that he was not an imposter, as had been stated; and, if those gentlemen who had said he was, could prove that he was an imposter, let them come forward and do it. He would be ready to hear and reply to their charges. He would inform them that he was not without credentials; he had letters to the most distinguished gentlemen, the most distinguished Abolitionists, in the country. He had been in Ireland for four months. and had delivered, during that time, no less, perhaps, than fifty lectures; but he had not, till he came to Belfast, been asked for his credentials – he was not asked for them in Dublin – the Abolitionists of Dublin had seen extracts from American papers respecting him, and he did not need to show them his letters of introduction. (Hear, hear.) But, what a sensible and cautious people the people of Belfast were! – (Laughter.) How very cautious and prudent they must be – how cautious, that they did not take into their fellowship such persons whose characters would not bear the strictest examination. He found that they were very cautious how they received a slave. (Hear.)

The laws of the several American States were such as to deprive the master of the privilege of emancipating his slaves. He believed that justice had no fellowship with injustice, that liberty could have no love for Slavery; and, therefore, no countenance should be given to those who united with slaveholders. There was not a single State in the American Union out of which a slave could not be taken by his master, by taking him across Mason and Dixon's line.[149] There was not, he would say, any individual who might not emancipate his slave; if anyone wanted to palm another opinion respecting the matter upon them, let them tell him, that they knew better. It had been said by some, that, when the slaveholder emancipated his slave, he became responsible for his maintenance; that was not true – those gentlemen who said so ought to know better – the facts were all on the other side; for the slaveholder, when he freed his slave, had nothing more to do with him whatever. Canada was open for them; and they might depend upon it they never would become chargeable upon Brother Jonathan. (Loud cheers.) Truth did not need many arguments – they had seldom to enter into long metaphysical details to assert it. They all felt that Slavery was wrong; they felt differently, when the word Slavery was mentioned, from the way in which they felt when liberty was mentioned. (Cheers.) Even among slaveholders themselves, the term freedom was musical. They loved the sound of the name of liberty. But, when it was mentioned to them in the presence of their slaves, they were stung to the very quick by it; and became, in the exercise of their barbarous cruelties, more like demons than men. (Hear, hear, and cheers.) Freedom had something sweet about it to the human heart – their very hearts leaped up at the name of freedom – (renewed cheers) – while they shrunk at the very name of slavery. They knew that the slaveholders were doing evil, and that continually. They knew that such could not be followers of the meek and lowly Jesus Christ. It was monstrous to say that they were Christian slaveholders. They might just every bit as well talk about sober drunkards. Did not the lash which was laid on his back by a Christian hand hurt him as well as that which he felt from the hand of one who made no profession of Christianity? He told them – and he uttered the words then as he had in his narrative – that, next to being a slave at all, he would regard it to be the greatest possible calamity to be the slave of a religious slaveholder. (Hear.) That he spoke of was no mere theory; he had had experience with respect to the fact. The slaveholder was a degraded being – a man stamped originally with the image of God, but which, in his person, became perverted. In him the image of God was lost. He was a fallen angel, sunk among demons. (Hear, hear, and cheers.) Men were said to be converted; but they were slaveholders, and that which they called religion was in them turned into the gall of bitterness. They were slaveholders, and women-whippers before conversion, as they called it. After conversion, backed up by their native cruelty, they were aided by the additional stimulant of religion; and their barbarities, so far from being put a stop to, were increased tenfold. (Hear, hear.) Let no man, therefore, say that it was a good thing to have religious slaveholders. (Hear, hear, and cheers.)

He would now call their attention to the doings of one or two of the churches in America. A Baptist brother had requested him to state to the meeting what the Baptist Church was doing to uphold Slavery. They were aware that the Baptist Church was congregational – that was, that each church was independent of the other. They met, however, triennially (as we understood Mr. Douglass to say) for the purpose of counselling as to the best means of spreading the Gospel among the heathen. At the meeting before the last, held in Baltimore, the Rev. Dr. Johnston, of South Carolina, presided; and what did they think were the views of this Rev. Doctor as to the duty of Christians, with regard to Slavery? – Why, at that meeting, he said, when any institution, such as Slavery, became established by law, in any country, every Christian was right in upholding it. (Cries of "Oh, Oh!") But they need not be surprised at his thus expressing himself, for he was a man-stealer, the Secretary to the meeting was a man-stealer, and the other officers were thieves. There was one noble-minded man, the Rev. Mr. Gallusha, on the Committee, who was a friend of abolition, one of the most eloquent of the delegates at the World's Convention, and who departed this life a few months since. That Christian man desired to see Slavery, which he denounced as a sin against God, abolished; and what was the consequence? Why, his friends on the Committee had him struck off, and that for no other offence than because he hated Slavery. He was a talented man – one of the brightest stars in connection with the Baptist congregations of America; – he was a successful minister, and was an honor to the mission, except, indeed, that he was accustomed to denounce Slavery as a sin, and the slaveholder as a sinner.

The Rev. Lewis Boles said,[150] there was a vast amount of unknown sin among their brethren in the South, for they were slaveholders. His friends did not associate with the pickpocket, with the cow-stealer, or the thief; but they did much worse – they associated with the murderer, not the murderer of the body, only, but the murderer of the soul. (Hear.) He repeated they were murderers of the soul, for they shut out from it the light of God's truth. (Hear, hear.) They would dethrone the Almighty from the hearts of the people, and compel them to worship man rather than God. (Hear, hear, hear.)

Mr. Douglass then read an advertisement, offering the property of a certain Baptist Doctor of Divinity, in the South, for sale. Among the items mentioned in the advertisement were, a library of works, chiefly theological; several mules; and a number of slaves. There, said Mr. Douglass, they had man associated in the old way: a library, chiefly theological, the property of a Doctor of Divinity; several mules, and a number of slaves! (Cries of "Oh, Oh!") These things, occurring in a Christian country, should make people hang their heads, and weep over such a man as this Doctor of Divinity; yet, that man was reckoned among the pious of the earth, and would have been received by the Baptists of Belfast, a few years ago, as a good Christian minister. He would not be so received now, he (Mr. Douglass) would venture to say. – (Cries of "No, no.") But that was not all, for there they had them setting aside the marriage state, by separating the husband from the wife, and selling them to different masters. There they had them entering into the trade of raising slaves, as the people of this country would raise cattle for the Smithfield market; and they had ministers of the Gospel, too, who could tear the husband from the wife, and send him away to the most distant market to dispose of him, – and these men wished their slaves, who were placed in such a position, to marry again.

One of these ministers (as we understood Mr. Douglass to say) sent a query to a brother minister, as to whether a man and his wife, separated as he (Mr. Douglass) had described, ought to marry again? and the answer given was, that when they were so separated, in the sight of God, they should be viewed as if they were dead, and by their marrying again, they would be saved from many temptations. (Cries of "Oh, oh!") There they had the Baptists of America sanctioning a wholesale system of adultery and concubinage, and yet calling themselves Christians! He would not proceed further with the Baptist Church. The Rev. Dr. Sharpe,[151] who was over here a few months ago, entertained similar views, with regard to Slavery, to those entertained by Dr. Chalmers, and other eminent men of the Free Church of Scotland; in his opinion, it was an evil that should be abolished; but its existence should not prevent persons or churches from holding Christian communion with each other. (Hear.) He knew he got not a little of the money which supported him from the slaveholders, and, therefore, he says, "Ministers are like other people, they feel they must live." (Laughter.)

George Bradburn, of America, speaking with a minister on the subject of Slavery, in connection with his Church, urged him to repudiate those who had anything to do with it. "You forget," said the minister, "that we are dependent upon our congregations for support; and we must live." "I deny the premises," said George, "I deny that any man should live, unless he live honestly." (Hear, and cheers.) The Ministers of the American churches felt that they must live; they never made a greater mistake, than to say they must live by such means as those by which they did live. What made it necessary that they should live by the blood of their fellow-man; for, was not the food they eat, were not the watches in their pockets, and the coats on their backs bought with the price of blood? (Hear, hear.) They considered, that if the slaveholders gave up their slaves, they would not be paid their salaries. – He (Mr. Douglass) did not believe that would be the case – (Hear, hear, hear) – for he knew that the ministers were better paid where there were no slaves – where freemen were the paymasters. (Hear.) But he wanted to say a few words with regard to the Congregational denomination, or Independents, as they were called here. – They were mostly to be found in the Northern States. But the way in which they were implicated in the crime of Slavery was the same as that in which the Free Church of Scotland was implicated. A large number in the New England States had taken a good stand as to Slavery; but the leading ministers and the leading papers all took the side of Slavery. And was it not a singular fact, that the farther they went

289

up, the higher grades of ecclesiastical officers were almost invariably to be found the most ardent defenders of the slaveholder; while the brethren that were below them, were on the side of humanity and Christianity? It was so, even in the days of our Saviour. They read of a man that fell among thieves, and was wounded, and left on the road-side, half dead; that a Priest, high in ecclesiastical distinction was journeying along the road where the man was lying; and that he passed by without noticing him; that a Levite came up after, who adopted a middle course. He went and looked on the wounded man, – and no doubt there was a struggle in his breast between humanity and office; the latter, however, prevailed, and he followed the footsteps of his illustrious predecessor, – and he [Mr. Douglass] was sorry it turned out that he was willing to follow the Priest, rather than to interfere in the cause of humanity. But they read of another who was journeying the same way, not of the school of the Priesthood, but rather a worshipper in what they believed in a wrong place – a Samaritan; and, when he heard the groans of the poor man, he had compassion upon him, bound up his wounds, pouring in oil and wine, set him on his own beast, and took him to an inn; gave the host two pence, and told him to take care of him, and that whatever he spent more, when he returned he would repay him. So it was even in Belfast; the people were on the side of the slave, – there would be no difficulty in getting from them an expression of their feelings in favor of the slave, – [Hear] – it was only in the higher or upper classes – the class of "Civis" – [alluding to a writer in *The Banner*.] that such a difficulty would arise. The leading Doctors of Divinity in America, and the Professors in the Colleges, were in favor of Slavery. There was Professor Stewart, of the Andover Seminary,[152] one of the first Biblical schools in New England – that gentleman had committed to him the instruction of the ministers of a large portion of the Congregational denominations, and he was an advocate for Slavery. The Rev. Dr. Fisk,[153] who some time ago, was welcomed by the Methodist Church, in Dublin, though they had shut him [Mr. Douglass] out, – this Doctor Fisk became uneasy, when he heard it said that Slavery was a sin, and, not willing to commit himself on the question, wished to have the opinion of Doctor Stewart on the subject. This man, who would have said that sheep-stealing was a sin, and would have decided so at once, had to consult a learned Doctor as to whether man-stealing was a sin – [Hear, hear] – but, then, they knew that it was necessary that he should live, and he could not do so, independent of his congregation. [Laughter.] Doctor Stewart sent him a reply, in which he referred to the case of Onesimus,[154] whom he stated Paul had sent back to Philemon for life. He [Mr. Douglass] would be glad to know where Dr. Stewart learned that Onesimus was sent back into Slavery for life; was it, he would ask, from that law? If it was he [Mr. Douglass] would tell him, that Jewish slavery was not for life; there was no such thing known among the Jews as slavery for life, except it was desired on the part of the servant himself. What did the Apostle say himself? He said, he sent back Onesimus greater than a servant; and told Philemon to receive him as he would receive him, Paul; not as a slave, who could be sold in the market, but as a brother beloved. After alluding to the case of a Mr. Jonathan Walker,[155] and a Mr. Torrey,[156] who were branded and cast into prison, for aiding some slaves to escape; and to the case of John L. Brown, who was sentenced to be executed for a similar offence against American law, but which sentence the voice of Great Britain prevented from being carried into effect, he observed, with regard to Brown it was said, there stood Brown, and there stood the law? and did not Brown know that he was violating the law? He [Mr. Douglass] would answer that Daniel knew he was breaking the law, when he would not worship as he was desired – [hear, hear] – and so did Shadrach, Meshach, and Abednego, when they refused to worship the golden image which the King had set up. He was sometimes led to think, that if some of the clergymen of the present day had been their advisers, they would have advised them to bow down, but not to worship the image; they would have told them that they had to live, that they should be very cautious, being the only ministers among the heathen; that if they lost their lives there would be no Minister of the Lord among them, and that then they would be left in the dark, to grope their own way. [Hear.] Such was the kind of wisdom they saw displayed by the Free Church of Scotland; but God was confounding the wisdom of the crafty, he was exposing the sophism of the worldly. He hoped the unanimous cry of the people of Belfast, to the Free Church of Scotland, and all the other churches, would be, "Have no communion with the American slaveholder;" and that the next thing the Free Church should do would be to send back the blood-stained money which they had received. That was the only safe course. They should tell the Americans that they saw the slave at their feet, they saw him dying, and divested of every religious opportunity; and that, therefore, they could not have fellowship with them; that they would gladly do so, but that the blood of the slaves forbade them to do so. If they would do this, they would give Slavery a blow that it would stagger under, among a large class of religionists in America. Mr. Douglass then resumed his seat, loudly cheered.

After a few observations from Mr. Gibson and Mr. Stanfield, Mr. Kier observed, that he was the person who had requested Mr. Douglass to state what connection the Baptist churches of America had with Slavery. Mr. Kier then read a remonstrance, on the subject, from the Baptists of Belfast, to their brethren in America.

Mr. Rose read a like document from the Independents of Belfast to their brethren in America; after which the Rev. Isaac Nelson read a reply from the Belfast Anti-Slavery Committee, to a letter which appeared in a contemporary newspaper, signed "Civis."

The thanks of the meeting were then moved to Mr. Standfield and Lieutenant Calder, the Secretaries of the Belfast Anti-Slavery Society, for their active exertions in the good cause.

Mr. Gibson then left the Chair; when, the Apostolic benediction having been pronounced by Dr. Paul, the meeting separated.

Advertisement
Publication: *Belfast News-Letter*
Date of Publication: Friday 26 December 1845
Title: 'Lecture this day'.

The Fugitive slave
Mr Frederick Douglass will give his SIXTH LECTURE ON AMERICAN SLAVERY
IN THE Presbyterian Church, Donegall-Street
this day at 12 o clock, Noon
John Clarke Esq. will preside
Friday Morning, 26 December 1845.

Anti-Slavery Meeting
Lecturer: Frederick Douglass
Date of Lecture: Friday, 26 December 1845
Location: Presbyterian Church, Donegall Street
Publication: *Banner of Ulster*
Date of Publication: Tuesday, 30 December 1845
Title: 'Anti Slavery Meeting – Mr Douglass's address'.

[from our reporter.] On Friday, twelve o'clock, Mr. Douglass delivered another address on American slavery, in the Rev. Mr. Nelson's Church, Donegall Street – John Clarke, Esq., in the chair. The lecturer read extracts from the laws of Louisiana, Alabama, Georgia, and other slave holding States, to show how much their enactments tended to perpetuate slavery, and render the condition of its unfortunate victims deplorable in the extreme. After commenting on what he had read, at some length, on the suggestion of Mr. Standfield, he resumed his seat for short interval.

Mr. Standfield [sic] improved the opportunity thus afforded him, to recur the charge brought by him and others against the *Banner of Ulster*, saying, among other things, that he thought those who had put forward 'Civis', *to damage the anti-slavery cause*, had, instead of injuring it, done it material benefit. After the learned gentleman had concluded,

Rev. Isaac Nelson rose and stated, that he been requested by the *Banner* of that day to retract the charge of unfairness which he had made against that journal, at their former meeting, but this he was not prepared to do. He then related what appeared to him to be the real circumstances connected with the non-appearance of the reply to 'Civis' in last Tuesday's number of the *Banner*, in order to justify his charge, which he again repeated, that foul play had been used towards the Anti-slavery Society, or those who acted for them, by the Editor of the *Banner*, Mr. Nelson was about proceed to some other subject, when

Your Reporter, anxious that the meeting should be supplied with at least the materials for coming to a right decision on the subject, appealed to the chairman, and requested that he would allow the explanation given in Tuesday's *Banner* to go before the meeting. Your Reporter, as one of the audience, was possessed of a general right to make that request, and as connected with the establishment against which charge of unfairness had been made, it was peculiarly his right to rise and endeavour calmly to repel, by a statement of facts, the accusation which had been thus publicly brought.

The Chairman thought different, and in a tone such as a magistrate would use towards a culprit, announced that they had met there for the specific purpose of hearing a lecture from Mr. Douglass, and this being the case, he would not permit any squabbling about the *Banner* to go on there.

Your Reporter, not wishing to appear disrespectful in contesting this decision, did not insist, and immediately after withdrew from the meeting, asking himself the following question: – How did it happen that the Chairman did not recollect when Mr. Standfield commenced, or, at least, before Mr. Nelson concluded, the specific purpose for which the meeting was called. And thinking of one of Aesop's stories about the man who said he could take such mighty jump, were he only at the Island of Rhodes; but, when asked to show his agility at home, could do no better than his neighbours, for all his boasting.

Anti-Slavery Meeting
Lecturer: Frederick Douglass
Date of Lecture: Friday, 26 December 1845
Location: Presbyterian Church, Donegall-street
Publication: *Belfast Vindicator*
Date of Publication: Wednesday, 31 December 1845
Title: 'Anti-Slavery Meeting'.

On Friday last, at twelve o'clock, Mr. Douglass delivered a long and very interesting address on American slavery, in the Rev. Mr. Nelson's Church, Donegall-street – John Clarke, Esq., in the chair. We were much pleased with the lecturer's manner throughout his brilliant discourse. His style is vigorous, and he has evidently a thorough knowledge of his subject – two very important requisites in a public speaker. The lecturer denounced, in withering language, the base conduct of those professing ministers of religion who, in America, uphold the villainous traffic in human flesh, which is there established by law. He showed how some of these ministers, themselves slaveholders, were actually guilty of whipping their helpless victims to death. He called on the Free Kirk to send back the blood-money of the slaves which she had received from America; contrasted her conduct with that of O'Connell, who had never, on any occasion omitted to denounce slavery – who had refused to let money into the Association from slaveholders, and concluded a most impassioned burst of eloquence, declaring that the conduct of the Liberator was 'as high above that of the Free Church as heaven was above earth.'

Advertisement
Publication: *Belfast Commercial Chronicle*
Date of Publication: Monday, 29 December 1845

This Evening.
Anti-Slavery Lecture in Lisburn.

The Fugitive Slave, Mr Frederick Douglass, will give a lecture on American Slavery, in the Presbyterian Church in Lisburn, on this (Monday) evening, at seven o'clock.

Anti-Slavery Meeting
Lecturer: Frederick Douglass
Date of Lecture: Monday, 29 December 1845
Location: Presbyterian Meeting-house, Lisburn
Publication: *Northern Whig*
Date of Publication: Thursday, 1 January 1846
No Title.

Mr. Douglass, the fugitive slave, delivered a lecture, on the horrors of slavery, in the Presbyterian Meeting-house, Lisburn, on Monday, to a large and respectable audience.

Anti-Slavery Meeting
Lecturer: Frederick Douglass
Date of Lecture: Monday, 29 December 1845
Location: Presbyterian Meeting-house, Lisburn
Publication: *Belfast Commercial Chronicle*
Date of Publication: Wednesday, 31 December 1845
Title: 'American Slavery. Lecture in Lisburn'.

Mr. Douglass, who is now well known to our readers as a most determined opponent of slavery, delivered a lecture on that infamous system, as it exists in America, in the Presbyterian Church, Lisburn,[157] on Monday, to a large and highly-respectable audience, who gave, as the lecturer proceeded, the most decided proof of their abhorrence of slavery, and their disgust at the conduct of slaveholders.

At seven o'clock, on the motion Mr. Robert M'Clure, the Rev. Alex Henderson, the Minister of the Church, took the chair, and after part of the 72nd Psalm had been sung, the Chairman made a suitable prayer, and then proceeded to say that he felt very much gratified at seeing so many present on so interesting an occasion. He trusted that they had a heart to feel for the oppressed, and that they would do all in their power to have the wrongs of those who were held in cruel bondage redressed. In opposing slavery in America there was much to contend against, and many difficulties to be overcome, but they were not greater than those against which Wilberforce, Clarkson, and others successfully contended, and they must not therefore be discouraged, nor cease to raise their voice in remonstrance, until the American slaveholder should be compelled, by the force of truth, to let the slave free.

Mr. Standfield then rose to introduce Mr. Douglass, and, before doing so, took occasion to speak of what the gentleman was doing for the freedom of his race, and, also, of the good that was sure to follow the agitation of the question in this country. The agitation of the question had been the means of banishing slavery from the East and West Indies, and Britain had been freed from the stain which was so long upon her; and now, though the sun never set on her widely-extended dominions, every man who touched her soil in every clime was a freeman. (Applause.) Mr. Standfield then alluded to the connexion of the Churches in America with slavery, and said they were the bulwarks which supported and kept it in existence; and, having dwelt forcibly on the duty of the various denominations in this country, and what was to be expected from their bearing a faithful testimony against the sin of the American Churches, he concluded a very eloquent address by introducing Mr. Douglass to the meeting. Mr. Standfield's remarks had, on two or three occasions, called forth applause from the audience and, after he sat down, the Chairman rose, and said he would take it as a favour if the meeting refrained from giving expression to their feelings by applause, as he did not consider such marks of approbation becoming in the house of God.

Mr. Douglass then came forward, and, in his usual eloquent and impressive manner, depicted slavery as he had witnessed it, and detailed the support which it received from churches called by the name of Christian, in a speech which occupied nearly an hour and a-half in the delivery. On several occasions, he held up the hideous monster of slavery in its naked deformity to the gaze of the audience, their indignation was such, that the request of the Chairman was, to a certain extent, disregarded, and expression was given to their feelings of disgust by suppressed applause. There has been so much respecting American slavery in our columns of late, in our reports of Mr. Douglass's lectures in this town, that we do not think it necessary to report, at length, his speech on this occasion, especially as only one lecture was to be delivered in Lisburn. He took a general view of the subject, and, in doing so, said very little that has not already appeared in our paper. After a few remarks on the gratification it gave him to see so large and respectable an audience, he proceeded to state that his object in visiting this country was to give accurate information regarding slavery as it existed in his native country, in order that he might excite sympathy for the oppressed, and procure the co-operation of the lovers of freedom on this side of the Atlantic for its suppression. Having answered most satisfactorily some objections made to the agitation of the question by persons in this country, as well as in America, he said, because the slaveholder did not like his evil deeds shown forth in England, he delighted to expose them; for whatever the slaveholder loved, he hated – and whatever the slaveholder hated, he loved. The slaveholder's deeds were evil, and could not bear the light of truth, and therefore they wished the world to be kept in ignorance regarding their horrible doings, and for that very reason he wished to expose them, in order that they might be execrated by all good men. Slaveholders, he said, were often in the habit of visiting this country, and he wished to make the people so well acquainted with their wickedness, that they would be shunned, not only by every Christian man, but, by every lover of freedom. He wanted to have the people prepared to give them that reception which slaveholders should meet with on account of their villainy. He had been asked, did not slaveholders profess to be good Christians? Did they not support bible societies and missionary societies? They certainly did support these and professed to be good Christians, but their religion was hypocrisy. The sound of the church bell and the sound of the auctioneer's bell announcing the sale of the bodies and souls of men, chimed in together – were not such doings a mockery of religion? While Mr. Douglass was pointing out the inconsistency of professors of religion in America, loud cries of "shame, shame," were to be heard from every quarter of the house, and, on hearing it, he said it did him good to elicit from them that expression of feeling. The bloody-minded men, who dared to take the name of the meek and lowly Saviour upon their lips, would receive no countenance from the assembly he was then addressing. They had not so learned from Christ. The Americans did not like to have slavery exposed in Great Britain, for, though they might affect to despise her, she was the model they copied after. When they would read his speeches, and hear how the people flocked to hear him wherever he went, they would feel deeply, and their conscience would smite them. Several of the lectures which he had delivered since he came to Ireland, had been published in the newspapers and had found their way against the western breeze, and been copied into American papers which were sent to him by friends. This showed the advantage of which the press could be to the slave.

As soon as Mr Douglass had resumed his seat, Mr. Standfield rose, and after some remarks, introduced the Rev. Mr. Buffin [sic], an American minister, who had been acquainted with Mr. Douglass from the time that he first began to lecture on slavery in America.

Mr. Buffin bore testimony to the good which had been done by the lectures of Mr. Douglass, and then spoke of what he knew of slavery, which went to confirm all that has been said against it.

After Mr. Standfield had stated that Mr. Douglass would lecture in the Methodist chapel, Donegall place, on Thursday evening, and that a public breakfast would be given to him on Tuesday morning next, a vote of thanks was passed to the chairman, and the benediction having been pronounced, the meeting separated.

Anti-Slavery Meeting
Lecturer: Frederick Douglass
Date of Lecture: Monday, 29 December 1845
Location: Presbyterian Church, Lisburn
Publication: *Belfast News-Letter*
Date of Publication: Friday, 2 January 1846
Title: 'American Slavery. Meeting in Lisburn'.

Mr Frederick Douglass, the eloquent lecturer on slavery, delivered an address on Monday evening in the Presbyterian Church, Lisburn, to a large and highly respectable audience. At seven o'clock, the Rev. Alex Henderson took the chair, and after a part of the 72nd Psalm had been sung and a suitable prayer offered by the Chairman, the Rev. gentleman proceeded to address the assembly. After expressing his gratification at seeing so many present on such an interesting occasion, he said, he trusted they had a heart to feel for the oppressed, and they would do all in their power to have the wrongs of those who were held in cruel bondage readdressed. In opposing slavery in America there was much to contend against, and many difficulties to be overcome, but they were not greater than those that Wilberforce, Clarkson and others successfully contended. And they must not, therefore, be discouraged, or cease to raise their voice in remonstrance, until the slave-holders shall be compelled, by force of truth, to let the slave go free.

Mr Standfield of Belfast then rose to introduce Mr. Douglass and, in doing so, took occasion to speak of what that gentleman was doing for the freedom of his race, and also to the good which was sure to follow the agitation of the question in this country.

Mr. Douglass, in a speech of great length, and in his usual eloquent and impressive manner, depicted slavery as he had witnessed it, and depicted the support it received from the churches "called by the name Christian". We have already so fully reported Mr Douglass's lectures in this town that we do not think it necessary to publish his speech on this occasion. When Mr Douglass had resumed his seat, Mr Standfield introduced the Rev. Mr Buffin [sic], an American minister who had been acquainted with Mr Douglass from the time that he first began to lecture on slavery in America. Mr Buffin then addressed the meeting, and bore testimony to the good that had been done by the lectures of Mr Douglass, and spoke of what he knew of slavery, which went to confirm all that had been said against it.

After Mr Standfield stated that a public breakfast would be given to Mr Douglass on Tuesday morning next, a vote of thanks was passed to the chairman, and the benediction had been pronounced, the meeting separated.

Temperance Meeting
Lecturer: Frederick Douglass
Date of Meeting: Wednesday, 31 December 1845
Location: Holywood, Co. Down
Publication: *Northern Whig*
Date of Publication: Thursday, 1 January 1846
Title: 'Holywood Total Abstinence Society'.

Mr Frederick Douglass, the fugitive slave, who is the advocate of total abstinence, as well as the abolition of slavery, kindly attended the fourth anniversary soiree of this Society, which was held on Wednesday evening, 31st ult. After due honour had been paid to 'the cup that cheers, but not inebriates', Dr McKittrick was called to the Chair. Having briefly alluded to the continued interest which the respectable portion of the community takes in the progress of the Society, he shewed the advantage of the tea party, in bringing all classes together for mutual improvement, reminded the ladies of the power of female influence, of their numerously signed petition to the Queen, on a former occasion, for the abolition of west India slavery, and suggested a remonstrance to the ladies of America, from the Holywood ladies, in the hope that such a movement might become general and give an impetus to the abolition cause. The Rev. C. J. McAlister then gave an account of the progress of the Society during the year. The Chairman said he would read the sentiment to which Mr Douglass was to speak, when he would have the pleasure of introducing that talented and eloquent stranger to the company. 'Freedom for the Mind and Body' – may the time speedily arrive when society shall be freed from the drinking customs by which men's best faculties and highest interests are enthralled, and then the word *slave* shall no longer be known in the vocabulary of professing Christians.

Mr Douglass was received with universal and continued applause. In the course of his address, he drew a striking parallel between the power exercised over the slave by his master, and that exercised over the drunkard by his bottle. He also alluded to the indifference of many Ministers to the teetotal cause. He then gave a very gratifying statement of the progress of tee-totalism in the New England states, mentioning several in which there was not a rum shop to be found. He attributed his heath and ability to undergo the various and important duties in which he was engaged to the practice of tee-totalism. He also made some striking statements on slavery. Mr Buffum, who is also an abolitionist and total abstainer for thirteen years, spoke of the progress and success of the Washingtonians in promoting temperance in America, and also on the subject of American slavery.

The Rev. Jacob Alexander, in a powerful and argumentative speech exposed the absurdity of the old temperance advocates monopolizing the name of Christian temperance, and their inconsistency in denouncing distilled spirit when mixed with pure water, while they continued drinking it themselves, as it was mixed in all the wines used in these countries. The next sentiment was 'Education', by which the humbler classes will be elevated, and all will better understand their duties, and the principles which contribute to the health and happiness of mankind. The Rev. H. Henderson was present, and prepared to speak on this sentiment, but, on account of the lateness of the hour, deferred it to another occasion, to give way to Mr Mulvenna, who had composed a poetical welcome and address to Mr Douglass. The next sentiment was 'The philanthropic efforts of the age, and may their happy results be speedily felt in the general improvement of society'. Mr Mulvenna spoke to this sentiment and, in alluding to the abolition of slavery, delivered in a very eloquent style, the address above alluded to, which was much applauded. During the evening several anthems were sung, by a choir instructed in the Hullah system,[158] by which tee-totalism was the means of introduction into Holywood. – *A Correspondent.*

Temperance Meeting
Lecturer: Frederick Douglass
Date of Lecture: Wednesday, 31 December 1845
Location: Holywood, Co. Down
Publication: *Belfast News-Letter*
Date of Publication: Tuesday, 6 January 1846
Title: 'Holywood Total Abstinence Society'.

Mr Frederick Douglass, the fugitive slave, who is the advocate of total abstinence as well as the abolition of slavery, very kindly attended the fourth anniversary soiree of this society, which was held on Wednesday evening, 31st ult.[159] Doctor McKittrick was called to the chair. We have not a space for a report of the proceedings.

Anti-Slavery Meeting
Lecturer: Frederick Douglass
Date of Lecture: Thursday, 1 January 1846
Publication: *Belfast Commercial Chronicle*
Date of Publication: Monday, 5 January 1846
Title: 'Anti-Slavery Society'.

On Thursday evening, another meeting of the friends of this society took place in the Methodist Meeting-house in Donegall Place. The Reverend James Griffin in the chair.

Mr. Standfield introduced Mr. Buffin [sic] and Mr. F. Douglass to the meeting. The Rev. Chairman briefly addressed the audience and expressed for himself and his congregation his abhorrence for slavery.

Mr. Buffin, in a plain and gentlemanly style, described the progress of the Society in the United States and the difficulties it had to contend with. The members were a few years ago mobbed at their meetings, but the march of intelligence on the subject had proceeded so well that they could now count thousands, for one who were formerly with them, and the cause was every day gaining friends and supporters. Yet much was to be done to counteract the odious system of slavery, and they looked to Britain to strengthen their hands. He bore ample testimony to his friend and neighbour, Mr Frederick Douglass; his early struggles for liberty – the hurdles and mortifications he had encountered – and how well he had overcome them all. Mr. Buffin, after many observations, concluded by exhibiting, for the execration the audience, the instruments of torture in common use among the slave-holders. The first was an iron collar with three long spikes thrown out from it, which prevented the slave from laying his head on a pillow, if he had one. The collar now shown had been taken from a young female slave, who had contrived to escape by concealing herself in the hold of a vessel, during a long voyage, till the ship got out of the cursed atmosphere of slavery; when taken from the girl's neck, some of the skin and hair were still attached to it. He next showed the shackles used when slaves were being conveyed from one part of the country to another; also a pair of handcuffs which had been put on a runaway slave by two slave-traders, who were conveying him back to slavery; the slave, however, observing on the road a sharp projecting rock, seized the opportunity, struck his fetters against it and broke free – although he at the same time fractured the wrist of his left arm. One of the slaveholders ran upon him to seize him, but the slave drew from his breast and stabbed him, though not mortally; the other coward wisely declined to encounter him, and so he escaped. In the town in which he lived he was told a runaway slave had come but that he was greatly burned. He (Mr. B.) sent for him, and would, never, while he lived, forget the awful impression the spectacle presented. The slave had run away with his wife and children into the Free States, and was endeavouring to support himself and his children by his labour. He was seized and carried back into slavery and in order to extort from him the secret of where his wife and family were, they stripped the poor man, and, with a red hot iron, ran it over his left arm, from his shoulder to the wrist, three times. He never saw anything like it. The poor creature, for a long time, lost the power of his left side, and probably would never recover. Mr B. then exhibited the cow-skin instrument of torture. When he first had it, it was covered with blood. A "thrill of horror" ran through the vast assembly on the exhibition of these accused instruments.

Mr F. Douglass then commenced his lecture on slavery, and depicted its horrors in animated and eloquent terms. And now, said Mr Douglass, I have something to say about Episcopalians. [Mr. Standfield called out "Don't spare them"). "Never fear me" said Mr. D. There are not less than 7,000 slaves held by high Episcopalians. They had not done their duty. There are six Methodist Episcopalian bishops in America, but it of course happens that one bishop must sometimes necessarily rule over both the slave and the Free States. Bishop Andrews married a wife, and obtained some slaves with her. It was all very well when in his duty he was visiting the southern States, but when he went north it was another thing. There, there was at least some shyness about the bishop being a slaveholder, and the congregated clergy, after three days earnest deliberation, came reluctantly to the conclusion that it would be right for Bishop Andrews, before ministering in the north, to get rid of this *impediment*. Many names have been given to slavery, but this was the first time that the horrid sin was characterised by the gentle appellation of im-pe-di-ment. In former lectures he had shown how many religionists of different persuasions were implicated in the injustice of slavery; he now described how far the good and worthy Society of Quakers were concerned in maintaining the system. They were, it was true, the earliest opponents of slavery; but they did not co-operate fully with the abolitionists, and, for political purposes, lent their powerful influence in the election of Clay[160] – a slaveholder, and worse – and received him to the seat of honour in their meeting-house, while the poor were shoved into the outer part the house – they were as the selvage of the web – like a black border round the extremity of the congregation. The Quakers were, nevertheless, the slaves' earliest friends, when their friends were fewer than now. When the slave escaped to the Free States, he anxiously sought for the broad brim and drab coat, in whom he was sure to find a friend in need. – On one occasion, when several slaves, by a strong impulse, ran off to get into freedom, they found, to their horror, that the slaveholders, with horses and hounds, were on their track. In this extremity, they applied to a Quaker near one of the border towns, and told him their fears. By stringent laws, great penalties are imposed on any one who would give a runaway slave a crust of bread or even a drink of water. The good Quaker, however, told the poor slaves to move on as fast they could, and he would try what he could for them. In a very short time afterwards, the man-stealers came pressing on, hot foot, and there they saw Jonathan, with all his might and main, hammering up his large barn. This was just what the slave-dealers wanted, for they were now sure that the slaves were concealed in the barn. They boisterously demanded their *niggers*. Jonathan told them to at least be civil and quiet, but nothing would satisfy them except their *niggers*. They threatened to break open the door. The Quaker asked them softly if they had a search-warrant from a magistrate? They had none. He told them to take care what they were about. So, thinking the runaways were safely nailed up in the barn, they left some of their party on the watch, and away they went for a search-warrant. It was several hours before they obtained it, and when they returned, and impatiently broke open the barn, nothing but empty darkness was there; so the poor slaves got clear off to a Free State. Mr. Douglass related, in capital style, many such occurrences, and concluded by calling upon the English, Scotch, and Irish people to aid the Society by abolishing for ever the inhuman system slavery.

The Rev. Isaac Nelson next addressed the meeting, and animadverted the conduct of the *Banner* of Tuesday, respecting a reply to an article signed Civis, which reply, he alleged, had been treated with neglect.

Afterwards the reporter of the *Banner* rose, and endeavoured to obtain a hearing, but the sense of the audience was against him, and he was obliged to desist and leave the meeting.

Some announcements were made respecting a public breakfast, intended for Tuesday next, to Mr. Douglass; when thanks were voted to the Chairman, and the meeting separated.

Anti-Slavery Meeting
Lecturer: Frederick Douglass
Date of Lecture: Thursday, 1 January 1846
Location: Primitive Wesleyan Church, Donegal Place
Publication: *Banner of Ulster*
Friday: Friday, 2 January 1846
Title: 'Anti-Slavery Meeting. Mr Douglass's Address'.

From Our Reporter.

Last evening, Mr. Douglass delivered another address on the subject of American slavery, in the Primitive Wesleyan Church, Donegall Place. The attendance was not large. After some excellent observations had been made by an American gentleman, appropriate to the occasion.

Mr. Douglass rose and addressed the meeting with his usual force and eloquence; and I deeply regret that the impression which his speech was calculated to make on the audience was marred by the shameful occurrences which followed. After he had concluded.

The Rev. Isaac Nelson rose, and commented at some length on the remarks made upon him in the *Banner of Ulster* of Tuesday.

301

When he commenced, the first impulse which I felt was to apply the same rule to him which was applied by the Chairman of a former anti-slavery meeting to me. 'That this meeting was called for the specific purpose of hearing a lecture from Mr. Douglass, and that no squabbling about the *Banner* would be allowed to take place.' I did not do this, however, but waited till the reverend gentleman concluded. In the course of his remarks he complained particularly of being accused in this paper of Tuesday of slandering the Free Church, when he only spoke what was the truth concerning that body; and being called a bearer of false witness when he charged the *Banner* with acting unfairly in the way in which they had treated the reply to Civis. The Rev. gentleman went on at some length, the whole scope and tendency of his remarks being intended to show that he had been the victim of foul play on the part of the *Banner*, not only in regard to the reply to Civis, but in reference to an article which he had written in his own defence in answer to the attacks made upon him in Tuesday's *Banner*. He had tendered his reply at the office of this paper, and it could not be received on account of the Editor's absence in Scotland. Such treatment was cruel in the extreme. He could not get his reply published in any of the papers; but would seek fair play, and he believed, too, that he would get it from the inhabitants of Belfast. When Mr. Nelson had sat down, I arose and addressed the Chairman, but that functionary remained adder-deaf. As I was resolved that he, and those who acted with him, should give a distinct aye or no to my request to be heard, I went upon the platform.

Mr. Nelson again arose, and was followed by Mr. Standfield, the very obvious design of both of these gentlemen being to defeat my intention of gaining a hearing, and, at the same time, save themselves from the shame of doing so by a deliberate act. In the meantime, the Chairman (one of the clergymen who officiate in the church where the meeting was held), said in *sotto voco* something about the arrangements of the committee being such as to prevent me from being heard, and Mr. Nelson chimed in the same tone, and to the same effect. Mr. Standfield *did* conclude at last, and I then put it distinctly to the Chairman whether I should be heard or not. He answered in the negative; and Mr. Nelson, as if to rivet the resolution more firmly, shouted out that the reporter of the *Banner* had no business to speak to the meeting, and that I had the paper in which to reply, if I wished to do so. I appealed from the decision of the Chairman and his supporters to the meeting, asking, repeatedly, 'in the name of truth and justice,' to be heard for a little in reply to the remarks made by Mr. Nelson, but the majority of the audience signified their disapprobation. Cries of 'Hear the *Banner*' rose from different parts of the church, and some cheers mingled with the storm of hisses, and other kindred and unanswerable arguments.

I left the meeting with a feeling of loathing which I cannot express. I have been in public meetings in a great many parts of the three kingdoms; but I never saw, far less experienced, injustice palpable and tyranny so gross as at the anti-slavery meeting last night, presided over by a minister. The parties who led the way in committing it knew well I had a few facts in my possession, the statement of which would have fastened the charge of foul play upon the real culprits; and, therefore, to shield themselves as they thought from the effects of one act of injustice, they perpetrated another. If men who act thus were the only advocates of the slave, his condition would be, indeed, hopeless.

Anti-Slavery Meeting
Lecturer: Frederick Douglass
Date of Lectures: Thursday, 1 January 1846 and Friday, 2 January 1846
Location: Methodist Meeting House, Donegall Place, Belfast
Publication: *Belfast News-Letter*
Date of Publication: Tuesday, 6 January 1846
Title: 'Anti-Slavery Society. Mr Frederick Douglass'.

On Thursday and Friday evenings, very interesting meetings of the friends of the Belfast Anti-Slavery Society took place in the Methodist Meeting House, Donegall place. On both occasions the building was packed to excess. On the former evening the chair was taken by the Rev. James Griffin and the speakers were the Chairman, Mr Buffum, Mr Douglass and Rev. Mr Nelson who animadverted on the conduct of the *Banner*, citing a letter signed 'Civis' (see Mr Nelson's letter inserted elsewhere). On Friday evening the Chairman was Dr Drew, who delivered an excellent address and expressed the great pleasure it afforded him to be called upon to preside at a meeting the object of which was the freedom of those who were in bondage. Mr Standfield then addressed the meeting in his energetic manner, after which:

Mr. Frederick Douglass rose – his coming forward upon the platform was greeted with applause which lasted more than a minute. He said – Mr. Chairman, Ladies and Gentlemen, according to the notice that has been given to this highly respectable and intelligent audience, I rise for the purpose of calling your attention to the subject of the Annexation of Texas to the United States. A question may rise in your minds as to what the Annexation of Texas to the States has to do with Slavery in America. This question I think I shall be able to answer during the remarks I shall have to make this evening.

I regret my inability to give you in one short lecture the history of the various circumstances leading to the consummation of the Annexation of Texas. If I were able to do so, you would see that it was a conspiracy from beginning to end – a most deep and skilfully devised conspiracy – for the purpose of upholding and sustaining one of the darkest and foulest crimes ever committed by man. But I will not attempt to give you a minute history of the incidents and occurrences which have led to the present position of the question.

Texas is that part of Mexico, north [south] of Arkansas and extending from the Gulf of Mexico to the Rio Del Norte. The extent of this country is almost equal to that of France, and its fertility is such that it is estimated as being able to support not less than twenty millions of souls. In 1820 this vast territory, as well as all the rest of Mexico, was subject to the Spanish Government. The history of the settlement of Texas by its present population is briefly as follows: In the year just mentioned, Moses Austin, of the State of Tennessee – a slave holding State – obtained a grant from the Royal Government of Spain to settle in that territory 300 families, on the condition that they should be industrious, sober, upright men, and professors – mark this – of the Roman Catholic religion. Austin obtained by this grant, great advantages to himself, and when he died his son Stephen Austin became the legal representative of his father, and prosecuted the work of settling the 300 families, for whom his father had obtained the large grants of land, with vigour, stimulating many who would not have otherwise thought of leaving their homes to go into this beautiful country, that they might enrich themselves, and lay the foundations of wealth for their children. During the prosecution of this design, however, the revolution broke out in Mexico, by which that country was severed from the Spanish government, and this event rendered the original contract of settlement null and void, so that Austin applied for and obtained a similar grant from Mexico, by which he succeeded in completing the number of families intended to be settled in Texas.

The settlers soon spread abroad reports of the fertility and salubrity of the country, and these reports induced a general spirit of speculation, and thus a way was opened for the practice of the grossest hypocrisy. Many persons were induced, from the love of gold, to pretend the profession of the Roman Catholic religion, thus obtaining large quantities of land. This spirit of speculation was entered into by the people of different nations, including many from England, Ireland, and Scotland. I have the names of several persons even from this town who took part in the settlement of Texas, but the territory was chiefly settled by the citizens of the United States – of the slaveholding states – of America. It was early seen by them that this would be a delightful spot to curse with slavery. They accordingly took their families and slaves to Texas, from the blighted and blasted fields of Virginia – fields once as fertile as any under Heaven – (hear) – and which would have still remained so had they not been cursed by the infernal spirit of slavery.

We do not hear of much confusion in Texas, until 1828 or 1829, when Mexico after having erected herself into a separate government and declared herself free, with a consistency which puts to the blush the boasted "land of freedom," proclaimed the deliverance of every captive on her soil. Unlike the boasted republic of America, she did this at an immense cost to her own slaveholders – not proclaiming liberty with her lips, while she fastened chains on the slave – not securing liberty for her own children but also for the degraded bondsman of Africa. (Cheers.) This act of the Mexican government was resisted at once by the settlers who had carried their slaves into Texas, though they were bound by a solemn agreement to submit to the laws of Mexico. They remonstrated with the government. They said their slaves were too ignorant and degraded to be emancipated. The Mexican government, desirous to treat amicably with those whom it had welcomed to its bosom, listened to this remonstrance, and consented that the Texian slaves should be only gradually emancipated under a system of indentured apprenticeship. Even this restriction was evaded by the Texians, making the indentures binding for

99 years. In fact they showed themselves to be a set of swindlers. Well, Mexico attempted an enforcement of her law, making it impossible for any man to hold an apprentice for more than ten years. This was resisted on the plea that the slaves would not be fit for freedom even then. One would think ten years long enough to teach them the value of liberty, but these wise Americans could not understand how that could be the case.

The Texians still persisted in holding their slaves, contrary to the express declaration of their legislature – contrary to the law of the land – to drive them before the biting lash to their hard tasks, day after day, without wages. Again, the Mexican Government attempted to enforce its law, but then Texas revolts – defies the law – and calls upon the people of the United States to aid her in, what they termed their struggle for religious liberty! (Hear.) Yes, they said they could not worship God according to the dictates of their conscience, alluding to the contract entered into by them as professing Roman Catholics. I am not prepared to say whether that contract was a righteous one or not, but, I do say, that after possessing themselves of the land, on the faith of their being Roman Catholics, they should be the last to complain on that score. If they had been honest, they would have said, in regard to their religious opinions, "We have changed our minds; we feel we cannot longer belong to the Church of Rome; we cannot, according to our contract, worship God as our conscience dictates; many of us are Methodists – many are Presbyterians; if you will allow us to worship God as we think right, we will stay in the soil; if not, we feel compelled to abandon it, and seek some other place." (Cheers.) That is the way that common honesty would force them to act, but the people of the United States – and here is one of the darkest acts of their whole history – understanding the terms upon which the Texians had obtained the territory, and well-knowing the exact nature of the contract – offered them the means of successfully resisting Mexico – afforded them arms and ammunition, and even the men who, at San Jacinto, wrested the territory from the rightful owners. Here was an act of national robbery perpetrated, and for what? For the re-establishment of slavery on a soil which had been washed pure from its polluting influence by the generous act of a "semi barbarous" people! (Hear.)

The man who goes into your ship on the high seas, puts out the captain, takes down the ensign and declares himself the owner – is no greater a robber than the people of the United States. And what are their excuses, their apologies, their reasons – for they always give reasons for what they do? One of them is, that Mexico is unable to defend her territory, and that therefore they have a right to take it! What do you think of a great heavy-fisted fellow pouncing on every little man he meets, and giving as his reason that the little man is unable to take care of himself? (Cheers.) We don't see this pretext made use of in the case of Canada. (Hear.) Mexico, nevertheless, is a sister republic, which has taken that of the United States for a model. But Mexico is a weak government, and that is the reason America falls on her – the British territories are safe because England is strong. (Hear.)

Oh, how superlatively base – how mean – how dastardly – do the American people appear in the light of justice – of reason – of liberty – when this particular point of her conduct is exposed! But here there was a double point to be gained – on the part of the Southern planters to establish and cultivate large plantations in the South – and on that of the Northern ones, to support what Daniel O'Connell says should not be called the internal, but the infernal, slave-trade, which is said to be worse than the foreign slave-trade, for it allows men to seize upon those who have sported with them on the hills, and played with them at school, and are associated with them in so many ways and under so many interesting circumstances. This is more horrible still than to prowl along the African shore and carry off thence men with whose faces at least we are unfamiliar, and to whose characters we are strangers. Still the chief object of the Annexation of Texas was the quickening of the foreign slave-trade, which is the very jugular vein of slavery, and of which, if kept within narrow limits, we would soon be rid. But the cry of slavery is ever "Give, give, give!" That cry is heard from New England to Virginia. It goes on, leaving a blighted soil behind – leaving the fields which it found fertile and luxuriant, covered with stunted pines. From Virginia it has gone to North Carolina, and from that to South Carolina, leaving ruin in its train, and now it seizes on the fertile regions of Texas, where it had been previously abolished by a people whom we are wont to call semi-civilized. They say they only want to increase their commerce, and add to their security. Oh what a reason to give for plunder! (Hear.) The pirate of the high seas might make the same excuse.

Mankind thinks that whatever is prosperous is right. Henry Clay said that what the law has made property is property, and that 200 years of legislation has made the negro slave property. With a *sang froid* more like that of a demon than a man he added, "It will be asked will not slavery come to an end? Why, that question has been asked fifty years ago, and answered by fifty years of prosperity." Prosperity is the rule of conduct. Justice is nothing – humanity is nothing – Christianity is nothing – but prosperity is everything. (Hear.) I was some time since, on the same principle, spoken to by a member of the church, who told me I was mistaken in my views and labouring against the will and wisdom of God, in this manner – "Don't you see," said he, "that we have been adding to our numbers, lengthening our cords and strengthening our stakes – don't you see the church growing in the favour of the world." This element of character is peculiar to the Americans; all they ask is prosperity, and therefore we see their bony fingers pointing towards the Pacific, threatening to overwhelm and destroy every other power which may dispute their claims. I am sorry that England, on this occasion, did not act with that high spirit of justice which led her to emancipate 800,000 of her own slaves elsewhere. I am sorry that she stepped forward with almost indecent haste to recognize the Texian banditti as an independent Republic. (Hear.) Oh, the love of money! rightly has it been called the root of all evil – with this lust for gold has England too been contaminated, and hence the result we witness.

Two years ago, I had hoped that there was morality enough, Christian-mindedness enough, love of liberty enough, burning in the bosoms of the American people, to lead them to reject forever the unholy alliance in which they have bound themselves to Texas. When I first heard of this event, at a meeting in Massachusetts, I was covered with confusion of face, for I believed we had religion enough among us to have prevented the horrid consummation. That event threw a gloom over the hearts of the struggling abolitionists, and led them to feel that the powers of darkness had prevailed against them. I hung my head, and felt that I was deceived in the people among whom I lived, and that they were hurrying their own destruction by dipping their hands in the blood of millions of slaves. However, I recovered when I remembered that ours was not a cause in which the human arm was the only agent – when I remembered that God was God still, I took courage again, and resolved to continue to pray to that God who has the destinies of nations in his hand to change their hearts.

We are still, however, strong, for the last intelligence I had from the United States was, that 40,000 good men and true, in Massachusetts, had petitioned the Government not to allow Texas to be received as a State until she had abolished slavery. (Cheers.) What will be the immediate result, I know not, but Texas in the Union or out of it – slavery upheld or slavery abolished – one thing I do know – that the true words now spoken, in Massachusetts, will create a resistance to this damning measure, which will go on under the smiles of an approving God, augmenting in power till slavery in the United States will be abolished. (Hear.) I know not how that consummation will be achieved. It may be in a manner not altogether agreeable to my own feelings. I do not know but the spirit of rapine and plunder, so rampant in America, will hurry her on to her own destruction. I hope it will not, for although America has done all that a nation could do to crush me – although I am a stranger among you – a refugee abroad, an outlaw at home – yet, I trust in God, no ill may befall her. I hope she will yet see that it will be her duty to emancipate the slaves. The friends of emancipation are determined to do all they can –

> Weapons of war we have cast from the battle, –
> Truth is our armour, our watchword is love;
> Hushed be the sword and the musketry's rattle,
> All our equipments are drawn from above.

Let no one accuse me of attempting to stir up a spirit of war. You may accuse me of being an impostor, or trying to make money – you may accuse me of what you please – but not of stirring up a war against that land which has done me and my race so much injury. For, though, if ever a man had cause to curse the region in which he was born, I am he – though my back is scarred with the lash of the driver – nature, law, and Christianity bind me to the United States of America.

Mr. Douglass then alluded to the charges which had been made against him, and which are fully disposed of in the letter in reply to "Civis," already alluded to.

He then spoke of 36 ministers of Belfast having signed a resolution to the effect that slave-holders should not be admitted as members of the Christian Church. That circumstance had cheered his heart, and he would remember the 2d of Jan. 1846, as a most glorious day, inasmuch as with the recollections of that day would always be associated with what 36 Christian ministers of Belfast had done in furtherance of the great cause he advocated. Their protest would cross the Atlantic, and fall as a bomb-shell amongst the slave-holders, filling their souls with terror and dismay.

Mr. Douglass then alluded to the many kind friends he had met with in Belfast, and said they would always be dear to his heart wherever his lot might be cast. Their Christian and fatherly advice would never be forgotten; and he would take care so to walk, that they would never hear that he had by any conduct of his retarded the progress of the holy cause of which he was the humble advocate, or that he had acted a part unbecoming an humble follower of the Lord Jesus. He then resumed his seat amid the warmest and most enthusiastic demonstrations of applause.

The Rev. I. Nelson then proposed a vote of thanks to Mr Douglass. He believed Mr Douglass had been raised up by God to do a great work and that he was destined to give slavery a blow from which it would never recover until it were finally overthrown. Mr Nelson concluded an eloquent address by wishing Mr Douglass prosperity in the cause in which he was engaged, and praying he might have that grace vouchsafed to him which would enable him to walk in the path of duty, no matter in what circumstances he might be placed.

The Rev. Mr Boyd in seconding the vote of thanks delivered an excellent speech. The motion was also supported by the Rev. Mr Hodges and the Rev. Mr Buffum.

The Chairman then rose and having made a few appropriate remarks on the duty they owed to the Americans in the way of warning, put the resolutions to the meeting, when the whole Assembly at once rose, and the applause which followed lasted for a considerable time.

A cordial vote of thanks was passed to Mr Nelson for the part he had taken.

It was announced that Mr. S. Crawford Esq., MP, would preside at a breakfast to Mr Douglass this morning, and that, on that occasion, a Ladies' Anti-Slavery Association would be formed.

Editorial
Publication: *Salisbury and Winchester Journal*
Date of Publication: Saturday, 3 January 1846
No Title.

Frederick Douglass, an American fugitive slave, is at present exciting a great interest in Ireland by a narrative, founded in his own experience, of the horrors of slavery in Maryland. Douglass is represented to be a young man of unusual ability, sound judgment, serious, of excellent character and with a degree of cultivation of mind quite extraordinary for the opportunities he had while in the Slave

States, where teaching slaves to read, or even giving them Bibles, subjects the offenders to severe penalties! The object of his visit to England is to escape the danger of his owner adopting means to recover and again place him in slavery. It is said that Douglass will in the ensuing spring pay a visit to Bristol.

Anti-Slavery Breakfast
Lecturer: Frederick Douglass
Date of Lecture: Tuesday, 6 January 1846
Publication: *Belfast Commercial Chronicle*
Date of Publication: Wednesday, 7 January 1846
Title: 'BREAKFAST TO MR FREDERICK DOUGLASS'.[161]

The friends of this gentleman entertained him at a public breakfast in the large room of the Commercial Buildings, yesterday morning at 10 o'clock.[162] The room was entirely filled by a most respectable party composed of about an equal number of ladies and gentlemen. The breakfast was supplied by Mr. Hall of the Commercial Hotel and was all that could be desired. A little inconvenience arose from more being present than was expected but this was soon got over, and everything proceeded most agreeable. Among those present we noticed the following: –

Wm. S. Crawford Esq. M.P.[163] Rev. Isaac Nelson, Rev. Mr Buffon [sic], Rev Mr. Boyd, Rev. Mr. Hodgens, Rev Mr. McAllister, Holywood; Rev Jacob Alexander Derry; Dr. Thompson, Roselands; Dr Aikin, Dr. Thomas Thompson, Messrs Robert Blackwell, Thomas Tennent, John Boyd, James M'Tear, James Gibson James Blair, Samuel Vance, Edwin Blow, Geo. Pim, R. Neill, J. Standfield, A. F. Calder, T. Hardy, Captain Hardcastle, Freeman Hardy, Robert Workman, J. Workman, Jr., T. Tripp, J. Henderson, York-street; John Owden, Wm. Valentine, C. Duffin, D. M'Connell, J Arnold, Maxwell Sanders, J. M'Vicker, S. Edgar, Wm. M'Peake, Ballymena; J. Girdwood, J. Gray, J. Marshall, Wm. Webb, J. Lamb, J.C. Trotter, James Ireland, Alexander Robb, J. B. Ferguson, J. M'Conkey, R. Boag, J. Workman, &c &c.

Mr. Crawford, Mr. Douglass, and Rev. Mr. Nelson, were loudly cheered on entering the room.

The Rev. Isaac Nelson said grace, and thanks were returned by Rev. Mr. Hodgens; after which, on the motion of Mr. Halliday,

Wm S. Crawford, Esq. M. P. took the chair amid loud applause. The Chairman rose and said he felt proud of the honour which the meeting had conferred upon him, by calling upon him to preside on that very interesting occasion. (Cheers.) When requested by the committee of the Belfast Anti-Slavery Society to preside, he did not for one moment hesitate to comply with the request, and he could assure the meeting that it gave him sincere pleasure to be called upon to perform any act that might in any way help forward the great and glorious cause of freedom. (Applause). In being present, he did nothing more than what he conceived to be his duty, and he trusted he would be always ready, at the call of humanity, to perform the same. He considered that there were two objects before the meeting, and for which they were assembled. In the first place, they were assembled to do honor to the gentleman who sat on his right hand. (Applause.) Mr. Douglass was worthy of the amount of praise which they wished to give him. His exertions on behalf of those of his race who were held in bondage, deserved the praise of every man who loved freedom, and especially of every Christian. (Applause.) They had assembled to do honour to a man who had been a slave, and who knew the horrors of the accursed system of slavery, but who was no longer such. (Cheers.) He was then a freeman; he had escaped from slavery, and had set his foot on British soil, where his liberty was secured. (Cheers.) It was one of the most glorious features of the British Constitution, that every man who touched its soil, no matter what was his clime or colour, was a freeman. (Hear, hear, and cheers.) On British soil, no slaveholder dare make his appearance for the purpose of claiming the slave, and dragging him back into bondage. (Cheers.) The laws of Britain made the slave free, and secured him his liberty. (Applause.) This, as he had said before, was one of the most glorious features of the British law. Another object of the meeting, and which perhaps as the more important one, was to denounce American slavery. (Cheers.) As lovers of freedom and those who enjoyed its blessing, they were called upon to denounce all those countries which held men in slavery, but more especially the Americans, who professed to have a Constitution founded on liberty, and yet kept three millions of men in bondage the most cruel – (Cheers) – who refused to them all civil rights. It was bad enough for any country to hold men in slavery, and to deprive them of those rights to which all men were entitled, but it was ten times worse, and called for stronger reprobation, when a nation did so that professed democratic principles of government. (Cheers.) As a member of the British Legislature, and the representative of a constituency who were attached to the great principles of freedom, he could not refrain from denouncing slavery wherever it was to be found. The Constitution of America was founded on the principles of liberty, and the system of slavery which was upheld in that country was in discordance with its Constitution. (Applause.) [Mr. Crawford here read part of the Declaration of Independence, which asserts the principle that all men are born equal, and that liberty is the inherent right of all men.] These were the views put forth by those who founded the American Constitution, but the establishment of slavery gave the lie to the principles on which their constitution was founded, and stamped them with inconsistency. (Applause.) The Americans wish all men to believe that their Constitution is based on principles of justice; but he would ask, is the system of slavery, which takes from the slave all the rights of man, compatible with justice? Is a system which deprives men of all the privileges of citizens, in accordance with just principles? No man who had any correct notion of justice could say so. (Hear, hear.) Look at the infamous laws which existed in a country that boasted of freedom, and their tendencies. No black man's evidence could be received against a white man, and the tendency of that law was, that the slaveholder might treat the slaves he possessed as he pleased, for they could not be witnesses against him. The most infamous deeds might be committed, and the perpetrator escape punishment. The slave had no means of obtaining redress, as the slaveholder had only to avoid the commission of the crime that would subject him to punishment, in the presence of a white man, and he was sure to escape. That was a most iniquitous law, and gave the lie to the statement put forth by Americans, that their laws were founded upon just principles. (Applause.)

Mr. Crawford then read some extracts from the works of an American writer, which contrasted the quiet that existed in the Free States with the turmoil in the Slave States, occasioned by attempting to keep in bondage those who were born to be free. There never could be tranquility in America while such a state of things existed. The Americans have put it to the world that they have established liberty, but could there be any liberty in a country where slavery existed? Could there be liberty where the slaveholder could shoot his slave and escape punishment? The Americans should have their attention called to the fact, that their conduct was in direct contradiction to the principles which, as a nation, they professed, and it was the duty of every lover of freedom, and especially of Christian men, to point out to them their inconsistency. According to the Declaration of Independence, slaves are men born free, but they have, by American law, become chattels, and are bought and sold without any regard to the relations of life – the wife may be separated from her husband, and the child from the parent. This was a state of things against which every man should raise his voice, who professed the love of liberty. Humanity rose up against such a state of things. Christian man should denounce it, as it was in direct opposition to the laws of God. No man who professed to be guided by religious principles could tolerate, or in any way countenance such a system of iniquity. How any minister could go into the pulpit, and read the word of eternal truth, and not denounce slavery as opposed to that Word, he could not comprehend. He would refer anyone who professed to hold the principles of Christianity, and would, at the same time, make a difference between the white and black race, to what the apostle Peter said to Cornelius after God had taught him not to call any man common or unclean. His language then was – 'I perceive that God is no respecter of persons, but in every nation, they that fear him, they are accepted,' though before he thought, in common with his nation, that the Jews alone were God's favored people. (Applause.) If they wanted any proof that black men were not inferior, in point of intellect, to white men, they had it in the gentleman they had met to honour. (Applause). He would be borne out when he asserted, that the black race, when placed in similar circumstances would be found equal to any, therefore, on the ground of inferiority, the argument in favour of slavery was futile. (Cheers.) He could not see how the slaveholder, who was in the habit of using the lash, could say that portion of the Lord's prayer which said, 'Forgive us our trespasses as we forgive them who trespass against us.' To use such a prayer would be praying not to be forgiven. It would be calling down curses instead of blessings on the head of the slaveholder who would use it. How could the man who held his fellow-man in bondage read that portion of the word of God which says, 'Do unto others as you would they should do unto you,' and still keep him fast bound in his chains?

The Honorable gentleman then proceeded to account for the Americans having become so degenerate, and said he attributed it to the democratic principles which as a nation they held. Irresponsible power was dangerous to liberty. The conduct of the Americans proved to the world, that those who held democratic principles were, for the most part, the greatest tyrants. This might appear strange, coming from him, who had always been the advocate of the rights of the people. He had, however, only advocated democratic principles in so far as they were consistent with monarchical government. He, as an advocate for the people's rights, felt called upon to raise his voice against those who disgraced the principles of which he was, to a certain extent, the advocate. He then alluded to the efforts that were made to abolish the slave trade, and said those efforts would never be successful so long as slavery existed in America, for so long as there was a market for slaves, there would be men found to carry on the trade; and the best way, therefore, to put an end to the slave trade, was to do all in their power to have slavery abolished. It was the duty of Christian men, by the reprobation of slavery, to do all in their power to cause those who made a profession of Christianity to abandon it. The slaveholder should be made to feel that the practices in which he was engaged were reprobated by all good men. (Cheers). He trusted the voice of that large and respectable assembly would cross the Atlantic – that it would be heard by the slaveholder, and that he would feel that a Belfast audience execrated him on account of his connection with the horrible system of slavery. The voice of the British people had reached America before, and slaveholders and their abettors felt severely the castigation they received. Let it be so again. Let their voice be heard demanding the freedom of the slave, and he had reason to hope that it would not be heard in vain. After a few other remarks, Mr. Crawford resumed his seat amid loud cheers.

The Rev. I. Nelson then rose, and, having stated some things with regard to Mr. Douglass visiting Belfast. He said, when he did arrive, the Anti-Slavery Committee wished to make his visit as efficient, for the promotion of the cause in which he was engaged, as possible, and he was sorry to say that in doing so, they had met with difficulties they had not anticipated, and opposition from quarters where they did not expect it. They had to submit to have obloquy cast upon them, and hard things said of them; but he had no desire to dwell upon them at that time, and would, therefore, merely remark, that they were fully compensated for all they had endured by the proceedings of that morning. – (Cheers.) To see such an assembly made up for all. (Renewed applause.) He had, from the very first, no fears as to the result. He knew when the people of Belfast would have the matter fairly brought before them, they would be found on the side of the oppressed, and respond to the call made on their sympathy and support – (hear, hear, and cheers) – and he had not been disappointed. He would not then occupy the time of the meeting with saying anything upon the evil of the accursed system of slavery. It was quite unnecessary for him to do so. The burning words of Frederick Douglass had produced their effect: he had made those who had the privilege of hearing him feel for the wrongs of his race, and he then had the pleasure of seeking the response in the large and respectable meeting there assembled. (Cheers.) Mr. Nelson then spoke of the chairman in very complimentary terms, and said, when the Committee decided upon asking him to take the chair in which he then sat, he for one had no fears of a refusal; his character was too well known for the thought to be for a moment entertained, that he would not throw his great influence into the side of the oppressed. – (Cheers.) He trusted it would not be the last occasion on which he should be found presiding at an anti-slavery meeting, and denouncing slavery as they all had heard him do that day. (Cheers.)

Mr. Nelson then read a very excellent Address to Mr. Douglass, and presented him with a beautiful Pocket Bible, splendidly bound in gold, and clasped. The following is the inscription on the first page: – 'Presented by the Belfast Auxiliary to the British and Foreign Anti-Slavery Society, to Mr. Frederick Douglass, a fugitive slave from the United States of America, in testimony of which he delivered in Belfast, on American slavery, in December, 1845, and, also, as a tribute of respect and esteem for his personal character. The Committee hoped he may be long enabled, in the strength of the Lord, to persevere in the noble cause in which he is engaged, and, by the torch of Divine truth, to expose all who attempt to defend or palliate slavery. When far separated, they trust that the possession of this Bible will remind him, that in Belfast, there are many who sympathize with those who are in bonds, and who are also the personal friends and well-wishers of Mr. Frederick Douglass. Signed by order, and on behalf of the Committee.

Jas. Standfield, F. A. Calder – Honorary Secretaries. Belfast, 6th January, 1846.

Mr. Douglass, on rising to respond, was received with the greatest enthusiasm. He spoke as follows:

It would be useless for me to attempt to conceal my embarrassment in rising to respond to the eloquent and highly complimentary address, together with the golden gift with which I have just been presented, by the Belfast Anti-Slavery Society. (Cheers.) I am unequal to the work: my feelings are too deep, too strong, too big for easy utterance. I have often, in the course of my short, though not uneventful life, been called upon to respond in accents of warm and heartfelt gratitude for noble deeds and generous favours conferred upon me by the friends of my long enslaved and deeply outraged fellow-countrymen, but never have I been more at a loss for language to fulfil that duty than on the present thrilling and interesting occasion. (Applause.) –

The incidents of this morning will form a period in my humble history – a period to which, with all my hopes and aspirations, I never looked forward; but one to which, while memory holds its place, I shall ever look back with the most grateful emotion. I accept, thankfully, this Bible; and while it shall have the best place in my house, I trust, also, to give its precepts a place in my heart. (Great applause.) The happy incidents of this morning, have called into remembrance some of my early struggles after knowledge, and the difficulties that then lay in the way of its attainment. I remember the first time I ever heard the Bible read, and I tell you the truth when I tell you that, from that time, I trace my first desire to learn to read. I was over seven years old; my master had gone out one Sunday night, the children had gone to bed, I had crawled under the centre-table, and had fallen asleep, when my mistress commenced to read the Bible aloud, – so loud that she waked me – *she waked me to sleep no more!* I have found since. I learned that the chapter that she then read was the 1st chapter of Job. I remember my sympathy for the good old man; and my great anxiety to know more about him, led me to ask my mistress – who was at this time a kind lady – to teach me to read. She commenced, and would have, but for the opposition of her husband, taught me to read. She ceased to instruct me, but my desire to read continued, and, instead of decreasing, increased; and, by the aid of little boys, obtained at different times, I finally succeeded in learning to read. (Applause.)

After learning to read, my desire for the books was equal to my early desire to learn how to read. I have frequently, with my fingers, from the mud and filth of the gutter, raked leaves of the sacred volume. These I have washed and dried, and read the words of heavenly wisdom which they contained with a glad heart, considering myself fortunate to enjoy such a privilege. I trust I shall not be deemed presumptuous or egotistical, when I say, that, from my present position, I see points in my humble history which seem marked by the finger of God. (Applause.) Twenty years ago, while lying, not unlike a pet dog, at the feet of my mistress, in her house in Philpot-street, Fell's Point, Baltimore, I was roused from the sweet sleep of childhood, to hear the narrative of Job. A few years afterward found me searching for the Scriptures in the muddy street-gutters, and rescuing its pages from the filth into which neglect and wastefulness had plunged them. A few years later, I escaped from my chains, gained partial freedom, and became an advocate for the emancipation of my race. During this advocacy, a suspicion obtains that I am not what I profess to be, to silence which, it is necessary to write out my experience in slavery, and give the names of my enslavers. This endangers my liberty. Persecuted, hunted, outraged in America, I have come to England, and behold the changes! – The chattel becomes a man. (Applause.) I breathe, and I am free. (Applause.) Instead of culling the Scriptures from the mud, they come to me dressed in polished gold, as the free and unsolicited gift of devoted hearts. (Applause.) I will take it, and while I live preserve it, and long after I have gone hence to my reward, if my will is carried out, it shall be preserved by my children, and remain a memento in the house of Douglass till times shall melt it into dust. (Applause.)

I assure you, gentlemen of the Committee, you have selected a proper mode of expressing your regard for me. What could be better than the Bible to me, contending against oppression, fraud and wrong? (Applause.) It is full of wisdom and goodness – faith, hope, and charity sparkle on every page, all of which deal death to slavery. An attempt has been made to press the Bible into the service of slavery. The abolition party in America find no more determined opponents of the cause which they advocate, than the expounders of the word of God. That, to this audience, might appear strange, but such is the fact. I thank God that a change for the better is taking place; a purer and a higher grade of men are finding their way into the ministry, and brighter days are beginning to dawn upon my country.

(Applause.) You could not have given to me a token so appropriate as this Bible. It contains all that is right, and is opposed to all that is wrong. (Applause.) It knows no one by the colour of his skin. (Applause.) It treats all alike, and says to all, 'Whatsoever you would that men should do unto you, do you do so unto them.' If you claim liberty for yourself, then grant it to your neighbour, is the doctrine it inculcates. I feel much struck with the changes in my circumstances; only a few months ago, I was in a land where I was hated and abhorred – where the blood-hound might have been put on my track, and I have been hunted down and carried back into slavery. I left that land, and in 11–12 days I set my foot on British soil, and was free. (Applause.) I now find myself surrounded by kind friends, the very expression of whose countenance beams with sympathy such as I never expected to meet with, and which has quite overcome and unmanned me. (Applause.)

I could expose slavery in the midst of those who would uphold it – I could contend for the great principles of liberty in the face of the most determined opposition – (Applause) – but I am not equal to address those who sympathy has been excited for my race, and who have showed me so much kindness. I shall always remember the people of Belfast, and the kind friends I now see around me, and wherever else I feel myself to be a stranger, I will remember I have a home in Belfast. (Applause.) I will look forward with pleasure to the day which will find me with you again – (Applause) – and, in the meantime, you shall hear from me wherever my lot may be cast. (Applause.) – Let me thank you with my whole heart for the address and the beautiful present you have made me, as well as for the deep interest you have taken in the cause of the wronged and oppressed slaves of America. You have discharged your duty nobly, and as Christians should do. When I came a stranger among you, I was taken by the hand, and, I may say, my hand has been held throughout. – The Committee have endeavoured in season and out of season, to give effect to any feeble efforts for the emancipation of my race. Without the Committee, I could have done nothing; to them all the praise is due. Once more, accept my thanks for all the kindness I have experienced at your hands, and I bid you all farewell until I shall meet you again in July. Mr. Douglas then resumed his seat amid the warmest demonstrations of applause.

The meeting was then addressed in eloquent terms by Mr. Standfield, but our space will not permit us giving his excellent remarks. The Rev. Mr. Nelson then rose, and, after making some observations very complimentary to the ladies, moved that a number of ladies, (whom he named,) with power to add to their number, compose the Belfast Auxiliary Female Anti-Slavery Society. [The first 19 ladies were read out by Mr. Bell, who had obtained them in the neighborhood of Bangor.] It was then moved by Mr. Standfield, and seconded by Mr. Calder – 'That the thanks of this meeting are justly due, and hereby given, to the congregation of the Presbyterian Church, Donegal-street, for the efficient aid given by the pastor and people to the Belfast Anti-Slavery Society, and for their co-operation with its members to wipe off the foul stain from Christianity, put on by those inconsistent professors, who say, that *they have authority in the word of God for 'the wild and guilty fantasy, that man can hold* property *in man'.*'

Mr. J. B. Ferguson returned thanks on behalf of Mr. Nelson and the congregation, and the meeting was then addressed by Mr. Gibson and the Rev. Mr. Buffum, after which, Mr. Gibson took the chair, and the cordial thanks of the meeting were voted to Mr. Crawford. The meeting separated at 1 o'clock.

Two Temperance Meetings
Lecturer: Frederick Douglass
Date of Lectures: Tuesday, 6 January 1846 and Wednesday, 7 January 1846
Locations: Lancasterian School Room and Presbyterian Meeting House Donegall Street
Publication: *Belfast Commercial Chronicle*
Date of Publication: Monday, 12 January 1846
Title: 'LECTURES ON THE EVILS OF INTEMPERANCE AND THE BENEFITS OF TOTAL ABSTINENCE FROM ALL INTOXICATING DRINKS, BELFAST. LECTURE BY FREDERICK DOUGLASS, THE FUGITIVE SLAVE'.

On Tuesday evening last, the friends of total abstinence from all intoxicating drinks (believing this the only effective remedy for destroying intemperance in every land) held their annual meeting in the Lancasterian School-room. After the Report had been read, which detailed the onward progress of this cause in every part of the world, with the exception of Belfast and the North of Ireland, where, as in the case of slavery, little assistance is given by those who ought to be foremost in this good work, and where, in consequence, intemperance and its attendant evils flourish – orphans are made, and the progress of religion obstructed – thousands of the poor never attending a place of worship – spending on whiskey, beer, ale, &c. that money which ought to go to the support of their families; while the Sabbath is constantly desecrated by 500 open public houses, in which about £2,000 are spent weekly on strong drink and tobacco, and showing that the Sabbath, to the lovers of drink, is no day of rest – that our country will never be prosperous, nor Christianity respected or extended, either abroad or at home, while such practices prevail, and while professing Christians, of all denominations, remain apathetic or lukewarm on this important subject.

The Rev. Jacob Alexander, of the Covenanting Church, being then called on, spoke in favour of total abstinence, and the blessings this system would confer on the Church and world, were it universally adopted – were there no distilleries or breweries to destroy the good grain which kind Providence has sent for the food of man, and were there no public houses to demoralise the people.

Mr. Buffum, an American minister, and a zealous abolitionist and temperance reformer, from the United States, next spoke on the subject. He had been in the South as well as the North of Ireland, and was struck with the contrast. In the former, temperance and sobriety; in the latter, much intemperance yet prevailed. Was not this not a shame on Protestants, who in many things thought themselves superior to Roman Catholics? He and his friend, Douglass, had been most kindly, and hospitably entertained by Father Matthew [sic], who, under

God, had been rendered the blessed instrument of carrying forward a great reformation. – An astonishing reformation had taken place likewise in America, and
there the greatest, best, and most learned Christian ministers were advocates of
the total abstinence movement. They had all tried the old pledge of moderation,
which did good to a certain length, but did not reach the extent of the evil. In
the United States the people were now total abstainers. On this principle there
were now about 4,000,000 members. The state of Massachusetts alone, contained 16 counties, and in only one of these were any licenses granted for the sale
of strong drink! The poor-houses and gaols had been emptied; the schools and
churches had been filled! and many saved from ruin. Irishmen who were sober
got immediate employment and high wages, while those addicted to drunkenness were universally despised. Mr. B. gave illustration of this in the case of his
own servant or caretaker, an Irishman, whom he had rescued from intemperance
and degradation, and whom he had since found to be the most grateful, faithful, and trustworthy friend he had in the world; so much did he depend on this
man, that now, in his (Mr. B.'s) absence from home, he had the charge of all his
property. He proposed the formation of a female total abstinence association
whose chief duties like that of a kindred society in America called the Martha
Washington Association, would be to visit the poor, and clothe the drunkard
when he renounced his evil ways. A resolution was proposed at the meeting,
and passed, concurring in the benevolent exertions of the Belfast Anti-Slavery
Society to extinguish this great evil abroad and home. At the conclusion of the
meeting, which was closed, as it had been opened, singing a temperance hymn,
several persons came forward and signed the pledge, as about 550 had done
previously during the past year. In the report, the names of Andrew Mulholland,
Esq. the late excellent Mayor, of Robert Workman, Esq., James Campbell, Esq.
&c. were mentioned with praise for their liberality and kindness to the society
during the year.

On Wednesday evening, the 7th inst. a very large and respectable assembly
of the friends of temperance met in the Presbyterian Meeting-house, Donegall
Street. There appeared on the platform the Rev. Isaac Nelson, the Rev. Mr. Hodgens, Rev. Jacob Alexander, Mr. Douglass, the celebrated anti-slavery lecturer,
Mr. Buffum, the American merchant, Mr. R. J. Bell, of Bangor, Mr. Robb, Belfast,
the Secretary of the Ballymena Total Abstinence Society, and others.

The Rev. J. Alexander having been called to the chair, opened the meeting with
several eloquent and appropriate remarks on the evils of intemperance, and the
means to be used for its removal, and concluded by calling on

Mr. Douglass, who, in the course of a long and eloquent speech, edified and
entertained the meeting, proving from reason and experience, and Scripture, the
excellence and benefit of the system of total abstinence from intoxicating drink,
and the necessity for its adoption in this professedly Christian land. Mr. Douglass
alluded to the progress of total abstinence in the United States, and attributed much
of his health and ability to perform labour to his being an abstainer. He answered
several of the objections made by professedly religious men, moderate drinkers

and others, against the society, showing, when weighed in the balance of Scripture and common sense, their utter weakness and futility. Even when a slave, he had not degraded himself by this vice, and inwardly felt his superiority over his drunken white master, who in this respect was the greater slave of the two. The one evil held the body in cruel bondage – the other destroyed both body and soul. Man was made in the image of God, and was intended to glorify his name; but did the drunkard in the gutter exemplify this character or glorify God? Having often seen his master riding home drunk and incapable, he was led to determine to be a total abstainer. He had wrought in the field, in the store, in the ship-yard, at various kinds of heavy and fatiguing work, and found himself, as a teetotaller, more able to endure hardships than the men who were constantly tippling and drinking. If a robbery or murder is committed, what an outcry is raised in the town and neighbourhood; but hundreds may be destroying their lives and properties, injuring their families and friends, making their wives widows, and their children fatherless orphans; and yet it attracts little or no attention – the priest and the Levite pass on unmoved, till, perhaps, some poor despised Samaritan calls public attention to the subject. If a house were on fire, what excitement and exertion is called forth until it is put out; but the devouring flame of intemperance, leading to everlasting burnings, may go on unheeded, because men get familiar with it, and accustomed to the evil. There may be more than 550 public houses in Belfast, and only 20 places of worship, and yet the matter attracts little attention. How appalling to find, in a professedly Christian country, the worshippers of Bacchus and the bottle so much more numerous and earnest in their work than the worshippers of the true God! Should not every Christian awake to his duty and make an effort to remove intemperance, and its accompanying evils, from the country? Though you should not drink yourself, yet join the society, and give the benefit of your example. Some object, and say, as they have said in this town, oh, they are only the low and vulgar that are joined this society. Such, perhaps, said the Scribes and Pharisees of old, respecting the Saviour and his humble followers, who, through the noblest and wisest of men, were esteemed the offscourings of the world. Others say – I will not take a pledge – I will not sign away my liberty. This, at first, may seem like a plausible objection, but, like the others, it is without foundation. If the thing is right, there is no harm: it is our duty to resolve to do it. The landlord signs covenants, agreements, leases; the merchant signs checks, bills, letters – he pledges himself to pay his lawful debts. I pledge myself every day. The Christian vows and resolves to pay; he pledges himself to the service of God, to truth and righteousness. This we ought all to do every day. I pledged myself not to touch, taste or handle, that which I saw destroyed its thousands and tens of thousands. I early resolved to look down upon my desperate oppressors and to be free. We know that young men will pledge themselves, and that young women are not afraid sometimes to sign away their liberty in other cases; why should they be afraid of this. Another objection against the Society was that the advocates were not learned or refined, or college bred. The objection might be urged against Christianity itself – its first advocates were unlearned, unrefined men. This is not the fault of the Society if there be a fault; it is rather the fault of those who are learned, pious and eloquent, and yet will not come forward in this glorious cause. After many eloquent illustrations, and the detail of several appropriate anecdotes, Mr. Douglass sat down, as he had commenced, loudly applauded – counselling the ministers, members and friends present to renew exertions in this work.

After several appropriate and eloquent speeches from Mr. Buffum, Mr. Bell, Rev. Isaac Nelson, the Chairman and Rev. Mr. Hodgens who, as well as Mr. Douglass, had witnessed the happy effects of temperance in the South of Ireland, the meeting was concluded at an early hour, when several ladies, and others, came forward and voluntarily put their name to the pledge – the pledge of abstinence from all intoxicating drinks, except when used medicinally or in a religious ordinance.

Article
Publication: *Liverpool Mercury*
Date of Publication: Tuesday, 6 January 1846
No Title.

The members of the Belfast Anti-Slavery Society have presented Mr. Frederick Douglas [sic], the fugitive slave from the United States, with a beautifully-gilt Bible, in rich binding, in testimony of their admiration of the several eloquent lectures delivered by him in that city on American slavery.

Article
Publication: *Liberator* (from the London Inquirer)
Date of Publication: Friday, 27 February 1846
Title: 'FREDERICK DOUGLASS'.

A correspondent of the *London Inquirer*[164] writes from Belfast (Ireland) as follows: We have had the 'runaway slave' Frederick Douglass, in Belfast, for the last week. He has delivered a course of four lectures, to crowded audiences, on American Slavery. I myself had not an opportunity of hearing any, except the last; and if that can be regarded as a fair specimen of Mr. D's lectures, a rich treat was theirs who heard the entire course. I had expected a good deal from Mr. Douglass, from what I had seen of him in the public prints; but high as were my expectations, they were more than realized. He is, in truth, a wonderful man. A man of color, born in slavery, and an oppressed slave till within the last few years, without instruction or the means of self-improvement in his youth, now attracting to the halls in which he lectures, assemblies large and respectable, assemblies which are drawn around him, perhaps, in the first instance, by the novelty of the matter, but which cannot fail to be delighted and electrified by the addresses of the lecturer. On the evening I heard him, he dealt chiefly with the apologists of slavery, having shown, in the introduction to his lectures, that slavery, as it now exists in the United States, is totally opposed to the teachings of both the Old Testament and the New.

In his remarks on the principal subject of his discourse, he was exceedingly severe on those divines (both on this and the other side of the Atlantic) who justify traffic in human blood. Dr. Chalmers and the *Free* Church of Scotland came in for a heavy share of well-merited censure on this subject. The representation of the lecturer, that this self-styled Free Church,[165] and the transatlantic '*Orthodox*' churches, generally countenanced American slavery, was received by the meeting (which was almost entirely composed of members of Orthodox churches) with strong marks of disapprobation, – while the announcement, at the conclusion of the lecture, of the noble stand against 'the accursed thing,' lately taken by upwards of 170 Unitarian ministers in the United States, called forth as expression of feeling stronger and warmer than I could have anticipated from an *Orthodox* assembly, in this hotbed of prejudice and religious animosity, for any Unitarian 'action,' however commendable, however noble. Mr. Douglass leaves this afternoon, for Birmingham, where he is to lecture on his favorite topic, American slavery, on Tuesday evening. He has promised, however, to return to Belfast, and to deliver another lecture on the evening of the 23d inst. After that, it is his intention, I believe, to make a thorough tour of Scotland. He is resolved, I understand, to embrace every opportunity, while there, to expose the 'F' *Churches* as apologists of slavery.

May God strengthen him to carry out his purpose! Let the 'apologists' but go to hear him: and though they had previously even resolved to reply to his observations, they will be struck dumb in his presence. Who could listen to his heart-rending description of the horrors of slavery, and not heartily hate the institution? His picture of its evils and cruelties, how dark! how black! how affecting! This communication I need not extend, as I am sure you will invite Mr. Douglass to London, to have an opportunity of hearing him for yourselves.

NOTES

1 The *Liberator* was the main newspaper of the American Anti-Slavery Society. Founded in 1831 by William Lloyd Garrison (1805–1879), the paper represented a more radical approach to abolition, arguing that it should be immediate and total. Despite some personal antagonism, Garrison was an admirer of the Irish nationalist leader, Daniel O'Connell (1775–1847), and frequently reprinted copies of his speeches. The *Liberator* was published weekly out of Boston.

2 The Hutchinson family were a large musical family from New Hampshire, who wrote and performed about social issues, including slavery. The musical quartet consisted of three brothers, Judson (1817–1859), John Wallace (1821–1908), Asa (1823–1884) and Abigail (1829–1892), but their brother, Jesse (1813–1853), accompanied them on their visit to the United Kingdom in 1845. In 1848, Douglass criticized the singers for performing in front of the leader of the American Whig Party, Henry Clay (1777–1852).

3 Bela Marsh (1797–1869) was a Boston bookseller and stationer.

4 James Haughton (1795–1873), a successful Dublin businessman, was also a prominent abolitionist, social reformer and temperance advocate. He attended Ballitore, the Quaker School in Co. Kildare. Raised a Quaker, Haughton joined the Unitarians in 1834. Together with two Dublin Quakers, he founded the Hibernian Anti-Slavery Society in 1837. Although a supporter of O'Connell's Repeal movement, he was critical of the Irish leaders' initial acceptance of financial support from slave-owners in the U.S.

5 Addressed to William Lloyd Garrison, editor of the *Liberator*.

6 Since the 1820s, Texas had been part of Mexico. Although Mexico abolished slavery in 1829, Texas remained ambivalent, largely because much of its cotton industry was based on slave labour. To safeguard its position, in 1836 Texas declared its independence and legalized slavery. In 1840, the British government recognized its independence – an action that was condemned by the Hibernian Anti-Slavery Society and by Daniel O'Connell. In 1845, the U.S. annexed Texas and moved troops into the territory. This action led to the Mexican-American War of 1846–1848. Within the U.S., the Texan question was controversial, polarizing opinion along pro-slavery and anti-slavery lines.

7 Richard Davis Webb (1805–1872) was a Dublin-based printer and abolitionist. He was a Quaker. Together with James Haughton and Richard Allen, Webb was a founder of the Hibernian Anti-Slavery Society in 1837, which allied with Garrison's American Anti-Slavery Society. He was responsible for publishing the Irish editions of Douglass's *Narrative*. Richard's wife, Hannah Waring Webb (1809–1862), from Waterford, was also active in the movement, working with women abolitionists in Ireland, Britain and America. Hannah was a talented editor and assisted in Richard's printing and publishing business – her special gift being to spot and eliminate 'Yankeeisms' used by American abolitionists. In his diaries, their son Alfred claimed that his

mother's premature death was due to her working so hard for the cause of abolition and other reform causes.

8 The 'old organization' referred to Garrison and his followers, the 'new organization' including the British and Foreign Anti-Slavery Society. Garrison's main support in the U.K. was in Dublin, Scotland and Bristol.

9 Probably Nathaniel Peabody Rogers (1794–1846), who gave up a lucrative law practice in New Hampshire to edit an abolitionist newspaper. In the 1840s, he fell out with the Garrisonians.

10 Probably George Bradburn (1806–1880), a Unitarian minister in Massachusetts known for his abolitionist views. He attended the 1840 Convention in London. In 1843, he and Douglass toured together, and they were both physically attacked. In 1844, Bradburn and Garrison disagreed publicly over the question of abolitionist involvement in party politics.

11 Packets were the ships that carried mail across the Atlantic. They also carried passengers and freight.

12 James Needham Buffum (1807–1887), a businessman and politician from Lynn, Massachusetts. A friend of Garrison since 1831, he had defended Douglass from a mob attack (see, Obituary, *New York Times*, 13 June 1887).

13 The *Cambria*, which had been built in Scotland in 1844, was part of the Cunard Shipping Line transatlantic fleet. It could carry a maximum of 120 passengers. It also carried mail. A paddle-steamer, it could complete the crossing in two weeks.

14 The town of Lynn was a centre of the abolition movement, leading Douglass to move there with his family in autumn 1841. According to C. H. Webber in *Old Naumkeag: an historical sketch of the city of Salem, and the towns of Marblehead, Peabody, Beverly, Danvers, Wenham, Manchester, Topsfield, and Middleton* (Mass, Salem: A. A. Smith and Co., 1877), 'Around the corner on Washington and Church streets, stands Lyceum Hall, built in 1831. Its exterior is unpretentious, its auditorium small and plain, but for lectures, readings and such entertainments it is most convenient. The hall is semi-circular in form, the rows of seats rising one above the other on an angle of thirty-five degrees'. The wooden hall was destroyed by fire at the end of the century.

15 Henry Clapp (1814–1875) was originally from Nantucket, but associated with Lynn in Massachusetts, where he edited a series of newspapers, including the *Pioneer*. Although he was critical of the radicalism of the Garrisonians, he was frequently quoted in the *Liberator*. Initially a supporter of temperance, he later adopted a bohemian lifestyle, inspired by time spent in Paris. He died in poverty.

16 Charles Henry Evan Judkins (c. 1809–1876) was the English-born captain of the *Cambria*. He worked for the Cunard Line for over 40 years, making over 400 trips across the Atlantic with no loss of life. He died at his home in Liverpool. See Obituary, *New York Times*, 9 October 1878.

17 The *Southern Reporter and Cork Commercial Courier* was an avid supporter of O'Connell and Repeal.

18 Together with Garrison's *Liberator*, the *National Anti-Slavery Standard* was an organ of the American Anti-Slavery Society. It was published in New York City and had first appeared in 1840 under the editorship of Lydia Maria Child (1802–1880) and David Lee Child (1794–1874). It ceased publication in 1870 when the Fifteenth Amendment granted African Americans the right to vote.

19 A weekly Boston newspaper that commenced publishing in 1836. It was founded by Rev. Thomas F. Norris, a Methodist minister, but had no formal affiliation with any religious organization.

20 James Gordon Bennett (1795–1872) was the founder and editor of the *New York Herald*. Born in Scotland, he emigrated to North America in 1819. After 1841, his son, also James Gordon Bennett (1841–1912), took over the editorship of the paper. At

that stage, it had the largest circulation in America, partly because of its sensationalist approach to news reporting. The *Herald* was pro-slavery.

21 Rev. Thomas Folsom Norris (c. 1792–1853), who was born in Vermont, was a Methodist minister and president of the New England Conference. He moved to Boston in 1818 where, in 1836, he founded the *Olive Branch*, a Christian journal, which he edited with his brother. The journal ceased publication in 1857.

22 Thurlow Weed (1797–1882) was a New York newspaper publisher and politician. He was a vehement abolitionist but sought to distance himself from the radicalism associated with the movement.

23 Reprinted in the *Liberator*, 16 January 1846.

24 The home of the Webb family (Richard Davis and Hannah Waring), who were Douglass's hosts while he was in Dublin. They lived above Webb's printing shop at Great Brunswick Street, in the centre of the city. Pettigrew & Oulton's *Dublin Directory* for 1842 lists R. D. Webb's address at 160 Brunswick Street, Great (p. 535). *The Dublin Almanac and General Register of Ireland* for 1847 lists them as living in '176, Brunswick Street, Great'. This seems to have resulted from a renumbering, not because they moved. In the twentieth century, Great Brunswick Street was renamed Pearse Street, after Patrick Pearse, the republican nationalist executed in 1916.

25 Cassius Marcellus Clay (1810–1903) was a wealthy Kentucky planter, politician and abolitionist. In 1843, he freed slaves on his farm and reemployed them as free labourers. In 1845, Clay began publishing an anti-slavery newspaper, *True American*. A mob regularly attacked him and his printing press, forcing him to relocate his business to Cincinnati. Clay helped found the Republican Party in Kentucky and became a friend and advisor of Abraham Lincoln.

26 The *Nation* had been established in 1842 by a group within the Repeal movement who, because of their age, were mockingly referred to as Young Ireland – a name that stuck. The paper sought to revive a sense of cultural and historical awareness amongst the Irish people. By 1845, the *Nation* claimed to have a readership of 250,000, making it the most widely read newspaper in Ireland.

27 The *Nation* responded to Haughton's criticism in the next issues, printing his letter and saying, 'On many other things we differ from him – on this we heartily agree', 'Temperance – Mr. Haughton', *Nation*, 6 September 1845. They were later to fall out over the issue of their support of slavery.

28 Father Theobald Mathew (1790–1856) was an Irish Catholic priest who gained an international reputation as the 'apostle of temperance'. Douglass greatly admired him and was administered the pledge by Father Mathew in 1845. He was also an abolitionist and in 1842, along with O'Connell and 60,000 other Irish people, had signed a petition condemning slavery. However, when Father Mathew visited the U.S. in 1849, he refused to comment on the issue, which drew the wrath of Douglass and many other abolitionists.

29 Father John Spratt (1798–1871) was a Dublin-based Carmelite friar. Initially a coadjutor to Fr Mathew, the latter came to see him as a rival in the temperance cause. Because of his extensive charitable work, especially during the Famine, he was regarded as a friend to Dublin's poor.

30 Royal Exchange, later City Hall, was completed in 1779. It was one of the most prestigious, and central, venues in Dublin.

31 According to *Dublin Weekly Register*, 6 September 1845, and the *Pilot*, 8 September 1845, this meeting took place on Thursday, 4 September. However, the Hibernian Anti-Slavery Society did usually hold their monthly meetings on Wednesdays; see *Freeman's Journal*, 9 April 1841.

32 The *Glasgow Argus* was a Scottish newspaper that was published twice weekly from 1833 to 1847. It was known for its progressive views, supporting abolition and opposing the Corn Laws.

33 There is no evidence that this lecture took place. The paper may have confused it with Douglass's first lecture in the Royal Exchange.

34 The full title was *The Chronicle and Munster Advertiser*, and it was printed in Waterford. It was published by Cornelius Redmond and appeared on Wednesday and Saturday mornings. It cost 5d. Redmond was an ardent supporter of O'Connell and Repeal. He served as mayor of Waterford in 1869.

35 The Dublin Mechanics' Institute opened in 1824. Its purpose was to promote scientific education amongst artisans. In 1839, women were permitted to attend lectures.

36 The full article was reprinted in 'Anti-Slavery Meeting', *Belfast Commercial Chronicle*, 13 September 1845, and in the *Freeman's Journal* on the same day.

37 The first recorded meeting of Quakers in Ireland took place in County Armagh in 1654. Meeting Houses were established in Dublin in 1686 and 1692. The second venue expanded into what became their premises on 6 Eustace Street, which was the location of some of Douglass's early lectures.

38 The Dublin Music Hall opened in the early nineteenth century as a concert and public venue for the lower classes. It could seat 4,000 people. Belfast also had a smaller Music Hall, where Douglass (and later, he and Garrison) would lecture.

39 'Inst.', an abbreviation of 'instant', is a Latin word meaning 'the present or current month'.

40 Irish Methodism had its roots in the mid-eighteenth century. In 1816, there was a split between the Primitive Wesleyan Methodists who retained their link with the Established Church and the Wesleyan Methodists who allowed their ministers to administer baptisms. At the time of Douglass's visit, there were approximately 23,000 Wesleyan Methodists in Ireland. As early as 1830, the Methodist church in Ireland had passed a 'strong resolution . . . in favour of the abolition of negro slavery'. See, Charles Henry Crookshank, *History of Methodism in Ireland: Modern Development* (London: T. Woolmer, 1888), p. 149.

41 Father John Spratt was a Dublin-based Carmelite friar. Initially a coadjutor to Fr Mathew, the latter man came to see him as a rival in the temperance cause.

42 *The Tablet* was established in 1840 by Frederick Lucas, who was a Quaker convert to Catholicism. It was published in London.

43 Sir Simon Bradstreet (1771–1853) was born in Clontarf near Dublin to an Anglo-Irish family. He was a supporter of the Repeal Association and a personal friend of O'Connell.

44 A bill to establish Queen's Colleges in Ireland, with locations in Belfast, Cork and Galway. The intent was to make university education available to members of all religious denominations, but the secular approach was opposed by O'Connell and most of the hierarchy of the Roman Catholic Church.

45 William Smith O'Brien MP (1803–1864) was a member of the Anglo-Irish Ascendancy class, but he had supported Catholic Emancipation and, after 1843, was openly associated with the Repeal Association. Following the split in 1846, he became leader of the Young Ireland group. He was sentenced to death, but eventually transported to Van Diemen's Land (Tasmania), for his part in the 1848 rising.

46 John O'Connell MP (1810–1858) was the third son of Daniel O'Connell (out of seven children), but he was increasingly regarded as his father's political successor. He lacked his father's skill and charisma, but similar to Daniel, John was a fervent abolitionist.

47 Thomas Davis (1814–1845) was a Protestant nationalist who was a leader of the Young Ireland group until his premature death from scarlet fever. He was one of the founders of the *Nation* newspaper.

48 Probably Christopher Moore (1790–1863), a Dublin-born sculptor who was known for his portrait busts.

49 A nationalist club formed in memory of the eighteenth-century Irish Volunteers, who were sometimes attributed with establishing the paramilitary tradition in Irish politics.

50 Probably Sir Frederick William Burton (1816–1900), who had been born in Country Clare. Burton and Davis had been friends.

51 One pound (£) in British currency. There were twenty shillings in a pound, and twelve pennies (pence) in a shilling.

52 The Devon Commission – officially 'The Commission on the Occupation of Land (Ireland)' – had been appointed in 1843 to inquire into land occupation in Ireland. It reported in February 1845. The expectation that land reforms would follow did not materialize; however, it provided a comprehensive insight into Irish society on the eve of the Great Famine.

53 To counter the sympathetic findings of the Devon Commission, the London *Times* appointed Thomas Campbell Foster to travel around Ireland and provide an 'accurate' – and unsympathetic – account of the Irish countryside and its people. Foster was particularly harsh in his criticisms of O'Connell.

54 Soft sawder – to butter-up, or flatter.

55 Ribbonism referred to Irish agrarian secret societies that were overwhelmingly Catholic. It generally sought to protect tenants from ruthless landlords. O'Connell was opposed to its use of secrecy and violence; his outspoken condemnation, in turn, lost him support.

56 François-Ferdinand-Philippe-Louis-Marie d'Orléans, Prince de Joinville (1818–1900), was the third son of Louis Philippe, the king of the French from 1830 to 1848.

57 Diocletian (244–311) was Roman emperor from 284 to 305. He was notorious for his persecution of Christians.

58 A farthing was a coin used throughout the United Kingdom and equal to a quarter of an old penny.

59 Richard Brinsley Butler Sheridan (1751–1816) was born in Dublin, but with his family moved to London in 1758. He entered the British parliament in 1780 and proved to be a powerful orator on a number of reform causes. Sheridan died in poverty but was buried in Poets' Corner in Westminster Abbey. He is remembered for his plays, poetry and political writings. It is possible that Douglass at times confused Sheridan with another Irish politician, Arthur O'Connor.

60 The *Liverpool Mail* was published between 1836 and 1880. It supported conservative and High Church principles, and the paper disliked O'Connell.

61 O'Connell trained as a lawyer but stopped practicing to work on the Catholic Emancipation campaign. After 1829, he sat in the British Parliament until his death. MPs did not receive any income, so he lived on 'rent' donated by the supporters of his various campaigns. He was frequently pilloried in the British press for taking money from the poor people of Ireland.

62 Foxwell Buxton (1786–1845) was an English abolitionist and social reformer. Although an Anglican, he had Quaker relations who introduced him to social issues. By profession he was a brewer and, after 1818, a member of Parliament. In 1823, he helped found the Society for the Mitigation and Gradual Abolition of Slavery, and, following Wilberforce's retirement from public life in 1825, he became leader of the abolition movement in the House of Commons. He attended the 1840 Anti-Slavery Convention in London.

63 This incident is explored in Kinealy, *Saddest People*.

64 Shambles is an archaic word for a butcher's slaughter-house.

65 Richard Allen (1803–1886) was a successful Dublin draper. Along with Webb and Haughton, he founded the Hibernian Anti-Slavery Society, serving as their secretary. Like Webb, he was a Quaker, and related to him through marriage. All three men were advocates of temperance, world peace and a number of other reform movements. During the Famine, Allen raised considerable sums of money for relief. He married Anne Webb in 1828, who was also actively involved in abolitionism. See, Hannah Maria

Wigham, *A Christian Philanthropist of Dublin: a Memoir of Richard Allen* (London: Hodder and Stoughton, 1886).

66 This article was reprinted in the *Freeman's Journal* of 4 October, thus giving the incorrect impression that the meeting took place on Friday.

67 Reprinted in *Dublin Evening Packet* and *Waterford Mail*.

68 In 1772, Wexford Corporation purchased some land in the town for the purpose of building a market house, which was also referred to as the Assembly Rooms. They were opened in 1776 and consisted of a large room downstairs for traders and a ballroom for supper dances. Most concerts and lectures were held at this venue. John Wesley preached in the Rooms and described them as one of the largest he had ever seen. In the early twentieth century, the building became home to the Wexford Arts Centre.

69 This article was reprinted in other newspapers, including *Southern Reporter and Cork Commercial Courier* of Tuesday, 14 October 1845.

70 Part of the Quaker Poole family of Growtown in Wexford. Joseph was a cousin of R. D. Webb. He had two sisters, Lizzie and Sarah, who were also involved in anti-slavery.

71 The *Waterford Mail* was a conservative and Protestant newspaper that started publication in 1823. It was bi-weekly, being published on Wednesdays and Saturdays.

72 The outlook of the paper was conservative, Protestant, and pro-Union. It was opposed to O'Connell and the Repeal movement. The paper was published three times a week out of Tralee. It ran from 1813 until 1917.

73 Adam Clarke (c. 1761–1832) was a Methodist theologian born in the north of Ireland. He wrote a commentary on the Bible, which took forty years to complete. He died of cholera.

74 Possibly a reference to a pamphlet by James W. Taylor of the same name, which showed the strength of the Union and the weakness of slavery in the mountainous districts in the South of America.

75 Anti-Catholic riots took place in Philadelphia between May and July 1844, which included the burning of a number of churches. They were provoked by anti-Catholic nativists.

76 Or 'colly-west', meaning nonsense. The etymology is uncertain but may refer to a village in England where people ended up when they were lost.

77 George William Frederick Howard, the 7th Earl of Carlisle (1802–1864), was more generally known as Lord Morpeth. He was an English politician who served as Chief Secretary for Ireland between 1835 and 1841. His involvement in Irish affairs was regarded as benevolent and, when he left office, thousands of Irish people signed a testimonial thanking him (the Morpeth Roll). A statue of him was erected in the Phoenix Park in Dublin in 1870, but it was blown up in 1958.

78 Globe Lane was a continuation of French's Quay.

79 Theobald Mathew was born on 10 October 1790.

80 Ald. An abbreviation of Alderman, a local government official.

81 Richard Dowden (1794–1861), a Unitarian, was born in Bandon and was mayor of Cork in 1845. He was active in the local temperance movement in Cork and managed a local company producing soda water and magnesia. Dowden was also a supporter of the Repeal Movement. A plaque in his honour is located in the Crawford Municipal Gallery. His papers are in the Cork City and County Archives (IE CCCA/U140). Alfred Webb, son of R. D., described him as having a 'hearty laugh' (Narratives, p. 20).

82 Abraham Beale (1795–1847) was a Corkonian Quaker businessman. He owned an ironmongery at Patrick's Quay and a spade mill at Monard. Similar to many other Quakers, during the Famine he worked tirelessly to support the starving poor. He contracted 'famine fever', which proved fatal. He died 22 August 1847, aged 54.

See *The Annual Monitor and Memorandum Book (or, Obituary of the members of the Society of Friends) for 1847* (York: C. Gilpin etc., 1847), p. 162.

83 Rev. William Whitelegge M.A. was a minister at the Presbyterian Chapel, Princes Street, Cork.

84 John Besnard was a justice of the peace for the borough of Cork.

85 John Francis Maguire (1815–1872) had been called to the bar in 1843. He was an abolitionist and a Repealer. Maguire served as mayor of Cork in 1852 and again from 1862 to 1864, and as a Liberal Member of Parliament between 1852 and 1872. In 1841, he founded the *Cork Examiner* newspaper.

86 William Martin, a Quaker shopkeeper and a friend of Father Mathew, was founder and leader of the Cork Temperance Society. In 1835, he founded the Cork Total Abstinence Society, but it made little headway. Together with Father Mathew, he was a governor of the local House of Industry.

87 A number of Douglass's speeches in Cork were reported in the British press. The whole of this speech was reprinted in the *Hampshire Advertiser*, 8 November 1845.

88 The Wesleyan Chapel on Patrick Street in Cork had opened in 1828. In the 1840s, two ministers preached there, Mr Bowers and Mr Newton.

89 Richard Furman (1755–1825) was raised in South Carolina. Initially opposed to slavery, he came to champion it. He published, in 1822, an 'Exposition of the Views of the Baptists Relative to the Coloured Population of the United States', which remained influential up to the Civil War.

90 In 1835, Amos Dresser, a theological student, was found selling Bibles in Tennessee. Due to a suspicion that he was an abolitionist, he was sentenced to receive twenty lashes of the whip.

91 *Summum bonum* is a Latin phrase which means the highest good or the ultimate goal.

92 The Imperial Hotel in Cork had first opened as commercial rooms for meetings in 1813, but three years later this extended into a hotel.

93 For booksellers in Cork, see, *1844–45 Aldwell's City of Cork Directory*; Ibid., the Varians are listed as 'Brush and Bellows Makers'.

94 The monthly *Truth-Seeker and Christian Thinker* first appeared in January 1845. It described itself 'an organ of free enquiry in Literature, Philosophy and Religion'. It was also an advocate of temperance. The paper was published in Douglas, in the Isle of Man, the site of many temperance newspapers and journals. It was edited by Dr. F. R. Lees, F.S.A., of Leeds, and G.S. Phillips. It had an estimated circulation of 4,000.

95 Strangely, the text of this speech does not appear in the local newspapers, but it was reprinted in the *Truth-Seeker*, apparently submitted by Ralph Varian. It was reprinted in John Blassingame et al. (eds). *The Frederick Douglass Papers: Series One – Speeches, Debates, and Interviews* (New Haven: Yale University Press, 1979. Vol. I), p. 55.

96 The Imperial Hotel in Cork, also known as the Imperial Clarence Hotel, was owned by C. McDowell, Esq.

97 Francis Parkman (1788–1852), a Unitarian minister of New North Church, Boston, who was visiting the United Kingdom. Because of his moderate position on antislavery, Haughton accused him of being pro-slavery. See letter of 3 October 1845 by Haughton to *London Inquirer*.

98 Madison Washington was an American slave who led a revolt in 1841 on board the *Creole*. Douglass wrote a novella, *The Heroic Slave* (1853), the hero of which was based on Washington's actions.

99 Theodore Wright (1797–1847) was an African American abolitionist born to free parents. He was the first African American to attend Princeton Theological Seminary, graduating in 1829. In 1833, he became a founding member of the American Anti-Slavery Society, but left in 1840, he disagreeing with Garrison on a number of issues including the woman question. He and the Tappan brothers founded the more moderate American and Foreign Anti-Slavery Society.

100 The *Nenagh Guardian* was published in Co. Tipperary. It was conservative and pro–Church of Ireland, often including articles that were anti-Catholic, anti-Repeal and anti-O'Connell.

101 Daniel Casey (1820–1885) was a local poet and noted wit. He authored *Cork Lyrics* (1857) and *Gems from the Cork Poets* (1883).

102 This is the date provided by Douglass, but it is incorrect. The event took place on Tuesday, 28 October 1845.

103 This handwritten poem was in Douglass's private papers. The introduction to it reads: The following lines written by one Daniel Casey, a poet of some local repute, in Cork, [were] read at a Soiree given the late Frederick Douglas [sic] at St Patrick's Hall, Cork, Monday, 25 October 1845.

104 More usually, *Cead Mille Failte*, meaning 'One hundred thousand welcomes'.

105 This article was in the *London Inquirer* of 18 October 1845 and, in full, the *Liberator* of 12 December 1845. The *Inquirer* had been founded in London in July 1841. It was the first newspaper founded on Nonconformist principles. It was published weekly.

106 Ralph Varian, and his brother Isaac, were brush manufacturers in Cork. Ralph was a member of the Repeal Association but sided with the more radical Young Ireland group. The family was of Huguenot origins.

107 The Oberlin Institute in Ohio was founded in 1833 by John Jay Shipherd (1802–1844) and Philo Penfield Stewart (1798–1868), two Presbyterian ministers. It was founded on liberal, progressive principles and, only two years after opening, became the first college in the U.S. to admit student of all races. In 1837, four women students were admitted.

108 Charles Lenox Remond (1810–1873) was born in Massachusetts to a free man of colour. In 1838, he was appointed an agent for the Massachusetts Anti-Slavery Society, and in 1840 travelled with Garrison to Britain. In 1841, he lectured in Ireland, including as a guest of the Hibernian Anti-Slavery Society. He subsequently lectured with Douglass in America.

109 From the Latin phrase *pro tempore*, meaning 'for the time being'.

110 This could be a mistake, as Henry Clay led the Whig Party in the U.S. from 1844 to 1848.

111 *Heywood's Manual* was a digest of laws in force in North Carolina at the time of its publication in 1818.

112 The meeting place of an independent Methodist congregation, the church having opened in 1821. The first conference of the Irish Methodists Church had been held in Limerick in 1752, and it was chaired by John Wesley.

113 Benjamin Clark Fisher, whose family hosted Douglass during his stay in Limerick.

114 Sir Charles Lyell, 1st Baronet (1797–1875), was a British lawyer and the leading geologist. In 1845, he published *Travels in North America*.

115 The Hutchinson Family.

116 John Philpot Curran (1750–1817) was an Irish lawyer and politician who was a champion of Irish civil liberties including Catholic Emancipation. His writings were greatly admired by Douglass.

117 He was described in adverts as 'the inimitable Bateman', who in his act would 'perform and delineate the various characteristics of Negro life, manners and customs', see *Freeman's Journal*, 6 September 1845 and 12 September 1845.

118 The Limerick Philosophical Society built these premises in 1840.

119 The mayor of Limerick in 1845 was William Geary M.D. See, Maurice Lenihan, *Limerick; its History and Antiquities* . . . (Dublin: Hodges, Smith, 1866), p. 708.

120 The song 'The Battle and the Breeze' appears in *The Standard Book of Song for Temperance Meetings and Home Use* ed. by T. Bowick and pub. in 1883.

121 Rev. John Brahan was the parish priest in St Mary's in Limerick. In 1847, he opened a soup kitchen for his parishioners, *Limerick Reporter*, 12 January 1847.

122 The *Belfast News-Letter and General Advertiser* was founded in 1737 by Francis Joy. Its principles were stated to be 'Loyalty to the Throne; Devotion to the religion of the Bible; and Unswerving attachment to the Protestant constitution of these lands'. It was the town's first newspaper. It the 1840s, it was published three times a week. Since 1844, the editor had been James Alexander Henderson (1823–1883). See www.news letter.co.uk/news/history-of-the-news-letter-1-3516204, accessed 12 October 2017.

123 It cost four and a half pence.

124 Founded in 1832 in Belfast, the *Northern Whig* had a liberal pro-Union focus. It was published three times a week, on Mondays, Thursdays and Saturdays.

125 Andrew Mulholland (1792–1866) was mayor of Belfast in 1845 to 1846. During the Great Famine, he contributed £200 to Famine relief. In 1862, he donated a magnificent organ to the Ulster Hall.

126 The *Banner of Ulster* was founded in 1842 by the Rev. William Gibson, minister of the Rosemary Street Church, to uphold orthodox Presbyterian principles. Its editor at the time of Douglass's visit was Scottish-born George Troup, who had been a founding member of the Free Church of Scotland.

127 Reprinted in the *Liberator*, 6 February 1846.

128 James Standfield (c. 1809–1861) was a local wholesale grocer and one of the secretaries of the Belfast Anti-Secretary Society. According to *Slater's Directory* (1846), he resided at 44 York St.

129 In most accounts, it is 'Mr Gough of Dublin'.

130 William Cowper (1731–1800) was an English poet and writer of hymns. As a result of his friendship with John Newton, he became interested in anti-slavery. He subsequently wrote a number of poems on this topic, including 'The Negro's Complaint' (1788), which was famous at the time and is quoted here by Douglass. In the twentieth century, the poem was quoted by Martin Luther King.

131 Probably Henry David Erskine, 12th Earl of Buchan (1783–1857). Dryburgh Abbey is situated on the River Tweed in Scotland.

132 This church opened in 1816.

133 John Stevelly (1795–1868) was a professor of natural philosophy at the Royal Belfast Academical Institution before taking up a position at Queen's College in 1849.

134 The church of Rev. Isaac Nelson (1809–1888), a Presbyterian minister and supporter of Douglass.

135 The Evangelical Alliance, which was formed in 1846, was a union between evangelical ministers from Britain and the United States. They were divided on the issue of slavery, some suggesting there was a distinction between slavery (which was a sin) and the slave-holder (who could be a Christian).

136 Rev. James Hodgens was a minister in the Independent Chapel on Donegal Street in Belfast.

137 There is evidence of Presbyterian worship at this site in the seventeenth century. Since 1799, Rev. Samuel Hanna, DD (c. 1772–1852), had been the minister.

138 Isaac Nelson (c. 1812–1888) was a Presbyterian clergyman who ministered in the Donegall Street Church, Belfast. He was a member of the Foreign and British Anti-Slavery Society. In 1880, Nelson was elected to the British parliament as a nationalist candidate for County Mayo.

139 Commander Francis Anderson Calder, RN (1787–1855), with Standfield, was a secretary of the Belfast Anti-Slavery Society. Both Calder and Standfield attended the 1843 Anti-Slavery Convention in London. Calder was also an animal rights activist. In 1859, the Calder Fountain was erected in his honour. See *Illustrated London News*, vol. 35 (17 September 1859), p. 284.

140 James Gibson was an elder in the Rosemary Street Presbyterian Church. He had served briefly as a Liberal MP for Belfast, from 1837 to 1838.

141 Rev. James Hodges, possibly a confusion with Hodgens.

142 William Brisbane (c. 1803–1878), a slave-holder who freed his slaves in South Carolina, became an abolitionist and moved north.

143 James G. Birney (1782–1857), born into a slave-holding family in Kentucky, allegedly received slaves as a wedding gift. He purchased his own cotton plantation and slaves in Alabama in 1818, which was financially unsuccessful. By the late 1820s he was opposing slavery and became a supporter of the American Colonization Society.

144 Elon Galusha (1790–1856). Born in Vermont, Galusha became a lawyer. He served as the first president of the Baptist Anti-Slavery Society and attended the 1840 Anti-Slavery Convention in London.

145 Probably Rev. Lucius Bolles, D.D. (1779–1844), who served for 22 years as pastor of the First Baptist Church of Salem, Massachusetts.

146 Dr Smyth of Charlestown, who had been born in Belfast. His dispute with Douglass ran for months in 1846.

147 Dr George Bradburn (1806–1880), a Unitarian minister who had been born in Massachusetts. He attended the 1840 Anti-Slavery Convention in London and was depicted with his hand to his ear. There, he defended the right of women to attend. In 1843, he and Douglass were attacked when lecturing in Indiana.

148 A letter had been published in the *Banner of Ulster* on 19 December 1845, written under the pseudonym of Civis, objecting to Douglass's unforgiving, didactic tone when it came to the churches in America, especially in the slave-holding states.

149 The Mason-Dixon line was an area that had been surveyed in the 1760s. In the years prior to the American Civil War, it was regarded, together with the Ohio River, as marking the dividing line between slave states south of it and free states to the north of it.

150 Probably Rev. Lucius Bolles D.D. See endnote 145.

151 Daniel Sharp, a Baptist minister in Boston who had been born in Britain. He was opposed to slavery but did not support ex-communicating slave-holders.

152 Possibly Moses B. Stuart (1780–1852), an American biblical scholar who suggested that slavery was permissible in the Christian faith. He expanded these views in his 1850 pamphlet, *Conscience and the Constitution*.

153 Willbur Fisk (1792–1839) was a Methodist minister and theologian. He favoured a repatriation of slaves to Africa, fearing the abolitionist position would split the Methodist Church. In 1835, he toured Europe, visiting Ireland.

154 'O' (died c. 68 AD) was a runaway slave. He was mentioned in a letter from Paul to Philemon.

155 Jonathan Walker (1799–1878) was a Massachusetts-born mariner who increasingly devoted his life to reform and abolition. He achieved notoriety in 1844 when he was branded and imprisoned for a year for helping runaway slaves.

156 Rev. Charles Turney Torrey (1813–1846) was born in Massachusetts. He attended Yale when aged 16 and, following graduation, became a Congregationalist minister. He is sometimes referred to as the 'Father of the Underground Railroad' because he moved beyond the 'moral suasion' tactics of Garrison, instead actively encouraging people to flee from their enslavement. His activities led to his imprisonment and early death.

157 The Church, which opened in 1768, was located on Market Street. The congregation dated back to the late seventeenth century.

158 John Pyke Hullah (1812–1884), an English composer who used his songs to promote teetotalism.

159 Sometimes abbreviated to 'ult.', a Latin word meaning 'in the month preceding the current one'.

160 Henry Clay (1777–1852) was an American lawyer and planter and politician. He ran unsuccessfully for the presidency in 1824, 1832 and 1844. He opposed the annexation of Texas and the Manifest Destiny policy. He owned slaves but freed them in his will.

161 A manuscript copy of Douglass's speech is available in the Frederick Douglass Collection held by the Library of Congress, www.loc.gov/resource/mfd.21002/?sp=11, accessed 15 September 2017.
The article was reprinted in full in the *Liberator*, 27 February 1846.

162 The Commercial Buildings were situated at Waring St. and Bridge St. See *History of Belfast*, 1823, p. 90.

163 William Sharman Crawford (1781–1861), an Irish landowner and politician, was known for his liberal views, including supporting Catholic Emancipation and opposing slavery.

164 The *Inquirer* was a London-based Nonconformist newspaper.

165 Free Church of Scotland, formed through a schism in the Presbyterian Church in 1843.